*Bosphorus Nights:*
*The Complete Lyric Poems of Bedros Tourian*

Harvard Armenian Texts and Studies, 10

# *Bosphorus Nights: The Complete Lyric Poems of Bedros Tourian*

The Armenian texts, with English translation and commentary

by

James R. Russell

**Published by**

**Department of Near Eastern Languages and Civilizations Harvard University**

**and**

**Armenian Heritage Press National Association for Armenian Studies and Research**

**Distributed by Harvard University Press Cambridge, Massachusetts 2005**

Library of Congress Cataloging-in-Publication Data

Duryan, Petros, 1851-1872.
[Poems. Armenian & English]
Bosphorus nights : the complete lyric poems of Bedros Tourian / Armenian texts, with English translation and commentary by James R. Russell
p. cm. -- (Harvard Armenian texts and studies ; 10)
Armenian; with translation and commentary in English.
Includes bibliographical references and index.
ISBN 0-935411-22-4 (hardcover : alk. paper) 1. Duryan, Petros, 1851-1872--Criticism and interpretation. I. Russell, James R., 1953- II. Title. III. Series.

PK8548.D6A28 2006
891'.99215--dc22

2005024714

Printed in the United States of America

This Publication Was Made Possible By a Generous
Grant From the Dolores Zohrab Liebmann Fund.

*Յարգս չգիտցան, բայց պիտի փնտռեն զիս։*

They did not recognize the honor due me, but they will seek me yet.

Bedros Tourian

# Contents

# Preface and Acknowledgements

When I was a callow stripling of seventeen naively striking out on the thorny path of Armenian studies, my dear departed teacher Miss Vartarpi Tarpinian, a native of Erzerum (Garin), Western Armenia, gave me a copy of the critical edition of Tourian's lyric poems, Petros Duryan, *Erkeri žołovacu (erku hatorov)*, vol. 1, Erevan: Haykakan SSH GA hratarakč'ut'yun, 1971 [*Collected Works in Two Volumes*, Academy of Sciences of the Armenian SSR], ed. by A.S. Šaruryan and Paruyr Sevak. Miss Tarpinian (and though the lady was of a certain age, she insisted on Arm. *oriort*—"Miss") was a survivor of the Armenian Genocide: her father was hanged by the Ottoman authorities and her mother and sisters were sent on the death march with its terminus at Raqqa, in Syria. They survived, but the family still was divided: the mother and sisters went to Istanbul, Vartarpi to various orphanage schools in Greece, Marseilles, and Paris. She attended the *Tbrots'aser* (Դպրոցասէր, "Scholastophile") academy of the latter, spent a few years in Germany after the Second World War, and eventually moved to New York to join her mother and sisters. The sisters had married in Turkey in the interim and had moved to the United States. Miss Tarpinian got a job at the Lycée on the East Side; and on Sundays she taught at the Holy Cross Church of Armenia Sunday School in Washington Heights.

In the summer of 1969 I traveled to the Soviet Union on the Choate School's Russian Summer Program, saw Erevan and the Matenadaran Institute of Ancient Manuscripts, and determined to study Armenian. When I returned, Mrs. Maritza Tsaggos, an Armenian and a history teacher at my school, the Bronx High School of Science, learnt of my interest and began tutoring me. She was like a second mother, and we remained friends till her death in 1990. When she had taught me all the Armenian she knew, she found a tutor at Holy Cross: Miss Tarpinian's one-hour tutorials lasted, on average, two or three, with weekend supplements. She gave me about a book a week, everything from stories about the life of St. Mesrop Mashtots' (which I smuggled into Physical Education class and was caught reading in the gym when I was supposed to have been developing a healthy body for my healthy mind) to the novels of Raffi. We did Western Armenian, and of course Miss Tarpinian and her family provided a wealth of knowledge about the vanished customs and speech of what was once called Turkish Armenia. Miss Tarpinian and I stayed in touch as I went to college, then grad school, then got an academic job. All her relatives died. She ended up frail and alone and afflicted by dementia. I was by then living in Cambridge. Another pupil of hers, Mary Missirlian, told me Miss Tarpinian remembered me with fondness towards the very end— and left a folder with every letter and card I'd ever sent her. We had not read Tourian together, though. At Columbia, Prof. (now the Very Reverend Father) Krikor H. Maksoudian, one of the finest scholars of his generation, taught me Eastern and Classical Armenian, and we read the robust poems of reformers and revolutionaries like Step'anos Nazarian and Michael Nalbandian. Later, I read Ch'arents' and Isahakian. But Tourian's mood seemed to me then lethally sombre; and his language, unnecessarily rebarbative. I preferred Armenia's poet of the Revolution, Yeghishe Ch'arents'; and when tenderer moods came, it was the limpid voice of Avetik' Isahakyan that I loved.

For years, the volume of Tourian languished untouched: the poet's morbidity seemed, whether one's mood was ardently passionate or loftily Promethean, an annoying affectation. When I first taught Armenian literature, at Columbia in 1980, I must confess I still did not much appreciate Tourian, even terming him, Demirjibashian, and others "the Sickly School" in my first lectures. (This is the sort of thing students remember, and I still get condign echoes of it.) Such disdain is not altogether unusual: Mr. Haig Messerlian, former director of the Manhattan branch of the AGBU, told me at a dinner at my former pupil Lola Koundakjian's home in New York on 25 March 2001 that he belonged to a group of alumni of the Hovagimian-Manugian school in

Beirut who call themselves still the *P'ch'ats'adz Yeridasartut'yun,* the "Spoiled Youth." It is still the custom of these gentlemen, now prominent in many fields, scattered all over the globe, and no longer young, to call a bad loser at backgammon Bedros Tourian—because of the plaintive poem "Murmurs" (*Drdunchk*)! There is something in the epicene, sorrowful posture of the Romantics that invites ridicule by both cheerful, ambitious young men and hardened veterans of the world alike. Experience can sometimes foster insight and enable one to perceive what those poets did, with greater profundity. In these middle years of life, I see Tourian differently than a quarter century ago: the tragic dimension is clearer and the sombre colors are not at all artificial.

My path back to him, even if it has been exceedingly long, is not unique: many Soviet Armenian poets rejected the Western Armenian Romantics and Symbolists as hopelessly naïve and incurably bourgeois. But Yeghishe Ch'arents' (of whom there will be much more to say in this book), the greatest of their number, prophesied even in the heady, early days of Soviet rule that the time was to come when Tourian, Siamant'o, Varuzhan, and the rest would be published and appreciated in the workers' paradise. A sixtieth part of wisdom (though not, I hope, of prudence) comes with age. I have now the pleasure to have worked with Susan Barba, now a Ph.D. candidate in the Department of Comparative Literature at Harvard, on the poet whose work I was too raw to savor in youth. This book benefits from her careful reading and suggestions. I am grateful also to my students Maria Kosovskaya and Arie Zakarian for being a patient audience of my revisions, and for their insights. Mr. Haig Tekeyan, of Hamadan, Iran, and now Massachusetts, loaned me his copy of the Mekhitarist edition of Tourian of 1922, from which are reproduced here the line drawings accompanying some of the poems—for "The Turkish Woman," "My Death," and "Whispers." Marc Mamigonian of the National Association for Armenian Studies and Research in Belmont, MA, a noted Joycean scholar and experienced editor—and, thus, no stranger to literary arcana and the problems of their lucid unveiling—has read and commented upon the manuscript in minute detail. My gratitude to him as a friend and colleague is particularly great. I am grateful to two Armenian gentlemen of Constantinople who have devoted their lives to collecting and preserving the precious ephemera of the nineteenth-century City: Mr. Mihran Adman, now resident in Long Island, New York, and Mr. Berj Fenerci, of Montréal. Both have very generously provided and given permission to publish tickets, postcards, etc., from their archives that illustrate the everyday world in which Bedros Tourian lived. I am also grateful to the Dolores Zohrab Liebmann Fund for their generous financial support of this publication.

Not long before he was murdered on the eve of 9/11/2001 by a pair of Arab Muslim terrorists posing as newspapermen, the Afghan freedom fighter Ahmed Shah Massoud said that, whether or not one enjoys it, life passes—so one may as well devote oneself to something worthwhile, in order not to look back with regret. In fact many people probably regret a great deal in their lives, however well they have tried to live them. W. H. Auden once said, "Man is not the center of the Universe, / And working in an office makes it worse." Perhaps, but the life of the academic, particularly in this age of the corporate, atomized university, does not lack for the sense of alienation and futility. The mages of the Renaissance recognized melancholy as the particular bedevilment of the scholar. I do not think they meant depression, and Tourian bears all the signs and emblems of *melancolia*; so perhaps a common disposition has assisted me to comprehend him.

The great American writer William S. Burroughs spent his undergraduate years where I work and live now. He commented succinctly on the matter that he detested both Harvard and Boston, and he resolved after graduation never to return. Some years later, he explained that he was forced by personal tragedy to write his way out of death. Harvard is better and worse than it was in Burroughs' day, and the phrase "Banned in Boston" is a quaint, ugly remnant of an unlamented past. But one needs friends to warm the atmosphere of New England, and in this respect I have been more fortunate than the reclusive Mr. Burroughs. (His pet ferret and pistol practice with live ammunition probably did not endear him to his fellow denizens of Adams House, anyway.) I've come to love Tourian's ghost; but the living friend to be celebrated here is a woman, some years my junior but in her unfailing charity and sweetness very much of the same golden ancient Armenian Christian coinage as those great elders, Mrs. Tsaggos and Miss Tarpinian. If one wishes to believe in angels who visit one's life, then she must belong to that Old Testament Trinity. It is time to express thanks for many lifts to Arax Market in Watertown, many meals shared, the days she fed Cat when I was away, and our evening walks from Memorial Drive to Harvard Square and back. So I offer this book to the daughter of *Yeretsgin* Varteni and Father Arsen Barsamian: Lucine, the light of whose friendship is no pale fire but a sun of righteousness. Առ Լուսին անսահման երախտապարտութեամբ և սիրով՝ որուն լոյսը սոսկ դժգոյն հուր մը չէ՝, այլ արեգա՛կն արդարութեան, իմ կենաց արահետը միշտ լուսաւորող։

A note on the title of this book. Mak'sud Mihrdatiants' wrote a letter at Armash monastery near Constantinople on 18 September 1891 to the literary scholar Arshag Ch'obanian, who was then engaged in research for a biography of Bedros Tourian: he had sent a list of queries to Tourian's younger brother Mihran—by 1891 Father Eghishe, soon to be Patriarch of Jerusalem—who dictated his answers to Mihrdatiants'. "He had apparently begun a novel entitled *Bosphorus Nights* (*Վոսփորեան գիշերներ Vosp'oryan kisherner*), which he did not finish, and which is lost. 'When I read it,' he [Eghishe Tourian] says, 'I was deeply moved. It began with a series of meditations, and after that people and events appeared in their midst. It remained incomplete—he had reached the point where he was describing our home.'"[1] Bedros Tourian's home was not only the streets, hills, theaters, houses, schools, churches, gardens of Scutari, Pera, Constantinople—but the great waterway of the Bosphorus that divided and united them, over which the ancient capital bestrode two continents. His passions were the light on its waters, the mystery of the deep—and a glance of passion on a ferry. *Bosphorus Nights* resumes, on a distant continent and in a strange tongue: may Bedros find a home in the hearts of his new readers.

---

[1] *Documents*, no. 32, p. 56 (see p. 328).

## List of Illustrations

6. Clockwise from left, the wonder-working image of the *Ch·arkhap·an Surp Astvadzadzin* ("Evil-Defeating Holy Theotokos"), Balat; a ten-*para* voucher of Tourian's parish church, *Surp Garabed* (St. John the Forerunner), Scutari; and a view of the altar of the church. Courtesy of Mr. Berj Fenerci, Montréal, Canada.

7. There are no known photographs of Bedros Tourian, nor any picture of the poet made during his lifetime. These two pictures, from boyhood and early manhood, of Tourian's cousin Ghevont (1879-1933)—who was ordained an Archbishop and was murdered in New York City by members of the *Dashnaktsut'iun*—may afford some idea of how Bedros might have looked.

8. A horse-drawn *araba*, "carriage," with veiled Turkish ladies inside: perhaps the kind that inspired Tourian's poem "The Turkish Woman" (from Albert Smith, *A Month at Constantinople*, London, 1851, p. 75).

9. An illustration from the Constantinople 1922 edition of Tourian's poems of "The Turkish Woman."

10. An illustration from the Constantinople 1922 edition of Tourian's poems of "My Death."

11. An illustration from the Constantinople 1922 edition of Tourian's poems of "Whispers."

12. Zabelle Boyajian's illumination (in her anthology *Armenian Legends and Poems*, London and New York, 1916) of the scene of the marriage of King Artaxias and Princess Sat·enik, from the *History of the Armenians* of Movses Khorenats·i with the fragmentary epic verses in Classical Armenian, Տեղ ոսկի տեղայր ի փեսայութեանն Արտաշիսի՝ տեղայր մարգարիտ ի հարսնութեան Սաթինկան։ "Rain of gold poured down when Artashes was groom; pearls rained when Sat·enik was bride." Tourian loved the epic and its imagery and employed them in his lyrics.

13. Albrecht Dürer's engraving *Melencolia, I.* The Romantics, especially Gérard de Nerval, were inspired by Dürer and by other artistic renderings of saturnine mood. They adopted the ancient, tragic image of the artist as a melancholic brooding beneath the rays of a black sun. Tourian, the Armenian Romantic, seems to have read Nerval, for he appropriates the latter image in a letter.

14. A sketch by Tourian in his first manuscript Notebook of cover art for a collection of his poems: on his deathbed, he implored his friends to publish the volume. On the left is a seraph, whose head is perhaps a self-portrait of the poet, with a lyre surmounted by two Crosses. On the right is a volume with the inscription Պ. Դուրեան, ՏԱՂՔ "B. Tourian, POEMS."

# The Poet of the City: An Introduction

"So it was in vain that Bedros Tourian came into the world. For our poets of the end of the [nineteenth] century he was still just a miserable youth who had released a few bitter cries and gone to lie down in the cemetery of Baghlar Bashi. People still could not perceive the road he had opened up, rescuing the Armenian lyric from dissipating into fragments by binding it to the human heart and to its immediate emotions."
—Hagop Siruni.[1]

"All of us were born of Bedros Tourian."
—Hovhannes Toumanian.[2]

Poetry is "Speaking of what cannot be said / To the person I want to say it."
—David Schubert.

A country may be fortunate enough to have its City. And the City may be blessed with its Poet. Karl Marx in the *Communist Manifesto* wrote of the idiocy of rural life. Great cities attract people who re-

---

[1]Y.Č. Siruni, *Polis ew ir derə* ("Constantinople and its Role"), 4 vols., Beirut and Antelias, 1965-1988, vol. 4, p. 150: Ի կո՛ւր աշխարհ եկեր էր ուրեմն Պետրոս Դուրեան։ Դարավերջի մեր բանաստեղծներուն համար ան հէք պատանի մըն էր դեռ, որ արձակեր էր քանի մը աղեկտուր ճիչ ու գացեր պառկեր Պաղլար Պաշըի գերեզմանատունը։ Դեռ մարդիկ չէին տեսներ անոր բացած ճամբան, հայ քնարը փրկելով հոեւտորութենէ ու ծեքծեքումէ ու կայն կապելով մարդկային սրտին ու անոր անմիջական յուզումներուն։

[2]Մենք բոլորս ծնուել ենք Պետրոս Դուրեանից։ Cit. by A. S. Šaruryan, *Petros Duryan: kyanḱə ev gorcə* ("Bedros Tourian: His Life and Work"), Erevan: Erevani Hamalsarani hratarakč'ut'yun, 1972, p. 44.

fuse to resign themselves to that sort of life. Marx also said, though only the latter part of his thought is generally cited, that the human condition is so heartless and full of suffering that men embrace religion as an opiate. But of course people who do not wish lives of idiocy are unlikely to surrender to stupid mythologies. If they require opiates, they take them straight: absinthe, heroin. Some of these special urbanites are poets and writers. Among them are the ones of fable who live short, hard lives: depression and alcohol take them away early. In the nineteenth and early twentieth centuries, consumption, a disease ideally suited to the Romantic temperament, helped to speed their departure from the world. In Russia, there were duels (Pushkin and Lermontov) and suicide (Yesenin and Mayakovsky). The death of poets became a sort of separate narrative, ancillary to poetry itself: Svetlana Boym's study, *Death in Quotation Marks,* explores the Russian and French forms. Perhaps the sublime untruths of faith promote longevity; but then the work of poets is satisfying in that it has all the aesthetic power, even the transcendence, at times, of scripture, without requiring of the reader an intellectually demeaning suspension of disbelief on the global scale religion requires. Even religious poems—the *Gathas* of Zarathustra, the Psalms of David, the divine poems of John Donne, perhaps St. Gregory of Narek's *Book of Lamentation* to a lesser extent—can be read without the prior acceptance of the unseen and unprovable.

But most poets do not talk about God that much, focusing instead in their ecstasies of distress on human unsuccess. The work of the poet of the great city lives in an urban landscape and gains from it. Hart Crane and Walt Whitman devote their songs to the sea and the island Mannahatta of New York, to its White Buildings and its Brooklyn Bridge. Allen Ginsberg's heroes enact their suicidal dramas in the cliff-dwellers' landscape of the West Side. Alexander Blok, Osip Mandelstam, Anna Akhmatova, and Joseph Brodsky determine the literary texture of twentieth-century St. Petersburg, one of the most literary of cities (Julie Buckler's *Mapping St. Petersburg* is the best study of the Northern Palmyra and of the cultural artifact as literary text). All of them are equally unthinkable without Peter the Great's city—without its metal Bronze Horseman and the spectral one of Pushkin, their own poems, Russian literature itself, could not have come into being.

"Warum huldigest du, heiliger Sokrates,
Diesem Jünglinge stets?..."

("Holy Socrates, why always with deference
Do you treat this young man?")

—Friedrich Hölderlin, "Sokrates und Alkibiades"

The great city is mother, and refuge, inspiration and laboratory for a poet; but it is also prison and hell. One is bound to it and discovers one cannot escape. Sardonically, it combines with anonymity the myriad, meticulous witnesses to aging and loss, all the acts of the tragedy that is human life. Despite the propensity of poets—and especially the poets of cities—to die young, one wants to observe a poet in age as well, with the many strata of his Troy stacked and strewn roundabout him. For this I choose Lawrence Durrell's Poet of the City: the city is Alexandria; the poet, Constantine Cavafy (29 April 1863-29 April 1933), a Hellene and a Christian in an ancient town that was both, was from its birth cosmopolitan as well, and was doomed to be reduced to being Muslim alone. The situation is analogous to that of Constantinople, a place where Cavafy lived for three years of his youth (1882-1885) as well. But it is Alexandria that is his *polis* and *tykhe* ("fortune"), its canvas of polymorphous ethnicity and historical depth the scene of his meditation—his beloved, and his private inferno.[3]

Cavafy wrote a vigorous, highly idiomatic modern Greek, tinged, as the scene demanded, with the Greek of other ages, from Attic to Byzantine. His laicism placed him outside the *katharevousa*, or purist, school, rather in the way that Bedros Tourian was consciously

[3]See Robert Liddell, *Cavafy: A Critical Biography*, London: Duckworth, 1974; and Edmund Keeley, *Cavafy's Alexandria: Study of a Myth in Progress*, Cambridge, MA: Harvard University Press, 1976.

to oppose Armenian neo-classicism by his own innovative employment of the vernacular. In the poem *He Polis,* "The City," Cavafy depicts a man telling himself he is trapped by the literal and metaphorical landscapes of his life; and in *Ho theos apoleipein ton Antonion,* "The god abandoning Antony," the noble Roman on the eve of Actium is bidden to face his end and ruin bravely, since he has been fortunate and worthy to enjoy the pleasure and sophistication of an Alexandrian. Though Cavafy was no Romantic, death is a nearly-ubiquitous theme in his poems: a pagan lover looks in at his beloved's Christian funeral, the poet muses upon the ancient epitaph of a youth, an old man looks out of his loneliness and isolation at the loveliness of the young and contemplates his own wreck. Art and memory alone, in every case, make bearable the despairing prospect of annihilation.

Cavafy's loves are all very young and all homosexual, almost all in the past—either the distant antiquity of Hellenistic Alexandria, or the bygone years of the poet's youth. If the setting is not Alexandria, it is still an ancient metropolis of the Eastern Mediterranean: Seleuceia, Antioch, or even, in one little-known poem, the Armenian capital Tigranocerta.[4] The beloved, generally of slight intellect and with the soul of a street hustler, dies in flower; only the thoughtful lover—the artist—survives into decrepitude, cursed to observe and perceive. Bedros Tourian was twelve when Cavafy was born; and by the time the young Greek poet came to the Ottoman capital, Tourian was long dead. But imagine a slight adjustment of time and dimension: the Greek poet sees a young student with thick chestnut hair parted in the middle like a girl's, and combed upwards (rather like Arthur Rimbaud's locks). His beautiful black eyes sparkle beneath long lashes, below arched brows and a high forehead. His aquiline nose, with its slightly flared nostrils, is set in the middle of a round face with smooth, fresh skin, above delicate lips—the perfect type of a handsome boy, with a soft, feminine beauty. His friends would joke, "Shave off a few of the whiskers under your nose, and we'll sell you as a girl." This descrip-

[4]For a translation and commentary see my article, "The Lost Epic of Tigran: A Reconstruction Based upon the Fragments," in J. R. Russell, *Armenian and Iranian Studies,* Harvard Armenian Texts and Studies 9, Cambridge, MA, 2004, pp. 1031-1050 (Henceforth cited as *AIS.*)

tion of the young Tourian—and Bedros Tourian was to die at twenty-one, never to grow old and lose his loveliness—belongs to the Armenian writer and literary historian Arshag Ch'obanian, who based it on the testimony of Tourian's mother and close friends.[5]

But this exotically delicate Armenian youth is no languid, cold-hearted, empty-eyed object. Stare at him, as into Nietzsche's Abyss, and he will gaze back; write poems, and you will hear his, lyrics whose language and imagery is fresh and new, whose own emotions of longing, love, and loss are as sharp as a wound. The scene of his verses is Constantinople: the park of Baghlar-bashi and the hill of Camlica in Scutari, the waters of the Bosphorus observed from there in many weathers and times of day, the crowds on the ferry, a girl hastily glimpsed over the edge of a newspaper. He is a black butterfly grieving amongst the dark masses of the cypresses. He and a friend suck insatiably the black milk of the grave in their conversation. If only he were a stone, so his beloved's tear might dampen him! The dawn brings commingled dew and fire. Were they to open his heart, they would find no tome, but a conflagration. Old Alexandrian Greek bard, old graybeard, behold your Constantinopolitan Armenian love. Lonesome voice, be answered at last. Poet of the City, meet the Poet of the City.

Rae Dalven and many others have translated Cavafy into English. There is even a recent collection of articles, *Russkaya Kavafiana*. English and French selections of Tourian's poetry all date from the turn of the twentieth century. The few monographs about him are all in Armenian. His poetics cannot be fairly said ever to have been studied at all.

* * * * * * *

This volume presents for the first time the complete lyric poems of Bedros Tourian (1851-1872) with Armenian text and English translation, and a commentary. The poet was a native of Scutari, now Üsküdar—the "Asiatic" district across the Bosphorus from Constan-

---

[5]Cited by A. S. Šaruryan (Sharuryan), *Petros Duryan*, Erevan: Erevani Hamalsarani Hratarakč'ut'yun, 1972, p. 53.

tinople (ancient Byzantium, Istanbul today), the capital of the vast, cosmopolitan Ottoman Empire. Its streets teemed with Greeks, Turks, Armenians, Jews, Kurds, Russians, Italians, and people of many other nationalities. Bedros Zembayan—i.e., Peter, the Western Armenian form of Petros; Zembayan is a surname formed from Turkish with the Armeno-Iranian patronymic ending *-yan*, of which Tourian is the poet's Armenized version[6]—was born on 20 May 1851 to Apraham and Arusyag (d. 1905). His father was a blacksmith who owned a two-story wooden house in Cukur-bakali Türbe lane (Tk. *sokak*), in the Yeni Mahalle (Arm. Nor T'agh, "New Quarter") neighborhood of Scutari. Bedros resembled his mother in appearance and facial expression; and in his feminine gentleness, too, he was like her. Bedros' second-floor bedroom's windows seem to have set the scene early for his verses: they looked out over a garden with two cypress-shaded graves onto the Bosphorus and Constantinople.

The boy was sent to school at age four, to memorize the Psalms in Classical Armenian. At the second level of the Scutari *Jemaran*, the Armenian Academy, he studied the *Narek*—the *Book of Lamentation* of the tenth-century Armenian mystic St. Gregory of Narek. He began French, too, and seems to have been a poor student and the class joker. But his work improved when in 1865 he first read the poems of the French Romantic Lamartine. He was good at drawing; and his sketch for the cover of a volume of his own poems has survived. He sang in the choir of the *Surp Garabed* (Սուրբ Կարապետ՝ St. John the Forerunner) Armenian Church of Yeni Mahalle.

Tourian's education was very thorough for his time and circumstances. He studied the Gospels, Psalter, and Narek in Classical Armenian (reading the Narek for the first time at the *Jemaran* school in 1858, where he remained till 1867, rubbing shoulders with Turkish, Italian, and Jewish boys as well as fellow Armenians). Later on he read the Classical Armenian *History of Vardan and the Armenian War* of Yeghishe

---

[6]This was a typical procedure of the period: cf. Allahverdian (Tk. *Allah verdi*, "God has given") to Arm. Asdvadzadrian, Güllü ("Rosy") to Vartovian, etc. Many Armenians from the Anatolian interior who spoke Turkish as their everyday language switched over to Armenian in the freer environment of the capital, in the period of burgeoning national awareness.

*vardapet*—he wrote a poem to its hero, St. Vardan Mamikonean. Under the guidance of his teacher Srapion Tghlian, he read also the neo-Classicizing works of the Mekhitarist Frs. Arsen Bagratuni and Ghevont Alishan, as well as Movses Khorenats'i, Aristakes of Lastivert, and Ch'amch'ian's multi-volume *History* of the Armenian people. He would often browse and read at the Seghpos Khan bookshop in Galata, which specialized in Mekhitarist editions from Venice, including the scholarly journal *Bazmavep* with its serialized translations into Armenian of Shakespeare, Rousseau, Lamartine, and other European authors. Tourian read in Modern Eastern Armenian the works of the revolutionary reformers Raphael Patkanian and Michael Nalbandian. The latter's tragic death in Siberia inspired at least one early, defiant ode. He read Musset and Chateaubriand, translating the latter's *Les Martyres* as a school exercise.[7]

Apraham Zembayan regarded his son's early absorption in the theater and poetry as frivolous. At night, when Bedros wasted candles on work, his father would yell *Dzo! daha nsder es, lus ge varres?* Ծո, տահա նստե՛ր ես, լո՞ւս կը վառես՝ "Hey, Boy! Why are you still sitting around burning the light?") Tourian describes the scene in a letter, and in his poem "Love one another." In 1866, Apraham forced Bedros to leave school and become a pharmacist's apprentice. But he relented, and the boy returned to the *Jemaran*. By age twelve, Tourian had seen a play for the first time—his teacher Tghlian's tragedy "Eleonora," produced at Pera: a dramatic account of the evening is provided by Arshag Chobanian (Արշակ Չոպանեան), and translated in the final chapter of this book. The teacher recalled that Tourian had been his most Romantic pupil, entranced by Victor Hugo and Shakespeare. In 1867, Tourian began to write plays himself. He disliked the *kraparkharrn voj*, "mixed-classicizing style" of Armenian translations of French drama, and did eight himself, of which three are known, including one of Victor Hugo's (the Arm: *Ark'ayn g'zbosnu*, "The King enjoys himself"). He

[7]See Boghos Levon Zekiyan, "Personal Tragedy and Cultural Backgrounds in the Poetry of Bedros Tourian," in Vahe Oshagan, ed., *Armenia, Review of National Literatures* 13, New York, 1984, pp. 121-149.

translated *Macbeth* into Armenian. He translated Hugo's 1837 poem "La Jeune Fille," too; but this and other translations are lost.[8]

Constantinople provided opportunities for social mobility unimaginable in the Armenian interior: despite his modest background and severe constraints of health and finances, Bedros Tourian achieved a measure of renown, even celebrity, in his very short lifetime. Other members of the Tourian clan went on to build illustrious careers as archbishops and patriarchs of the Armenian Church, from Trebizond and Jerusalem to New York,[9] well into the first half of the twentieth

---

[8] In his monograph, *The French Influence on the Western Armenian Renaissance, 1843-1915*, New York: Twayne, 1964, p. 203, James Etmekjian suggests that Tourian in the poems "Love One Another," "The Child to the Cross," "Murmurs," and "Remorse" is influenced, not only by the poetry of France, but also by its Roman Catholicism. I perceive no such influence: quite the contrary. Tourian expresses overt contempt for the cruelty and stupidity of the Western church and its Inquisition. And most of his poems involving religion are protests against it.

[9] Bedros had three brothers: the youngest, Mihran (1860-1930), named Yeghishe (i.e., Elisha) at ordination, went on to become abbot of the Armenian Seminary at Armash, near Nicomedia/Izmit, then Patriarch of Jerusalem. Abp. Yeghishe Tourian was a great and prolific scholar: for my own doctoral dissertation on pre-Christian Armenian religion (published as *Zoroastrianism in Armenia*, Harvard Iranian Series 5, Cambridge, MA, 1987), I relied frequently upon his short but densely erudite work, *Hayoc' hin krōnə kam haykakan dic'abanut'iwn* ("The Ancient Religion of the Armenians, or, the Armenian Pantheon"), *Durean matenadaran, t'iw 3, Ambołǰ erker Ełišē Patriark' Dureani*, 2 (Tourian Library, no. 3, Collected Works of Patriarch Yeghishe Tourian, 2), Jerusalem: St. James', 1933. He is mentioned below in connection with the erection of Tourian's tombstone. There is a serviceable, if rather florid, biographical chapter on Yeghishe, with good bibliography, in Dickran H. Boyajian, *The Pillars of the Armenian Church*, Watertown, MA: Baikar Press, 1962, pp. 363-370 and 423-424. Another scion of the family, Bedros' younger cousin Archbishop Ghevont Tourian (b. Zembayan, Scutari, 1879; English, Leon Tourian), moved to the New World and became Primate of the Armenian Church in North America in 1931. He was seized and disembowelled with a dagger while celebrating the Divine Liturgy in December 1933—by grim irony, at the end of the same year his kinsman's monograph was printed in the Holy Land—by members of the New York chapter of the Armenian Revolutionary Federation (i.e., the "Dashnaks"), an Armenian political party that began its journey committed to Socialism, but, like its analogues in Germany, Italy, and elsewhere, eventually embraced an ideology of

century. His own work, considered the greatest Romantic[10] poetry in

---

ultra-nationalism with fascist and anti-Semitic leanings. In the 1930s the Dashnaks sponsored the "Race Worship Society" (Arm. *Ts'eghakron*) in the U.S.; and in World War II two heroes of the Party, General Drastamat ("Dro") Kanayan and Karekin Nzhdeh, raised an Armenian legion that participated in the Nazi invasion of the Soviet Union and served Hitler on other fronts as well.

In the early 1930s, the ARF leadership decided the Archbishop had betrayed the cause of Armenian independence by refusing to attend functions at which the tricolor flag of the short-lived postwar Armenian republic (now restored as the banner of the post-Soviet Republic of Armenia) was displayed, and by making accommodation with the Communist régime in Erevan (under whose control the Holy See of the Armenian Church at Echmiadzin had to function). Tourian's murder took place at the Holy Cross Church of Armenia in the upper Manhattan neighborhood of Washington Heights. The murderers were arrested and punished. See the leaflet *Patmut'ean hamar: Durean Srbazan Anmeł Zohə eŕagoyn drōšin,* New York: Matenašar Durean Yanjnaxumbi, 3, 1934 ("For History: Abp. Tourian, the Sinless Sacrifice to the tricolor flag"). The murder, which horrified the American public, was front-page news in *The New York Times* on Dec. 25 and 26, 1933 (I am grateful to my friend Ms. Helen Anahid Sahagian, formerly of Arlington, MA, a descendant of immigrants from Sebastia/Sivas, for photocopies of the *Times* articles.) Since I grew up in Washington Heights and first studied Armenian with Miss Vart Tarpinian, a teacher at the Holy Cross Sunday School, the Tourian case was both local lore and an early lesson in Armenian history. In February 2001 the Dashnak weekly *Hairenik,* Watertown, MA, published an article on Holy Cross Church, describing in exhaustive detail the history of the place from its foundation down to the present—but without one word about the assassination, the only event of historical importance that ever actually occurred there. When I pointed out this omission, in a letter published in the Social Democratic *Armenian Mirror-Spectator,* the editor of *Hairenik* offered as justification the argument that Tourian had not actually been **pastor** of the church; and pamphlets supplied to the author of the article did not mention the matter.

Archbishop Tourian is buried in the church, to the left of the high altar, and the sanctuary shelters also a copy of the miracle-working painting (whose original is still at Armash, near Constantinople— the monastery and seminary where Abp. Yeghishe Tourian, Bedros' brother, had served as Abbot) *Č'arxap'an surb Astuacacin,* the Mother of God who Expelleth Evil—before which hang the *ex votos* of the faithful.

[10]Romanticism was a European movement in arts and thought that reached the Western Armenians of Constantinople principally through the medium of

the language, achieved an instant fame that has never waned. It has been edited and anthologized in dozens of volumes and is studied to this day in most every Armenian school. But the poet, who died in the bloom of youth, saw none of those places or future times. His verses belong to the years 1867-1871, and mostly to the last two years of that period: they are intensely passionate, full of unrequited love, shattered faith, and, finally, impassioned resistance to the darkness he saw closing in upon him. His work far surpasses in its importance the achievements of his longer-lived kin, even beyond the bounds of its literary significance. For without it, modern Western Armenian poetry, perhaps even the modern Armenian literary language and its secular culture as we know it, would not have been. At least it would have been much impoverished.

Notice of the poet's work reached Europe relatively soon, though it cannot be said that appreciation and understanding were universal. In 1887, one Alexander P'anosian translated the poem "My Death" into French and published it at Paris, altering the text radically and adding stanzas of his own, justifying this barbarism by the claim

---

French literature. The Romantics rebelled against what they regarded as the cold rationality and ruthless, mechanistic optimism of the eighteenth-century Enlightenment. They sought truth in personal feeling, so the sorrow and pessimism of the tragic human state found validation with them: suicide was understandable; and death, almost laudable. Love meant all, and all is pain: woman to them is often the *femme fatale*. They had a neo-Gnostic tendency, too—one might even say they re-invented Gnosticism—to see the soul in society as an alien and pure being sunken in dross, oblivious of its joyous preexistence and its true state of oneness with a Nature from which Civilization, itself a mere construct of man's inner genius and therefore susceptible to radical amendment or abolition, has sundered us. The emotions, fired by art, help the soul to find liberation, through a retuning of its perceptions and responses. (See the seminal essay by Northrop Frye, "The Drunken Boat: The Revolutionary Element in Romanticism," in his *The Stubborn Structure: Essays on Criticism and Society*, Ithaca, NY: Cornell University Press, 1970, pp. 200-217.) All of this we will see in Tourian: the fascinated dalliance with death, longing, the near-consummation of love as death's aspect, the deification of an imagined and highly romanticized Nature. Had the scythes of Turkish massacre and Stalinist purge not cut the shoots down, a remarkable Modernism might have grown in the fields Tourian and lesser Armenian Romantics had fertilized.

that Tourian's fame exceeded his "unripe" and "artless" talent—an illustration of the Persian expression, *'ozr ke az gunah badtar ast,* "the excuse that is worse than the offense." The Russian Orientalist and literary scholar Yu. Veselovsky regarded Tourian as a minor poet obsessed with his own personal sufferings. Minas Tchéraz (Մինաս Չերազ) published an article on Tourian in *Le Muséon* (Louvain, no. 13, 1894); Alice Stone Blackwell heard Tchéraz lecture in Boston and wrote to him the same year about her fascination with Armenian poetry. She began publishing translations of Tourian's poems in the Boston papers, then in her 1896 collection *Armenian Poems* (repr. 1917). (Both Blackwell's and Tchéraz's translations are cited and compared with mine throughout this book.) The Italians were perhaps the most appreciative: Gianpietro Luccini published at Bari in 1913 a small volume of Tourian's verse; and other Italian critics compared the Armenian to their own Leopardi. In the Introduction to his great *Anthology* of Armenian poetry, published in 1916, the Russian poet and translator Valerii Bryusov declares that Tourian "cut across the vault of the sky of Armenian poetry like a bright meteor" (... *prorezavshego nebosklon armyanskoi poezii kak yarkii meteor*).[11]

In some ways, Tourian's short and intense life as a writer parallels that of Arthur Rimbaud, who began his sojourn in Paris in the ruins of the fallen Commune, even as Tourian was dying. Both invented a future that they did not live to see. Like the French youth, Tourian was a revolutionary innovator, a genius. His taut, fine lines, sometimes so terse that it is easy to miss the complexity of pattern and image that fires them within, liberated the Armenian language from the suffocating, pious pomposity of contemporary convention and thematic propriety. A watered-down kind of Classical Armenian, parallel to the pseudo-Attic *katharevousa* that was to afflict modern Greek letters and particularly officialdom for a much longer time, dominated prose and poetry in the language. The Greek word is an active present participle meaning literally "cleansing": the intention of its users was to return to an imagined national ideal and to remove from Greek the numerous

---

[11]On p. 68: see the note below on Bryusov's *Antologiya armyanskoi poezii* and its contents.

loans from Ottoman—Turkish, Persian, and Arabic—accreted over nearly half a millennium of *tourkokratia*, Turkish rule. In the Armenian case, the refinement of *grabar* (գրաբար՝ literally, the language of books, as opposed to *ashkharhabar*, աշխարհաբար՝ literally secular language, i.e., the vernacular) served similar purposes. The 18th-century scholar-priest and convert to Roman Catholicism Mkhit'ar Sebastats'i (Մխիթար Սեբաստացի՝—Sebastia is modern Sivas, in Western Armenia) founded the monastic order that came to bear his name at Pera, then on the island of San Lazzaro of Venice.

The Mekhitarists promoted the study of *grabar* with the aim of teaching the speakers of the diverse Armenian dialects a common, refined idiom into which works of Western literature, science, philosophy, and theology were to be translated, and of making accessible to educated readers the primary works of ancient and medieval Armenian historiography. Though Tourian's knowledge of the *History of the Armenians* of the Classical writer Movses Khorenats'i indicates that he benefited from the Mekhitarist project, he did not attend a Mekhitarist school. Though he was saved from the arid neo-classicism of *grabar* in his own writing thereby, that did not prevent his teacher Simon Felek'ian, a devotee of what Sirouni rightly terms the *zhamanagavreb bashdamunk'*, "anachronistic cult," from attempting to *grabar*-ize his pupil's poems (and, later, to bowdlerize them as well)![12]

Sirouni calls Tourian and Hagop Baronian (Յակոբ Պարոնեան) the two giants of the Armenian vernacular of their epoch: the former, of verse; the latter, of the stage. He rightly observes that Baronian's idiom was far more conversational that Tourian's—as befits his comedies of everyday Armenian life in the capital. Of the poet, Sirouni says, "Tourian's vernacular Armenian, though, is the most limpid and literary language that was ever employed in his day, and for many years

[12]Sirouni, *op. cit.*, vol. 4, pp. 72-73, who notes also that the learning of some teachers of Tourian's day in Constantinople did not extend beyond the Psalter, the Acts of the Apostles, and the Narek (a cycle of 95 mystical prayers of the tenth century, which Tourian studied as a boy, and on which see further *infra*).

thereafter."[13] The great Armenian writer, scholar, and critic Arshag Chobanian, one of the leading authorities on Tourian, valued so greatly the poet's role as the first fully to bring the vernacular to the level of art, that he was unable to see a masterful and intricate early poem in the Classical language as anything other than a triviality.[14] Tourian's concise poetic oeuvre was nothing less than a whole new literary style in the spoken language of his native city—one that was sufficiently powerful and refined to replace outmoded forms.

---

[13]Sirouni 4.76: *Dureani ašxarhabarə sakayn amenēn včit u amenēn grakan lezun ē or erbewic'ē gorcacuac əllay ir ōrov, u ankē šat tariner yetoy*. He regards Tourian as the exemplar of modern Armenian epistolary style, too, as in this letter of 5 September 1871 anthologized in Simon Karamajian's *Hawak'acoy əntir gruacoc'* ("Collection of choice writings"), 1890, pp. 108-109: *Nerec'ēk´ et'ē patasxans k'ič' mə erkarajgec'i. Šnorhakal em jer ayd ołǰunēn: sirec'i ayd ołǰoynə— carawi hanǰari mə ayd ǰerm əndgrkumə. Čēk' xabuir: ayn hamest gałap'arnerə, oronk' orotalu het burel, šant'eru het bužel giten—ayn gałap'arnerə patrast em šinel im kołmēs... Xōsec'ēk' ew sawaŕnec'ēk', perčaxōs barekam, ew t'oyl tuēk' or beweŕayin erkri pēs c'urt— txur ew dalkahar čakti mə vray—lok luŕ xoršomner calluin— c'aweru t'ert'er...*"Forgive me if I have put off answering somewhat. I am glad of your salutation. I loved it—that warm embrace of a thirsting genius. You are not deceived: those modest ideas that know how to be fragrant whilst thundering, to cure even as their lightning strikes—for my part, I am prepared to fashion those ideas ... Speak and soar, my eloquent friend, and allow that on a sad and pallid brow cold as the polar clime only silent furrows will unfurl, petals of my pains..." Though the anthology of 1890 presents this epistle as a model for emulation, what recommends it to one's attention now is its kinship to the imagery of the lyrics. There is the jaundice-stricken epithet *dalka-har* that Tourian loved and bequeathed to the Symbolists and Ch·arents·. We meet familiar wrinkles of care, here compared to petals, rather than to stilled waves. And there is the typically vivid concatenation of contrasting images, itself concealing more complex structures: *vorodal* "thunder" to *purel* "be fragrant," *shant'* "lightning bolt" and *puzhel* "to cure." Here lightning strikes to heal; and perhaps there is more to the opposition of harsh thunder and gentle fragrance when one considers that the Indo-European root of the Armenian for thunder may be **perd-* "fart": the smells of foul brimstone, delicate rose. And note how the *buyr*, reminiscent of a flower garden's (*burastan*) fragrance, is resumed lower down by *t'ert'*, petal!

[14]See the commentary on the second (undated) poem, "Now Soars the Joyful Day" (*Aha srana orn yerchanig*), page 322.

Bedros Tourian was thus the Romantic who made Armenian Modernism possible. His vocabulary is rich and sometimes exceedingly difficult, his symbolism complex and rooted in traditions going back to the glories of Armenian mediaeval literature and the mythology of the pre-Christian era; so although his syntax is close to that of Modern Western Armenian as he spoke it in everyday life in the streets and salons of what Armenians still call simply *Bolis*, "The City," it makes sense—it is necessary—still to deploy the philological methods of minute analysis proper to the study of Classical Armenian texts written a thousand years earlier, in interpreting him. For instance, the invented word *anali*, "wave-less," which he uses in one of his most famous poems, "Murmurs" (*Drdunchk'*), is arcane enough to have been regarded by some editors as a typographical error in recent editions. The Soviet Armenian poet and scholar Paruyr Sevak (editor of the authoritative edition on which is based the present book) emends it to *ahali* "full of fear," in the text, though in an essay translated in this volume (p. 329ff.) he himself probes the nuances of the *lectio difficilior*. The image in the poem of a ladder to heaven has deep resonances within Armenian tradition that is explored in the commentary in the present volume, in seeking to understand the full implications of the poem.

The European Modernists express a self-conscious indebtedness to their own Classical heritage—T.S. Eliot and Ezra Pound stand out in poetry in this regard. Tourian was well educated, as was observed above, in the works of the Classical Armenian historiographers, especially that of the *Patmahayr*, "Father of History"—Movses Khorenats'i (Մովսէս Խորենացի), whose *History of the Armenians* he mined for its rich poetic, mythological, and epic lore. He seems to have been well-acquainted with the great monument of high mediaeval Armenian spiritual literature, the *Matean voghbergut'ean*, "Book of Lamentation," a cycle of ninety-five penitential prayers and mystical meditations by St. Gregory of Narek (Arm. Grigor Narekats'i, Գրիգոր Նարեկացի). Tourian's lexicon is informed by the monuments of *grabar*; even more significantly, the phonetic and semantic patterns of his poems belong to the deep structures of ancient Armenian poetics. His learning, and the complexity of his art, justify a close reading that both focuses on the intricacies of the verse in itself and fully engages the tradition in depth. Because, like Rimbaud, Tourian was a poet of the future, in the analysis of his poems it is appropriate for the discussion to touch upon works that came to be written long after his physical death, works by poets such as Daniel Varuzhan, Yeghia Demirjibashian, Misak' Medzarents',[15] and Yeghishe Ch'arents', of which he is, however, a living creative part. Tourian belongs to the same Christian tradition as Eliot or Pound, still, but it is an Eastern one rich and strange—and with a modern Levantine identity of which all Eliot might have perceived was *The Waste Land's* Smyrna merchant, Mr. Eugenides. And the language of Tourian, for all its nineteenth-century locus in an imperial capital at the dawning edge of Europe, is Armenian, an archaic tongue of Asia, a root language of the Indo-European tree, a great survivor of antiquity, with gnarled and far-flung roots in the civilizations of eastern Anatolia and the Caucasus, of Aramaic-speaking Syria and of pre-Islamic, Zoroastrian Iran.

At the turn of the twentieth century, the Armenians were a vital and striving, ubiquitous community of the Ottoman Near East, and their political predicament was the focus of international attention. Their intrinsically fascinating language and culture, correspondingly, attracted the interest of scholars and literati. Prof. Peter Balakian, exploring the American response to the Armenian Question, concludes in his study *The Burning Tigris*[16] that activities on behalf of the Armenians formed the embryo of the modern human rights movement. So it is to be expected that almost all translations of Tourian's verses into ma-

[15] The tribute in verse by the young Symbolist Medzarents' to Tourian—the great poet of the preceding, Romantic epoch—is provided and translated on page 367.

[16]Reviewed by J. R. Russell, "When the Tigris Burned and the Euphrates Ran Red," in the weekly *Forward*, New York, 23 January 2004, where the book is appreciated as a monument of humanism and scholarship, but it is suggested also that its optimism is unjustified. No human rights movement has halted or even retarded genocides; and the latter have multiplied arithmetically through the twentieth century and into what one might with some justification call the present dark age. The message of the Armenian Genocide seems to be, rather, either effective self-defense for small peoples or collective security within the framework of a multi-ethnic civil society like America.

jor Western languages were done in this period. Subsequently, with the extinction of the Armenian communities of Turkey and the disappearance of eastern Armenia behind the *cordon sanitaire* thrown up by the Western powers around the Soviet Union, Armenia and its people ceased to interest humanity and all further studies of Tourian were done only by Armenians.

The Armenian Romantic and Modernist movements differ from their European and Russian namesakes considerably—as one might expect in the different circumstances of the Near East. The influence of a profoundly different cultural background can be felt even in poems that are composed consciously on Western models. The social setting that conditioned the interaction of poet, work, and audience was entirely different, too: literary journals, the theater, the existence of a definable intelligentsia, the idea of cultural and political liberty in writing—all of this was developed in Europe and America but new to Ottoman Turkey. The economic and social possibilities open to Armenian poets were very much more circumscribed than those of their European counterparts. Arthur Rimbaud at age sixteen arrived penniless in the French capital when the ashes of the Commune were not yet cold,[17] yet his work found an immediate reception and understanding with Verlaine and his circle. He was in a thriving literary society, in a revolutionary present, writing the script of the future. Tourian, four years the French youth's senior and very near death, had published some of his work, though he was not to live to see a volume of his poems in print. He produced his plays and enjoyed the attention of readers and

---

[17]An Armenian of Constantinople by the name of Step'an Vosgan interrupted his university studies in Paris to fight on the barricades in 1848; and he wrote in an April 1859 number of the journal *Arevmudk'* (*Արեւմուտք՝ The East*) about his experiences (Sirouni, 2.374): Tourian would have had ample opportunity to read the piece. The Ottoman Turkish reformer Ibrahim Shinasi, who was in Paris at the same time, also participated in the uprising, even climbing the dome of the Panthéon to fly the tricolor flag. Shinasi, who founded the first Turkish newspaper and translated a number of French writers including Racine and Fenelon, wrote a poem declaring that his only fatherland was the cosmos. It is not surprising that many Armenian liberal reformers felt a complete kinship with their Ottoman fellow citizens and could not imagine the fate that was to overtake them.

critics. When he died, a crowd attended his funeral. But Ottoman Constantinople was still no Paris. His editors and teachers were at worst prudish philistines. His poems hint at leaps he might have made, but anything like Rimbaud's daring was unthinkable.

It is not surprising that he struggled with Victorian propriety like a fly caught in resin hardening to amber, since his nation was captive, too, to a social and political position of relative backwardness. The Armenians were a minority people crippled for centuries by the degradation of Muslim rule. Particularly in the eastern provinces of the Ottoman Empire—the heartland of Armenia—they could not develop the cultural resources, nor, as a political entity, secure the freedoms that Western Europeans enjoyed. Still, Armenians in the relative haven of the Turkish capital enjoyed a measure of self-administration under the *millet* system.

Armenians were not newcomers to Byzantium. If we are to believe Koriun, the pupils of St. Mesrop Mashtots', the inventor of the Armenian alphabet, studied Greek texts there. Several Byzantine emperors were Armenian. The Armenians were different from the Greeks, but not sufficiently different to be defined as a distinct minority *ethnos*;[18] and there were very many Armenians residing in the Christian capital. Their numbers increased under the Ottomans: throughout the late fifteenth century, Sultan Mohammed Fatih brought Armenians to the newly-conquered city; in the next century, their numbers were augmented by Sultan Selim by Armenians brought from Tabriz. The flow of internal migrants was steady; by the middle of the nineteenth century, the Armenian population of the capital was reckoned at *ca.* 125,000, for a time narrowly exceeding the numbers of the Greeks—the next largest minority community. They prospered, their institutions grew, and changes in Ottoman society encouraged modernizing trends. The successive reforms of 1839 and 1856 (the *Tanzimat* or *Hatt-i Sherif* and *Hatt-i Humayun*), bringing legal guarantees of religious liberty, judicial due process, and protection of person and

---

[18] See J. R. Russell, "A Scholium on Coleridge and an Armenian Demon," *Journal of the Society for Armenian Studies* 10, 1998-1999, pp. 63-71 (*AIS*, pp. 989-997).

property, encouraged Armenians to seek a viable life within the framework of the Ottoman state. In 1863, at around the same time as the emancipation of the slaves in America, and shortly after the freeing of the serfs in Russia, the Sultan granted the Armenians a communal Constitution. It was greeted with great enthusiasm—Tourian celebrated its commemoration in verses of 1870 and in a prose poem of the following year to be considered below, in the discussion of his poetics. Soviet Armenian literary historians, with the embittered hindsight of the 1915 Genocide, dismissed the Ottoman legal reforms as worthless paper, but they were in fact of some benefit. And they served, no doubt, to buttress the sheer vitality of the Armenians of the capital.

Numerous philanthropic societies (ընկերութիւններ *engerut'iunner*) were founded through the 1850s, to aid education and the publication of books— from grammars, texts on geography, political economy, and anthologies of ancient Armenian literature to the novels of Jules Verne (Քսան Հազար Փարսախ Ծովերու տակ՝ *K'san Hazar P'arsakh Dzoveru dag—Twenty Thousand Parasangs Under the Sea*!) and Eugène Sue. Tourian himself was most closely associated with the Society of Lovers of Reading (Ընթերցասիրաց Ընկերութիւն *Ent'erts'asirats' Engerutiun*) of Scutari; his close friend Hovhannes Janfesjian was a leading member of the Society of Lovers of the Poor (Աղքատասիրաց *Aghk'adasirats'*) of the Yeni Mahalle district of Scutari. The latter half of the nineteenth century also witnessed the proliferation of newspapers and journals, principally in the capital but also in the provinces, in both Armenian and Armeno-Turkish (Turkish printed in Armenian script). Tourian himself was a correspondent of *Orakir* (*Օրագիր*՝ *The Daily*, founded 1868); others that published his work or articles about him include *Masis* (*Մասիս*՝ *Mount Ararat*, founded 1852), the satirical journal *Mamul* (*Մամուլ*՝ *The Press*, founded 1869), *Yep'rad* (*Եփրատ*՝ *The Euphrates*, founded 1869), *P'unch* (*Փունջ*՝ *The Garland*, founded 1860), *Arevelk'* (*Արեւելք*՝ *The East*, founded 1884), *Hayrenik'* (*Հայրենիք*՝ *The Fatherland*, founded 1870), *Endanik'* (Ընտանիք՝ *The Family*, founded 1883), and the Armeno-Turkish *Ceride-i Havasi* (Tourian's schoolmate and friend B. Dikran Atamian edited the latter) and *Manzume-i Efkar*. Armenians excelled in every field: the architect Nicholas Balian (1826-1858) came from a family of architects whose numerous masterpieces in Constantinople include the Dolmabahçe palace; Hovhannes Vahanian wrote on chemistry; Hovhannes Duysuzian, on viticulture; Parunag K'rdik'ian (1824-1868), after obtaining a medical degree at Galata, wrote a travel book on Anatolia and Mesopotamia.

After 1917, in the Russian-controlled sliver of the country that was mainly untouched by the Genocide, Armenian was proclaimed the state language of the Armenian Soviet Socialist Republic, and every aspect of culture thrived. But Soviet rule brought to the Armenians, as to everybody else, also the purges of the 1930s and the murder of hundreds of writers and poets, notably Yeghishe Ch'arents'. The latter, a poet who combined the visionary qualities of the medieval mystic, the sweet lyricism of the 18th-century bard Sayat'-Nova, the linguistic enchantment of the Symbolists, and the ardor of Mayakovsky, was of world stature, the father of a stillborn Armenian avant-garde counterculture. If Tourian had a spiritual heir, it was Ch'arents'. Though Ch'arents' was a convinced Communist and revolutionary fighter, writing strident, futuristic verses, he treasured the poetic inheritance of earlier generations and themes: M. Mazmanyan testifies that as early as 1921-22—after the Great October Socialist Revolution but before the formation of the Soviet Union—Ch'arents' was already planning an anthology of verse to be entitled *Dimankarner* (Դիմանկարներ *Portraits*), beginning with Tourian, followed by T'umanyan, Isahakyan, Medzarents', Siamant'o, Teryan, et al. The writer Gurgen Mahari said Ch'arents' told him the time would come "when we'll publish Tourian, Medzarents', T'ek'eyan, Varuzhan, Siamant'o..." Vagharshak Norents' said Ch'arents' was the first Eastern, Soviet Armenian writer to speak of publishing Western Armenian literature—the division of Eastern and Western Armenian was for Ch'arents' only a "conditional concept" (*paymanakan haskats'oghut'yun*).[19] And after Ch'arents' came only the poet Paruyr Sevak, who wrote a doctoral thesis on Sayat'-Nova, edited Tourian, and produced an astonishing corpus of work.

---

[19] See A. S. Sharuryan, *Petros Duryan: kyank'e yev gortse*, "Bedros Tourian: His Life and Work," *op. cit.*, p. 17.

Despite these tragedies and limitations, the success of the modern Armenian literary language that Tourian and a few others shaped (especially, perhaps, the satirical playwright Hagop Baronian) did have a real influence in the political arena: as the medium of a burgeoning secular, periodical press, it served as a powerful enabling factor for the diffusion of secular, nationalist, and reformist ideas in the Armenian community of the time. These ideas enjoyed fairly rapid development and led to great social advancement in the large urban centers of Western Turkey, and, to a lesser degree, in the eastern hinterland of Armenia proper. One turns briefly, therefore, to the political background of the poet and his age.

In his patriotic verses, Tourian follows with emotion the events in remote Eastern Anatolia. In 1828, Russia conquered the nominally Persian-ruled Khanate of Erivan: a part of historical Armenia, including the sacred city of Echmiadzin, was for the first time in centuries under the rule of a Christian state. Though Tiflis (Tbilisi), the capital of Georgia, was to remain till the early twentieth century the center of Armenian population, economy, and culture in the Transcaucasus—Erevan was a small provincial town, most of whose inhabitants were in fact Muslim Tatars (i.e., present-day Azeris)—the significance of the conquest escaped no one. Armenians had agitated since the mission of Israel Ori to the court of Peter the Great, at the beginning of the eighteenth century, for Russia to make its move. The uprising of 1722 in the Transcaucasus led by David Bek against Ottoman rule is further evidence of the strength of a native ideology of political liberation. So Armenians everywhere hailed the liberation of the northeastern part of their country as the dawn of a new era, and many from the Ottoman Empire emigrated to Russian Armenia. Tsar Nicholas I and his successors introduced a stiflingly repressive, autocratic order, with Russification as one of its main features, however; and many Transcaucasian Armenians subsequently joined the revolutionary movements sprouting up across the Russian Empire: they formed Workers' Councils even as their Russian comrades did; and Armenian socialists in the great industrial cities of Tiflis and Baku were to be the vanguard of the Bolshevik Revolution. Step'an Shahumian and Alek'sandr Myasnikian were the most famous: thanks to their efforts, the Dashnak, Menshevik, and Mussavatist régimes in Armenia, Georgia, and Azerbaijan were swept into the dustbin of history and the Transcaucasus became Soviet.

Back in the Ottoman Empire, as was noted above, there had been reforms in 1839 and 1856; and in 1863 the Sultan promulgated a constitution which provided for the formation of a National Assembly. According to the old *millet* system, the Patriarch of the Armenian Apostolic Church at Constantinople governed the Armenian community in many respects and represented it at the Sublime Porte. This clerical yoke, however often it was derided by secularists, became steadily less onerous; and from the priestly ranks emerged such charismatic and brilliant figures as the national leader Catholicos Mkrtich' Khrimian, called *Hayrig*, "Little Father" (Մկրտիչ Խրիմեան Հայրիկ), and the scholar Garegin Srvandztiants' (Գարեգին Սրուանձտեանց), whose ethnographic fieldwork brought to light the Armenian national Epic of Sasun in 1874. Tourian dedicated a number of his early, patriotic verses to the "Little Father."

The Armenians of Turkey began in the 1840s to publish periodicals, principally at the capital; at the same time the vernacular (*ashkharhabar*) of Constantinople began to be promoted as a literary language to replace Classical Armenian (*grabar*). Some impetus for this movement came even from the Catholic Armenian clergy—the Mekhitarist fathers of the monastery of San Lazzaro in Venice: in 1858, the great scholar Father Ghevond Alishan (Ղեւոնդ Ալիշան) published there a book of romantic verses in the European style, *Nevagk'* (*Նուագք*՝ "Melodies").

Linguistic reform was one way for the Vatican to advance its interests among the laity, bypassing the authority of the Apostolic Church, which was the custodian, as it were, of Classical Armenian tradition. The American Protestant missionaries who opened schools, hospitals, and other institutions in the main towns of Turkish Armenia (Harput, Aintab, Sivas, etc.) adopted a similar strategy, rendering the liturgy of prayer itself into Modern Western Armenian and publishing Bible translations in the vernacular. This way the faithful could read and understand the words of Christ directly, like good Congregationalists; but they also became reliant on the institutions of the missionaries. The missions printed Bibles and other books and periodicals also in Armeno-Turkish in regions like Cilicia where most Armenians spoke Turkish better than their national language, if indeed they knew the latter at all. In his Preface, Friedrich Engels mentions a (Western) Armenian translation of *The Communist Manifesto* of Karl Marx confiscated by the Ottoman police. It would be the earliest into an Oriental language— and it was neither a Mekhitarist nor a Congregationalist undertaking. Along with secular and vernacular publications, secular cultural institutions such as the theater proliferated. The first Armenian theater, *Arevelian t'atron* (Արևելեան թատրոն՝ "The Oriental Theater"), was opened in 1861 at Constantinople: actors from there opened the *Osmaniye* ("Ottoman") theater at Gedik-pasha, where Tourian's plays were to be produced.

By the middle of the nineteenth century, all the indigenous Christian minorities of the Empire, encouraged by the constitutional reforms, were engaged in a struggle for autonomy or at least equality within the Anatolian heartland and for complete independence outside it (in such peripheral possessions as Greece and the Balkans). Foreign intervention by the European powers, which was motivated partly by philanthropic concern, partly by an imperialist agenda—and was expressed in warfare and peacetime concessions of extra-territorial status—served to strengthen these centrifugal tendencies. Growing Turkish nationalism, as distinct from the supra-national Ottoman ideology, was from the start infused with alarm, and was destined, inevitably, to collide most violently with the strivings of the Armenians. For they were commercially and culturally prominent and closest to the Turks in the life of the country—and were, just as uncomfortably, also the only non-Muslim minority whose ancient homeland lay almost entirely within the confines of the Ottoman-ruled Anatolian peninsula.

When Tourian lived, hope and energy were already being met with systematic repression and massacre, but Armenians were numerous and prominent in every town, their new schools and hospitals everywhere, their press active, their language and culture studied with respect in most of the world's great universities, their national fate debated at most international gatherings. The state was crisis, but the mood was hope. None then could have predicted or imagined then the

Genocide—the premeditated and unprecedented mass murder that was in World War I to eradicate Western Armenia entirely and to cast the remainder of the nation, most of it in exile, into systemic crisis; its millennial cultural heritage into an obscurity that the enlightened, civilized societies of nineteenth-century Europe and America would not have thought possible. In retrospect, how could it have been otherwise, for a people whose ubiquity, prominence, and progress threatened their rulers—the rulers of a backward empire in swift decline—and who enjoyed no real political power, and no military power at all? It is the tragedy of Armenian history that a nation whose best members have striven to become part of Western civilization has been isolated in an Islamic world that for some centuries has closed itself to liberal political and social development and economic and technological progress. The result of the Armenian encounter with Islam has all too often been stagnation and worse.

Tourian's poetry is shaded by the obvious and imminent prospect of the young poet's death; but it is inevitable that the gathering clouds that eventually plunged Anatolia into the stormy darkness of the Armenian Genocide should cast a darker shadow still over it in retrospect. It requires great effort to convince oneself imaginatively of the fact that Tourian's society—the Constantinople of the mid-nineteenth century—was vital and optimistic: the personal tragedy of his work was felt by a burgeoning literary culture that cherished him and drew eagerly from his work, though, except for a few of his poetic brethren, it did not really understand him. For these are the poems of a subtle mind in the conflagration of youth, in a fabulous city of the East. Meeting Tourian is not always, despite early dark, a mooring on Böcklin's isle of death. Though Tourian himself manifests deep concern in a few patriotic poems for the plight of the Armenians of the hinterland, nobody in multi-ethnic Constantinople, full of hopes for social and economic progress and reform, could have imagined, much less foreseen, the industrial mass murder of the Genocide, any more than Europeans troubled by the Russian pogroms and the Dreyfus affair could have imagined the Holocaust.

So Tourian's main focus in his poetry is not political but personal: adolescent angst, pangs of love, wonder at the glory of nature, fury and remorse, and the fear of impending death. He lived in privation, and in a letter of 21 December 1870 written at Scutari to his friend B. D. Atamian, Tourian affords a glimpse into his everyday working conditions, which must have exacerbated his illness:[20] "If you want some information about me, then my condition is the same. In order to be alone, I retire often to a cold cell [Arm. *khuts'*, with its monastic overtones, presumably to give the extra ascetic flavor to the Romantic garret!] of my house, and with cold-dulled [*muyk*] fingers I scratch and blot with my pen, I burn, I stare wide-eyed, I growl, I press my hand to my brow, I groan in impatience, I ponder, I give off smoke ... the result of this is a play ... Of course I want by all means to be a playwright or a poet—a desire that finally will be smothered, against my will, in the corner of a poor hovel, under the black blankets of hunger and cold ... In any event, I'll endure it as long as I can: I don't despise cash, but I do love the pen."

**On Tourian's Poetics**

An essay on Bedros Tourian must include at least a preliminary discussion of his poetics. The commentaries to the individual poems provide detailed discussion of the intricacies of Tourian's lexicon, his description and development of themes, and the metrics and sound-patterns of his art. In this introductory discussion, though, I will approach Tourian's poetics obliquely, explicating a poem in prose that is not included in the corpus of the lyrics. Through close analysis and citation of selected lyrics, I will show how the poetics of this concise, controlled sample typifies his *oeuvre* in general.

Between the years 1867 and 1870, by Sharuryan's count, Tourian wrote eleven poems; in the last full year of his life, 1871, he wrote twenty-six. At the midpoint of that year—24th May 1871—not too long before the final onset of his fatal illness, but at a moment when the poet's particular sense of his art can be considered complete, Tourian published three prose-sketches in the Constantinople paper *Orakir*. The last of these is a prose poem in celebration of the anniversary of the promulgation by the Ottoman Sultan in 1863 of a Constitution for the

[20]Sevak, letter 2, p. 158.

Armenian community. In 1870, Tourian had written a poem for the anniversary—his last political ode, with the sole exception of "New Black Days" (No. 33). The Constitution seemed for many liberal Armenians an epochal document, in the context of the other reforms of the Ottoman social and governmental structure and in a period of unprecedented economic growth and development in the capital. It was to be the beginning of the vindication of their centuries-old national aspirations, the threshold of a freedom about which they had scarcely dared to dream. The hindsight of the twenty-first century does not help to recapture the euphoria: knowing what was to come, it is hard to experience the feeling of boundless optimism, the crypto-religious faith in progress, of the nineteenth century.

The piece is related thematically to Tourian's impassioned patriotic poems celebrating the Patriarch Khrimian *hayrig*, the Russian-Armenian democratic activist Michael Nalbandian, the ancient warrior-martyr St. Vardan Mamikonian, etc. They constitute a good quarter of his entire output. These poems, all of them pre-1871, are, in my view, not his strongest works. That is not because they are political *per se*, but because their themes and language are stilted and affected, with grandiose visions of Mt. Ararat, distant ruins, and past events read about in textbooks. They have none of the keenness of the poet's authentic personal feelings and none of the immediacy of his own experience. Tourian as a public figure was strongest in drama; but his lyric voice achieves its greatest power in the exploration of the regions of the inner universe of love and sorrow—the emotional provinces to which the things and senses of nature are signposts. The prose poem to be discussed here is of some documentary historical importance, but its principal interest, I think, lies rather in its lyric qualities and structure. For it has nothing in common with the ode to the Constitution that the poet had composed only a year before: the setting is, rather, Scutari, the Bosphorus, and Tourian's inner cosmos of natural symbols and the imaginal afterlife. Its emotions are those of the love lyric, not the soapbox oration. A close analysis yields insights into some of the fundamentals, in fact, of Tourian's developed poetics. Accordingly, the analysis is illuminated, not by other political verses, but by the lyric poems in which Tourian achieved his authentic voice. The text is published in Sevak, I, pp. 123-124 (I have restored here the pre-Soviet orthography of Tourian's own Western Armenian.):

Վարդի և արշալոյսի ամսուն՝ Մայիս 24ը կը մօտի։ Կրակոտ յիշատակի մը սրտագրաւ թուական։ Տե՜ս սա կապոյտ եթերին ձիւնատիպ ամպիկը. տե՜ս սա Վոսփորի խաժագոյն ալին.– Ձգե՛նք, եղբա՛յր, թող երկին ու ծով իրարու նային։

Տե՜ս սա կանաչագեղ թաւուտքը։ Շուք և փափսուք ունի.– Ձգե՛նք, եղբա՛յր, թող հոն սիրեն։ Տե՜ս սա դափնեվարդ և դրօշաւոր շոգենաւները, որոնք Վոսփորի խաժագոյն լանջը պատռելով կը թռչին։ Անոնց մէջ խուռն ու կուարթ ամբոխ մը կայ։ Հոն սրտերը շոգենաւին անիւներէն ուժգին կը բաբախեն։ Կարծես թէ եռանդը զիրենք կը տանի, քան թէ շոգենաւին մեքենայն։ Հոն կիներ ալ կան։ Հաստատուն աստղերու պէս զիրենք շրջապատող մոլորակներուն լոյս տուող էակներ։ Ծածանող դրօշակներ, բոցավառ ճակատներ, դիւթեալ նայուածքներ, կցկտուր ձայնարկութիւններ, նուագարանաց թրթռումներ...։

Ո՜հ, ուր կ'երթայ այս սրտագրաւ շէնքը։

Հոն, ուր կան նաև ամպիկներ, ալի, թաւուտք, շուք ու փափսուք։ Գեղ, գոյն, բոյր, ամեն բան կայ հոն։ Բայց հոն ա՛յլ է սէրը։ Հոն շատեր իրար կը սիրեն, հոն հոգիները կը սիրեն, հոն հայրենիք մը կը սիրեն։ Հոն կայսերաշնորհ Սահմանադրութեան մը յիշատակը կր տօնեն։ Հոն ազգային հանդէս մը կը կատարուի։

–Այդ շոգենաւը նետուինք ուրեմն, եղբա՛յր, որ կարծես թէ Վատիկանը վարնող շանթէն շուտ այն սրբավայրը կ'ուզէ նետուիլ, հոն, ուր հոգիներու բուրում մը կը ծաւալի։ Ազգային հանդէսները ազգի մը շնչառութիւններն են։

Բայց բա՛բէ։ Ո՛րչափ կարճ կը տևէ այս սիրային օրը։ Արևը կը փութայ իր ճառագայթները լերանց գագաթը մարելու։ Իսկոյն օդը կը տարաժամի, մինչդեռ սրտեր դեռ կը բաբախեն և շուրթեր դեռ կը դողդոջին խօսելու համար։

Շոգենաւները կը սուլեն։ Բաժանում կր գուժեն։

Տեսե՞ր էք այն ալին, որ հանդիսականները ի ծով կամ ի վերադարձ հրաւիրելու համար ծովափին աւազներուն վրայ կը շփշփայ։

Լսե՞ր էք այն հսկայ ծառերուն սօսափած տխուր Երթայք բարեաւ—ը, որոնք իրենց շուքին տակ հիւսուած մտերմութեանց վկայ հանդիսացան։

Ցիրաւի դառն է այս ժամը։ Բայց ամբողջ տարի մը դառն չըլլալու համար երանի թէ այն բոցավառ ճակատները չը մարին, երբ այն օրուան վերջալոյսը հորիզոնին վրայ մարի։

Translation:

In the month of the rose and of dawn, May 24th approaches. A heart-arresting date of fiery memory. Behold the snowy cloudlet in this blue aether. See the azure wave of this Bosphorus. Let us leave it, brother: let heaven and sea gaze upon each other.

Behold this copse, luxuriantly verdant. It has shade and sussurus. Let us leave it, brother: let them make love there. Behold these steam-ships adorned with laurel wreaths and banners that fly, cleaving the azure flanks of the Bosphorus. A motley, gay crowd are aboard. There, hearts beat more powerfully than the steam-ship's wheels. You would think fervor, rather than the ship's engine, conveyed them. There are women there, too: beings like the fixed stars, illuminating the planets that circle round them. Snapping flags, fiery brows, bewitched glances, snatches of shouts, the trill of musical instruments ...

Oh! Where is this heart-stopping edifice going?

There, where the cloudlets also are, wave, copse, shade, and whisper. Beauty, hue, aroma—everything is there. But love is different there! Many love each other there, there the souls are in love, there they love a fatherland. There they celebrate the memorial of a constitution granted by the emperor. A national feast is consummated there.

Let us hie ourselves, brother, to that steam-ship: faster than a lightning bolt striking the Vatican, it seems, it wants to hasten to that holy region—there, where the fragrance of souls is wafted through the air. National festivals are a people's respiration.

But look! How short this loving day lasts! The sun hurries to extinguish its rays upon the mountains' peak. The very air untimely perishes, even as hearts still throb and lips are still atremble to speak.

The ships sound their whistles, a dire knell of parting.

Have you seen the wave that hisses upon the seashore's sands to invite celebrants to sail away, or to return?

Have you heard that vast, sorrowful, shuddering *Bon Voyage!* the trees make—who were present to witness the tendernesses twined 'neath their shade?

Truly, bitter is this hour. But lest the entire year be bitter, would that those enflamèd brows not grow cold when that day's last light on the horizon expires.

The prose poem, like some of the verses, starts with bright morning and moves to dusk and darkness. In other poems Tourian moves from the sunlit upper world of life to the tenebrous pit of the grave: in general, the temporal and spatial movement of Tourian's poems, then, is downwards. Tourian's poems also have chromatic and olfactory patterns; and this piece begins with a delicate scene dominated by the color red. The blush of the rose and the glow of dawn establish a chromatic unity, and the rose suggests also a sweet fragrance. Spatially, this setting establishes the position of the observer, whose gaze moves outward and away to the next scene, one marked this time by the contrastive unity of the color blue: the blue (*gabuyd*) sky of full morning, and the azure (*khazhakuyn*) waters of the Bosphorus. With the naming of the strait, it becomes plain that the narrator's coign of vantage is Tourian's home ground, Scutari. In a number of poems, he gazes down at the Bosphorus and the city beyond from Camlica hill, or from Baghlar-bashi. So it is here, too.

By then summoning sea and sky to gaze at each other, the author introduces an affective element to his piece, that of love— and in a manner that stresses its spiritual, ethereal quality rather than its passionate and sexual aspects. The theme of duality is very important here, too. The archetypal natural pair in Armenian poetics is not sea and sky, but sky and earth (Clas. Arm. *erkin-erkir*). In the ancient Song of the Birth of Vahagn preserved in the *History of the Armenians* of the mediaeval scholar Movses Khorenats'i, the sea (Clas. Arm. *cov*) comes later as a tertiary, intrusive element, with a different sound pattern than the preceding pair. So earth by its loud absence makes itself known here; and in the next stanza it appears, further separated from the first pair by the refrain ("Brother, let's leave ...") from the observed scene.

The duality of the Song of Vahagn finds a changed reflection centuries after its composition, in the tenth-century Melody of the Nativity of the mystical poet St. Gregory of Narek. In the Melody, the loving eyes of the Theotokos are described as laughing seas that dilate like two suns in the dawn. Tourian developed this inherently contradictory—and thereby most vivid—image of two suns in his verses: Ես չը-սիրեմ սա կապոյտ զոյգ մ՛երկիներն գինովցած, ոյր մէկուն մէջ պաշտի նա, և միւսին մէջ ալ՛ Աստուած, "I would not love these blue and drunken heavens twain [*gabuyd zuyk m'erginern kinovts'adz*], in one of which is worshipped She; and in the other, God." (27.17-20) The tipsy eyes are left both mystically intoxicated and profanely drunk on passion. Or, Եթէ մօտի հողակոյտիս թուխ—մոխրագոյն ւ աչեր ներա թէ ջուխտ մարգրիտ թափին իմ վրայ, չը ցաւագնիր ոսկերոտիս, "If she approach the heaped earth [of my grave] and her eyes shed upon me pearls twain [*chukhd markrid*], then my bones will grieve not." (No. 32, "My Rest"—a poem in the shape of a tombstone.) In this case each eye sheds a precious tear, the beloved's body in the bright world above—pearls shine—thus touching the poet's newly-buried corpse in love, though he be in the lightless pit below. This image hints also at a marriage scene: the poet wrote a play on the pre-Christian King Artashes (Artaxias I) and mentions him in his poems also (cf. 28.16). In the oral epic cited by Movses Khorenats'i on the wedding of Artashes to the Alan princess Sat'enik, gold and pearls are said to rain down on their nuptials (see also the discussion of No. 11). Tourian's funereal variation introduces additional intricacies of theme: water nourishes the earth, but salt tears will bring no new life to the soil of the grave, any more than a girl can fertilize her dead boy-lover. I stress these details because the prose poem under discussion here will also move to darkness and death—and none of the love described in it is requited for the narrator. The text moves to an evocation of earth.

Tourian's Earth is a grove of trees, marked by a hissing, alliterative pair of words for shade and whisper, Arm. *shuk' yev p'sp'suk'*. It is not clear whether the trees themselves are whispering. It is possible to use the verb, of course, which properly describes articulate human speech, to describe the rustling sound of leaves—for which Armenian has the splendidly onomatopoeic *shrshyun*. Lovers, we are shortly to learn, are concealed in the *shuk'*, shade, of the trees—so perhaps the secretive, cautious whispering is theirs. This intentional ambiguity, though, is the basis for a richly allusive and polysemantic word, *sosap'-adz*, its reduplicative form linking it to *p'sp'suk'*, which is to be introduced in the resumption of the scene of the trees at the prose poem's conclusion. The chromatic signature of this segment of the text is the color black. Though the copse is *ganach'akegh*, beautifully green, the overall hue of the earth element is still dark—shadowy, secretive, concealing. In the lyric poems, the trees are usually high, dark cypresses, the trees of the cemetery; and in one poem black butterflies flit through the crepuscular air amongst them. In his exploration of the possibilities of darkness in the midst of his cypresses at Baghlar-bashi, Tourian was even to craft a proto-modernist image of black milk. But quite suddenly one is urged to leave this large, mysterious image to the delights of lovers who have not been anticipated, introduced, seen, or named.

The Bosphorus becomes again the focus, with several new images introduced to stress its vivid energy: flags snapping, wheels spinning, crowds milling, hot brows, glances, fragments of shouts. The focus is the steam-driven ferry. Again, all this is very familiar to the reader of Tourian's lyric poems. For he did not only look out and down at the Bosphorus from the green shades of his introspective, lazy days: he crossed it as a teenager for a memorable evening at the theater, followed by a night of boisterous carousing with his friends (an account is provided in the documentary section at the end of this book). On another ferry crossing, the face of an anonymous fellow-passenger captivated his emotions and he scribbled down the poem *Hayuhin*, "The Armenian Woman" (see discussion of No. 23). The ferry was a personal and general symbol of life exultant, of Constantinople itself growing with unprecedented swiftness into modernity. It was Tourian breaking free into the wider world of art, creativity, and amorous possibility. Balzac had compared Paris to a steamship. Our poet employs this strong symbol to bear, literally, the weight of his message of a nation progressing and celebrating the crossing of its Deluge, its Jordan, its Red Sea. He calls it not just *shokenav*, "steamship," but *shenk'*, "building, edifice, dwelling," as though it were Noah's Ark.

The next paragraph, then, must cause perplexity: if we have already seen cloud and wave, copse and shade, with their beauty, color, and scent, as the background or starting-point of the narrative, then why does Tourian make these same things, now recalled telegraphically in sharp, pointillist bursts of monosyllabic color—*kegh, kuyn, puyr*—the destination of the steam-ferry, the Ark of the Armenian nation, as though they were another place than the one mentioned before? The simple explanation is that the Constitution granted by the Sultan will transform the world we now inhabit, leading the Armenians to a promised Fatherland where human nature will be purified to idealism and devotion, where nature will be edenic, and love will be requited and everlasting. That is the political text; and the rather odd, shocking simile—shocking for its geographical remoteness and total lack of foregrounding—of lightning striking the Vatican underscores the political message. Tourian had wanted in childhood to be a priest, and at thirteen he would even celebrate the Divine Liturgy at a little table at home. He was a choirboy; all his short life, he loved to sing the *sharagans*, or hymns of the Armenian Church. But at school he would also deliver fiery Jacobin speeches; and the anti-clericalism of some of his pronouncements is so bitter that there is a sense of rejection and disappointment in it. His association of the Roman Catholic Church in particular with obscurantism, when there were so many other possible symbols available, seems to have to do with the same obscure embittered feelings. There are many possible sources for these. Several poems, culminating in the dark, titanic "Murmurs," decry the injustice of poverty and sickness of the human condition and condemn the divine author of the cosmos for having made such a world. Tourian as a patriotic Armenian would have deplored the attempts of Roman Catholic missionaries to make converts from amongst the Orthodox (they were forbidden, of course, to preach to Ottoman Muslims). He probably realized as he grew older that the reality of the Church often falls far short of Christian ideals. And the rather cowardly refusal of Bishop Khoren Nar-Bey to render promised financial help to the young poet must have been a source of deep disappointment. However the place the ship is steaming towards so swiftly is also farther than an industrial paradise or Armenian republic. It is the Otherworld.

Before proceeding thither, though, let us look at some of the formal usages of the passage. Armenian has a far greater proportion of polysyllabic words in its basic vocabulary than English does— like Russian, it is a "longer" language. It takes special effort, then, to produce lines of shorter words, and Tourian does this to great effect. Գիշերն երկնի կայծից, լուսնոյն սխրադէմ, Ցերեկն ալե՛աց, ծաղկանց ժպտիս… մէկուն գէթ (*Kishern yergni gaydzits, lusnuyn sekhratem/ Ts'eregn alyats', dzaghgants' zhbdis... megun ket'*) "At night to heaven's sparks, to the sharp-visaged moon,/ To day's billows, flowers, thou smil'st... but to one." (No. 2, var. 1, lines 5-6) In these lines, the syllable count of the words is of four words in the body of the line, with final variation: 2+2+2+2/+3//2+2+2+2/+3+1. Each line has four nouns; each word conveys a swift, concise impression, with the syntactical sense resting not on word order but on the case endings, which are in Classical Armenian (dat. pl. *-its'*) rather than Modern Western (*-erun*) for the sake of brevity. So the result is a rapid series of images, which might be rendered into English monosyllables, excising the three-syllable groups at the end of each line, as: /night-sky-sparks-moon/day-waves-flow'rs-smil'st/. The next two lines of the poem are a discursive expansion: Իսկ քեզ համար ես արցունքով կ'աղօթեմ, Դու չ'ես շնորհեր նայուածք մ'ինձ հուր աչերէդ։ (*Isg k'ez hamar yes arts'unk'ov g'aghot'em,/ Tu ch'es snorher nayvadzk' m'ints hur ach'eret.*) "But I pray for you in tears:/ You do not grant me a glance from your fiery eyes." (No. 2, var. 1, lines 7-8) The syllabic scheme is: 1+1+2+1+3/+3//1+1+2+2+1+1/+3. The first line contains only one noun; the second, two. So the purpose of the contrastive syllabic character of the two couplets is related directly to the intended lexicon itself: the nouns are crisp, numerous, hard in the first couplet; in the second, speech softens and widens into reflective thought.

One of Tourian's monosyllabic bursts merits some detailed comment: this is *puyr* (Clas. Arm. *boyr*), "smell, fragrance," a significant term for Tourian's imaginal world and his poetics. It derives from Iranian *bauda-*, "awareness, smelling," hence Persian *boy*, "fragrance," Arm. *purastan* and Pers. *bostan*, "rose-garden," etc. (see discussion of No. 18). Դու, որ գիտես լոկ բուրել, Գիրգ սրտերու վէրք փորել, Եւ կը սիրես, երբ կարի Քեզ պաշտող սիրտն արիւնի։ (*Tu, vor kides log purel,/*

*Kirk srderu verk' p'orel/ Yev ge sires, yerp gari/ K'ez bashdogh sirdn aryuni.*) "You, who know but how to be fragrant, / To pierce tender hearts with wounds, / And love when severely / The heart of your worshipper is bloodied." (No. 11, var. 1, lines 33-36) Here the verbs *purel,* "be fragrant" and *p'orel* "puncture" are homonymically linked: the association of *puyr* with the usages of the church through incense and the բուրվառ *purvarr,* "thurible (lit. scent-carrier)," supports the subsequent image of the *bashdogh,* "worshipper." The redness of the rose that is the lyric source of scent comes, thanks to the collocation of scent and wounding, in the image of blood, *aryun*; and for a Christian that wounding must be the laceration of Christ, who is the Rose ever blooming—though here the sanctity of the theme of divine love and self-sacrifice is inverted. For the beloved is cruel, and takes pleasure in the sacrifice of others. In Armenian, there is a further stratum of complexity, for the suffix *-varr,* "carrier," was early misunderstood to mean "burning" from the unrelated verb *varrem.* Thus the old Armenian summer holiday of Rosalia, *Vartavarr* ("rose-carrying"), retained in the church as the Feast of the Transfiguration, was thought to mean "rose-burning" and the like. So Tourian's lines summon the strongly-tied associations of rose, burning, incense, wound, worshipper, and sacrifice all together. The Armenian word for a kiss is համբոյր, *hampuyr,* literally meaning shared *puyr*: what word could mean more to a poet, the power of whose intense, synaesthetic perception of the world of the senses was equalled only by the black suffering of his intolerable loneliness and unrequited longing? *Puyr* is the signature of pleasurable sense, but also of grievous emotional pain; and this fits well into the changing emotional direction of the prose poem, too.

Here is another, even more striking example of Tourian's employment of short noun-bursts in a lyric: Էակ չէր նէ, այլ սէր, հուր, ժ(ը)պիտ, ցաւ։ (*Eag ch'er ne, ayl ser, hur, zh(e)bid, ts'av.*) "She was no creature, but love, flame, smile, pain." (No. 6, var. 1, line 26; var. 2, line 28) The syllabic form: 2+1+1+1/1+1+2+1. Here the word *zhbid,* "smile," formally a monosyllable and appropriate as such to the staccato litany of the second part of the line after the caesura, is lengthened to a disyllable for the purpose of metric balance. The parallelism of the two disyllables, *eag* "creature, being" (pron. with a glide as /*eyag*/, the glide necessitated by the vocalic hiatus) and *zh(e)bid* "smile," is thematically sensible, since it takes a physical creature to produce a visible smile—all the other things are either unhuman (fire) or invisible (love, pain). The vocalic pattern is interesting, too: e-a-e-e-ay/e-u-e+i-a. The only diphthong marks, syntactically and metrically, the caesura; and the intrusive, marked vowel is the u of the correspondingly powerful, striking *hur*, "fire," thus highlighted as the sole metaphor of the line: love, pain, and smile can be human; but fire cannot be, except metaphorically. Monosyllables, or concatenations of shorter words, especially nouns, in Tourian's poetics, thus have the intentional function of arresting and dazzling the consciousness with primary emotional or physical impressions that may be expanded and expounded elsewhere. Let us return to the Otherworld of our prose poem.

The words "But there love is different; the souls love, there" suggest a spiritual, otherworldly destination, as well as a change of condition, for to speak of souls loving implies disembodiment, a state of existence not dependent upon physical being. In Tourian's poems, there are often two worlds mirroring each other—this transient one, where colors fade and the sky darkens and lovers perish; and the Platonic, imaginal one after death, where flowers do not fade and love is deep and full and unending. A good example is the short poem "To May" (No. 30), where the first stanza describes the earthly vernal month; the second, a pallid, endless May beyond the grave. This division into two worlds becomes even clearer from the final section of the prose poem, where the day is coming to an end in the sublunar world. Tourian in this section uses thrice the verb *marel*, "to extinguish," as well as *kuyzh* "grievous tidings," *tarrn* "bitter" (twice), and *darazham* "untimely": as at the end of so many of the lyric poems, he is talking about death. He asks whether his listener has heard the trees' *Ert'ayk' paryav*, "Bon Voyage!" But how can one hear this? The answer is the encoding of sound in the words preceding the greeting: *hsga dzarrerun* ***sosap'adz*** *dkhur*, "the giant trees' frightened sad ..." Arm. *sosap'*, "fright," Clas. *sawsap'*, from **sap'sap'- < *sarsap'* by dissimilation perhaps, is a reduplicative form, cf. *sarsap'*, "*idem*"; and for an analogous construction cf. *t'ot'ap'em*, Clas. *t'awt'ap'em*, from **t'ap't'ap'em* (discussed in the commentary to No. 11); but it has the same phonetic and metric signature as *sheshunch, shrshyun* and *sawsiwn* (pron. *sosyun*), "soughing"—and the *sawsi* (*sosi*), "plane," was, Movses Khorenats'i informs us, the tree the ancient Armenians used for divination, by listening to the rustle of its leaves! (Cf. also 24.33-34: "The leaves by their sussurus / Our kisses kept.") Tourian has superposed the sound of a tree's voice upon the homonym expressing the feeling of fear, to produce sad words of parting. The rustling is a voice; and that voice harks back to the *p'sp'suk'*, "whispering," of the beginning of the piece. And whisper and grief, kissing and parting, passion and death are brought together by Tourian's deft strategy of sound. For the greeting offered the traveller, ***Ert'ayk'*** *paryav*, lit. "go well," must remind one of the greeting the traveler returns his well-wisher as he departs on his journey, ***Mnas*** *paryav*, lit. "remain well," that Tourian used as the title of a poem (No. 11, var. 3)—and the latter means, as a phrase at parting, Farewell.

Now, the reduplicative sibilant form of *p'sp'suk'-sosap'* (*sap'sap') is a signature, not just of death and parting, but of love and passion (never entirely separate from death, of course): ...Շրջակայիս Պաղլար—Պաշի, Գիտե՛ս թէ սիրտս ո՛րչափ մաշի՝ Շրջազգեստիդ լոկ շրշիւնով։ (*Shrchagayis Baghlar-Bashi,/ Kides t'e sirds vorch'ap' mashi/ Shrchazkesdit log shrshyunov?*) "When you perambulate through Baghlar-bashi, / Do you know how my heart is worn out / Just by the rustle of your frock?" (17.13-16) The signature sounds of these lines is *sh/ch*: the first line has three; the second, two; the third, four. The second line has the fewest, with its negating verb *mashi* (infinitive *mashel*, "wear out, expire," from Iranian *marsh-*, with -r- elided, thus related thematically and phonetically to the *marel*, "extinguish," of the prose poem, both linked to death: cf. Avestan *merethyu-* "death" > Arm. *ma(r)h—*, i.e., regular *mah*, "death," but dialect *mrhnore*, "on the day of death, with the -r-, and *merrnel*, "to die"< **merhnem*). Another example: Համբոյրի մը յիշատակն էր սիւքին շունչ՝ Իր դողդոջ ձայնն՝ տերևներուն սա շըշունչ Գունատ ճակտին տխրիկ պատկերն այս լուսին... (*Hampuyri me hishadagn er syuk'in shunch'/ Ir toghtoch tsaynn derevnerun sa sheshunch,/ Kunad jagdin dkhrig badgern ays lusin...*) "The zephyr's breath was the memory of a kiss; / Its tremulous voice, this rustling of the leaves: / The sad visage of the pale brow, this moon ..."

The first line has three *sh/ch* sounds; the second, four: in the first line, the collocation is of memory-breath, of a kiss; in the second, of tremble-rustle, of leaves. Thus the trees echo, phonetically and semantically, the soft breathing, whispered words, and trembling, passionate breathing of two lovers kissing each other.

"The very air untimely perishes ..." The waning of the day interrupts hearts that yet throb, lips that quiver at the edge of speech. In the formal context of the passage, this means most likely nothing more than that people who might have begun a conversation are now hurrying home. But, given the lyric subtext of love and death, this *loquentia interrupta* must mean something more: death prevents the fulfillment of self-expression, of communion with another soul, of full mutual understanding. Tourian writes, Խօսինք, ըսաւ՝ո՜հ, խօսի՜լ, Հատնիլ է լոկ ինծ համար։ Աչերու բոցն երբ մարի, Դադրի տըրոփն երբ սրտին, Լոկ այն ատեն հարկ է որ Անզօր շուրթերը խօսին։ (*Khosink', esav—Oh! khosil! / Hadnil e log ints hamar. / Ach'eru pots'n yerp mari, / Tatri derop'n yerp srdin, / Log ayn aden harg e vor / Anzor shurt'ere khosin.*) "She said, "Let's speak." O, to speak! / Is only to perish, for me. / When the eyes' flame dies (*mari*), / When the heart ceases to beat, / Only then must it be / That strengthless lips speak" (24.15-20). True speech, then, is possible, only in that Otherworld of perfection and requital. T. S. Eliot, in part five of "The Hollow Men," expresses this sense of loneliness and frustration: in a litany whose refrain is broken snatches of the Paternoster—cf., perhaps, Tourian's fragments of shouts?—the Shadow (of death) falls between idea and reality, motion and act, conception and creation, emotion and response, desire and spasm, potency and existence, essence and descent.

In an allegorical poem written to commemorate the constitution of the Ottoman Armenian community, Tourian has deployed many of the phonetic, thematic, lexical, and other features of his lyric art. Tourian's poetics is both utterly personal and vastly demiurgistic: he writes into being rosy dawns and fields of dewy flowers glowing red. From the quiet vantage point of Camlica's cypresses and gardens, he sketches the geography of the vast, sea-girt, fabulous capital; and in almost satanic verbal collocations he evokes the noisome, strait, black pit of the tomb. In intricate acrophony, he constructs and juxtaposes emotional and sensual heavens and hells, cleaves universes, charts a path to love beyond the grave. His poetic locutions and patterns are as ancient as the etymological pairs in the pre-Christian songs recorded by Movses Khorenats'i, as novel as the variations on those old themes in the songs of Grigor Narekats'i, the tenth-century mystic of Van. He is the comet, the fleeting miracle of nineteenth-century Armenian letters. But he is an enfranchised citizen of the cosmos of letters—this Constantinople schoolboy, this Armenian Romantic nourished on Lamartine, Nerval, and Hugo, bears within him the seeds of the modernism of T. S. Eliot, even the post-Auschwitz articulations of Paul Celan.

**A Note on the Plays**

Though his principal contribution is the small corpus of lyric poems presented here, Tourian was the author also of a number of plays and sketches of plays. One of the latter, for instance, is a suspenseful drama, full of elopements, conspiracies, and betrayals, about the Armenian king Tigran II ("the Great," r. 95-56 B.C.), whose short-lived empire merited the attention of Plutarch. Tourian's "Fall of the Arsacid Dynasty" was produced in 1870 at the Ottoman (*Osmaniye*) Theater in Gedik pasha, receiving good reviews; in March 1871, his "Tamerlane's Invasion of Armenia" and "Persian Raids into Armenia, or, the Destruction of the Bagratid Capital Ani" were also performed there. G. Fesjian, writing in *Ep'rat* ("Euphrates"), 15 January 1870, described the atmosphere of the theater: on the one hand, there were Western-style curtains and props; but there were also the cries of Oriental street hawkers—*Sucu!* ("Water-carrier"), *Fistik!* ("Pistachio nuts"), and *Hararet sündürü!* ("Thirst quencher!"). And the audience behaved raucously, clapping loudly and whistling.[21] Since the themes of these plays are unabashedly nationalistic, they were often omitted from editions of the poet's work published in Ottoman Turkey in the decades between his death and the reforms following the revolution of

[21]See A.S. Šaruryan, ed., *Petros Duryanə vaveragrerum ev žamanakakic'neri hišołut'yunnerum* ("Bedros Tourian in documents and the reminiscences of contemporaries"), Erevan: Erevan Univ. Press, 1982, p. 11.

1908. They are of only modest literary interest, but they do attest to Tourian's careful reading in Armenian history, and references to the ancient kings and their epic romances crop up in the lyric poems. Tourian is considered an innovative master and exemplar of the epistolary style in Modern Western Armenian, too; and some of his letters are translated in the commentaries to the poems and in the final section of this book.

The plays have not aged as well, perhaps, as the poems, but they are of interest to the history of Armenian drama. Besides, it was the theater that provided escape and excitement to Tourian, a life in the arts, as an artist, that was otherwise largely inaccessible to him. That is important to an understanding of the poet's life, but the plays themselves fall outside the purview of this book, and only a few remarks are in order here. S. Sarinyan observes usefully in his monograph on Armenian Romanticism[22] that Tourian focuses more on the reasons for the decline and fall of the ancient Armenian kingdoms than on their glories, and stresses the immorality, callousness, and corruption of royalty and the palace elite. He departs in this respect from the attitude of previous writers who emphasized the grandeur of their ancestors. But Tourian's ideological position, Sarinyan admits, still fell far short of the sophisticated social critiques of the late nineteenth century: the poet calls rather feebly for renewed commitment to Christian love and commiseration with the poor. At age fifteen, Tourian wrote his first play, *Vart ev Shushan gam hovivk' Masyats'* ("Vart and Shushan, or, the Shepherds of Ararat": *vart* means "rose"; *shushan*, "lily"). Other characters embody Evil and Misfortune, but the bucolic heroes live for their love and will never be *siratruzh*, "love-betraying": the play addresses thus the major theme of Tourian's poems, indeed, of his tragically truncated young life—his longing to love and to be loved in return. His play on the invasion of Tamerlane has some stirring, martial passages, for instance: "By unity and heroism ... unity, unity is a nation's weaponry, its life ... O Armenians! Let us not seek hope in heaven's face; rather, let our heart and sword be our hope ... Rise, O

[22] S.N. Sarinyan, *Haykakan Romantizm* (Armenian Romanticism), Erevan: Armenian Academy of Sciences, 1966, p. 366.

sun, rise! By your setting on this day Armenia will either descend with you, to its grave; or else its star will shine forth with the first luminary of the evening. I do not doubt, though, that the latter will happen, as long as every Armenian takes up arms in unity and wavers not ..." National unity is of the essence: "No, no, Tamerlane did not destroy those cities. A spirit more powerful than Tamerlane did: it was discord that eclipsed Armenia's sun ... O emissary (*badkamavor*), think not that the Armenians lack for valor. Had they as much unity of purpose as they have bravery, Tamerlane would not have attacked, trampling this country underfoot—he would not even have imagined plundering it." The latter passage may have a significant echo in the poem *Patgam* ("Message": the Eastern Armenian pronunciation, in Western Armenian *badkam*) in the *Girk' chanaparhi* ("Book of the Journey," 1933) of Yeghishe Ch'arents'. The second letters of each line spell out the challenge: Հայ ժողովուրդ, քո միակ փրկությունը քո հավաքական ուժի մեջ է՝ "Armenian people! Your sole salvation is in your united strength." The Soviet censors missed the encoded message, Ch'arents' boasted of it to an acquaintance, the latter informed the authorities, the entire edition of the book was confiscated and burnt, and a few years later Ch'arents' was executed. But some of Tourian's lines, for all their admirable patriotic fervor, seem stilted today, as in this colloquy:

Hope: Do not despair, Armenia … those chains may shatter yet; you've still a star.
Armenia: Ah! Heavens be blessed … but who are you? Might you be the angel of death?
H: I am Hope, who smiles even before the icy gateway of the tomb, upon crown and coffin with indifference.
A: And which is it you bring me—crown or coffin?
H: A crown! If the Armenian loves his brother, then Armenia will rise again [Armenia makes a joyful movement]. Armenia will not grieve, but smile [throws the crown of thorns away]. Armenia is not captive, but shall be free [breaks the chains]. It is the alien who smites Armenia's head, by love and light Armenia to Paradise is led, disunity is the plague that strikes Armenia dead … soon a new star will shine upon

the visage of the heavens—the nation's fortune, ascend! [Sweet light is suddenly diffused.]
A: Armenia lives! … Armenians, clap your hands! [The throne of Disunity is shattered.]
Love [appearing]: Give me your hand, Armenia.
A: Indeed. [They are entwined in an embrace.]
H: So the Armenian people will rise again."

*******

Tourian's death from tuberculosis, described in heartbreaking detail in later years by his brother Yeghishe (see the final section of this book for a translation) was announced on 21 January 1872 in *Oragir* by his brother Harut'iun (1848-1873). The funeral was scheduled for nine in the morning the next day, Saturday, at the church of *Surp Garabed* (St. John the Baptist) at Yeni Mahalle, where the poet had been a choirboy only a few years before. Writing on the 24th in *Manzume-i Efkar*, Tigran P'ap'azian reported that some three thousand people attended the funeral (other reports have four thousand). Such an enormous crowd saying farewell to a poet was something new for the business-minded capital: it was a sign of the great social and cultural changes that were taking place in Armenian and Ottoman society. Writers editorialized that Tourian would be better remembered by history than the son of a rich man or *Amira* (Armenian grandee). Elegies poured in to the papers, some couched in a pompous pseudo-Classical Armenian at variance with Tourian's own innovations. "Alas! Dark clouds of a gloomy dawn over Byzantium are descending ..." A classmate writes:

Only a month ago, when I said "Let's talk,"
"I am to die; death—speak!" he said,
"And when next you come to Baghlar-bashi,[23]
Cry over my black earth," he said.
Alas, silent boy, how can I sing to your soul
When my own voice is gone?[24]

---

[23]Baghlar Bashi is the park at Scutari that provides the setting for Tourian's poem "Whispers" (*Hdzdzyunk'*, no. 17) and a number of others as well. Ironically, it is also the cemetery where he was interred.

[24]Šaruryan 1982, pp. 30-31.

*Masis* reported on 12 February 1872 that a committee had been formed to publish Tourian's works: an octavo volume of some 500 pages was planned, to cost 1.25 silver *mejidis,* with the proceeds to go to the erection of a monument at the grave site. (On the monument, see my note to poem No. 37.) Bedros' brother Harut'iun protested two months later in *Sion* that the committee were engaged in "correcting" the poems. What this was in fact, as becomes clear from the notes to Paruyr Sevak's critical edition, which cite readings from that publication, was the substitution of simple vocabulary for some of Tourian's intricate, complex terminology, with some bowdlerization of his references to religion and sex. The writer and critic Arshag Ch'obanian, a major authority on Tourian, castigates Felek'ian in particular for his role in this. Later editors, and of course Sevak himself, have restored what they could; and I have noted the variants where they materially affect the meaning of the text.

**A Note on Transliteration.**

In transliterating most references—the titles of books with author's name and publication data—lexical items from Classical Armenian (*grabar*), and some other terms demanding historical or philological precision, I employ here the system required by the *Revue des Études Arméniennes,* Paris, which is based upon the transliteration devised by Profs. Heinrich Hübschmann and Antoine Meillet in their studies of Armenian historical linguistics. This schema corresponds to the reconstructed pronunciation of the language some fifteen centuries ago, and, with some significant exceptions (such as the change of the dark *l,* rendered as *ł,* to a guttural *gh*) to the phonology of the Modern Eastern Armenian standard literary dialects of the Republic of Armenia and the Armenian communities of Iran today. It specifically enables one to transcribe a given word in Armenian script with complete precision. But this system, already inadequate to Modern Eastern Armenian, utterly distorts the actual sound of *Western* Armenian, the form of the language Tourian himself used. The latter is also the form of Armenian employed as a standard literary language by the overwhelming majority of Diaspora Armenians, since their communities were formed mainly of refugees and survivors of the Genocide from the Ottoman Empire.

In Western Armenian the voicing of the unaspirated stops of Classical (and Eastern) is reversed in most environments: *p* becomes *b*, *t* becomes *d*, *k* becomes *g*, *ts* becomes *dz*, and *ch* becomes *j*; so the Classical name Petros, i.e., Peter, is pronounced Bedros. The *REArm* system also employs a plethora of diacritic symbols that are not readily comprehensible to the uninitiated. Nor does the Hübschmann-Meillet system account for such an important feature of the living language (in both its Western and Eastern types) as the on-glide, whereby the name of the city Erewan is pronounced Yerevan, or the relative pronoun *or* is pronounced *vor*, so the name Yeghishe (Armenian for the name of the prophet of Israel, Elisha; it is, as we have seen, the name of Tourian's brother, too) is rendered as Ełišē. And Bedros Tourian becomes Petros Durean, in a precisely orthographic (but un-phonetic) rendering of *ea-*, the way Classical Armenian orthography renders the diphthong *-ya-*. (I've generally spelled Western Armenian surnames with –ian, the usual form for Armenians in the USA; for Eastern/Soviet Armenians I've kept –yan.) Never mind the transliteration of Turkish words, with *iw* for *ü*! Part of studying a poem involves knowing the way it was meant to *sound*. Here, no accepted system of transliteration is of any help. Armenian orthography often reproduces clusters of consonants without the unwritten short vowel *shva* (Armenian ը) that is inserted into them in actual speech. It is customary in editions of poetry to print the *shva* where the poet intended it to be stressed for metrical purposes: this is called a *sugh vang* (սուղ վանկ), and I have respected the convention in the text and transliteration (where the *shva* is, as elsewhere, rendered as an e). In most cases I also use a simple apostrophe (') after a stop that is aspirated.

And the modern historical and cultural context is also important to choices in transliteration. The Armenians were the minority for many years closest to the Turks themselves in everyday life, commercial intercourse, and political affairs—the "loyal *millet* (national-religious group)." The second language of most Ottoman Armenians was Turkish[25]—for many, it was their mother tongue, and the syntax and morphology of Western Armenian are deeply informed by Turkish, as well—so I render words and names from it as they sound in spoken Turkish, not as a system designed for the historical study of Classical Armenian would transcribe them: the name of the poet Yeghia (i.e., Elijah) Demirjibashian (i.e., son of the head of the ironworkers, Tk. *demirci*) becomes a nonsense as Temirčipašean. So I will use at liberty phonetic transliterations of Western (or, when appropriate, Eastern) Armenian, trusting fellow savants will recognize the utility and sense of the compromise, which reflects more nuanced scholarship than slavish adherence to an arcane and often plainly inappropriate system. The Armenian text of every poem is provided, in any case. So for spoken Western Armenian, these Latin equivalents are employed (except for the diphthongs at the end, the Armenian letters are given in upper and lower case), the Hübschmann-Meillet system where it differs being added in brackets:

Աա a
Բբ p [b]
Գգ k [g]
Դդ t [d]
Եե e, and ye- in initial position
Զզ z
Էէ e [ē]
Ըը e (mostly as the definite article in postposition: a *shva* sound) [ə]
Թթ t′ [t′] aspirated, as in "tar"
Ժժ zh [ž] as in "mirage"
Իի i always long, as in English "eel"
Լլ l
Խխ kh [x] as in Scottish "loch"
Ծծ dz [c]
Կկ g [k]

---

[25]In areas of Ottoman-ruled Armenia proper, as in the environs of Diyarbakir, it was sometimes Kurdish. The Armenian script was employed extensively, especially in Cilicia, where many Armenians spoke only Turkish, for Armeno-Turkish printing. For Kurdophone Armenians there were schoolbooks in Kurmanci printed in Armenian letters, though these are rarer.

Հհ h

Ձձ ts [j]

Ղղ gh [ł] a guttural sound, the gh of Arabic *baba ghanoush*

Ճճ j [č]

Մմ m

Յյ y in diphthongs where pronounced, otherwise initial h-

Նն n

Շշ sh [š]

Ոո o, or vo- in initial position except in some monosyllabic words

Չչ ch′ [č′] aspirated, as in "cheese"

Պպ b [p]

Ջջ ch [ǰ]

Ռռ r [ŕ] trilled, as in Spanish "Carramba!"

Սս s

Վվ v

Տտ d [t]

Րր r

Ցց ts′ [c′] aspirated, as in "cats"

Իւ v (but see diphthongs below) [w]

Փփ p′ [p′] aspirated, as in "park"

Քք k′ [k′] aspirated, as in "kick"

Օօ o [ō]

Ֆֆ f

աւ av [aw]

եա ya, and ia or ya in the Armenian family ending –ian or –yan (the latter in Eastern/Soviet Arm usage) [ean]

իւ yu [iw]

ու u, or v before a vowel [u]

և ev, or (y)ev alone as "and" [ew]

**Text Edition.**

The critical edition of the great Soviet Armenian poet and literary scholar Paruyr Sevak (Պարույր Սևակ) and the eminent Tourian scholar A. S. Sharuryan (Ա.Ս. Շարուրյան) is the basis of this book. Though it is the first complete translation of Tourian's lyric poems into

English, numerous individual poems were translated long ago.[26] There

---

[26]Kevork Tourian, the "martyred archbishop of Trebizond," himself assisted Alice Stone Blackwell to translate Bedros' poems, some of which were printed in 1896, after the first wave of massacres of Armenians in Turkey; all her translations were published in *Armenian Poems,* Boston, 1917. Blackwell translated the following poems, which are all lovely to read but are in a few cases, sadly, paraphrases, and abbreviated at that: "Little Lake" (pp. 13-15), "Wishes for Armenia" (pp. 16-18), "To Love" (pp. 19-21), "New Dark Days" (pp. 22-24), "What are you, love?" (pp. 25-27), "I have loved thee" (pp. 28-29), "In memoriam of Vartan Lutfian" (pp. 30-31), "She" (p. 32), "Little Gifts" (p. 33), "My Grief" (p. 34), "Complaints" (pp. 35-37), "Repentance" (p. 38); and, in Part II of the book, "At Evening" (pp. 214-215), "To May" (p. 216), and "My Death" (pp. 217-218). In his masterful study of the response of Americans to the Armenian Genocide, *The Burning Tigris* (2003), Prof. Peter Balakian explores Ms. Blackwell's romantic attachment to a young Armenian cleric studying in the United States, whose concern for his people inspired her to work on *Armenian Poems.* In the introduction to her book, Blackwell asserts that the Armenians are of "Aryan race" and "pure Caucasian blood"—one may as well address this kind of nonsense now; and it will be necessary to do so at points in notes to the translations. Her motives were kind: she wanted to galvanize the support of white Christians in America for Armenia, and to do this it was helpful to explain that the Armenians were "white," too. There was a race-based quota for immigrants, and presumably it did not help that the Caucasian *Ch'en* (Greek *Tzan*) ethnos from which the noble house of the Mamikonians were descended was thought to be Chinese! Racialism and eugenics were then respectable here: in 1936, with the Nuremberg Laws in Germany in force, Harvard University's Peabody Museum published a monograph whose purpose was to provide an answer to the pressing question whether the Armenians were of Semitic "race"—with measurements of skulls and noses. It was concluded that they were not "Semites" (Carl C. Seltzer, *The Racial Characteristics of Syrians and Armenians,* Papers of the Peabody Museum, Harvard, Vol. 13, No. 3, Cambridge, MA, 1936). 101 Armenian males (no women) living in Boston but of foreign birth were measured for the study in 1931. The study determined that there are Syrians of "Armenoid" type, but Armenians themselves have a stronger "Nordic" strain. What a relief. I have not bothered, gentle reader, to ascertain whether there were all of 101 Armenian males, Nordic or other, enrolled at this institution in that year of grace. President Lowell, who had devised the *numerus clausus* somewhat over a decade earlier, had at least ensured that the number of Jews would be kept down at Harvard. There is a dormitory named after the man, who had also participated in the commission to whitewash the judicial murder by the Commonwealth of Massachusetts of the Italian immigrant workers Sacco and Vanzetti in 1927. In a famous painting that outraged the

have also been significant translations into French[27] and Russian.[28]

---

ruling classes of the day, Ben Shahn portrayed the decrepit blackguard in his crimson robes hovering over their corpses. Under Lowell's rule, Harvard also held secret tribunals to identify and expel homosexuals throughout the period. That was the benighted society, steeped in bigotry, class stratification, lynchings, and state violence, that decent Armenian immigrants and their children were trying to live and work in—when they could find work. For, while Harvard students sipped champagne in their faux-Colonial supper clubs, the real America was in the throes of the Great Depression.

27Minas Tchéraz, *Poètes Arméniens,* Paris: Ernest Leroux, 1913, pp. 1-79, offers for the first time in any foreign language *all* the poems, in excellent strophic prose translations faithful to the text, with critical commentary on the Armenian edition of 1872 and an introductory essay: "A la vierge," "Souhaits," "Chagrins de l'arménien," "Chants de guerre des compagnons de Vartan," "Le petit père des arméniens," "A propos de l'élection au patriarcat de Mgr. Khrimian," "A la rencontre du patriarche Khrimian," "Aimez-vous les uns les autres," "Souhaits à l'Arménie," "Je t'ai aimée," "Il faut mourir," "La vierge abandonnée," "L'enfant à la croix," "Petits cadeaux," "Au mois de mai," "A la violette," "Elle," "Un regard," "Les boutons de fleur de la vierge," "Nouveaux jours noirs," "Ma douleur," "Souvenir dédié à M.H. Djanfesdjian," "Gémissements sur la tombe de mon cher ami Vartan Loutfian," "La turque," "Aimer," "Le l'adore," "Avec elle," "Ma mort," "Murmures," "Perfidie," "Noir! Noir!" "Que dit-on," "Mon repos," "Petit lac," "Plaintes," "Repentir," "La brume de soir rampait pour accumuler ses voiles..." The 1913 printing, which includes also translations of Sayat´ Nova, Mik'ayel Nalbandian, and others, itself is a collection and reprint from serialized publications in the journal *Arménie,* commencing 1 July 1894. I refer to the comments of Tchéraz in the notes to my translations.

28Valerii Bryusov edited the massive anthology *Poeziya Armenii s drevneishikh vremyon do nashikh dnei,* Moscow: Izdanie Moskovskogo Armyanskogo Komiteta, 1916 ["The Poetry of Armenia from earliest times down to our days," published by the Moscow Armenian Committee]. The volume was published to acquaint the Russian reader with the depth and wealth of Armenian literary and spiritual culture and to encourage thereby support for the survivors of the massacres even then taking place on the southwestern frontiers of the Russian Empire. Five poems by Tourian are offered in translation in the volume: *"Moya smert',"* (no. 37, *Im mahe*) *"Bliz okeana golubogo,"* (from its first line, but it has a title: no. 35, *Nver hishadagi arr B.H. Janfesjian*) and *"Ropoty,"* (no. 25, *Drdunchk'*) tr. by Bryusov; *"Borolsya den',"* (from the first line, but it has a title: app. no. 3, *Mnas paryav*) tr. by E. Syreishchikova; and *"Moya skorb',"* (no. 34, *Im ts'ave*) tr. by K. Bal'mont. On p. 508, Bryusov notes that

Generally I mention the translations of Blackwell and Tchéraz in the commentary following each poem, with more or less detail depending on controversial readings, contextual remarks, etc. The editors of the 1971 critical edition represent the best scholarship and taste in the subject: Sharuryan is the modern scholar who has done the most work on Tourian's life and times: he is responsible, for example, for the reprint of Arshag Chobanian's important memoir and study of the poet. Sevak, whose vivid essay on Tourian is translated in the concluding section of this volume, was the greatest Eastern Armenian poet after Yeghishe Ch'arents'. The latter was murdered by the Soviet Armenian secret police in 1937. Sevak himself died in a car crash in the spring of 1971 in Armenia: it is often alleged that this was a deliberate accident arranged by the Soviet Armenian régime. Both left the world as young men. I have never seen any evidence to support the charge in the case of Sevak, and it is not clear why the government of the time should have wanted to kill him. That does not lessen the pain of the early loss of so great a poet. The wound of Tourian's early loss is reopened over and over: this is the tragedy of Armenian literature. The translations here follow the established text and numeration of Sevak and Sharuryan. They used the new orthography. In transcribing the texts I have restored, however, the pre-Soviet orthography that Tourian himself adhered to, which is still standard throughout the Armenian Diaspora for Western Armenian, and in all editions of Classical Armenian texts.

---

other Russian poets have translated Tourian before, including the important literary scholar and ethnologist Yuri Veselovsky (whose rather disparaging assessment of the Tourian is noted above). I refer to the Russian renderings, which are sometimes very loose, in the notes to my own translations.

# The Poems

## 1. Untitled, 1864 (?) (Sevak pp. 11-12)

**Text.**

Գարնանային կենացս մէջ
Սիրոյ ծաղկունք մինչ փըթթէին՝
Սիրտըս վառուած սիրովն անշէջ
Առաքինուոյն և գեղեցկին։

Մահագուշակ խորշակն անդէն
Հասաւ տիրեց սրտիս բոլոր,
Թառամեցան ծաղկունք ամէն
Ծըլած փթթած սրտիս մէջ նոր։

Այն, որ տուաւ երկրիս գարուն,
Ծաղկունք, մարգերն ալ վարդ նորին
Եւ մարդկային վեհ սրտերուն
Ուսոյց սիրել գեղն ու բարին։

Ինչո՞ւ արդեօք խորշակահար
Կ'ընէ ծաղկունք դեռափըթթիթ,
Ինչո՞ւ արդեօք Նա սիրահար
Սըրտերն պեղու արտասուօք միշտ։

Ահա կ'իջնեմ, ո·հ, ես այժմէն
Առջևս բացուած գերեվման խոր,

Բայց սա տըխուր տեսարանէն
Ի·նչ կայ արդեօք հաճոյք մ'Անոր։

**Translation.**

In the springtime of my life
As the flowers of love bloomed,
My heart was aflame with an inextinguishable love
For the virtuous and the beautiful.

Suddenly a sirocco, death's harbinger,
Came and overmastered my heart entire:
All the blossoms withered
That in my heart had newly sprouted and grown.

He who gave springtime to my land,
And flowers and meadows, too, for its adornment,
Who taught noble human hearts
To love the beautiful and the good—

Why does He strike with desert wind
The flowers still unfolding?
Why does He always overwhelm
Lovestruck hearts with tears?

Behold! Oh, I descend to the deep grave
Yawning open before me now.
But from this grim spectacle
Is there pleasure He may derive?

**Commentary.**

In his notes to the text, Sevak (I, pp. 223-224) mentions the manuscript was kept by the poet's friend H. Janfesjian, about whom see the Commentary to No. 35: Arshag Chobanian copied it out by hand, but it is unknown whether the original has survived, and it is not to be found in any of the poet's notebooks. The poem was first published in 1894 by Chobanian in his study of Tourian; subsequently it appeared in various collections. Janfesjian stated to Chobanian, "It is [Tourian's] first verse or at least one of the first" (առաջին ոտանաւորն է կամ գէթ առաջիններէն մին *arachin vodanavorn e gam ket' arrachinneren min*) and dated it to Tourian's thirteenth year. Step'an P'ap'azian, it was reported to Chobanian, severely reproved the boy for writing such a sinful (*amparishd,* the Arm. word for a sinner used in Psalm 1!) thing and bade him never do it again.

The reproach was in vain, since most subsequent poems of Tourian's deal with the same themes: spring flowers and new love cut down by the simoom of sickness, a vision of the grave, and a sarcastic, embittered protest against the Creator. The poet's powerful verse "Murmurs," No. 25, is famous for the latter aspect. The base *p't'it'-*, "blossom," was to become a favorite in later poems, too; so the poem foreshadows the lexicon of the later, better-established work. Even though the lover's tragically early death is the very soul of the Romantic vision, Tourian was not yet ill in 1864. The poem is notable, then, not only for its precocity but for fate's, or the author's, ironic prescience. Were it not for Janfesjian's testimony and Chobanian's unerring scholarship, these considerations might call into doubt the early date proposed for the poem, or, given the archival record, the very authenticity of the verse. At the very least, it was not one the poet himself chose to preserve, so it owes its prominence in the collection solely to chronology.

**2. "If Only"** (*Its'iv t'e*) and variant "I Love You" (*Ge sirem zk'ez*), 1867 (Sevak, pp. 13-14, 99-100)

**Texts.**

**1. ԻՑԻ՛Ի ԹԷ**

Ո՛հ, ի՞նչ ես դու, սէ՛ր, երկնի հուր կամ ժըպի՞տ...
Զ՛ունի երկին աչացդ կայծերն ու կապուտ,
Վարդն չ՛ունի քու լանջդ ամբիծ, լուսափթիթ,
Զ՛ունի լուսինն վարդերն շիկնոտ աչերուդ։

Գիշերն երկնի կայծից, լուսնոյն սխրադէմ,
Ցերեկն ալեաց, ծաղկանց ժպտիս... մեկո՛ւն գէթ...
Իսկ քեզ համար ես արցունքով կ՛աղօթեմ,
Դու չե՛ս շնորհեր նայուածք մ՛ինձ հուր աչերէդ։

Արդեօք էա՞կ մ՛ես թէ երկնի վըուարթուն,
Կը նախանձին փայլիդ վըրայ վարդ, լուսնակ.
Ձայնիկդ ապշած լըսելով քաղցր ու թրթռուն՝
Նոճերու մէջ կ՛սըգայ լըռիկ լուսինեակ։

Ծնէի իցի՛ւ թ՛ հևացող հով մ՛անուշիկ,
Եւ գգուելով երապ ք ճակտիդ այդ անսուգ՝
Տայի շունչըս շուրթերուդ մէջ ես յուշիկ,
Լոկ սրբելով՝ եթէ շողար աչքդ արտսուք։

Պարտէզդ իցի՛ւ թէ փթթէի վարդ լացող,
Եւ երբ գայիր այգուն շաղին ժպտով պերճ՝
Գունովս ներկել այտերդ, թափել գոգդ իմ ցօղ,
Թոռմէի գիրգ ձեռքըդ տայի կեանքիս վերջ։

Բխէի ես իցի՛ւ թ՛առու մը վըճիտ,
Եւ երբ յուշիկ նստած մօտ իմ եզերքին,
Ցօլանար իմ հայելւոյն մէջ քու ժըպիտ՝
Պղտորելով կապոյտ ալիքս՝ ցամքէին։

Ա՜հ, իցի՜ւ թէ լինէի ես ճառագայթ,
Շողշողայի դէմքիդ վըրայ վայրիկ մի,
Խաբէի քեզ թ՛ես աւելի գեղապարդ,
Ի՛անուշաբոյր մազերուդ մէջ մարէի։

Այլ ո՜չ, անգո՜ւթ, եթէ տրուիր մեկուն սէր,
Իցի՜ւ թ՛անոր գերեզմանին քարն լինիմ,
Եւ դու թոշնած գաս շնչե՜լ շուրջս… արտասուե՜լ…
Քեզ հըպելու համար հարկ լոկ գոլ շիրիմ…

**2. ԿԸ ՍԻՐԵՄ ՔԵԶ**

Ո՜հ, ո՞վ ես դու, սէ՞ր, երկնային շո՞ւնչ կամ հո՞ւր,
Քու սև անո՜ւշ աչերդ չ՛ունի գիշերը,
Վարդը չ՛ունի քու լանջդ ամբիծ ձիւնաթոյր,
Լուսին չ՛ունի քու վարդագոյն այտերը։

Ցայգն՝ աստղերուն փաղփուն, լուսնոյն սիրադէմ,
Ցերեկն՝ ալեաց, ծաղկանց ժըպտիս, մէկուն… գէթ.
Իսկ քեզ համար ես արցունքով կ՛աղօթեմ,
Դու չես շնորհեր նայուածք մ՛ինձ սև աչերէդ։

Արդեօք էա՞կ մ՛ես, թէ երկնից վըււարթուն.
Կը նախանձին գեղոյդ վըրայ վարդ, լուսնակ,
Ձայնիկդ ապշած լըսելով քաղցր ու թըթուն՝
Նոճեաց խորերն կը սգայ լըռին լուսինեակ։

Այլ ի՜նչ քաղցր է, եթէ ըլլամ ես պեփիւռ,
Եւ գըգուելով մազերդ խարտեաշ ու անօսր,
Տամ շունչս յուշիկ այտերուդ վրայ վարդափիւռ,
Սըրբեմ, եթէ կայ աչերուդ մէջ արտօսր։

Պարտէզկիդ մէջ իցի՜ւ թէ վարդ մ՛ըլլամ ես,
Եւ երբ դու գաս առաւօտուն ժըպտով պերճ,
Որ քու այտերդ կարմիր գունովըս ներկես,
Թոռմիմ… փափկիկ ձեռքիդ մէջ տամ կեանքիս վերջ։

Երանի· թէ վըտակ մ'ըլլամ ես վըճիտ,
Եւ երբ յուշիկ նըստած մօտ իմ եզերքին՝
Պատկերանայ հայելոյս մէջ քու ժըպիտ,
Պըղտորելով կապոյտ ալիքըս ցամքին։

Այլ ոչ, անգո·ւթ, եթէ ունիս սիրահար,
Իցի·ւ թ'անոր գերեզմանին վէմն ըլլամ,
Եւ հոն թափած դառն արցունքներդ ծըծեմ յար,
Ըզգամ դէմքդ… այլ ոչ, թէպէտ վէմն, այլ կու լամ։

Ո·հ, դու սիրէ·, գըգուէ·, ժըպտէ·, Հայ աղջիկ.
Քեզի համար պիտի մեռնիմ, թո·ղ պլպլուն
Արցունք մ'հեղու դագաղիս վրայ սև աչիկդ,
Տըխուր շիրմիս վերև երգէ թո·ղ պլպուլն։

**Translation.**

1. *If Only*

O love, what are you—fire from heaven, or a smile?
Heaven has not your eyes' lightning sparks, their blue,
The rose lacks your unblemished flanks aflower with light,
The roses of your hot blushed cheeks are wanting to the moon.

To heaven's sparkle and the keen-faced moon by night,
To flowers and waves by day you give, at least to one, a smile,
But I for you in tears must pray
And you grant no glance to me of your fiery gaze.

Are you a being or an angel celestial?
Rose and moon are envious of your glow;
At your soft voice's lilting sweet sound
The moon, smitten to silence among the cypresses, mourns.

Were I but born a sighing wind,
Then caressing the dream on your never-mourning brow

I would gently impart breath to your parted lips,
Only brushing away the tear that dared to glimmer in your eye.

If only I could sprout, a rose in your garden, and cry
When you came to water it with resplendent smile,
But to bedaub your cheek with my hue, to shed at your bosom my dew,
I would wither, giving my life's end to your arms' embrace.

If I were but a limpid rill,
When you paused to sit upon my banks
In my mirror your smile might glimmer:
Stirred to confusion, my azure waves would go dry.

Ah, were I a ray of light
Shining for but an instant on your face,
I'd trick you into thinking me more bright
And in your sweet-scented tresses then, I'd die.

But no—if, pitiless one, your love you ever gave,
Would I were of his tomb but a stone,
And you, wilted, came to breathe near me, to mourn—
To touch you I must be a grave.

2. *I Love You*

Oh, *who* are you, love, a *heavenly breath*, of fire?
The night has not your *black* eyes;
The rose lacks the *snowy stream* of your unblemished flanks;
The moon has not the *rosy hue* of your cheeks.

*At dawn, to the shining stars and the moon's loving face;*
*By day, to the waves and flowers—at least it is to someone!—you smile.*
But I for you in tears must pray
And you grant no glance to me of your *black eyes*.

Are you a being or an angel celestial?
Rose and moon are envious of your glow;
At your soft voice's lilting sweet sound
The moon, smitten to silence among the cypresses, mourns.

*What could be sweeter* than for me to be a breeze,
And caressing your *golden* tresses *fine*
I would give my gentle breath to your *rose-strewing cheeks,*
Touching them but to brush away a tear.

If only I were a rose in your garden,
And when you came in the morn with resplendent smile
*To rouge your cheeks with my crimson hue*
I would wither, giving my life's end to *your gentle hand.*

If I were but a limpid rill,
When you paused to sit upon my banks
In my mirror *the shape of* your smile *might be seen*:
Stirred to confusion, my azure waves would go dry.

But no, pitiless one! *If you have a lover*
Would I were of his tomb but a stone:
*There ever I'd sip the bitter tears you shed,*
*And touch your face—but no, still I'd cry, although a stone.*

*O, love on, Armenian maiden, and smile and embrace:*
*For you would I die. Let the shining*
*Tears pour down upon my casket from your dark eyes,*
*And over my sad tomb may the nightingale sing.*

**Commentary.**

The poem was first published in the Constantinople journal *Meghu* ("The Bee") after Tourian's death, in June 1871. A variant entitled "I Love You," the fate of the manuscript of which is unknown, was published by Melk'on Gyurjian (under the *nom de plume* Hrant) in the journal *Hayrenik'*, Constantinople, 5 August 1891, no. 19. Gyurjian states that the text came into his possession "by chance" (*tibvadzov*: see Sevak, I, p. 290). The variant omits one stanza and adds another; where there are differences in parallel lines, these are italicized in the translation. The refinements are clear. In line 2, it is better to say the *night* lacks sky-*blue* eyes than to try to deprive it of *black* ones! In line 3, it is obvious roses lack a snowy slope. If the girl addressed already has a lover she is mourning, then it makes no sense for her to be crying Tourian's own casket a river in the last quatrain. Before that, the assertion by the poet that he'd cry even if turned to stone is an awkwardly put contradiction of the common image of cold-heartedness, "tears from a stone"; and the needless confusion spoils also the image of the calcified bard absorbing (literally, sucking—like milk!) the *girl's* tears. And so on. Having made the necessary alterations, Tourian didn't keep the variant poem "I love you" in his notebooks.

The only significant textual variant in the *final* text, a change which Sevak (p. 224) regards as a distortion, is of the line "I would wither ...": *Verchin shnch'igs i kirgd arner elevech*, "My last little breath would rise and fall in your embrace." It is a vivid one: the leap of happiness at union with the beloved, followed by expiration. In line 9, Tourian asks whether his beloved is a (created) being (*eag*) or angel (*zevart'un*): the latter term is a translation of Greek *(e)gregoros*, Aramaic *'ir*, and refers to the ranks of the heavenly "Watchers." The more usual Armenian for "angel," which the poet also uses, elsewhere, is *hreshdag*, a literal translation of the Greek *angelos*, "messenger." The *Zevart'unk'*[1] are probably to be understood as more remote, staying always in heaven, the implication perhaps being that the beloved is unattainably perfect and distant. But the word is as likely just a rhetorical flourish, to make the wings of the angel a little more vivid. Tchéraz, in the note to his translation ("Souhaits," pp. 12-14), comments that the sixteen-year-old author "Tourian essaye ses ailes."

The procession of imagery of this early poem sounds themes to which Tourian returns in his later work: his beloved in the final draft

[1]The famous, round church Zvart'nots', built in the seventh century, bears their name; the nearby airport of Erevan is named after it.

has sky-blue (*gabuyd*) eyes (in the draft they're black, *sev*), which can be likened to the sky, with its luminaries; the rose sacrifices his color to make her cheeks red and bright. In the draft version, her hair is golden-blond, *khardyash*: the word is found in the pre-Christian song of the birth of Vahagn preserved by Movses Khorenats'i, where it is an epithet of the god of fiery tresses. The nocturnal scene of the moon grieving amongst the cypresses, trees associated with death and grave-yards,[2] anticipates the unsettling final stanza, where all previous colors invoked fade away: lines painted black.

In those closing lines, the beloved has given her love to another man, who has died: no longer aflower with light or rosy health, but wilted (*t'oshnadz*), she comes to mourn him; and Tourian, himself petrified into a gravestone, his voice become an epitaph, can at last touch her—there is, he says, no other way. So, after all his self-effacing timidity, after all the delicacy of the previous stanzas (the repeated word *hushig*, "careful," the incessant diminutives in *-ig*, *-ag*, *-yag*) in fact he is Death, robbing Love, the ultimate and violent ravisher. Before this Romantic *Liebestod*, there is in literature the famous tomb scene of *Romeo and Juliet*, a work Tourian the Romantic teenage playwright knew very well. There, too, Death is the final lover.

---

[2]Cypresses are ubiquitous in Tourian's poems. Three decades after Tourian's death, the Constantinople writer Mihrdat Chrakian (known by his Vedic and anagrammatic *nom de plume* "Indra"), who is most famous for his lexically innovative, impressionistic prose work *Nerashkharh*, "Inner World," was to write a lyric cycle *Nojastan*, "The Cypress Grove." Cypresses loom blackly over the Isle of the Dead in Böcklin's painting. The use of the cypress this way is a departure, though, from the context of *Eastern* tradition, that in which Armenian poetry grew. In Iran, the slender, sinuous ever-green cypress (Pers. *sarv*) is likened to the youthful beloved, graceful and arrogant, standing hips akimbo or swaying in dance. Arm. *noch(i)* "cypress" (*noji* in Tourian's Western pronunciation) is a loan from Iranian; and in Persian mythology the Hippolytus-like boy-hero Siyavakhsh, also named Noch, becomes a cypress when he dies.

**3. "The Armenian's Griefs"** (*Vishtk' Hayun*), 1868 (Sevak, pp. 15-17)

**Text.**

ՎԻՇՏՔ ՀԱՅՈՒՆ

Փոխանակ քաղցր օրորներու, հայրենի՛ք,
Օրրանիս քով մայրիկս ըլքեկ միշտ ողբաց,
Համբոյրին հետ շիթ մ'ըլգացի արտասուաց,
Աչերս տեսան արցունքներու լոկ երկինք։
Աւերակաց ծաղկանցըդ սոսկ այցելու
Զեփիւռն չ'ելաւ նժդեհ ճակատս շոյելու.
Փառաց դարեր ծընող՝ ընկնող հայրենի՛ք,
Մամռոտ աւէրք և դամբարան յօրավիգ
Արարատեան հսկայից,
Ուր ծոր ճակտով վիրալից
Հեծէ ոգին հայկական…
Բայց ի կո՛ւր, ողբ, վայ, կական
Եւ արտասուք ու հառաչ
Քեզ ըսփոփել չ'են կարող,
Այլ վեհ ճակատ քրտնաշող
Ի'արիւնաբուխ կող ու լանջ։

Մոխիր հագած, արիւն ծըծած սև հողե՛ր,
Ուր կը տիրեն սոսկում, տըխուր յիշատակք,
Ալ ծոցէդ թուեր են յուսոյ քաղցր հրեշտակք
Եւ արիւնոտ դափնի մ'անգամ չ'են հողեր…։
Սև շղթաներ եղան ինձի խանձարուր,
Մըթութեան մէջ սըրտիս վըրայ հսկեց սուր,
Միթէ Հա՞յ եմ՝ մինչդեռ չ'ես իմս, Հայաստա՛ն,
Եւ հոյակապ, վէս կոթողներդ պատուանդան
օտարաց, գահդ՝ յիշատակ,
Եւ ճակատըդ կրես պըսակ
Արդ փըշահիւս, սև նոճի…
Ալ չըկա՛յ վառ թագդ առջի,
Որուն ականց տեղ անգին՝
Դառնաթախիծ մըտածմանց

Քրտունքներ սառ՝ քար կտրած՝
Կնճռոտ ճակատդ պճնեցին։

Երբոր տեսաւ արիւնլուայ վարդին ծոց՝
Վարդատարփիկ բուլբուլն դողով թռչեցաւ,
Սուգին փափկիկ թեւքն արցունքով թրջեցաւ՝
Սիրատրոփ լանջք կուսից տեսաւ երբ սրախոց...
Լռեցին քնար, համբոյր, գեղգեղ և մրմունջ,
Հրաժե՜շտ տիրեց... և սիրակաթ շուրթերը մունջ
Համբուրեցին սև հողեր, ժայռ և ալիք,
Բոյլ բոյլ, բիւր բիւր ոգիք թըռան տրտմալիք
Մասեաց մուսայք դողահար՝
Թողուցին պսակ և քընար.
Դաշտեր, ձորեր և սարեր,
Ալիք, ժայռեր և սառեր,
Հէ՜գ հայրենիք Հայաստա՜ն,
Ըզքե՜զ, ըզքե՜զ ողբացին,
Որ ուրացողք քեզ բացին
Բիւր բիւր, սև սև գերեզման։

Հայն էր, որ թագըդ գըլորեց փայլարձակ,
Եւ ալևոր ճակտիդ բարդեց սև ամպեր,
Յետոյ վայեց, երբ գերեզման կը շտապէր,
Այլ շնչասպառ էր, չ'ունէր ձեռքը կայծակ,
Որ այն ամպերն փոթորկաբեր փարատէր,
Եւ հայրենիքն շղթաներէ ազատէր.
Նոճեաց խորքը մահուան շունչը սօսափեց,
Սոսկմամբ ցնորած Հայն իր երկրէն խուսափեց,
Թողուց աւէր և արիւն,
Թաղեց հօն փառք և աւիւն,
Արդ կը տեսնէ բօթաբեր
Ներկայն՝ ճիգ մը չը թափեր,
Հայաստա՜ն, քեզ փրկելու,
Անզգայ դարձած դարէ դար՝
Չը յիշեր քեզ, չը փութար
Քեզ անձկանօք գրկելու։

**Translation.**

*The Armenian's Griefs*

Instead of sweet lullabies, fatherland,
My little mother lamented you ever by my cradle:
With her kiss I felt a falling drop
And all my eyes beheld was a tearful sky.
From the flowers' midst your ruins no stray
Zephyr even chanced to caress my exiled brow.
Dejected fatherland, parent of glorious epochs,
Mossy ruins, mighty tombs
Of titans Araratian[3]
Where with brow new-wounded
The Armenian spirit mourns ...
But in vain are cries of woe and groans
And tears and moans—
They cannot comfort you—
Only a lofty, sweat-shining brow
And blood-bedaubed flank and torso.

Black lands dressed in ashes, drinking blood
Where fright and gloomy recollections reign,
Sweet angels of hope have flown from your breast
Without leaving even a laurel incarnadine ...
My swaddling clothes were black chains
And the sword in the dark over my heart kept vigil.
Can I be Armenian when, Armenia, you are not mine?
When your splendid, mighty monuments are the pedestals
Of others; your throne, a memory,
And the diadem that on your brow you bear
Is black cypress and woven of thorns ...
No more, your fiery crown of yore,

---

[3]Tcheraz, p. 14, emends the adjective *araratean* to the Classical genitive singular *Araratay*: "les géants de l'Ararat, où gémit le génie de l'Arménie..."

And in place of its priceless jewels
The cold sweat has crystallized
Of bitterly sorrowful cares
To adorn your furrowed brow.

When the nightingale aroused by the rose beheld
The rose's breast all blood, with a shudder he flew,
His soft wings with lamentation's tears bedewed,
When he saw the virgin bosom that beat for love by a sword run through ...
Lyre, kiss, loveliness and murmur fell silent:
Parting reigned... and love-streaming lips mute
Kissed darkened earth, rocks, waves,
Throngs and myriads of souls full of sorrow flew away;
Atremble the muses of Ararat
Abandoned diadem and lyre,
Plains and dales and peaks,
Waves and rocks and glaciers:
Armenia, sad fatherland,
You, you they lamented,
For traitors had dug you,
By the thousands, a black grave.

It was the Armenian who threw down the spark-scattering crown
And heaped black clouds upon your brow
And then cried woe as he hastened to his tomb
Out of breath, no lightning-bolt in hand
To scatter those storm-bringing clouds
And free the fatherland of his bonds.
Death's breath from the deeps cypresses scared him
And, scared by spectres, the Armenian from his land fled,
Leaving ruins and blood,
Burying glory and inspiration,
And now he sees the ill tidings
Of the present day and does not strive,
Armenia, to save you,

For centuries now benumbed
He remembers you not, does not run
Eagerly to your arms.

**Commentary.**

There is a variant of the first seven lines that was published as an appendix to “Farewell” (*Mnas paryav*), which belongs itself to a set of three variant poems (see No. 11):

Փոխանակ քաղցր օրորուելու…
օրրոցիս քով մայրիկս զքեզ միշտ ողբաց
Երբ համբուրեց զիս՝ իւր այտերն էին թաց.
Թշուառ մ'էի, աչերս արցունք նախ տեսան.
Սիրուն գրկէդ հեռու աչերս ես բացի
Այլ բնապդմամբ ես քեզ համար նախ լացի, իմ անուշ
Նոճեպարդ տխուր դամբան այդ անյուշ՝…

Instead of being sweetly rocked...
My mother ever lamented you by my cradle
And when she kissed me, her cheeks were wet.
I was unlucky, my eyes first beheld tears.
Far from your sweet embrace I opened my eyes
But by natural impulse first for you I cried, my sweet
Sad tomb of oblivion adorned by cypresses...

This is one of several early poems on patriotic themes—except for the plays, Tourian’s later works are personal in content—aroused by the charismatic figure of Patriarch Mkrtich’ Khrimian (called *Hayrig*, “Little Father”). As Minas Tchéraz puts it (p. 14), “Le poète a mis dans ces vers toute son âme patriotique, ulcérée par l’indifference des certains de ses compatriotes.” But the intimate focus is still present in this public verse: patriotic grief is a sorrow conveyed by a mother’s tears falling into the cradle, a sense of darkness and imprisonment felt in earliest childhood. Though Tourian invokes, vaguely, the massy, mossy ruins and cyclopean tombs of the Araratian past, one has the feeling he did not really know what these looked like; and only when he brings in the local cypresses, romantically symbolic of death, which will be so prominent in his later poems about his own doom, is there any sense of real sight of a place, even though the locus is Constantinople. The titans or giants of Ararat whom he describes, though, seem to be the *k'ajk'*—the supernatural beings who, according to the medieval superstitions transmitted by the Armenian historiographers such as Movses Khorenats'i, hold captive the Promethean king Artavazd. The lines about the dethroned and entombed king may refer to him.

The image of the rose and nightingale, altered to suit the theme of a ravaged beloved from whom the lover flees in horror, may seem at first painfully trite and awkward, but it is stylistically intricate, and some study of it may reveal deeper feeling. *Yerpor desav aryunleva vartin dzots' / Vartadarp'ig bulbuln toghov t'rrch'ets'av, / Sukin p'ap'gig t'evk'n arts'unk'ov t'rchets'av.* The character—something "awash in blood" (*aryun-leva*) of the thing seen (*desav*) appears before the thing itself—breast (*dzots'*) or the two subjects (rose, nightingale): this conveys the solid shock coming upon a murder, the expected person an inanimate reddened thing. The genitive *vartin* "the rose's" links the horror to its viewer, who is defined by the passion for the living being he had expected to see: *varta-darp'ig*. Arm. *darp'-ank'* is hot, sexual passion, and Tourian both evokes a strong emotion and makes it gentle with the addition of a diminutive suffix. In sex one trembles, and ejaculates (in Classical Armenian idiom, "wetting" means adolescence[4]); but instead of the expected *t'rch-* "to get wet" that would follow *darp'-*, we have *t'rrch'-*, "fly away," with trilled r (lines 42-43 end with a similar variation, *sarer/sarrer*, "mountains/glaciers" but without semantic contrast); the nightingale is wet with tears, and now the diminutive is transferred to *sukin p'ap'g**ig**,* "(wings) very soft with mourning."

In this poem, Armenia is a faraway place. Tourian himself is an exile (*nzhteh*, from OIr. **nizh-dahyu*, "away from (one's own) country"; cf. the *nom de guerre* of the twentieth-century Dashnak general Garegin

---

[4]On the ancient conceptions in Armenia of the symbolism of wetness and semen, see my article "Some Iranica in Eznik," *Journal of Armenian Studies* 8.1, 2004 (*AIS*, pp. 1333-1346).

Nzhdeh). The Armenians themselves Tourian regards as having abandoned their country, for lack of the courage their ancestors had.

**4. "Desires for Armenia"** (*Ightsk' arr Hayastan*), 1869 (Sevak pp. 18-20)

**Text.**

ԻՂՁՔ ԱՌ ՀԱՅԱՍՏԱՆ

Երբոր ցօղին փաղփուն շիթերն գիշերուան
Խոտի, թերթի, ծաղկի վըրայ կը շողան,
Երկինքն երբոր աստղեր փալփլին գիշերը՝
Յայտեն արցունք, կայծ իմ ցաւած աչերը.
　　Ի·նչ, Հայաստա·ն, քեզ մոռնա·լ…
Երբէ·ք, այլ սև նոճի մ'ըլլալ, քեզ շո·ք տալ։

Զ'իս աստղազարդ երկին սփոփել չ'է կարող,
Մասեաց սարին արտասուալից է նա քող,
Ձեր յիշատակն ինծի համար հեշտագին՝
Նըման կուսին սիրոյ առջի արցունքին.
　　Դամբա·նք, աւե·րք, Ձեզ մոռնա·լ…
Երբէ·ք, այլ ուղխ մ'արցունք ըլլալ, Ձեզ թա·ց տալ։

Երկաթ, շղթայ, կնդան, անդունդք ու վըհեր,
Ամպրոպ ու շանթ, մահուան կանգակ ու ջահեր,
Չ'է, չ'են կարող պահ մը Ձեր վառ յիշատակ
Ծածկել սևի ու սուկումի՝ վէմի տակ.
　　Ապա·տ օրե·ր, Ձեզ մոռնա·լ…
Երբէ·ք, այլ հուր մ'ըլլալ և Ձեզ Հայո·ւն տալ։

Ջուարթ բնութեան այն կամարներն ծաղկահիւս,
Բոյր, կայծ ու գեղ, նայուածք, ժըպիտ սիրուհւոյս,
Անուշ հովեր, արծաթ ալիք վըտակին
Ձեր հուրն սրտէս պահ մը առնել չը կրցին.
　　Փառա·ց օրեր, Ձեզ մոռնա·լ…
Երբէ·ք, պատրոյգ մ'ըլլալ այլ Ձեզ, ու լո·յս տալ։

Արշալոյսին տժգոյն աստղեր երբ փալփլին,
Գողտըր գեղգեղ վարդակարօտ բուլբուլին,

Բնութեան դաշնակք, ո·հ չ'են կրնար նուաճեր
Ձեր հառաչներն որով մռընչեն նոճիներ.
Սև· սև· օրեր, Ձեզ մոռնա·լ...
Երբէ·ք, արիւն մ'ըլլալ և Ձեզ կարմի·ր տալ։

Թերևս ժպտին Մասեաց մըթին սարերը,
Կամ արտասուին Սիպերիոյ սառերը,
Բայց սև հոգիք ու սև ճանկեր չ'են կրնար
Խեղդել իմ ձայնս, փշրել փըշուտ իմ քնար.
Արդարութի·ւն, քեզ մոռնա·լ,
Երբէ·ք, այլ սուր մ'ըլլալ, սրտեր քեզ մուտ տալ։

Մինչ ց'ե՞րբ գոչեմ, ձայնըս մէկը չը լըսեր,
Հայն իւր ժանգոտ շղթան երբէ·ք չը սարսեր...
Վայրկեան մ'ինձ հետ դեռ իրաւունք չ'թոթովեց,
Հայն կ'իս ծաղրեց, և ձայն մը կ'իս չը թովեց.
...Դեռ կը գոչեմ Ձեզ, Հայե·ր,
Որ դամբանիս մէջ չը լըսեմ Ձեր վայեր։

Հարուստն ու կղեր թէ ազգ ըզգան ու վառին,
Թէ «լոյս և սէր» Հայ սրտերուն մէջ թառին,
Թէ լուսոյ դարն երկնէ «ազատ զաւակներ»,
Թ'եղբայրութեան, սիրոյ վառին կըրակներ,
Թէև ըլլամ ես մեռել,
Դամբանէս դուրս կ'նետուիմ ԱԶԱՏ Հայն տեսնել։

**Translation.**

*Desires for Armenia*

When the resplendent dewdrops of the night
Glimmer upon the grass, the leaf, the flower,
When the stars glitter in the night sky,
Tears gush, sparkle in my anguished eyes.
What, Armenia—forget thee?
Never! Rather I would be a black cypress and shade thee.

The star-bedecked heaven cannot console me,
For it is but Mount Ararat's tear-gemmed veil:
Your delightful recollection for me
Is like a maiden's love's first tear.
        Tombs and ruins—forget you all?
Never! Rather may I moisten you as a rill of tears.

Irons, chains, dungeon, abysses and pits,
Thunder and lighting, torches and the knell of death—
No! Not for a moment your bright recollection
Can they hide beneath a boulder of darkness and fright.
        Days of freedom—forget you?
Never! Rather make me the fire that to the Armenians conveys you.

Those blossom-woven trellises of nature gay,
Fragrance, glint and glance, loveliness, my beloved's smile,
Sweet breezes, the silver lapping stream
Could not for an instant remove from my heart your fire.
        Days of glory—forget you?
Never! Better I be your candle flame and give light.

When the pale stars at daybreak gleam
Upon the tender lovely nightingale for his rose pining,
Harmonies of nature! Oh, those melodies cannot hide
Your sighs that the creaking cypresses groan.
        Black, black days! Forget you?
Never! Better I become blood and redden you.

Perhaps the summits of Ararat smile in the dark
Or the ice of Siberia weeps.
But black souls, black talons cannot
Strangle my voice, shatter my sharp lyre.
        Righteousness! Forget you!
Never! I should be instead a sword, into hearts to cleave your way.

How long shall I shout? None hears my voice,
The Armenian shakes not his rusted chains.
Justice has not stammered for an instant a single word:
The Armenian mocked me: no voice brought me enchantment.
    Shall I summon you, Armenians, still,
So that I do not hear your wailing even in my grave?

If the feeling for their nation enkindles the rich and the priest,
If "light and love" in the Armenians' hearts come to dwell,
If an age of enlightenment to "free sons" give birth,
If fires of fraternity, of love burn bright,
    Then even if I am dead
To behold the Armenian liberated—from my tomb I shall arise.

**Commentary.**

The poem is copied in two of Tourian's notebooks and has been published in numerous editions. In Blackwell's *Armenian Poems* it is entitled "Wishes for Armenia" (pp. 16-18); "Souhaits à l'Arménie" in Tchéraz's anthology (pp. 30-32). A number of lines in the poem are very similar to verses of Tourian's poem (No. 7) written 27 September 1869 in honor of the election of Mkrtich' Khrimian as Armenian Patriarch of Constantinople; so it is likely that this poem was written around the same time (and perhaps before rather than after No. 7, since it refers, as we shall see presently, to events of 1866). The reference to Siberia in line 32 indicates that the poem refers to the persecution by the Tsarist régime in Russia of Armenian liberals, particularly Michael Nalbandian (b. 1829). The latter, a native of Nor Nakhichevan—the Armenian colony at Rostov on the Don—worked as a teacher of Armenian at the Lazarev Academy at Moscow. He also published as a prose writer, poet, and publicist in the influential Russian-Armenian liberal journal *Hyusisap'ayl* ("Aurora Borealis") edited by the poet Step'anos Nazarian.[5] He went on to earn a doctoral degree

---

[5]Step'anos Nazarian, 1812-1879, wrote the famous poem *Mayreni lezu*, "Mother Tongue." In what may be a deprecating reference to the Tsars' policy of Russification, Nazarian writes in that poem (in Simonian's edition, p. 57: see the following note):

Ո·ճ, ինչպէս պըղտոր էր սըրտիս օրը.

at St. Petersburg University in 1860. He spent the last two months of the same year at Constantinople and travelled on to London, where he was befriended by the writer Ivan Turgenev, whose novel *Fathers and Sons* exemplifies the social conflicts of the great Sixties. He associated also with the Russian democrat and publicist Alexander Herzen and the anarchist Mikhail Bakunin. On Bastille Day 1862 he was arrested in his native town and incriminating, encrypted letters from Bakunin were found in the police search of his lodgings. He was transferred for trial to St. Petersburg and imprisoned for three years under harsh conditions in the capital's Peter and Paul Fortress. Then, "more dead than alive," as he wrote in a letter, he was sent into exile at Kamyshin in the province of Saratov, where he died of lung disease, on 31 March 1866. After an elaborate funeral, his remains were interred in the Armenian

---

Երբ պանդուխտ էի օտարի տանը,
Եթէ հարկ էր ինձ այլազգի լեզուով
Իմ միտքը յայտնել օտար բառերով,
Որ երբէք սիրել կարելի չէ ինձ,
Որ ձայն ողջունի բնաւ իսկ չեն ինձ։

(Oh! How gloomy was my heart's day / When I was a stranger in an alien's land / If I had in a foreign tongue / To express my thoughts in alien words, / Which I can never love, / Whose sound can never be welcoming to me.") But in the anthology *Գոհարներ Հայ գրականութեան* (*Koharner Hay kraganut'ian*, "Jewels of Armenian Literature"), Boston: Hayrenik', 1916, the above stanza is omitted and replaced with this milder one, which the Imperial censor of a book printed in the Russian Empire might have liked better (neither Nazarian's nor Nalbandian's poem found its way into Bryusov's *Anthology*; the two mention only a fleeting mention in the Introduction, in connection with *Aurora Borealis*):

Ամէն տեղ փչում է Աստուծոյ շունչը,
Սուրբ է, այո՛, միւս, այլ ձև ու ոճը,
Բայց թէ աղօթել, գոհանալ պէտք էր,
Իմ սրտի սէրը յայտնել արժան էր.
Իմ երանական մտածութիւնքը–
Ապա կը խօսիմ իմ մօրս խօսքը։

("God's breath in every clime is breathing, / And truly other forms and styles are holy. / But if there be need of prayer and praise, / Meet to express the love of my heart, / My beatitudinous musings, / Then it is my mother's language that I speak.") In either case, Nazarian's poem is also a plea for the literary use of spoken Armenian—a sentiment very close, of course, also to Tourian's heart.

Monastery of the Holy Cross at Nor Nakhichevan, and a large monument was erected over the grave. Nalbandian's death sent shock waves of grief and anger through the Armenian world. Constantinople learnt of the tragedy relatively soon afterwards, in May 1866, from the Tiflis paper *Haykakan Ashkharh* (*Հայկական Աշխարհ՝ Armenian World*). In the journal *Dzaghig* (*Ծաղիկ' Flower*), Smyrna/Izmir, 15 October 1867, Matt'eos Mamurian wrote: "There is still not yet a stone above the tomb of the body of Nalbandian ... But before the shrine of his soul every Armenian heart will forever burn incense." In 1867-1868, Tourian wrote a play, *Darakir i Siberia* (*Տարագիր ի Սիպերիա՝ Exile to Siberia*), in which Nalbandian personifies the struggle for freedom; Armenia, the Armenian people; and Siberia, tyranny.[6]

Tourian's poem, as it seems to me (though Blackwell, Tchéraz, and Sevak do not mention this in their notes to translations and texts, perhaps because it was too obvious to them!), reflects beyond any doubt the particular and strong influence, in both theme and lexicon, of Nalbandian's famous *Erg azatut'yan*, "Song of Freedom."[7] Blackwell, whose translation of the latter is entitled "Liberty" (pp. 39-40), wrote in her biographical note two decades before the Great October Socialist Revolution: "It is forbidden in Russia to possess a picture of Nalbandian; but portraits of him, with his poem on 'Liberty' printed around the margin, are circulated secretly."

ԵՐԳ ԱԶԱՏՈՒԹԵԱՆ

Ազատն Աստուած այն օրից,
Երբ հաճեցաւ շունչ փչել,
Իմ հողանիւթ շինուածքին
Կենդանութիւն պարգեւել,
Ես անբարբառ մի մանուկ՝
Երկու ձեռքս պարզեցի

---

[6] Sirouni, III, p. 190.

[7]The text given here is from Simon Simonian's anthology *Arevelahay kraganut'yun* (*Արեւելահայ գրականութիւն՝ Eastern Armenian Literature*), Beirut: Sevan, 1965, p.61; the translation is my own.

Եւ իմ անվօր թեւերով
Ապատութիւն գրկեցի։

Մինչ գիշերը, անհանգիստ,
Օրօրոցում կապկապած,
Լալիս էի անդադար
Մօրս քունը խանգարած,
Խնդրում էի նորանից
Բազուկներս արձակել,
Ես այն օրից ուխտեցի՝
Ապատութիւնը սիրել։

Թոթով լեզուիս մինչ կապերը
Արձակուեցան, բացուեցան,
Մինչ ծնողքս իմ ձայնից
Խնդացին ու բերկրեցան,
Նախկին խօսքն որ ասեցի՝
Չէր հայր, կամ մայր, կամ այլ ինչ՝
Ապատութի·ւն դուրս թռաւ
Իմ մանկական բերանից։

«Ապատութի՞ւն» ինձ կրկնեց
Ճակատագիրն վերևից.
«Ապատութե՞ան դու պինուոր
Կամիս գրուիլ այս օրից։
Ո·հ փշոտ է ճանապարհդ.
Քեզ շատ փորձանք կը սպասէ.
Ապատութեան սիրողին
Այս աշխարհը խիստ նեղ է»։

-Ապատութի·ւն,- գոչեցի,-
Թող որոտայ իմ գլխին
Փայլակ, կայծակ, հուր, երկաթ,
Թող դաւ դնէ թշնամին,
Ես մինչ ի մահ, կախաղան,
Մինչև անարգ մահու սիւն
Պիտի գոռամ, պիտի կրկնեմ

(40) Անդադար՝ Ազատութի·ւն։

*Song of Freedom*

God, the Free, from the day
He was pleased to breathe
Spirit into my earthly form,
And life to bestow:
I, a child without speech
Spread both my hands
And with strengthless arms
I embraced Freedom.

When at night, unquiet,
To my cradle bound,
I ceaselessly cried,
I disturbed my mother's sleep
And sought of her
My arms to release.
From that day I swore
To love Freedom.

When the bonds of my stumbling tongue
Were sundered and released,
And my parents might rejoice
And be glad at my voice,
The first word I pronounced
Was neither father, nor mother, nor anything else
But Freedom, that flew
From the confines of my childish mouth.

"Freedom?" repeated
My fortune from on high:
"Is it as Freedom's fighter
You wish this day to be inscribed?
Oh, thorny is your path,

And many tribulations await.
For the lover of freedom
This world is severely strait!"

"Freedom!" I cried:
Let lightning strike my head
And thunder, iron, fire rain,
Let the enemy hatch his schemes:
Until death, the gallows,
The pillar of a dishonored end,
I will repeat, without cease,
Freedom! will I cry out!

Several lexical correspondences may be cited. In Tourian's poem, line 13 reads: ***Yergat'***, *shght'a, zntan, antuntk' u veher*; in Nalbandian's, line 35 has *P'aylak, kaytsak, hur,* ***yerkat'***. Tourian, line 39, has the verb *t'ot'ovets'* ("stammered"); line 17 of Nalbandian's, the adjective *t'ot'ov*. Both poems end with references to death, though Nalbandian's farewell is an arrogant challenge; Tourian's, the despairing farewell of a prophet unheard, with the bitterly sarcastic remark—following an anti-clerical passage—that if the Armenian ever achieves freedom, the poet will be resurrected. Nalbandian is a revolutionary; Tourian, the Romantic rebel. It is also striking that Tourian mentions Armenia constantly; Nalbandian, not even once. The latter's life glows in the rainbow-spectrum of Russian radicalism; Tourian, for all his appeals to mankind to love one another, cannot quite see beyond the idea of nationhood. Despite his patriotic fervor, Tourian has still written what is essentially a lyric and private poem, full of stars and streams, cypresses and the beloved's glances. For all the evocations of the twin peaks of Ararat, vaguely imagined and never seen, it is a reverie of the poet's beloved Camlica, above the Bosphorus, with night giving way to dawn.

**5. "Love One Another"** (*Sirets'ek' z'mimyans*), 1869 (Sevak, pp. 21-22)

**Text.**

ՍԻՐԵՑԷ՛Ք Զ՛ՄԻՄԵԱՆՍ

Վարդակարմիր Գողգոթային վեհ գագաթ
Միշտ փայլփըլող, սիրոյ անշէ՛ջ ճառագայթ,
Դէռ կը սպասե՞ս թափել սրտից քու սըլաք.
Զ՛ո՞վ կը հըսկես, վիհ և անդունդ, թէ կըմախք.
Ո՞ր սև ժայռից մէջ մարեցաւ այն բեկբեկ
Բարբառն վըսեմ, թէ՝ «Ըզմիմեանս սիրեցէ՛ք։»

Ծածկէ ամպով կարմիր կողերդ, Գողգոթա՛յ,
Եւ թող խայտան ցաւոտ ոսկերք սև Յուդայ...։
Ժանգոտ ու գուլ թուրերն առին կարմիր փայլ,
Նոր կրօնին հետ արեան հեղեղն առաւ քայլ...
Թնդանօթին առջի բոմբիւնն խեղդեց սէգ
Զհագագըն քաղցր, թէ՝ «Ըզմիմեանս սիրեցէ·ք։»

Մարդապոհով Վատիկանի մըխացին
Ծխնելոյկքը, կամարքը՝ «Փա·ռք» գոռացին,
Փոխ-Քրիստոսք խաչն ըրին դաստակ կացինի՝
Սև դրօշ մը ատելութեան արիւնի.
Դարուց մոխրէն կամ ամպերէն յուսայ հէք
Զրկեալն լսել, թէ՝ «Ըզմիմեանս սիրեցէ·ք։»

Տնանկին դամբանը կ'անհետի ոտնակոխ,
Տընակին մէջ մարի առկայծ կանթեղն հող.
Այն մութին մէջ նօթի տըղեկք կը հեծեն,
Դղեակըն խրախ մինչև լոյս ջահք կը հիւծեն.
Հարուստին կառք ժխորով կ'անցնի սըրարշաւ,
Հէքին դագաղն իր գերեզմանն լուռ իջաւ...

Գեթսեմանին իջնող հրեշտակն դալկահար,
Որ գեղ, ծաղիկ, արցունք ու փառք չը ճանչնար՝

Նորա ցուրտ գոգն աղքատը սոսկ կ'ըսփոփի.
Ճոխն ու տընանկ պատանին մէջ կ'ըլլան մի.
Կայծակնաթև թէ մըռընչեն մըրրիկներ
Թէ «սիրեցէք զ'իրար», հէքն հոս չեն սիրեր։

**Translation.**

*Love One Another*

On Golgotha's rose-red summit high,
Love's inextinguishable, ever-shining ray of light,
Do you still wait to plunge your lance into human hearts?
Over whom—chasm and abyss, or a skeleton—do you stand guard?
On what black cliffs did that broken noble maxim,
"Love one another!" die?

Veil your red flanks in cloud, Golgotha,
And let the bones of pain-wracked Judas dance.
Rusted, blunt sabers glinted red
And with the new faith the blood-red tide advanced:
The cannon's thunder proud impending
Choked the sweet utterance, "Love one another!"

The Vatican's smoke stacks belched human sacrifice,
Her arches thundered "Glory!"
And the Cross became the handle of Christ's vicars' axe
And a black banner of sanguinary enmity.
From the ash of ages, or from the clouds, the destitute
Disfranchised man hopes yet to hear, "Love one another!"

The grave of the pauper vanishes, trodden down,
And in his hovel the faltering lamp gutters on the ground.
In that dark his hungry children howl,
While at the palace banquet the torches flame till dawn.
The rich man's carriage rockets past with a roar
As the poor man's casket is lowered to a silent tomb.

The pale angel, on Gethsemane descending,
Who knows not beauty, flowers, tears, or fame:
Only in his chill embrace does the poor man find consolation.
Pauper and rich man become as one in the shroud;
Yet though the storms on pinions of lightning proclaim
"Love one another!" no one loves the poor man here.

**Commentary.**

The poem exists in two manuscript notebooks, and was first printed in the 1872 edition of Tourian's works; in 1893, the second and third stanzas were omitted as incomplete. Minas Tchéraz emended *vih* ("rock chasm") to *veh* ("noble"). Before the word *gaydzagnat'ev* ("with wings of lightning") in the final stanza, Tourian crossed out the adjective *aheghasasd* ("with awful stricture"). The repeated Biblical injunction "Love one another" is from John 13.35. A few lines in Tourian's last poem (no. 39, "A")—on the wretched poet's own hovel with its guttering candle—are drawn from here.

The colors red and black dominate the poem. The catastrophic red dusk of Friday flaming out on Golgotha, and the blood and fire of the holy wars and inquisitions of fanatical Roman Catholicism, are all violence. Night descends (cf. the verb *marets'av,* in line 5), and what fire has burnt, or poverty ground down, becomes black Judas fleeing from the scene of betrayal, black ash, the shadows advancing across a poor man's room as his only candle melts away and gutters out, the dark pit of the grave in potter's field. In the first line, the qualifier of (Clas. Arm.) *vardakarmir,* rosy-red, may encode with Christ's self-sacrifice the martyrdom it inspired—that of *karmir Vardan,* "red (St.) Vardan (Mamikonean)," who led the Armenian Christian resistance to the Sasanian campaign of the mid-fifth century to force the Armenians to return to the Zoroastrian fold: cf. No. 10, Tourian's song dedicated to Vardan and his men.

The latter poem is a call, not to victory, but to martyrdom: the warrior-saints were still the principal paradigm available to Armenians thinking about liberation from tyranny. In 1874, two years after Tourian's death, Bishop Garegin Srvandztyants' published the first transcript of the epic of Sasun, whose heroes do not bend their necks to the oppressor. Four years after that, in his famous "iron ladle" sermon at Kumkapu, Khrimian Hayrig was already invoking the valor of the fighters of Moks and Sasun. Tourian did not live to see this. As for social protest from the standpoint of the class struggle, rather than that of national liberation, a Western Armenian translation of the *Communist Manifesto* (1848) of Marx and Engels might already have existed by the time of Tourian's youth, though the Ottoman authorities confiscated it (the first published translation we have is into Eastern Armenian, from the first decade of the twentieth century). In any case, the limit of Tourian's social consciousness is this earnest appeal to universal love. It is worthy of note that to the poet as an Armenian Orthodox Christian the exemplar of cruel fanaticism in human history is not Islam (not that he could have said it was in print in Ottoman Constantinople, even if he'd believed it), but Catholicism. The fire and ash of this poem will reappear, though, in Tourian's despairing, bold challenge to God, "Murmurs" (No. 25).

**6. "One Must Die!"** (*Bedk' e merrnil!*) and variant (untitled), 1869 and 10 August 1869 (Sevak pp. 23-24, 101-102)

**Texts.**

**1. ՊԷՏՔ Է ՄԵՌՆԻ·Լ**

Դժգոյն գիշեր մ՛էր քաղցրաբոյր աշնային,
Երկինքն աստղեր վերթ «սիրոյ վէրքք» ցոլային·
Դեղնած ու չոր թերթից՝ լուսինն իր բեկբեկ
Շողքը ցողէր ամրան վարսիցն աղեբեկ·
Շամբերուն մէջ կը սողոսկէր ուղխ մ՛անհետ,
Կայծեր, աստղեր կը խաղային ալեաց հետ·
Սիւքը խաղար տերևներուն հետ թեթև,
Կը շողէր գլուխս՝ այրած ճակատս վառէ թև,
Նա իր շնչովն իս գոհ ընել կը կարծէր,
Բայց կ՛արծարծէր, ո·հ, իմ սիրոյն բիւր կայծեր…
Ոգի մ՛անցաւ սրտէս՝ թողուց հոն ըստուեր,
Աստեղց բոյլ մը… միայն գիտեն կ՛այս աստղեր…։
Համբոյրի մը յիշատակն էր սիւքին շունչ,
Իր դողդոջ ձայնն՝ տերևներուն սա շրշունջ·
Գունատ ճակտին տխրիկ պատկերն այս լուսին…
-Ո·հ, կեանք պէտք է տալ՝ սիրտ տրուի թէ կուսին։
Կը սիրէ նէ, նայուածքին մէջ կը թառմի·
Ո·հ, ի՞նչ է նէ- ձիւնով շաղուած մի անդրի,
Վըսեմ ճակտին վըրայ կոյգ մը աստղեր վառ՝
Եթէ սիրէ՝ հալի, թ՛ատէ՝ կտրի սառ…։
Լոկ հուր աչեր, ժըպիտ, արցունք տեսի նախ,
Կուրծս ուռուցիկ լանջ մը ըկգաց սիրաբախ,
Սիրոյ մրմունջ, հառաչ լսեցի բեկբեկ խօսք,
Դողդոջ ու գիրգ՝ պաղ ձեռք մ՛ըկգաց ձեռքըս սոսկ·
Թևերուս մէջ լոյս մը, հով մը մարեցաւ·
Էակ չ՛էր նէ, այլ սէր, հուր, շունչ, ժըպիտ, ցաւ·
Գոհար աչեր, վարդ այտ, այլ ինքն էր թախիծ·
Այն գիսաւոր աստղէն «քար մը» մընաց ինձ…
Յիշատակ մը, գերեզման մը… սո·ւրբ սափոր,

Ուր հեկեկով սիրտըս կ’ընէ միշտ թափօր…։
Երանի՛ թէ ըլլամ ես շիթ մ’արտասուք
Եւ անհետիմ դամբանիդ քով սիրասուգ.
Իցի՛ւ թէ խոտ մ’ըլլամ ու ես ցամքիմ հող,
Ծաղիկ կ’ըլլամ, բայց առանց քեզ չ’ունիմ հոտ.
Լոյս թէ մութ, քուն, շուքըդ պիտի չ’անհետի,
Հառաչելով ուշ պիտ’ ըլլամ ոսկր ու դի,
Շիրմիդ վարդքը չը թոռմած քեզ գրկեմ ես…
«Կեանք կու տաս՝ սիրտ թէ տաս» ըսեն ետևէս։

2.

Աշնան տըժգոյն գիշեր մըն էր ձմրահուպ,
Կը ցոլային երկինքն աստղեր բիւր՝ ասուպ.
Զոր թերթերուն խորերն լուսինն իր բեկբեկ
Շաղն կը ցօղէր՝ ամրան վարսիցն աղեբեկ.
Շամբին մէջ թարմ կը թաւալէր վըտակը,
Փաղփուն աստղեր կը շողային յատակը,
’Ի անոր ալեացն հեշտիկ մրմունջը միայն
Սիրոյ քնարին վերջին լարին էր ողբ՝ ձայն…
Սիւքը կ’սուլէր տերևներուն մէջ թեթև,
Դէմքիս վըրայ կը սահեցնէր շղարշէ թև.
Նա իր շնչովն կիս գոհ ընել կը կարծէր,
Բայց կ’արծարծէր սրտիս սիրոյն վառ կայծեր։
Ոգի մ’անցաւ սըրտէս, չ’թողուց հոն ըստուերն՝
Յիշատակ մը… միայն գիտեն այս աստղերն…
Համբուրից տխուր յիշատակ մ’էր սիւքին շունչն,
Իր դողդոջ ձայն տերևներուն այս շրշունջն.
Անոյշ ժըպիտն ու վեհ նայուածքն այս ալին,
Մետաքս վարսերն սև հողին տակ կը հալին…
Տըժգոյն ճակտին տըխուր պատկերն այս լուսին…
Ո՛հ, կեանք պէտք է տալ՝ սիրտ տրուի թէ կուսին…
Կը սիրէ նա, նայուածքիդ մէջ կը թօշնի…
Ոխի մէջ՝ քար, սիրոյ մէջ՝ վարդ, սիրտ մ’ունի…
Անոյշ աչեր, ժըպիտ, արցունք տեսայ լոկ,
Կուրծըս վարսեր լանջ մ’ըկգաց սիրատրո’փ

Սիրոյ մրմունջ՝ հառաչ լսեցի բեկբեկ խօսք,
Դողդոջ ու գիրգ պաղ ձեռք մ’ըկգաց ձեռքըս սօսկ.
Թևերուս մէջ լոյս մը՝ հով մը մարեցաւ…
Էակ չէր նա, այլ սէր, հուր, շունչ, ժըպիտ, ցաւ…
Ըստուեր մ’էր նա, որ սահեցաւ վերթ թախիծ,
Բայց կանգ առաւ՝ փոս մը, քար մը ցըցուց ինձ՝
Յիշատակ մը՝ գերեզման մը՝ սուրբ սափոր…
Ուր կը յածի հեկեկով սիրտս ցօղաթոր…
Երանի թէ ըլլամ ես շիթ մ’արտասուք՝
’Ի անհետանամ դամբանիդ քով սիրասուգ,
Եւ կամ թէ խոտ մ’ըլլամ ու հոն ես ցամքիմ…
Ո·հ, կեանք պէտք է տալ՝ սիրտ տրուի թէ կուսին.
Դարեր անցնին շուքըդ պիտի չը մեռնի,
Արցունքներով կեանքըս պիտի ուշ թոռմի,
Շիրմիդ վարդերն դեռ չը թօշնած գըրկեմ քեզ,
«Կեանք կու տաս սիրտ թէ տաս» ըսին ետևէս…

**Translation.**

1. *One must die!*

It was a dim night in a sweet-scented autumn;
And the stars in the sky like “wounds of love” sparkled.
The dry and yellowed leaves the moon with broken
Beams upon the summer’s greying tress bedewed.
A rill within the canebrake crept and disappeared
As stars and sparks toyed with its ripples.
A breeze among the leaves was lightly playing
And caressed my head—with gossamer arm, my burning brow—
Thinking to please me with his breath,
But, Alas! fanned the myriad embers of my love...
A soul passed from my heart and left a shadow there,
A nebula of stars ... this the stars alone can know ...
The zephyr’s breath was the memory of a kiss;
His quavering voice, and in the leaves this rustling sound,
And this moon, whose pitiful visage is of a pale brow ...

—O! one must surrender one's life if one give one's heart to a girl!
She loves, and in the very look exchanged she fades.
O! What is she— a statue shaped of snow,
A pair of flaming stars upon her lofty brow;
And if she loves, she melts. She freezes solid, if she hates ...
I saw first only eyes of fire, tears, a smile,
My swelling breast felt her flank athrob with love,
Love's complaint: I heard some broken words, a groan,
Trembling, tender, a cold hand felt my hand alone.
In my arms a light, a wind died away:
She was no earthly being, but love, flame, breath, smile, pain:
Her eyes were gems; roses, her cheeks—but she herself was grief.
Of that comet star to me remained "a stone" ...
A memory, a grave ... sacred urn!
That my heart ever circles in lamenting procession...
If only I were the single globule of a tear
And near your tomb of love lamented disappear!
Would I were a blade of grass to dry up there:
I shall be a flower, but without you I waft no savor to the air.
Light or dark, sleep, your shadow departs ne'er;
Groaning, a memory I'll become of skull and bone
And embrace you before upon your tomb the roses scattered fade.
Thereafter of me all will say: "Give up your life, if your heart you give away."

2.

It was a dim night in autumn, *with winter at the door,*
And the *myriad* stars of heaven sparkled, *shooting stars.*
*The dry leaves' depths* the moon with broken
Beams upon the summer's greying tress bedewed.
*A stream within* the canebrake *rushed,*
*The glittering stars at its bottom agleam,*
*And only a soft plaintive murmur 'midst its* ripples
*Was love's lyre's last chord—lamentation's voice ...*
The breeze amongst the leaves was lightly *whistling,*

*And swept his gauzy* arm *across my face,*
Thinking to please me with his breath,
But he fanned the *burning* embers of my *heart's* love.
A soul passed from my heart and left *no* shadow there,
*A memory* ... this the stars alone can know ...
The zephyr's breath was the memory of a kiss;
His quavering voice, and in the leaves this rustling sound,
*The sweet smile and noble regard, these white*
*Silken tresses that moulder 'neath the black ground* ...
And this moon, whose pitiful visage is of a pale brow ...
—O! one must surrender one's life if one give one's heart to a girl!
She loves, and in the very look exchanged she fades.
*In anger she is stone; a rose, in love—she has a heart* ...
I saw *but sweet* eyes, a smile, and tears:
My heart felt her *tresses at her side*, the *throb* of love.
Love's complaint: I heard some broken words, a groan,
Trembling, tender, a cold hand felt my hand alone.
In my arms a light, a wind died away:
She was no earthly being, but love, flame, breath, smile, pain:
*Wafting* as grief *does, she was a shade*.
*But she stood, and shewed me a pit, and a stone*:
A memory, a grave ... sacred urn!
*Where* my heart *lingers* shedding its lamentation's dew ...
If only I were the single globule of a tear
And near your tomb of love lamented disappear!
Would I were a blade of grass to dry up there:
O! one must surrender one's life if one give one's heart to a girl!
Centuries will pass—your shadow shall not die,
And as a memory *will my life in tears expire*:
I shall embrace you before upon your tomb the roses scattered fade.
Thereafter of me all will say: "Give up your life, if your heart you give away."

**Commentary.**

The poem exists in both Tourian's manuscript notebooks: it was first printed in the 1872 volume and subsequently in numerous print editions. Ekserjian believes the girl is the same B. to whom Tourian addressed No. 27, "I worship her" (*Z'ne bashdem*) (see Sevak, I, p. 230). Tchéraz summarizes the poem in the note to his translation ("Il faut mourir," pp. 35-37): "Le jeune amoreux, qui cherchait la mort dans un moment de désespoir, pleure celle de son amante, dont la perte lui rappelle le beau rêve du passé." As to the variant version, nothing is known of the fate of the manuscript text. Dikran Arp'iarian published it in the Constantinople journal *Arevelk'*, 18 July 1892, no. 2544; and it was reprinted in numerous print editions of Tourian's poems. Arp'iarian writes: "16 [written a week after var. 1?—JRR] August 1869 ... I read that bygone date on a worn and yellowed sheet of paper which, after lying for twenty-three years in the corner of a school or at the bottom of a pile of papers, appeared all of a sudden one fine day and was brought to the editorial office to be published. It is a small square of paper, on both sides of which a trembling hand has inscribed one of those poems, marked by the breath of disease (*hivantapuyr*), which characterized the life of the poet, who died so early. And at the bottom it is modestly signed, Bedros Tourian. I unfold the four-fold crease, furrow of a quarter century, with cautious fear. The ink has already faded, but the writing remains forever, legible, a miniscule, lovely script, product of a fevered pen. There is neither title nor dedication; only through the initial letters (*sgzpnadarrerov*) one might find some trace, or discover, to whom it was addressed." Arp'iarian later reveals the manuscript belonged to a learned distant relative of Tourian's, Missy[8] Eugenie, whom he suspects of having bowdlerized it. Eghishe Tourian wrote to Chobanian that she had done nothing of the kind. Tourian himself once met Eugenie *dudu* after having heard of her passionate devotion to literature and remarked to his friend Hovhannes Janfesjian after the visit, "So that was Missy Eugenie? She's no big deal" (*Ays e yegher Yevgine dudun? Pan me ch'e.*) (Sevak, I, pp. 291-292).

[8]The word *dudu* is explained by H. C. Hony, *A Turkish-English Dictionary*, as "Old Armenian woman": presumably, an aged maiden aunt is delicately meant. Malkhasiants' explains it as a word for mother or an honorific given to women, or for a woman, her husband's sister (Clas. Arm. *tal*). See pp. 339-340.

In the translation, I have noted in italics significant differences in the draft from the final version. One is invisible in English: in the draft, Tourian uses the Classical Armenian third person pronoun singular, common to all genders: *na*—in the final text, it is *ne*, an artificial word invented by the mediaeval grammarians to translate the feminine pronoun, "she" (cf. Tourian's poems *Ne*, "she"; and *Nera hed*, "With her"). I think the poet employed the exotic word to achieve an effect of sensuous elegance and directness. Some changes were, it would appear, dictated by salutary considerations of sense: the word *tsmrahub*, "near winter" in the first line, for instance, is clearly superfluous, and making autumn "sweet-scented" is far stronger. For the sweetness of autumn has in it something of death; and the poet will commingle the sweet and sensuous memory of the beloved with the intolerable grief of tombstones, bones, ashes, and cold. Line three also underscores the mixed beauty and death of autumn with the use of the color yellow (*teghin*), which is both golden and sallow at once. In line two, the *asub*, "shooting star" of the draft is replaced by "wounds of love" (a comet will return in the final draft, line 28). This is a good early example of Tourian's phantasmagoria: the stars streaming light are wounds in night's dark skin; and to bare night's heart would be to reveal a conflagration—which is, indeed, what the poet in "The Lake" will declare is the substance of his heart. Another phantasmagoric effect Tourian often uses is the dizzying inversion of depths and heights; and in the draft of the poem, the stars shine on a stream-bed, a reverse heaven. But in the final version this interesting vision is omitted: instead, the stars toy and play, as the breeze is to do. Their activity is both amorous and ghostly, both sensuous and strange; and the conflicting impressions coalesce in the quality of memory, which brings together both love and death. Tourian's memory may justly be the inverse of Coleridge's: it is tranquillity recalled in a later state of agitation.

Contradictions are ironed out. In the draft, a shadow of the soul fled from the poet's heart does *not* remain as a shade (in the final version, it *does*); but then it stands like a wraith and points out a grave to him later (a Romantically grotesque scene the final version omits). In the draft, lines 17-18 introduce a chromatic contrast of the beloved's white tresses and the black earth. But white hair suggests age, and we are to imagine a girl who has died young; so Tourian in the final version, in line 18, makes the young woman snow—keeping the aspect of whiteness and linking it, by snow's melting, to the theme of fading and disappearing that pervades the poem. In the draft version of line 5, for instance, the stream (*vedag*) is described as spilling or tumbling (*t'avalel*) through a field of tall grasses; but in the final text the rill (*oughkh*) like the girl does a vanishing act and disappears, instead. The draft has more of *mrmunch*, "plaintive murmuring," than the final version—but the moan emerges into its own later in Tourian's short career, in his monumental poem *Mrmunchk'*, "Murmurs," No. 25. In the concluding lines, Tourian has replaced vague "lingering" (*hadzel*) about the girl's grave with the strong and vivid image of a religious procession, the *t'ap'or* "circumambulation" of Armenian Orthodox ritual. The poet is to embrace his beloved before the flowers left on her grave by the mourners have had a chance to wither (and we may expect to find, correspondingly, unwithered on the curls of the poet dying young a Housmanian garland briefer than a girl's): supernatural vindication of the Greek chorus of plain folks who comment that you die if you give your heart away. The declaration of the title acquires, then, its force—and in the poem's end is its beginning.

**7. "Upon the Election to the Patriarchate of Abp. Khrimian"** (*I badriark'agan endrut'yun Amen. Hayrigin*), 27 September 1869 (Sevak pp. 25-27)

**Text.**

Ի ՊԱՏՐԻԱՐՔԱԿԱՆ ԸՆՏՐՈՒԹԻՒՆ ԱՄԵՆ. ՀԱՅՐԻԿԻՆ

Այն սգալի սև նոճեաց ետևէն
Արշալոյսին շողք մեզի «Լո՛յս» կ'աւետեն,
Խուսեց խաւարն, փողփողէ լոյս արևուն
Հայոց կարմիր մարգաց սառուտ սարերուն.
Փըլատակաց մըթին խորքէն կու գայ ձայն-
Հայե՛ր, Հայե՛ր, դեռ Հայաստան չ'է՛ կործան...
        Ձայն տըւողը չ'է՛ ըստուեր,
        Հուր ներշնչողք չ'ե՛ն աստղեր,
        Եղբայրութեան է հուր, ձայն,
Հայը սիրող Հա՛յն է այն։

Նա գիշերուան հետ ազգ խոկաց ու լացաւ,
Եւ արևուն սըլաքաց հետ կրակ դարձաւ,
Հողմոց թևով միշտ սըլացաւ Հայկարան,
Տիգրիսի հետ թըրջեց աւերք տխրական.
Հայաստանի, եղբայրութեան սիրահար
«Հա՛յ» գոչելով շուրթերն եղան դալկահար։
        Աւարայրի նա վարդին
        Սոխակն եղաւ տրտմագին,
        «Վարդա՛ն» գոչեց նա, անդէն
Վասա՛կն ելաւ դամբանէն։

Նա իրաւո՛ւնք, ազատութի՛ւն գոչեց յար.
Փոշոտ ու խոնջ ոտքերն նետեց ուր Հայ կար,
Ուր որ Հայ կար ջերմ համբուրեց նա այն հողն,
Ուր Հայն շնչեց՝ հառաչ և հուր ղրկեց հոն.
Բոցաթըռիչ Հայէ ի Հայ նա թըռաւ,
Հարուած, ցաւ, դաւ՝ սէրն խեղդելու չ'եղան բաւ։

Այս հայկավնը չ՚ունէր սուր,
Այլ կուրծն ունէր Հայ, խաչ, հուր.
Կը հագնէր սէր և գրգլեակ,
Նա գո՞ւթ ունէր, ո՞չ քըսակ։

Ապա՞տ սիրեց, ապա՞տ գոչեց, չը թովեց.
Հայն վ՚այն ատեց, Հայ մը ձեռք չը թօթուեց.
Բանտ, կախաղան, աքսոր, Սիպիր և սուսեր
Չը կրցին ձայնն մարել, խեղդել իր յոյսեր.
Միշտ «Հա՞յ» կանչեց, բարձն էր գլխուն Մասեաց սար.
Նա սիրտն ըրաւ հայրենայուշ գոռ քընար.
Արդ հայրենեաց մեր շնչիկ՝
Հով մը կու գայ անուշիկ՝
Վառ ճակատուց այցելու,
Հայուն աչերն սրբելու։

Բա՞ց են թևեր, բա՞ց են սրտեր, բա՞ց ճակատ,
Եկո՝ օգնել տըկար Հայուն ապաբախտ,
Հո՞ւր հայրենեաց, եղբայրութեան դու հագա՞գ,
Քընարահար Հայու մը իղձ քեզ հրեշտակ.
Վէս Վոսփորին ալիք ըվքեզ բարևեն,
Ցրուէ՝ սև ձեռք՝ սև ամպ Հայոց արևէն.
Արտօսր ու քիրտդ թող փալփլին՝
Ջերթ աստղեր Հայ երկնքին,
Եւ սորուեցուր Հայուն դու
Սիրե՞լ, օգնե՞լ իրարու։

Արտասուաթոր՝ քե՞վ կը նային Հայ աչեր,
Սև շղթաներ քեզ ցոյց կու տան գոռ քաջեր,
Մըշոյ կտրիճք՝ աղջիկք ի քեզ ապաստան
Հայն ու դամբանն, տաճարն, հիւղակն՝ Հայաստան։
Թո՞ղ փլատակաց մոխրէն յառնեն յիշատակք,
Մութ մենաստանք վերափայլե՞ն նախնի փառք...
Լո՞յս, լո՞յս տեղան ամէն տեղ,
Գիտութի՞ւն, լո՞յսն Հայ աստեղ,
Լո՞յս հիւղակին, լո՞յս վըհին,

Լո·յս Հայ փառաց շէջ ջահին։

Ահա սրանայ մեղ ապագայ բոցագէս,
Մեր հայրենի աւերակաց տալ լոյս վէս․
Հարկ չ'են մեղի նիկակ և սուր ու վառօդ․
Իրաւունքի, սիրոյ, լուսոյ ենք կարօտ․
Եղբայրութեա·ն Հայն կը յենու, ո·չ թագի,
Բռնէ ձեռքէն, որ շունչ առնէ և հոգի․
    Եւ ալ մոռնայ հայկայն հէք
    Հին հարուածներն ու խոր վէրք․
    Եւ սիրտք ի տրոփ որոտան
«Կեա·ց միշտ, ՀԱՅՐԻ·Կ ԽԸՐԻՄԵԱՆ»։

**Translation.**

*Upon the Election to the Patriarchate of Abp. Khrimian*

Beyond the deep black grieving cypresses
Dawn's rays announce to us good tidings of light.
Darkness has fled, the sun's light shines
Upon the reddened meadows of Armenia's cold mountain clime.
From the dark depth of ruins a voice comes:
Armenians, Armenians, Armenia is not yet destroyed!
    The voice is not that of a specter
    And it is not stars that inspire flame:
    Fraternity is voice and fire,
    The Armenian who loves his kind.

By night he pondered his nation and cried,
And with the risen sun's darts he became fire.
On the wind's wings he sped where Armenians dwelt,
And with the Tigris drenched sad ruins.
In love with Armenia and brotherhood,
His lips from crying "O Armenian!" grew sallow.
    Of Avarayr's rose
    He became the nightingale of sorrow,

Crying "Vartan!" at which
From the grave Vasak arose.

He called ever for justice, for liberty,
Turning dusty, weary tread wherever Armenians were:
He kissed warmly the earth wherever an Armenian lived;
Where an Armenian breathed—thither he despatched a fiery sigh.
In flaming flight, from Armenian to Armenian he sped,
And blows, pain, treachery were insufficient to throttle him.
This son of Hayg had no sword,
But at his breast he had Armenian, Cross, fire.
He put on but love and rags,
Carrying only compassion, no money bag.

Freedom he loved, freedom he cried, he did not mystify,
Yet Armenians did not clasp his hand—he was despised—
But prison, the gallows, exile, Siberia and the sword
Could not drown out his voice, extinguish hope.
Ever "O Armenian!" he cried; Mount Ararat became his head's pillow.
A fierce lyre of the fatherland's remembrance he made his heart.
Now that slight breath of our homeland,
A sweet wind, comes
To visit fevered brows,
To cleanse Armenian eyes.

Open are our hearts, our brow, our arms:
Come to the aid of the Armenian, weak, ill-starred,
Fire of the fatherland, fraternity's sound;
An Armenian lyricist's wish be your messenger.
The waves of the proud Bosphorus greet you:
Scatter before the Armenians' sun, black hand, black cloud!
Let tears and perspiration gleam
Like the stars of the Armenian sky;
And teach the Armenian, thou,
To help and love one another now.

Armenian eyes streaming with tears look to you;
Proud heroes show you their blackened fetters;
The braves of Mush, maidens look to you as their refuge—
The Armenian, tomb, cathedral, hut—Armenia!
Let memories arise out of the ruins' ashes
And dark hermitages glow again with ancient glory ...
Light, everywhere light falls like rain!
Wisdom, light of the Armenian star,
Light to the hovel, light to the pit,
The Armenians' extinguished torch relit!

Lo! The future, fire-tressed, sweeps towards us,
Shedding on our fathers' ruins its sublime light.
We need no ammunition, no lance or sword:
We long but for justice, love, and light.
Upon no crown—on fraternity the Armenian relies.
Take him by the hand, that he may breathe, in spirit revive.
And let Hayg's poor offspring forget
Old blows and deep wounds;
And every heartbeat thunder
"Live forever, Archbishop Khrimian, Little Father!"

**Commentary.**

The poem, copied in Tourian's two notebooks, was first published on 2 October 1869 in no. 21 of the journal *Orakir dziln Avarayrvo* ("Seedling of Avarayr"), where it is dated 27 September and bears the title *Tson Arr Hayrign Khrimian Azkaser Norendir Bad. G. Bolso* ("Dedication to Little Father Khrimian, Newly-Elected Patriotic Patriarch of Constantinople"). The misprints were sufficiently serious that a letter to the editor from the poet to correct them was published on 6 October. The many subsequent printed editions, including Sevak's text, incorporate these corrections. The poem appears as "A propos de l'élection au Patriarcat de Mgr. Khrimian" in Tchéraz, pp. 21-25. Bishop Khoren Nar-Bey was so impressed by the poem that he summoned its young author for a conversation; and Tourian's brother Yeghishe wrote that the Little Father, Catholicos Mkrtich' Khrimian himself, confessed to him, Իմ Պատրիարք եղած ատենս շատեր գրեցին ինծի համար, բայց անոր գրածին պէս չի կար։ "During my time as Patriarch many wrote about me, but there was nothing like what he [Tourian] wrote" (Sevak, I, p. 233). The Little Father himself was a poet of some renown, so it is not surprising that he saw at once the talent of the young poet.

Mkrtich' Khrimian (1820-1907) had been elected Armenian Patriarch of Constantinople on 3 September 1869, whilst still in Russian Armenia; he embarked at Trebizond for the sea journey to the Ottoman capital. Patriarch Khrimian was to become Catholicos of All Armenians in 1892; but perhaps the high point of his career was his famous "Iron Ladle" sermon of 1878. After Turkey's defeat in the Russo-Turkish war of 1877, Article 16 of the peace treaty signed at San Stefano in March 1878 guaranteed Armenian rights. But when the Congress of Berlin, convened that June, failed to affirm the clause, the leader of the Armenian delegation, Patriarch Khrimian, returned to Constantinople and delivered a sermon at the Armenian Cathedral in Kum Kapu. He said the Western powers had placed a dish of freedom, a pot of the porridge called *herisa,* on the table; and the Balkan peoples had come with their armed heroes, who used their swords as iron ladles to serve themselves. But all the Armenians had was a paper petition that would dissolve in the hot stew. And they went away hungry: *Aynzham tartsuts'i eress yev ipr t'e ge p'ndrei im zeyt'unts'i, sasunts'i, shatakhts'i yev ayl lerrnts'i yev tashdets'i k'achers, payts' ur ein, zhoghovurt Hayots'?* "Then I turned my face and searched, as it were, for my mountain and plains heroes of Zeytun, Sasun, Shatakh—but, O Armenian people, where were they?" They should have been with him, so he might proclaim: *Desek', aha im ergat'ya sherep'nere, hos en, badrasd!* "See—here are my iron ladles, right here, and ready!"[9]

Tourian's poem disavows armed struggle as a means to the securing of justice for the Armenians. The poet invokes the memory of the fifth-century warrior-martyr St. Vardan Mamikonian (line 19), but only to stress how deaf Armenians had been to Archbishop Khrimian's exhortations: when he cried "Vartan!" the sole result was that the arch-

---

[9]On the sermon and the symbolism of *herisa,* see J. R. Russell, "The Praise of Porridge," *Le Muséon* 116.1-2, 2003, pp. 137-179, repr. *AIS*, pp. 1217-1260.

traitor Vasak Siuni rose from the grave! But Patriarch Khrimian's sermon, with its vivid symbolism deeply embedded in Armenian folklore, was to become a clarion call for self-defense in the decades leading to the Genocide. However touched he was by the lyricist's dedication, the Little Father, whose candid political statements alarmed both the Ottoman and Russian authorities, could scarcely have shared his dreamy, eirenic idealism. Even when he mentions the Armenian fedayeen of Mush, Tourian's imagination is immediately diverted to the consideration of the city's young women, who were famed for their beauty. And despite vague references to Mt. Ararat, ancient ruins, and archaic glories, Tourian's authentic landscape of black cypresses and Bosphorus waves still dominates the poem.

**8. "Upon the Reception of Abp. Khrimian"** (*I timavorut'yun Amen. Hayrigin*), 1869 (Sevak pp. 28-29)

**Text.**

ԻԴԻՄԱՒՈՐՈՒԹԻՒՆ ԱՄԵՆ· ՀԱՅՐԻԿԻՆ

Ո՞ է որ գայ մեկ ճեղքած օդն, ալին,
Ճակտին վրայ գոհարք, աստեղք կը փայլին.
Թագաւո՞ր մ'է Հայ, որ ցատկեց շիրմէն,-
Ո·չ, դէմքը վառողք արցունք, ըսպի են.
Նա կ'արհամարհէ ծիրանի, փառքեր,
        Նա սև է հագեր։

Նա մեր Հայ եղբարց արցունքն է քաւեր,
Ցոյց կու տայ մեկի արիւն ու աւեր,
Դիւցա՞կն մ'է, որ դո·ւրս թըռաւ դամբանէն,
Ո·չ, թուր չ'է· ձեռքն, այլ խաչ բռներ արդէն,
Չը ցայտեր աչքէն շանթեր, այլ սէ·ր, գո·ւթ.
        Դողայ անկէ Քուրդ։

Նա կու գայ Հայոց կարմիր մարգերէն,
Ապատեց Քրդէն հէգ Հայ գերիներն,
Խաչափայտով մը պանծացաւ յաղթող,
Հնչեցուց ի Հայս ապատութեան փող,
Տեսէ·ք, քուրձ հագեր, կարծես ինք դիակ,
        Բայց սիրտն է կըրակ։

Գայ Մասեաց սարէն, նա ձախն ու աջը
Մովսէսի քընարն՝ Ղևոնդի խաչը,
Աստղի մը նայուածք, քընարի մը ձայն,
Աղեաց խորերէն կը սիրէ նա Հայն.
Դեռ չը ճանչցա՞ք վ'այն, ճակա·տք վըշտակոծ,
        Հրեշտակն է Հայոց։

Ահա կը հնչէ նորա հեշտ սըրինգ,

Արձագանք կու տան Հայոց դաշտք, լերինք,
Երթանք իր շուրջը, Հայե·ր արտալած,
Զը խաբեր, մատներ նա մեկ օտարաց,
Զը սիրեր ոսկի, փառք ու վատ մարդիկ,
Հայուն է Հայրիկ։

Գլխիկը դըրած սըգաւոր սըքեմ,
Զը թափիր ճակտէն դեռ ալիք վըսեմ,
Բայց իր դիմաց վրայ կանուխ են փթթած
Անցքի ու վշտի խորշոմներ միշտ թաց.
Միակ վարձք մ'ունի՝ այն է կոչել պինք
«ԽԸՐԻՄԵԱՆ ՀԱՅՐԻԿ»։

**Translation.**

*Upon the Reception of Abp. Khrimian*

Who is he who comes towards us, cleaving the air and the waves?
Gems on his brow, stars that shine—
Is this an Armenian king, sprung forth from his tomb?
No, it is tears that burn and scar his face:
He scorns the purple, disdains fame,
And is clothed in black.

He has atoned the tears our Armenian brothers have wept,
And displays to us ruins, and blood:
Is this some hero of fable, risen from the grave?
No, that is not a sword in his hand, but the Cross that he clasps;
Not lightning, but love and compassion sparkle in his eye—
And that makes the Kurd afraid!

He comes from the Armenian meadows incarnadine,
Having freed hapless Armenians from the bondage of the Kurd.
It is in the tree of the Cross he exults, victorious,
And liberty's trumpet in Armenia he blows.
Behold his rough habit! He seems but a corpse,

Yet there is fire in his soul.

He comes down from Mount Ararat, in his left hand
Moses' lyre; in his right, the Cross of Ghevont.
The gaze of a star, the voice of the harp:
He loves the Armenian from his vitals inmost.
Have you still not recognized him, brows wracked with grief?
It is the Armenians' angel.

Lo! his lilting shepherd's flute sounds,
And the plains and mountains of Armenia echo:
Let us gather round him, O Armenians in exile,
For he betrays us not to the alien, deceives us not,
Loves not glory, gold, or evil men,
The Armenian's Little Father.

Upon his head the mournful cowl,
Gray hair not yet showing on his brow;
Yet early on his face are etched
The ever tear-stained furrows of care and sorrow.
His sole recompense is that we acclaim him
Little Father Khrimian.

**Commentary.**

The text exists in both Tourian's manuscript notebooks, and has been published in numerous editions. Tchéraz, in his introductory note to "A la rencontre du Patriarche Khrimian" (pp. 24-25), explains that the poem "a été composée alors que les Arméniens de Constantinople, réunis dans un grand nombre de bateaux, traversaient le Bosphore pour aller au-devant du vaisseau qui l'amenait à la capitale." Archbishop Khrimian, apprised whilst in Russian Armenia of his election to the Patriarchate, had taken ship at Trebizond: see the comments to the preceding poem, No. 7. Ekserjian explains the occasion differently: 1869-ին նորընտիր Պատրիարքն Սկիւտարու Ս. Կարապետ եկեղեցին կու գայ Վարդավառի տօնին՝ Ս. Պատարագ մատուցանելու համար։ Պետրոս Դիմաւորութեան առթիւ ոտանաւոր մը կը գրէ… և ձեռօք կը մատուցանէ նմա։ Սրբազան Պատրիարքը կը հաւնի և այն ատենէն մեծ համակրութիւն ցոյց կու տայ անոր… "In 1869 the newly-elected Patriarch arrives at the church of *Surp Garabed* [i.e., St. John the Forerunner, Tourian's parish church] at Scutari on the Feast of *Vartavarr* [i.e., the Feast of the Transfiguration] to celebrate the Divine Liturgy. Bedros writes a verse on the occasion of the reception ... and offers it by hand to him ... His Eminence the Patriarch likes it, and thereafter shows his great sympathy ..." Sevak, citing this testimony (I, p. 234), observes that in 1869 that summertime holiday would have preceded by some months the Little Father's arrival at Constantinople (on 6 November). Even poetic license could scarcely explain why Tourian would describe the Patriarch's visit to officiate at a church in Scutari as the advent of a sweating avatar breaking through air and waves, though Khrimian's sea voyage might inspire such imagery. The explanation by Tchéraz is more likely; and in his translation, too, he was right to emend the meaningless phrase (կարծես) ենք դրակ *(gardzes) enk' trag,* to ինք դիակ *ink' tiag,* "himself a corpse," a necessary correction which Sevak has retained in our text.

As in poem No. 7, dedicated to Archbishop Khrimian's election, Tourian invokes the heroism of St. Vardan by mentioning the latter's spiritual mentor and comrade in arms, St. Ghevond *yerets'* ("the Presbyter"), though as always he piously rejects armed struggle as a means of resistance against the Armenians' predators. Tourian repeatedly mentions the Kurds. The latter are speakers of a Northwestern Iranian language who have over the past century experienced repression and massacre at the hands of the Republic of Turkey and the Arab nationalist, Ba'athist dictatorship of Saddam Hussein in Iraq. Armenians have lived for at least a millennium with Kurds, whose language is called in medieval texts *mareren,* "Median"; and there were Kurdophone Armenian communities in eastern Anatolia, particularly in the Dikranagerd/Diyarbakir area, for whom educational foundations in Constantinople prepared textbooks in Kurdish printed in Armenian script. In the Ottoman period, Kurdish tribesmen were employed as tax collectors by the Ottomans with the intention to harrass the Armenians: they exacted tribute from the Armenians, whose homes and families they frequently attacked and plundered. In the Genocide, the Turkish and

German authorities encouraged the Kurds to wage *jihad*—Muslim holy war—against the Christian Armenians. In much of eastern Anatolia, it was thus Kurds, not Turks, who did most of the actual killing. Unlike Turkey, the Kurdish national leadership today has recognized both the Genocide and the partial complicity of Kurds in the crime. From the perspective of Bedros Tourian, a thousand miles away, the Kurds must have seemed the instigators, as well as the perpetrators, of anti-Armenian pogroms.

The attitudes of ordinary Kurds to the Armenians at present can be complex and contradictory. During a visit in Summer 1997 to the former Armenian village of Shushants' near Van, a middle-aged Kurd showed us proudly the few stones left of the Armenian church, which he had helped to destroy as a youth—the Cross, he averred, was a dangerous and potent sign of a powerful enemy. Yet he welcomed my friend, the poet and playwright Herand Markarian, whose ancestors had served in the church, as a returning native son fully entitled to be there. Several college-age Kurds listened attentively to a lecture I delivered during the same visit in the tenth-century Church of the Holy Cross on Aght'amar island in Lake Van: they were very interested in the history of the Armenian Christians, about whom information had been withheld from them at school; and we met again at a Kurdish restaurant in town that evening. Several months later, they managed to send a letter to Cambridge to me through a local bank, reporting that they had been arrested and beaten by the police (torture is routine in Turkey) for having spoken to the Harvard professor. The Kurds of the Van region generally preserve the authentic Armenian names of villages and shrines that the Turkish authorities have changed.[10]

Tourian blends national themes—old Armenian kings and heroes, Mt. Ararat, meadows and shepherds' flutes, St. Vardan's companion—with Biblical ones appropriate to the acclamation of a leader and prophet. The poem begins, as noted above, with Abp. Khrimian cleaving air and wave; and the image cannot but remind one of Moses

[10]On Kurdish-Armenian cultural and historical ties, see the Introduction, with refs., in J. R. Russell, tr. & comm., Karapet Sital, *An Armenian Epic: The Heroes of Kasht*, Ann Arbor: Caravan, 2000.

leading the Children of Israel from slavery to freedom between the parted waters of the Red Sea. In line 20, Khrimian is described holding the lyre of Moses; and in line 14 Tourian hails the Little Father as liberator.

**9. "The Little Father of the Armenians"** (*Hayrign Hayots'*), 24 October 1869 (Sevak pp. 30-31)

**Text.**

ՀԱՅՐԻԿՆ ՀԱՅՈՑ

Փութա·, հովուապե·տ, սիրող յար ապատ՝
Հարապատ,
Փարատի· սև ամպ, փայլի· արդ արև
Արդարև,
Փողփողի·ն դաշտեր, ապատ առնե·նք քայլ,
Առ նենգ գայլ
Ցըցո·ւր ցուպդ, Հայերն կանչէ· յ՛արօտ մի՝
Յար հօտ մի։
Ճանկեր արիւնոտ կուրծ մեր թափ առինք,
Թափառի·նք,
Եկո·, հովուէ· մեզ, սիրածդ, ազգասէ·ր,
Ազգ ա·ս էր։
Դու գըթոտ նըման երկնի Հայրիկին՝
Յ՛այր՝ ի կին՝
Յ՛օրոց և յ՛ալիս սփռէ· լոյս և սէր,
Լո·յս ևս, է՞ր
Ցաւի, չը պարթնու հըրճուած յ՛այգուն յ՛այն
Յա·յ, քուն Հայն։
Սոխակ մ՛էիր մերթ ի նոճս, ւ՛երգերդ
Վէրքերըդ
Առած բիւրաւոր՝ դեռ դու կանչեցիր,
Կա·ն, չ՛է· ցիր
Երգերդ միշտ մեր սիրտ, սիրոյ հոգւոյ ձա·յն,
Յ՛ոգւոց Հայն
Հանեց, վառեցաւ ձայնէդ, իմացաւ
Հիմա ցաւ.
Քե·զ խնդրէ Հայն արդ, ամբոխ ամբոխ չ՛է·,
Ամբողջ է.
Արդ ըսէ· Հայուն, ըրէ· ապդ անոր

Աստանօր.
-Ես կարօտ եմ վառ սրտից, ձեռքերի,
Ձեր գերի
Եղբարքն ապատե·լ, լո·յս տալ ի Մասիս,
Ի մաս յ՛իս
Առնել իմ նախնեաց արիւն արտասուքէն.
Արդ սուգէն
Ելնեն Հայք՝ օրէնեն սիրով յաւէտ իս՝
Յ՛աւետիս.
Ցանկամ որ Հայք ինձ ըսեն ա·հ, յամայր
«Ահա· մայր».
Այս իմ վերջին տենչ, միշտ ճետք կա·ն
Հայկական։

**Translation.**

*The Little Father of the Armenians*

Hasten! chief pastor, loving ever free,
Our own,
Dispel the black cloud, shine now the sun
In truth,
Let the fields shine, let us tread free;
Against the treacherous wolf
Your staff strike, summon the Armenians to pasture,
Ever one flock together.
We shook off the bloodied talons at our breast:
Let us wander.
Come hither, guide us, patriot beloved,
This was your people.
Compassionate as the Heavenly Father,
To man, to woman,
To cradle and gray locks dispense love and light,
More light! Why
Does it hurt, not waken, impassioned in that dawn,
Oh, Armenian somnolent?
You were once a nightingale in the cypresses, and your songs

Were your wounds:
Ingathering the myriads, still you summoned:
They remain, undispersed,
Your songs ever in our heart, voice of love and soul,
The Armenian groaned,
Was armed with your chant, learnt
Pain now.
The Armenian seeks you now: he is not this and that crowd,
But unanimity.
Say now to the Armenian, declare to him
Here:
I long for burning hearts and hands,
Your captive brethren
To liberate, on Mount Ararat shed light,
Making my communion bread
My ancestor's blood-red tears.
Now from mourning
Let the Armenians arise and bless forever in love
Me in good tidings.
I desire that the Armenians long to me profess
"Here is our Mother!"
This is my final wish, that progeny of Hayg there always be:
Armenians.

**Commentary.**

The poem exists in both Tourian's manuscript notebooks, and was first published on 27 October 1869; it has appeared in numerous editions. The version published in Tourian's lifetime, however (reproduced by Sevak, I, pp. 235-236), has a number of different readings and entire additional lines:

Preceding line 1: Սլացիր սարերէն Հայ փութով, հովիւ, Թով հովիւ "Speed from the Armenian mountains hither in haste, Enchanting shepherd."

The first words of line 5: Լոյս տեսնան ... "They see light ..."

The first words of line 15: Ցանմեղ և յալի տիրէ ... "Upon blameless babe and hoary elder reigns ..."

After line 18: Մերթ փըլատակաց եղիր դու լուսին, Դու լուսին
"Now you became a moon in the ruins, Thou moon."

In line 19: Սոխակ ծնար նոճեաց խորերն ու երգերըդ
"You were born in the depths of the cypresses, and your songs ..."

The final words of lines 35-36 are changed, and a strophe follows:
Առնել իմ նախնեաց արիւն քիրտերէն, Քիւրտերէն
Ինչպէս առի վրէժ, Հայեր փրկեցան, Փրկեց ան
"To take from my ancestors' sweat of blood, From the Kurds
As I exacted revenge, the Armenians were saved, He saved."

Lines 39-40 are altered, as two strophes:
Ցանկամ, որ օրհնենք ինձ տան Հայկարան՝ Հայկ՝ Արամ.
Ասեն ինձ Հայեր՝ թշուառք, ահ յամայր, «Ահա մայր»
"I desire that the Armenians—Hayg and Aram—give a blessing[11] to me, saying to me, 'Here is our mother!'"

And the final lines are replaced by these:
Մեռնիմ քեզ համար, Հայաստան անուշ, Տան անուշ։
"May I die for thee, Armenia sweet, Sweet home."

Tchéraz, pp. 18-20, evaluated it well: "Cette poésie, assez médiocre d'ailleurs, est encore un jeu d'esprit du jeune poèt; elle représente des vers en echo. Elle est très obscure et par conséquent très difficile à traduire." The sole difficulty of translation consists in the homonymic repetition as every even-numbered line of the last three syllables of the previous line—a nice *tour de force*. Thus, the two words

[11]Sevak has here օրհնենք *orhnenk'*, "(that) we bless," which is in context grammatically impossible and may be a typographical error for the noun օրհնէք *orhnek'*, "a blessing," which would then be the object of the subj. 3 pers. pl. *dan*, "they give."

*har azad,* "ever free" of line 1, are echoed by *harazad,* "an intimate relative" in line 2. But for such a conceit to succeed aesthetically, one thinks, it must have brilliance and ease. Tourian's constructions are forced, however, with much elision and classicizing abbreviation; and at one point, at the end of line 31, he is even forced to use a Modern Eastern Armenian genitive plural, *-eri* to achieve his desired echo (in Western Arm. the ending is of course *-eru[n]*). Susan Barba has observed that the final line of the poem breaks the pattern of echo in order to cast in high relief the final word, *haygagan,* "Armenian"—an interesting use of the difficult conceit Tourian chose. Whatever its artistic merits, the poem is of interest as a glimpse of the young poet experimenting, at swim in the seas of his language.

**10. "Song of the Battle of Vartan"** (*Yerk mardin Vartanants'*), 1869 (Sevak, p. 32)

**Text.**

ԵՐԳ ՄԱՐՏԻՆ ՎԱՐԴԱՆԱՆՑ

Արի՛ք, որդի՛ք Արարատեան,
Նըսեմ ճակատք ցայտե՛ն թող շանթ,
Դողդոջ ձեռաց մէջ սուր ցոլա՛ն,
Արդար վրիժուց ժամն հասաւ արդ,
Փշրի՛ Պարսկին անդուլ կացին,
Հայք բա՛ւ լացին.
Մեռնի՛նք Մասեաց շուքերուն տակ,
Յաւերժ կանգնե՛նք յաղթանակ.
Օ՛ն, ապատ ըլլանք
Եւ Հայաստան մեր,
Թող տան արձագանք
Մասիք անվեհեր.
Մեռնի՛նք յ'Արտաշ՝ Տղմուտի մօտ,
Ուսկից ծագի մեզ առաւօտ։
Մեր սուսերց փայլէն
Սասանին Սասանք,
Մեր ամէն քայլէն
Ծագի յաղթանակ։

**Translation.**

*Song of the Battle of Vartan*

Arise, sons of Ararat!
Your noble cohorts' lightning flash
Of swords aglitter in your trembling hands,
For now has come the hour of just revenge—
To shatter the Persian's never-resting axe.
Armenians have done with tears:

Let us perish in Ararat's shadow
To rise in victory eternal.
Oh, let us and our
Armenia be free:
Let mount Ararat echo the call!
Let us die in Ardaz, on the Deghmud's shore
Where our morning light may dawn.
Shake, Sasanian,
At our sabers' glare
And victory's sunrise break
At our every marching tread.

**Commentary.**

The poem refers to the War of Vardan, a defining episode in Armenian history chronicled by Ełišē (Yeghishe) *vardapet*, a priest who claimed to have been an eyewitness. Armenia in ancient times was situated squarely between the Roman and Iranian Empires, but in most aspects of life—religious, linguistic, political—the influence of Armenia's eastern neighbor was preponderant, and was indeed so great that Armenian was generally regarded as a language of the Iranian branch of the Indo-European family tree till Heinrich Hübschmann's groundbreaking work, published in 1875 (three years after Tourian's death), reclassified Armenian as the surviving member of the Thraco-Phrygian branch. In many respects, nonetheless, Armenia could be studied as a civilization of the Iranian periphery.

Armenia's cultural orientation turned westwards, though, with the conversion of the country's Arsacid royal court to Christianity early in the fourth century. The religion had long existed in the country; and with the creation of an alphabet for Armenian by St. Mesrop Mashtots' at the beginning of the fifth century, Christianity became deeply rooted throughout all layers of society. With the collapse of the Armenian Arsacids in 429 and the consequent loss of sovereignty, the Church became the focus of national cohesion and has remained so ever since. In Late Antiquity, the Persian Sasanian dynasty recognized the religious leaders of subject peoples as authorities empowered to govern their communities in some spheres of life: they were answerable to the King of Kings. In the seventh century, Iran and Armenia were among the early conquests of the Arabs, who instituted a similar structure of delegation of limited power to tolerated minorities. The Ottomans continued the practice, which is in Turkey referred to as the *millet* ("national/religious community") system. In Tourian's time, the leader of the Armenian community was the Patriarch of the Armenian Church at Constantinople.

Zoroastrianism, the official religion of all pre-Islamic Iranian dynasties (Persian Achaemenian, Parthian Arsacid, and Persian Sasanian), had been predominant among Armenians before Christianity; so when it appeared to the Persians that Christian Byzantium would exploit the potential dual loyalties of Christians living in Iran to create a hostile fifth column, King Yazdagerd II attempted to force the Armenians to abjure their new faith and return to the old ways. After some indecision, Vardan (W. Arm. Vartan) Mamikonean, scion of the noble clan who had been the hereditary commanders-in-chief of Arsacid Armenia, led a campaign of armed resistance which culminated in the Battle of Avarayr, on the banks of the river Tłmut (Deghmud) in the southeastern province of Artaz, in May 451. The Armenians were defeated and Vardan and his companions were martyred; but the military disaster was so costly to the Persians that the Armenians regarded it as a moral victory, and were encouraged to fight a guerrilla war.

The peace of Nvarsak in 484 guaranteed the Armenians religious freedom: in a way, it marked the beginning of that durable mechanism of tolerance in multiethnic states, the *millet* system. For Armenians, the church holiday of Vardanants', which commemorates the battle at Avarayr and the holy martyrs, was a paradigm for the armed struggle for national liberation. Sevak (p. 237) notes that the poem was published, doubtless from a manuscript copy, in September 1908 by the editors of *Hayrenik'i k'nar* ("Lyre of the Fatherland")—who were apparently unaware that it had been printed before and therefore hailed it as a discovery. The occasion was their celebration of the Constitutional Revolution of that year, which raised the Armenians' hopes, whether for independence or for a better life within Turkey. In the newspaper version, the epithet *antul* used of the Persian axe becomes *andash*, "blunt": it would have been easy to confuse the final three letters of անդուլ with the last two of անտաշ since the letters o and w of the diphthong pronounced in Modern Armenian as u are usually written together and can be misread as the three-toothed lower case a. And only the small curl on the left of the letter sh distinguishes it from l. As we now know, the reforms of 1908 did not stay the tireless axe, whether sharpened or not: in 1909 the Armenians of Adana were massacred, in what was clearly a dress rehearsal for the holocaust of 1915.

**11. "I Loved You"** (*Sirets'i k'ez*) (final version), 1869 (Sevak pp. 33-35);
**"I Loved You"** (first version), 1869 (Sevak, pp. 239-240);
**"Farewell"** (*Mnas paryav*)(alternate final version), 1869 (Sevak, Appendix no. 3, pp. 103-104)

**Texts.**

**1. ՍԻՐԵՑԻ ՔԵԶ**

Շաղի, շողի ժամք էին.
Վարդից հրդեհ կար յ'երկին՝
Փոխան ամպոց հուր հիւսքի.
Տեղա՛ր մարգրիտ և ոսկի։

Թաւուտքի մը խոր ծաղկոտ
Ընկողմանած նըւաղկոտ՝
Կը հևայիր դու դժգոյն,
Ամրան սիւքի մը հանգոյն։

Աչերդ սիրոյ Ատրուշա՛ն...
Եւ մատներովդ պերթ շուշան՝
Կը փետտէիր ծաղիկ մի,
Յառած շողից աչքդ երկնի։

Հիանայի թէ ի՛նչպէս
Փետտել թերթեր վարդին վէս՝
Եւ թափթըփել քու գիրգ գիրկ
Կը պօրէին մատներդ գիրգ։

Եւ նըւաղկոտ այդ աչեր
Նըշուլէին նո՛ր եթեր,
Եթեր մ'աստեղց ուր փոխան
Հրաշէկ սլաքք կը շողան։

(Ո՛հ, խոցեցիր իմ սիրտս ալ
Եւ ժըպիտըդ պըլացար,

Նըշողումն այն կենսատու
Այրէ ցաւեր սրտերու։)

Ըրիր աչացդ մէկ կայծին
Եւ մէկ վանկիդ կ'իս գերին,
Շղթայեցիր կ'իս, անգո·ւթ,
Նշոյլներովն վեհ հոգւոյդ։

Թո·ղ սիրտս, ինձմէ գնա հեռի,
Չ'ուզեմ հոգւոյս թագուհի
Քեզ, որուն կուրծն վարդի թերթ,
Այլ կըրանիտ սիրտն է գէթ։

Դու, որ գիտես լոկ բուրել,
Գիրգ սրտերու վէրք փորել,
Եւ կը սիրես, երբ կարի·
Քեզ պաշտող սիրտն արիւնի։

Թաւուտքի մը շուք նըսեմ
Երբոր մենիկ արտասուեմ,
Հոն ես դու, կը գտնես կ'իս,
Տերևներէ·ն կը խօսիս։

Երբ առուակին մէջ փաղփուն
Կ'ուզեմ մոռնալ դէմքըդ, դուն
Դարձեալ հոն կը գտնես կ'իս,
Ալիներէ·ն կը ժպտիս։

Երբ կը փախչիմ ժայռ ու սար՝
Ջախջախել սիրտս և քընար,
Հովին մէջէն միշտ մնչես՝
Թէ դու բնաւ կ'իս սիրած չ'ես։

Գրկեմ սրտովս արդ ցուրտ հող,
Ի'ալ չը դիպիմ քեզի թող.
Կոյս մ'է նաև գերեզման...
Կա՞յ խորունկ սիրտ մ'անոր նման...։

## 2. ՍԻՐԵՑԻ ՔԵԶ

Առտու մը դէռ մըթընշաղ՝
Կը ծաւալէր շող ու շաղ,
Ծաղկանց մէջ քեզ տեսայ ես,
Կէ ժըպտէիր լուսնոյ պէս։

Աչերդ սիրոյ Ատրուշան,
Մատներդ էին գիրգ շուշան,
Այտերդ վարդի նոր թերթեր,
Նայուածքեդ ծնէր նոր եթեր։

Սիրտըս թըռաւ ոտքիդ տակ,
Կոխեցիր հոն քաղցր հրեշտակ
Սիրով եղան ձիւն մակեր,
Ըսին՝ կեանքը երազ էր։

Մինչդէռ դու չես սիրեր զիս,
Մ'իշխեր գոնէ տկար սրտիս.
Ուր որ երթամ դէմքդ ինձ հետ՝
Նայուածք չէ այդ՝ մահու նետ։

Թաւուտքներու տակ նըսեմ,
Երբոր մէնիկ կ'արտասուեմ
Հոն ես դու, կը գըտնես զիս
Տերեւներէն կը խօսիս։

Երբ առուակին մէջ փաղփուն՝
Կ'ուզեմ թաղել դէմքըդ, դուն
Դարձեալ հոն կը գըտնես զիս,
Ալեաց մէջէն կը ժըպտիս։

Երբ կը փախչիմ ժայռ ու սար,
Երթալ հանգչիլ շիրմաց սնար,
Հովին մէջէն կը մըռնչես

Թէ դու բնաւ զիս սիրած չես։

Իսկ երբ գըրկեմ ցըրտին հողն
Քեզ չեմ գըտներ այլևս հոն,
Կոյս է մ'է նաև գերեզման,
Կա՞յ խորին սիրտ մ'անոր նման։

### 3. ՄՆԱՍ ԲԱՐԵԱՒ

Առտու մը դեռ մթնշաղ
Կը ծաւալէր շող ու շաղ,
Ծաղկանց մէջ քեզ տեսայ ես,
Կը ժպտէիր լուսնոյ պէս։

Աչերդ սիրոյ ատրուշան,
Մատներդ էին գիրգ շուշան,
Այտերդ վարդի նոր թերթեր,
Նայուածքէդ ծնէր նոր եթեր։

Սիրտըս թըռաւ ոտքիդ տակ,
Սիրեցի քեզ, իմս հրեշտակ...
Սիրով եղան ձիւն մազեր,
Ըսին՝ կեանքը երազ էր։

Մինչդեռ դու չես սիրեր զիս,
Մ'իշխեր գոնէ տկար սրտիս.
Ուր որ երթամ դէմքդ ինձ հետ՝
Նայուածք չէ այդ... մահու նե՛տ։

Երբ անտառին խորը նըսեմ
Կ'երթամ լալ՝ լուռ մենաձեմ,
Դարձեալ հոն կը գտնես զիս,
Տերևներէն կը խօսիս։

Երբ առուակին եզերքը
Նըստիմ սփոփել իմ վէրքը՝
Դարձեալ դու կը գտնես զիս,

Ալեաց մէջէն կը ժպտիս։

Երբ լեռները կը փախչիմ,
Որ չտեսնեմ քեզ, հանգչիմ,
Հողմոյն մէջէն կը խօսիս,
Թէ՝ դու բնաւ չես սիրեր պիս։

Լուսնի լուսով գիշերը
Երբ ցօղեն իմ աչերը,
Դարձեալ դու կը գտնես պիս,
Աստղերուն մէջ կը ժպտիս։

Իսկ գերեզման երբ մտնեմ,
Քեզ հոն չը գտնեմ…
Մնաս բարեա·ւ… Հայուհիս,
Անգո·ւթ, արցունք մ՛ալ չունիս։

**Translations.**

1. *I loved you* [Final version]

Those were hours of gleaming and dew:
A conflagration of roses there was in heaven,
Plaited fire in place of clouds:
Pearls and gold were raining down!

In the flowering thicket's deep
Reclining languidly
You expelled a discolored sigh
In harmony with the summer breeze.

Your eyes, love's Fire Temple! ...
And with your fingers like lilies,
You were plucking a blossom,
Fixed upon the beams, your eyes, of heaven.

I marvelled at how

Your soft fingers had the might
To shred the petals of the haughty rose
And scatter them upon your gentle breast.

And those languorous eyes
Glittered, an ether new,
An ether where in the stars' stead
Arrows glinted, burning red.

(Oh, you have pierced my heart as well
And withheld from me your smile,
That life-bestowing radiance
Which burns the hearts in pain.)

You made of your eyes' one flash,
One syllable said, your captive:
You enchained me, pitiless one,
By the beams of your lofty soul.

Leave my heart alone and go away:
I do not want you queen of my heart,
Whose breast is strewn with rose petals,
Yet a heart of granite is within.

You, who know only to be a fragrance,
To carve a wound in gentle hearts,
Love when greatly
The heart of your worshipper bleeds.

In the somber thicket's shade
When all alone I cry,
You are there, you find me
And speak out of the leaves.

When in the sparkle of a stream
I want to forget your face,

You discover me once again,
And smile out of the waves.

When I flee to the mountain rocks
To shatter my lyre and my heart,
You murmur ever from the wind's midst
That you have never loved me.

Now by my heart I embrace the chill ground,
And may I never touch you again.
For the grave, too, is a virgin maiden ...
And has any other heart her depth? ...

Variant 2. *I loved you* [First version]

Early one morning when it was still dark
Began the gleaming and dew to diffuse:
I beheld you in the flowers' midst
And you were smiling, like the moon.

Your eyes—love's Fire Temple;
Your fingers were lilies soft;
Your cheeks, petals of the rose all new,
And a new ether of your gaze was born.

My heart beneath your feet flew
And you trampled it, sweet angel;
Of love was that snow of hair:
Life was a dream, they said.

Since you love me not,
Do not, at least, command my frail heart.
Wherever I go, your face is with me:
It is no gaze, but death's arrow.

Below the sombre thickets,

When all alone I shed tears
You are there, you find me,
You speak out of the leaves.

When in the sparkling stream
I wish to bury your face,
Again you find me,
And smile from the midst of the waves.

When I flee to the stony mountains
To go and rest on the pillow of tombs,
You murmur from the midst of the wind
That you have never loved me.

But when I embrace the earth cold,
I will find you there no more.
The grave, too, is a virgin maiden:
Is there another heart deep as hers?

Variant 3. *Farewell* [First draft]

Early one morning when it was still dark
Began the gleaming and dew to diffuse:
I beheld you in the flowers' midst
And you were smiling, like the moon.

Your eyes—love's Fire Temple;
Your fingers were lilies soft;
Your cheeks, petals of the rose all new,
And a new ether of your gaze was born.

My heart beneath your feet flew,
My angel, I loved you ...
Of love was that snow of hair:
Life was a dream, they said.

Since you love me not,
Do not, at least, command my frail heart.
Wherever I go, your face is with me:
It is no gaze, but death's arrow.

When to the somber forest's deeps
I go to cry, silent, with lonely tread,
You discover me there again,
You speak from the leaves.

When on the steam's bank
I sit down to nurse my wound,
You find me again
And smile from the midst of the waves.

When I flee to the mountains
That I might not see you, and rest,
You speak from the wind
Saying you will never love me.

When by the moon's light
At night my eyes shed their dew,
You find me again
And smile in the stars.

But when I enter the grave
I will not find you there ...
Farewell, my Armenian maid,
Merciless! who hast not a tear.

**Commentary.**

The poem in its final form was printed twice in Tourian's lifetime, it would seem: first, in the periodical *Meghu* ("The Bee"), no. 46, 1 July 1871. It is excluded from some editions, being considered merely a variant of *Mnas paryav* ("Farewell," App. no. 3). Ekserjian discovered two drafts of *Mnas paryav* among Tourian's papers. These MSS. are lost, though a photograph of one was published. That poem was published in *Arevelk'* no. 2516, 13 June 1892. Tchéraz translated "Je t'ai aimée" (pp. 33-34); Blackwell has "I have loved thee" (pp. 28-29).

The sixth stanza of the *final* version, which I have printed in parentheses, was added to a subsequent edition in *Orakir* by the author, who then decided to delete it—Sevak publishes it in the notes to the text. And there is extant the second draft of the poem, bearing the title "I loved you" (Sevak, pp. 239-240, also dated 1869): this draft, intermediate between *Mnas paryav* and the final version, is presented and translated as text 2. I have given it this subordinate status only because Tourian chose not to print it. It is of anything but secondary importance, though, since, as Sevak points out, it is really the first poem, an Ur-version that underwent mitosis in its creator's mental womb: with some differences, stanzas 1-4 became the first four quatrains of *Mnas paryav*; 5-8 were reworked into 9-12 of *Sirets'i k'ez*. It enables one to observe in minute detail stages of the creative process as perhaps nowhere else in Tourian's oeuvre. For purposes of comparison, I will call the final version of *Sirets'i k'ez*, 1; the first draft, 2; and *Mnas paryav*, 3.

In the first stanza, 2 and 3 are in agreement; 1 is radically changed. Instead of the predawn dark (*mt'nshagh*, a word the later poet Vahan Teryan loved and used in the title of his cycle *Mt'nshaghi anurjner*, "Crepuscular reveries"), there is abundant, gorgeous light diffused through dew (see below how Armenian enables the poet to fuse the contrasting fire and water: *shogh* and *shagh*): a conflagration of roses and a fire of tresses in the place of clouds, as the first flame of dawn is reflected off their wispy coils and trails. Rose and tress prefigure the beloved girl, but appear first as metaphors of heaven. Such phantasmagoric collocations of rose and fire, of clouds and hair (note how later on hair is to be snow made of love, with the contradictory implication of love's warmth!), are the soul of Tourian's visionary poetics. In the poem "The Lake," his heart is called a "conflagration" (Arm. *hrteh*); and I think it is not perhaps too farfetched to suggest that this word is a marker of his own passion, touching the girl's ethereal and vast presence in the early morning sky. But how did he arrive here from the original shape of the stanza? His use of the verb *ge dzavaler*, "spread, dilated, diffused" might have been inspired by St. Gregory of

Narek's Song of the Nativity, much admired and emulated by subsequent poets, in which the visage of the virgin Mother of Christ is thus evoked: *Ačʿkʿn cov i cov cicałaxit cawalanayr yařawawtun / Erku pʿaylakajew aregakan nman* which would be pronounced in Modern Western Armenian /*Achken dzov i dzov dzidzaghakhid dzavalanayr harravodun / Yergu p'aylagatsev arekagan neman* /. "Her eyes, sea into sea dense in laughter dilated into the dawn/ Like two suns in the form of flares of lightning." Tourian retains the fusion of contradictory opposites—fire and water—of Narekats'i's image by the phonetic pairing of the phrase *shogh u shagh*, "ray and rain," as it were, the impossibly intensified fusion of opposing elements in an imagined sunshower. (Blackwell has for this "It was the hour of dew and light"; but Tchéraz, utilizing a text in which, it would seem, *shagh* "dew" is replaced by *vart* "rose," has "C'était l'heure de la rosée et des rayons.") Tourian might have perceived the closing image, of moonlight, as anticlimactic, after such a dawn. It is too pale; so he reworked the stanza entirely, introducing a very striking, marked phrase.

*Deghar markrid yev vosgi*. "Pearls and gold rained down." This is a paraphrase of the citation by the Classical Armenian historian Movses Khorenats'i of a strophe from the pre-Christian epic cycle of Artaxias I (Artašēs) in which is described the marriage of the king to the Alan princess Sat'enik. The passage, in *History of the Armenians* II.50, reads: *Doynpēs zharsaneacʿn ařaspeleal ergen, ayspēs aselov: Teł oski tełayr i pʿesayutʿeann Artašisi, tełayr margarit i harsnutʿean Satʿinkann*, "In that same way do they sing bardic songs about the nuptials, reciting thus: 'Golden rain fell when Artaxias became a groom; pearls rained down when Sat'enik became a bride.'" It is certain that Tourian read Khorenats'i, since he wrote a historical play, *Ardashes Ashkharhagal*, "Artaxias the World-Conqueror" (completed on 1 July 1869, printed in Sevak, Vol. II, pp. 133-193). Tourian also mentions Artaxias by name in "The Rosebud: Flowers of the Maiden" (No. 28). One notes there the similarity of the Armenian image to that of the myth of Danae, in the cognate Indo-European tradition of Greece.[12] Poem 1 inserts a second

[12]The king of Argos, Acrisius, had one daughter, Danae. An oracle had told him that his daughter would bring into the world a son by whose hands he was to perish. Acrisius built a subterranean bronze chamber—or, according

stanza to locate the languorous beloved in an earthly glade: all seems ready now for the earthly nuptials heaven has just celebrated in myth and fire. Stanza three of poem 1 further stresses the pagan joy of the poem: the girl's eyes are an *atrušan,* a Zoroastrian fire altar.

But from the static subsequent image of 2 and 3 (her fingers are lilies, *shushan,* softly rhyming but imaginally contrastive with *atrushan*) Tourian has the fingers pluck a flower. The verb employed is *p'ettel,* probably originally a reduplicative, **p'etp'etel,* which would then anticipate the overtly reduplicative *t'ap't'ap'el* "drop." But this verb can have the more forceful sense of "beat," and Prof. Jos Weitenberg has argued[13] that Classical Armenian *t'awt'ap'el,* "shake," may be derived from a reduplicative with the same base. So Tourian constructs a series of implied violent motions linked by the phonetic signature of a pair of simple syllables enclosed by aspirated labial and dental stops: repeated tearing, repeated casting down, the overtone of repeated tossing away. And the contrast of this cruelty to the beloved's softness (*kirk,* replaced before "lily" by *zert',* "like," in 1 and shifted to modify, alliteratively, *kirg,* "bosom") astonishes the lover, inducing a kind of awe. When the English-speaking reader considers the girl plucking at the flower and notes Tourian's strategic use of sharp reduplicatives (cf. also *chakhchakhel, infra*), he may be reminded of the deliberately vicious lines of T. S. Eliot in "Sweeney Among the Nightingales": "Rachel *née* Rabinovitch/ Tears at the grapes with murderous paws." The line is memorable for its tearing and plucking. But Eliot's intent is not awe at the power of woman, as is the case with Tourian's poem, but a particular, anti-Semitic misogyny. He reduces his Rachel to a wild beast; but it is his pen that proved the more feral.[14]

---

to other sources, a tower—and locked up Danae with her nurse. But Zeus, father of the gods, desired the girl and often visited her in the form of a shower of gold. In due course she gave birth to Perseus.

[13]See J.J.S. Weitenberg, "An early dialectal phonetic split in Classical Armenian: the cases of *t'awt'ap'em* and *p'lanim,*" in J. Greppin, ed., *Proceedings of the Fourth International Conference on Armenian Linguistics,* Delmar, NY: Caravan, 1992, pp. 295-318.

[14]Anthony Julius, *T. S. Eliot, Anti-Semitism, and Literary Form,* Cambridge: Cambridge University Press, 1995, p. 87, notes that the American poet Ezra

Following these initial stanzas, Tourian largely abandoned the phrasing of variants 2 and 3, while retaining the form of the beloved pursuing him in leaf, wind, and water through the refuges of his longed-for solitude. But he has refined his language to avoid the dreary repetition that weighs upon the two other poems, and has altered some images entirely.

Thus, instead of nursing his wounds (*sp'op'el im verk'e*), he accuses the girl of fragrance (*purel*), of stabbing deeper into them, *verk' p'orel*. Instead of *g'ert'am lal, lurr menajem,* "I go to cry, silent, with lonely tread," he prefers the simpler *erpor menig ardasvem,* "when I shed tears, alone," and the emphasis has shifted from locomotion to focus on his tears. Instead of the repeated *Tartsyal tu ge kdnes zis,* "You find me again," of 2 and 3, Tourian has in 1 *Hon es tu, ge ktnes zis* and *Tartsyal hon ge kdnes zis*. And the beloved no longer speaks (*ge khosis*) from both leaves and wind—she moans eternally instead (*mishd mnch'es*), in a fine alliterative phrase.

In 2 and 3, Tourian flees to the mountains to rest. But the hard ascent of stony cliffs intuits no calm; and in 1 he refines the image, introducing another reduplicative verb of action as well: *chakhchakhel sirds yev k'nar,* "to shatter my heart and my lyre." The strength of this image is not solely in the directness of the action of smashing, but in the actions that precede it: ascent of the mountain, and the swift plummeting down, the descent that shatters the poet's physical and spiritual body. These swift ascents and horrible plunges are the very soul of Tourian's vision of the tortured mind in motion; and here the crescendo recapitulates the movement up to heaven and the descent to earth at the beginning of the poem, in hues altered from sublime to lurid. The descent here implies not only an incarnation of earthly passion, but the further fall into the pit of the grave. Tourian altered the stanza of variants 2 and 3 about his visit to the banks of a stream, in order to stress this. In the drafts, he merely sits beside the stream; but in 1 he moves all the way into it, and it receives the reduplicative epi-

---

Pound in one of his broadcasts from Fascist Italy during World War II used the phrase "*née* Rabinovitch" to attack a (Gentile) woman in the Roosevelt administration. The hands of the fictional Rachel are metaphorically murderous—of the work of the real Eliot, the epithet is literally true.

thet *p'aghp'ghun*, "glittering" or "broken up by glints," which ought by its special, marked aspect to be an indication to the attentive reader of some more violent movement impending. He has gone in, to bury (*t'aghel*) the beloved's face. The completed pattern of reduplicatives forms a tripartite series, in which the first two members are related, and the third is marked by its affricate stops as radically different. None of this, we have to stress, is in the texts of either 2 or 3: 1 is a completely new poem. The consonantal pattern of the series is: *pt/tp > pgh/tgh>chkhchkh:* *p'etp'et>t'ap't'ap'>p'aghp'agh>chakhchakh ... t'agh-*. The pattern of two phonetically and typologically related elements followed by a radically different one marked by an affricate is elemental in Armenian poetics: cf., in the ancient song of the birth of Vahagn, preserved by Movses Khorenats'i, *erkin* (1), *erkir* (2), and *tsov* (3): heaven and earth, seen as two halves of a whole; and sea. On a conscious level, Tourian doubtless selected the reduplicative verbs whose sound and rhyming qualities he liked; but the deeper structures relating them were probably subconscious, and even as he created, moving in his chosen direction and revising, he was carried on the dark and strong currents of the Armenian language.

Tourian's mention of burial prepares us for the final stanza, which in 2 and 3 is little more than an embittered whine, an anti-envoi. There is something of a poetic conceit: the girl is everywhere, except in the grave— but it comes across as little better than a sarcastic parting jab. In 1, though, the poet does not enter the grave, but embraces it (*krgem*: cf. the plays on *kirg* and *kirk*) as he might a virgin (*guys*), restoring the nuptial theme of the first stanza in a shocking inversion. Instead of the heights of heaven, there is profundity of depth; and the latter not open and spatial, but the further, enclosed inwardness of a heart (*khorung sird*). Death becomes the only true lover: the title, "I loved you," moves from the multifaceted instant of nature's display of fire and dew and Armenian antiquity's stately showers of gold and pearls, to its true past tense: Tourian bears farewell to his unrequited life, two brief years before he leaves it, in what is his poetic comet-trail's golden dawn.

**12. "The Maiden Abandoned"** (*Guysn lk'yal*), 1870 (Sevak, pp. 36-37)

**Text.**

ԿՈՅՍՆ ԼՔԵԱԼ

Հալեց սառեր գարնան արև,
Ոսկի մատամբք ծաղիկ, տերև
Ցանեց, ցրուեց ամպ ու բալ փոյթ,
Պարկեց աստեղց կամարն կապոյտ.
Ո·հ, ինչո՞ւ կոյսին
Նայուածքն է մըթին։

Ոսկի սփռեց լերանցն արփի,
Ծիծաղեցաւ լուսինն յ'ալի,
Կա·յծ ու ծիծաղ, ծաղիկք համբուն,
Թերթեր, ուր սէր կարդայ կուսարթուն.
Ո·հ, ինչո՞ւ գունատ
Է կոյսին ճակատ։

Բուլբուլն թառեր թաւուտ թփին՝
Գեղգեղէ գե·լ աղիօք սրտին.
Թռչունք մըթին անտառաց խոր
Ձայնակցին, հեշտ սիրոյ ժըխո·ր...
Ո·հ, ինչո՞ւ լինի
Լուռ կոյս լեզուանի։

Ալիք սիրոյ ցոյց տան կայծ, նետ,
Մրմունջ, նայուածք տանելով հետ,
Ջըրել կ'երթան ծաղկոտ մարմանդ,
Թոթուէ խոտեն հովն ադամանդ.
Ո·հ, ինչո՞ւ արտսուք
Թափէ կոյսն ի սուգ։

Ի դրանց ոսկի արևելքին՝
Թռչտելով սիւքեր հեշտին՝

Ծաղկանց, ալեաց, թերթից համբոյր
Տալով՝ սահին թողլով համ, բոյր·
        Ո·հ, ինչո՞ւ հառաչ
Հանէ կոյսին լանջ։

Ո·, կոյս, ինչո՞ւ այսպէս տրտում
Սամոյր հոպոպքդ արտասուաթուրմ
Դէմքըդ սիրուն ծածկեն, վերցո·ւր
Ճակատդ, շնչէ սէր, լոյս ու բոյր·
        Անկողինդ ծաղկունք,
        Աստղեր քեպի շուք։

-Սիրէի ես աստղերն երկնի,
Ալին կ՛իս ցոյց տար գեղանի,
Վայլէր ծաղիկ Ճակտիս անսուգ,
Զեփիւռն ունէր հեշտ փըսփըսուք·
        Մատնելու պկուսիկ
        Հրապո·յրք խաբուսիկ։

**Translation.**

*The Maiden Abandoned*

The sun of spring has melted the ice
And with golden fingers flowers, leaves
Has raised, swiftly clouds and mist has scattered,
And the blue canopy of stars spread plain.
        Oh why so dark
        Is the maiden's gaze?

The sun's rays scatter gold upon the mountains
And the moon laughs on the wane.
Sparkle and laughter, the flowers assembled,
The petals where love cries gay.
        Oh why is the maiden's
        Brow so pale?

The nightingale nesting in the thicket's shade
Trills quavering her heart's inmost song.
The birds of the deeps of the dark forest
Accompany her—languorous love's clamor.
O why so eloquently
Speaks the maiden's silence?

Love's billow displays sparkles, arrows,
Murmurs of complaint and glances borne away
To shower the sparkling meadow
Rebuking in gentle burble the adamantine gale.
O why does tears
Of mourning the maiden shed?

At heaven's eastern, golden gate
Zephyrs luxuriating on the wing[15]
A kiss to flowers, waves, and petals
Give and glide, savor and aroma lingering behind.
Why does the maiden's bosom
Heave a sigh?

O maiden, why so sadly
Do your sable ringlets, tear-bedewed,
Conceal love's face? Reveal
Your brow, breathe love, light, fragrance:
The flowers, your bower;
The stars, your shade.

— I loved the stars of heaven,
The wave my loveliness displayed,

---

[15]Tcheraz, p. 38, relying on the 1872 text of l. 26 (see Sevak, p. 242) reading *Ichner zep'yurr ts'oghig heshdin,* which Sevak considers corrupt, further emends the first word of the line, Clas. impf. (or Mod. past subj.!) *iǰ(a)nēr* to 3 pers. pl. *iǰnen,* yielding thereby "La rosée et le zéphire voluptueux *descendent* des portes d'or de l'orient."

The flower was meet for my untroubled brow,
And the breeze whispered delight
    To betray the maiden,
    Charms of deceit!

**Commentary.**

The poem exists in both of Tourian's manuscript notebooks and has been published in numerous print editions; Tchéraz translated it ("La vierge abandonnée, pp. 37-39). The verse has a rhyming pattern of AABBCC. Internally, Tourian employs multiple alliterations in the first half: ***ts'****ane****ts'***, ***ts'****erve****ts'*** (line 3), *barze****ts'*** *asdegh****ts'*** ***ga****marn* ***ga****buyd* (line 4), ***dzidzagh***, ***dzagh****igk'* (line 9), ***t'a****rrer* ***t'a****vud* ***t'****p'in* (line 13), ***keghke****ghe* ***kel*** (line 14). There is a further deep alliteration, on the level of the Classical Armenian lexicon where the two are not phonemically distinct, of *l* and dark *l* (now pronounced *gh*). He seems in league with nature to lull the maiden to languorous sleep, for a seduction. In lines 26-27, he resolves *hampuyr*, "kiss" (where *ham-* is etymologically a prefix meaning "shared"), into luxurious sensations: *ham, puyr* "taste, aroma" (and the latter word is repeated in line 34). At the end of line 32, *Samuyr hobobk't ardasvat'urm*, the long compound "tear-streaming" stretches out all the sounds of the first word, "sable," to combine imagery of fur and water and evoke the maiden's long tresses as a dark and luxuriant torrent. The poet also plays upon contrasts of dark shadow and dazzling light, of hushed stillness and the joyful roar of vernal life.

In the case of line 13, it is interesting to note that Tourian originally wrote, Թառէր սոխակն ի խիտ սաղարթ *T'arrer sokhagn i khid saghart'*, "The nightingale nested in the dense green," using the older, Parthian loan-word (meaning literally, "speaker") for the bird, with an even more complex sound pattern than in the line finally chosen: initial *tar-* is mirrored by final *-art*, with an inner mirroring of *kha-* and *-agh* and a stress at the center of the line on the frontal vowel i, in the preposition *i* and the word *khid*. And *saghart'*, "greenery," seems lusher than *t'up'*, "bush." However in the realized line the nightingale is the Persian loan into the Western Armenian of Ottoman Turkey, *bulbul* (to be pronounced thus, although in Western strictly speaking one would have expected orthographic *p-*, not *b-*). Perhaps the reason for the choice is the immediate, subconscious association any reader will make with the allegory of the nightingale's love for the rose (*gol*) in the Persian formula *gol o bolbol*.

And indeed, as William Blake cries, "Rose, thou art sick!" The phallic worm has got her and Eden's immortality has fled. In the latter half of the poem, Tourian addresses the maiden directly, and in the final stanza she replies that all the forest's enchantments were deceptive charms (*hrabuyrk'*, which, unetymologically, contains the sounds of Tourian's alluring images of light [*hr-* <*hur*, "fire"]; *buyr*, cf. *puyr*, "fragrance") to betray (*madnelu*) her, to hand her over to an enemy—and one recalls that in the title she is betrayed, cast out (*lk'yal*, the Classical Arm. past participle). Since she is a virgin, a maiden (*guys*), one might think of Christ and of Mary, and then of His betrayal. The latter is signified by Judas' kiss, Arm. *hamboyr*, discussed above, whose dissected segments recombine at last into the final illusion. But of course the more obvious Biblical reference must be to Eve, deceived in Eden and sexually seduced by the Serpent, delivered to expulsion. Armenian tradition leaves little doubt about this: the bas-reliefs of Adam and Eve on the tenth-century Church of the Holy Cross on the island of Aght'amar, Lake Van, Armenia, show the four-legged Serpent coiled about the tree, erect in the air facing the naked Eve, who kneels and holds out her breasts to him.[16]

Tourian's evocation of Adam and Eve cannot be stressed too strongly. The myth of the first human couple looms large in Armenian folk imagination, not least because two of the four rivers that flow from Paradise, the Tigris and Euphrates, rise in Armenia and mediaeval commentators locate the Garden there, in the canton of Hark' northwest of lake Van. (Armenians identify local streams with the other two.) Six travelling monks are said to have espied Eden upon a

---

[16]Prof. Thomas Mathews of the Institute of Fine Arts, New York University, has stressed this erotic gesture, which Sirarpie Der Nersessian does not mention: in her monograph *Aght'amar: Church of the Holy Cross*, Cambridge, MA: Harvard Univ. Press, 1965, p. 19 and fig. 48, she writes, "Eve, kneeling, raises both hands and appears to be speaking or listening to the serpent, whose head almost touches hers."

mountaintop. Though the angel barred their way, they smelled the perfumes of the garden; and, the Armenian version of the legend adds, one went to inform St. Nerses Shnorhali (d. 1173) of their discovery, about which he wrote in a Commentary on Genesis that is now lost.[17] The rest remained to the end of their days at the foot of the mountain. There is another legend, also widespread in Christendom but especially popular in Armenia, according to which Adam after his expulsion from Eden was so terrified by the dark of the night— he had never seen it before— that he agreed to sign a pledge to Satan (a cheirograph, literally, writing signed by his own hand) that Adam and his progeny would serve him "till the unborn is born and the undying dies," if only the Sun might rise. Of course it did, soon thereafter. But the devil was outwitted by the Nativity and Crucifixion of the eternal and immortal Christ, Who destroyed the cheirograph. Armenians still call the hour that is darkest before the dawn *adamamut'*, "Adam's darkness." The story is an adaptation of the basic type of the wise god or warrior who defeats a sorcerer or demon who has tried to entrap him in riddles. The *locus classicus* is Oedipus and the Sphinx; closer to Armenia is the tale of the Parthian hero, Yoishta ("Youngest") of the Friyana clan and the sorcerer Akhti. But the myth of the genre closest to the Cheirograph of Adam is Indic: that of the god Shiva and the monster Hiranyakashipu. The latter could not be killed by man or woman, by day or night, indoors or outside. So Shiva transformed himself into the hermaphrodite god Ardhanarishvara and slew the creature at dusk, on a threshold.[18]

Overshadowed by the symbolism of Genesis, all the poet's persuasions turn out to be demonic and life-devastating; his adolescent love, the serpent's way into decay: he is "The invisible worm/ That flies in the night/ In the howling storm" of Blake's poem, and it is his

---

[17]See Nira Stone, *The Kaffa Lives of the Desert Fathers: A Study in Armenian Manuscript Illumination*, *CSCO* vol. 566, Louvain: Peeters, 1997, pp. 80-88 and color plate 6.

[18]See Michael Stone, *Adam's Contract with Satan: The Legend of the Cheirograph of Adam*, Bloomington, IN: Indiana Univ. Press, 2002, and this writer's review in *International Journal of the Classical Tradition*, Summer 2003, pp. 309-312.

"dark secret love" that destroys his rose. But that does not lessen the sensual beauty of his descriptions— any more than the association of two seeming opposites, sex and death, detracts from either— leaving an ambiguity between virtue and the pleasure of fulfilled desire that, as with William Blake's rose, transcends the customary pieties of good and evil.

**13. "Ode on the Seventh Anniversary of the National Constitution"** (*Nvag VII daretartsi Azkayin Sahmanatrut'yan*), 1870, Sevak pp. 38-39.

**Text.**

ՆՈՒԱԳ Է ՏԱՐԵԴԱՐՁԻ ԱԶԳԱՅԻՆ ՍԱՀՄԱՆԱԴՐՈՒԹԵԱՆ

Պատուեր են Հայոց դաշտերն արիւնոտ,
Հայկավն հըսկայից կըմախք կայթեն յ’ոտն,
Մոխրոտ ու մամռոտ աւերակք խայտան,
Մասիս բարձեր է վեհ ճակտէն պատան.
        Յիշատակն Հայն կը կանչէ,
        Հայն Հայաստան կը կանչէ։

Զինուո·ր Սիրոյ, դրօշդ ծալ ծալ ծըփացո·ւր,
Սորուինք խաչովդ սէր, ’քան թէ փայլել սուր,
Հեշտ արցունք թափեն սառք Մասեաց սարին՝
Երբ Հայեր աննենգ իրարու փարին՝
        Հայաստան դեռ ողջ է՝
        Թէ Հայն միշտ Հայը կանչէ։

Հայրենեաց տըխուր մէջ աւերակաց՝
Հուր հոգի մ’ըսկէր, կանթե·ղ սիրակայծ,
Միշտ դէպ ի հէք Հայն տանէր քայլ յառաջ,
Նա աղեաց խորն Հայն՝ կուրծն էր գամած խաչ։
        Ըսին թէ Հայն պայն կանչէ,
        Սէ·ր է, նոճեաց լոկ ձայն չէ։

Ծովե·պր, որ սիրոյ նախ տուիր արձագանք,
Արիւն չըր ծըծած հող, չըր թաղած գանկ,
Բաժակք հնչեցին՝ ո·չ սև թնդանօթ,
Հիւսեցան կամարք դափնեաց սիրայօդ.
        Սև վէտ յափունսդ թէ հնչէ,
        Հէք Հայն եղբայրն կը կանչէ։

Դառն են արցունքով մեր սիրոյ բաժակք,

Սիրոյ դրօշք՝ մեր քերց արցունքոտ լաչակք,
Թէ չ՚երդնումք, եղբա՛րք, յիշել զՀայաստան,
Արեամբ եւ պահել պատիւն Հայոց տան,
Կը տառապի՝ Հայրենիք,
Կամ Հա՛յ ըսուինք կամ մեռնինք։

**Translation.**

*Ode on the Seventh Anniversary of the National Constitution.*

Rent are the bloodied plains of Armenia
As the skeletons of the titan sons of Hayg leap to their feet.
The ashen, mossy ruins rejoice,
And Mount Ararat has removed the shroud from his noble brow.
Memory "O Armenian!" cries out;
And the Armenian "O Armenia!" shouts.

Warrior of Love, unfurl your banner, may it wave;
May we learn by your Cross to love, rather than polish the blade,
And the icy summit of Mount Ararat shed tears of joy
When Armenians cleave to one another without deceit.
Armenia is yet alive
If the Armenian ever for his fellow cry.

Amidst the Fatherland's sad ruins
A spirit of fire kept watch, a lamp glinting with love,
His step towards the wretched Armenian ever advancing,
Armenian to the depths of his vitals, the Cross to his bosom nailed.
They said that if the Armenian summon him
He is love, not the cypresses sighing.

Shore of the sea, who first to love gave echo,
Your soil has not absorbed blood, interred a skull;
Clashing goblets, not cannons, resounded,
And love-limbed laurel bowers there were woven:
If the black breaker sound on your banks,

It is the poor Armenian calling for his brother.

Our loving cups are full of bitter tears;
Our sisters' bloodied kerchiefs are the banners of our love:
Till we swear, brethren, to remember Armenia,
To protect even with blood the honor of the Armenian house,
Then the Fatherland will continue to suffer.
We either declare ourselves Armenians or go to the slaughter.

**Commentary.**

The poem was copied into both of Tourian's manuscript notebooks, and was first published in the T'eodik *Yearbook* for 1914, pp. 19-20, with a facsimile illustration of the final stanza and the caption: "The only unpublished poem that Abp. Yeghishe Tourian was pleased to supply to us." Yeghishe Tourian wrote "X" ("tenth"); but "VII" appears in both T'eodik and the index of Mihrdateants'. On 24 May 1860 the Patriarchate accepted the draft of a constitution drawn up by N. Rusinian, N. Balian, G. Odian, et al. for Armenian communal self-government; the Sublime Porte ratified it on 17 March 1863. Tourian's "VII" thus refers to the latter date.

A number of phrases in the poem are borrowed, with few changes, from the encomia Tourian had addressed in the previous year to Abp. Mkrtich' Khrimian, including even the scene of someone's arrival by sea (line 19)— here, a black wave propelled westwards by Armenian suffering to the Bosphorus, rather than Khrimian's ship from Trebizond. The recollection of the tribulations of their brethren in the homeland to the East transforms the wine in the Constantinopolitans' glasses to bitter tears, a sort of reverse Eucharist; and the flag becomes the bloodstained *lach'ag* ("kerchief, veil") of a village woman.

The year after this fulsome poem was written, Tourian commemorated the anniversary of the Constitution again in an intricate prose poem published in *Orakir*, which is translated and analyzed in the Introduction to this book (pp. 24ff.).

**14. "She"** (*Ne*), 1871, Sevak, p. 40.

**Text.**

Նէ

Վարդը գարնայնի
Թէ կոյսին տիպար
Այտերուն չ'ըլլար՝
Ո՞վ կ'յարգէր զ'անի։

Թէ չը նմանէր
Կապոյտն եթերաց
Կոյսին աչերաց՝
Երկինք ո՞վ կ'նայէր։

Թէ կոյսը չ'ըլլար
Սիրուն ու անբիծ,
Աստուածն այն Երկնից
Մարդ ո՞ւր կը կարդար։

**Translation.**

*She.*

Were the rose of spring
Not the type
Of the virgin's cheek,
Who would render it esteem?

If ethereal blue
Were not the semblance
Of the virgin's eyes,
Who would favor Heaven with a glance?

If the virgin did not exist,

(10) Lovely and unblemished,
The God of those Heavens–
Whither would man cry?

**Commentary.**

The title, *Ne*, is arresting. Modern Armenian has no grammatical gender: *an* means he, she, and it. Neither does the Classical language, in which the pronoun is *na*. Mediaeval grammarians, who translated and interpreted the Greek grammar of Dionysius Thrax, using it as a model for their own, very different mother tongue, were forced to invent a feminine pronoun, *nē*, "she." The word never gained currency outside learned treatises; so when the short, strange word stands absolutely alone as the title of a vernacular poem, it has a focussing, hieratic force: She, with a capital letter, is no mere girl, it would seem, but a divinity, an object of cult: Bulwer-Lytton's She, She Who Must Be Obeyed, *das Ewige Weibliche*, Anahit, Astarte, Cybele, the Magna Mater, devouring female, dominatrix. This theme of a slightly frightening, uncanny sanctity bestowed upon a physical being must inform our understanding of the three stanzas of simile that follow in an ascending trinity: rose-cheek, eye-sky, woman-God (Sophia, Daughter, Holy Spirit, and God the Mother, if you will).

Tourian's comparison of the face of his beloved to the red rose is one he has often used before, to which he returns; but his treatment is of an intricacy that belies the common simile: "Small Dedications" is perhaps the best example of his treatment of the theme. The comparison of blue eyes to the blue sky is also familiar, even a cliché, in Western poetry, though in Armenian it is a little strange.[19] At first it seems

[19]Tourian, again, does not praise blue eyes for the first time here—and it's important that the color enables him to compare the eyes to the sky by day. But it is worth stressing that most Armenians have *dark* eyes: the blue eye, *xaž akn*, was the feared evil eye of magical literature, apotropaically to be warded off with the eye-shaped charms of blue glass that are still ubiquitous in the Middle East. But there are Armenians with blue eyes and fair hair. By the late nineteenth century, when it was shown that Armenian is an independent branch of Indo-European with closer kinship to the ancient Thracian of southeastern Europe than to the Iranian tongues of the East, the myth took hold that this fairer physical type was a survival of a pure and ancestral proto-Armenian strain. Such a conviction gave pseudo-scientific support to

that this is the standard hyperbole of praise: the beloved is prettier than roses; her eyes, bluer than heaven; and so on. But it is more. Tourian argues that, were it not for the aspects of human beauty that we appreciate and love, we would be unable to find beauty in the natural world around us. Without the qualities we perceive in living human beings, we should have no inclination to turn to the sky we can see in worship, or to cry out towards a God we cannot see, Who is wholly transcendent. The poet does not actually devalue roses, or heaven, or God, as a talentless versifier reaching for hyperbole might do. His point is that we really do have aesthetic and religious feelings, but the starting point of human love makes them possible: "Man is the measure of all things" was not meant by the Presocratics as a slogan of narrow anthropocentrism, but as an honest observation about the necessary bounds of perception. What other measure, for a man, is there?

For crying out, Tourian uses *ge gartar*, impf. 3 pers. sg., employing the verb *gartal* in its Classical sense, endowing it with the power of its Biblical context: in modern Armenian the word means "to read," *goch'el* and *ganch'el* being the common verbs for "calling"; so its archaic usage here gives it a marked emphasis. Marked, unusual terms thus begin and close the poem, stressing its theological, metaphysical overtones. Though the poem is entitled "She," that word is not found in any of its forms in the body of the poem (elsewhere, Tourian uses the genitive of the pronoun, *nera*). Instead, every stanza contains *guyse*,

---

the Armenians' understandable hope that the Christians of Europe would help a nation of not only co-religionists, but racial brethren also, to achieve independence. Even without benefit of historical hindsight it is clear what such racialism had to lead to; and, as we have seen, Armenians are no more immune than any other group to such a bacillus. So on the eve of the First World War, even as the ultra-nationalist Young Turk party were planning the extermination of the Armenians as an inferior and pernicious race, the Constantinople literary periodical *Mehean* ("*[Pagan] Temple*") published edifying polemics about the heroic Aryan Christ, denying that the Savior had possessed any taint of Jewish blood. But what does it matter? Children with eyes like the sky and hair golden as a field of wheat in summer died in the death marches to Syria and later on in the gas chambers of the Germans, and neither Science nor Europe nor Christ rescued a single one.

"the virgin." (Propriety aside,[20] was she one, in the city of the seraglio, the place where girls and boys to satisfy any taste might be had with ease?) Sadly, I think the shadow fell very heavily for the young, ailing Tourian between the passion and the spasm. And there is a religious dimension to the sexual tension, for the repetition of "virgin" in this context forces one to think of Mary.

Eve's sin condemned us all, and stained in particular every woman to come after her with the curse of menses: the Virgin Mary, redeeming Eve, alone of the female sex was without blemish (*an-pidz*), and in the third stanza the virgin has precisely that cult epithet. The last two stanzas link her with Heaven, too (*yergink'*, line 8; *yergnits'*, line 11): in Armenian aretalogies the Virgin is high, lofty, or heavenly, almost superior to God the Father—she is His Mother. She is the object of extreme devotion, sometimes more so than Christ, and she seems to have inherited features of the goddess Anahit, reverence for whom amongst Zoroastrians was particularly strong in pre-Christian Armenia.[21] But Tourian's poem is about a virgin who is not Mary—a girl

---

[20]The only good place for it. Sexual prudishness has often bedevilled Armenian scholarship, not to mention social relations; and "inappropriate" is the stupid, witch-hunting word of the new American campus puritans. Philip Roth in *The Human Stain* has his hero, a college professor, muse upon a course on "appropriate" behavior in the Greek classics—it would be the world's shortest.

[21]It would be impossible to overestimate the importance of Mary, the *Tiramayr*, "Mother of the Lord," *Astuacacin*, "Generator of God" in Armenian tradition. As the *Marutʿa banjr surb Astuacacin*, "High holy Mother of God of Marutha," she is the principal divinity of the Epic of Sasun. In Diyarbakir (Amida, Dikranagerd) in 1997, I met a middle-aged Kurdophone Armenian woman of Sasun who had been converted to Islam as a small child. She knew—or would say—very little of her Armenian heritage, but when I mentioned the word Maratʿuk (the affectionately prayerful diminutive used by the Sasunts'is of Mary's shrine), her face was transfigured by joy and she said that even looking in the direction of the shrine could cure a person stung by a scorpion. St. Gregory of Narek invokes the Virgin Mary in chapter 80 of his *Book of Lamentation*, a work Tourian studied at school and every Armenian knew some of. She is the *erknawor arkʿayuhi* "heavenly queen," *anšałax əst nmanutʿean patkeri arusekin barjrutʿean* "unmixed in the likeness of the image of Venus of the height," *anarat* "unblemished" (her true worshippers have lips that are *anbic*, the epithet Tourian has), and a drop of the milk of her vir-

then, whom he would love, whose virginity he would take away. So beyond the poem lies an implied, unimaginable bliss, beyond even the sublime infinity of God, past the call of the human voice. And since Tourian says none of this, it is the act of reception of the reader that does all the imagining of the unimaginable, beyond the ultimate limits.

Let us look excursively at a love poem that employs familiar comparisons in a different but also unusual way, which relies for its full effect as Tourian's poem does on the act of reception by manipulation of the reader's expectation.

William Shakespeare, Sonnet 130.

My mistress' eyes are nothing like the sun;
Coral is far more red than her lips' red;
If snow be white, why then her breasts are dun;
If hairs be wires, black wires grow on her head.
I have seen roses damasked, red and white,
But no such roses see I in her cheeks,
And in some perfumes is there more delight
Than in the breath that from my mistress reeks.
I love to hear her speak, yet well I know
That music hath a far more pleasing sound;
I grant I never saw a goddess go—
My mistress when she walks treads on the ground.
And yet by heaven I think my love as rare

---

ginity, falling upon one's soul as rain, can restore life (*aha kat'il mi kat'in k'umd kusut'ean yanjn im anjreweal kenac' im zawrē*); she is the mother of Him who made both Heaven and earth. Anāhitā's name means "unblemished," and ancient Armenians called her *mayrn amenayn zgastut'eanc'*, "mother of all chastities." The planet Venus bears her name in Persian still, Nāhīd (the Arm. *aruseak,* "little white one," an Iranian loan itself, might have been a cult epithet originally). She has the cult epithet *barzokharā,* "from high Harā," on a monument from Cappadocia: her waters rolled down this mountain to a sea of broad shores, *Vourukaša,* which the Zoroastrian translator of the Avesta into Sanskrit, Neryosangh, calls the Sea of Milk (*kshirasamudra*): Narekats'i has *all* this. (On the cult of Anahit, see J. R. Russell, *Zoroastrianism in Armenia,* Harvard Iranian Series 5, Cambridge, MA, 1987, ch. 7.)

As any she belied with false compare.

Professor Helen Vendler of Harvard, who is at the time of this writing probably the most authoritative critic of poetry in the academic grove, and in many ways one of the most brilliant and exciting writers and teachers of American letters, maintains (*The Art of Shakespeare's Sonnets*, Cambridge, MA: Harvard University Press, 1997, pp. 556-7) that the poem is an answer to a poet who declares his lover's eyes *are* like the sun. Well, this one isn't: "She's a real woman." The final couplet, "And yet by heaven..." she says, is a burst of the Bard's "submerged irritation," and the whole is just "another case in which perceiving the accurate nature of the speech-act mimicked by the sonnet is indispensable to a correct understanding of the poem." She helpfully provides an example for us accurately to perceive, of the mimicked speech act—the kind of poem annoying Shakespeare so. It belongs to the hapless Thomas Watson's emotional holocaust, *Hekatompathia*: "...Her sparkling eyes in heaven a place deserve," etc. Watson's images, declares Vendler in her summing up of the case, are "preposterous when called to the bench of accuracy," and accuracy is, one must admit, not the strong suit of Watson. Shakespeare wins the judgment and Watson and his ilk go straight to Poetry Jail.

In a forensic sense, Prof. Vendler's analysis is beyond reproach. But so what? Is such plain accuracy the truth a *poet* strives for? If that is all Shakespeare has to say, then why do we respond to the sonnet as to a magical thing? And comparisons are trite: any number of characters in Shakespeare's plays wittily parody such hackneyed similes, or scoff, or admit—and their jocularity reduces the parody to a commonplace insight, the triviality that is the doorway to something more important. On this occasion, Professor Vendler does not walk through that doorway.[22] What do we feel when we hear the expression "nothing like the

---

[22]And that's strange by itself, since the importance of feeling bulks so large in her critical writings that one does not expect ugly courtroom metaphors about fact in a discussion of the Sonnets. On feeling, I have in mind Vendler's valediction about Allen Ginsberg in *The New Yorker*, shortly after the publication of the hardcover anthology of his poems, and, grievously, not long before his death. She writes there that his poems are better to the degree that they are more personal and less political. Ginsberg, as his friend Peter Lam-

born Wilson told me in conversation shortly after the piece appeared, was flattered at the attention of one of (Lou Reed's, I'd say) Prominent People. But he thought her standard of judgement of his work was all wrong.

I'd go farther than that. It seems to me a misunderstanding of just about everything Ginsberg was about, a distorted appreciation suitable to this de-politicized era in which it is private pleasure in the parlor or seminar room, and not public social commitment or change in the agora, that matters in, well, selling the product. There has always been powerful political poetry, anyway; but the whole point of the Beats' poetry was to go beyond that, to lead to the crucial, liberating declaration of my generation: The personal is political. How could one fail to see this? Both *Howl* and *Kaddish* (not to mention numerous shorter poems) are rooted in anarchist ideals and Old Left pathos and praxis. To be gay and personal was to be closeted; to make one's homosexuality political was to challenge the establishment on every level, from the church and state right down to people who take their poetry at Harvard with tea, rather than out loud on the streets of New York City. If you obscure this, the two great poems are inevitably reduced to the level of irresponsible, self-indulgent, adolescent ranting—which is where the neo-Conservative critic Norman Podhoretz, whose animosity pursues Ginsberg beyond the grave (since even as play he sees the poet's work as dangerously corrupting), would have them. (I refer to his noxious rant against the poet, shortly after Ginsberg's death, in *Commentary*.) Making personal matters political and poetic ennobles and gives voice to that public space, those general concerns, which are part of the common experience of men and women without private funds, privilege, and power—the luxury to be detached that in fact is maintained precisely through the fragmentation of the weaker classes of society into alienated individuals co-opted into taking vicarious pleasure in the glamor of the wealthy. Disarming political verse serves this anti-human agenda.

The technique favored at Harvard of "close reading," a method of literary study, is of undeniable value. Most of my own work on Tourian is close reading, since very often the wide context outside the poem is not important–the poem is intimate. But close reading can be misused disingenuously to remove from the field of one's attention in studying a book the social and economic context of its author's life and times. (And since that means less historical study and arduous acquisition of context, it's also a method favored by the *jeunesse dorée*—who then have less work to do and more time to go to parties and network with other members of the ruling class.) Aesthetics alone matters, then, and it is a short walk from there to an analysis that is entirely formal, which, as it seems to me, is what has happened to Shakespeare's sonnet in Professor Vendler's sumptuous, learned tome (which includes a compact disc of the Professor reading Shakespeare). Taking verse that is already deeply personal and emotional (Shakespeare's Sonnets, for example) and imprisoning it in technical discussions remarkable for their sun," which Anthony Burgess used as the title of his impressionistic novel about the mind of Shakespeare? (Borges, too, attempts to enter Shakespeare's memory, in a short, visionary tale.) "Nothing" in Shakespeare (cf. the colloquy between Lear and Cordelia) can mean everything. It's a short shocker word that startles a reader to attention. What I feel, roused by the startling first line, is curious apprehension, *wonder*, of course—an expectation upon reception of the poem that the beloved's eyes are more, not less. Since we'll never see anything brighter than the sun, the unspoken shaping of a greater luminary is the thing of which poetic suggestion plus the reader's emotionally-charged imagination are capable, and of which Nature is incapable. But then we return to Nature—to the woman's dun, dim, reeking body, but with more. With more. For the poet has *seen* roses—but in her cheeks he does not see them. What, one asks, then, *does* he see? There is some kind of unseen flower, like that of Coleridge's dream of paradise, perhaps, the one left at waking, behind the words. *Some* perfumes are more fragrant than her breath. When a poet says "some," one asks of the others—again, there are fragrances hidden. He loves, he says, to hear her speak, but admits music sounds more pleasing. Everyone knows this, so perhaps there is another point: music is a language, it has been said, that is intelligible but untranslatable. The beloved's speech is both, though; and the poem, in which Shakespeare speaks to her, is by its essence musical language, or as close as language can come to music, the ghost of musicality hovering just beyond view (the Russian poet Osip Mandelstam, his widow wrote, said he heard a kind of music in his head before a poem came to him, that was resolved

---

cold-heartedness seems to me to belong to the same continuum, for such poems, thought once to be the common inheritance of English-speakers, of the world really, now are presented as the rightful property of an academic technocracy. For it is inevitable that where the personal is no longer allowed to merge with the political, the political—in our era, corporate culture and its alienating, repressive, anti-sexual neo-Puritanism—will reach in to dominate the personal. The free and emotional contact with Shakespeare is severed, the Sonnet made an intricate, arcane, bloodless exercise. And this grayness is what has happened to American education in the Humanities, too.

gradually into words). So this plain statement, like the others, is not so plain, thanks to the strategy of its reception.

Shakespeare continues that he never saw a goddess go; but his beloved walks on the ground. "Go" is short and vague and pregnant—like "nothing" above, it makes one think. The going of a goddess: well, is it flight, or (from the next line) treading—but not treading on the ground (cf. the way Ariel goes, including walking over water, in Shakespeare's *Tempest*)? And from "ground" Shakespeare pulls us up in the very next line up to heaven, returning to the locus of the sun in the first line, in an instantaneous flight, and at the same time affirms one's inkling: all the beloved's qualities are *rare*, that is, both precious and hard to see: and *she* belied the comparisons made; not they, her. Vendler's analysis seems to me to reach a kind of artistic and emotional untruth through facts. By analyzing the sonnet through the analysis of emotional expectation and reception, we can see how Tourian's deceptively simple poem uses some strategies like Shakespeare's. He takes familiar similes and homologies and then both enriches and inverts them, to arrive at a stronger effect which also brings one to emotional truth.

**15. "To the Virgin"** (*Arr guysn*), 1871, Sevak, p. 41.

**Text.**

ԱՌ ԿՈՅՍՆ

Ո՜հ, մինչև ց՛ե՞րբ, ըսէ՛, ո՛ կոյս, հոգիս ըլլայ գեղոյդ գերի,
Եւ մինչև ց՛ե՞րբ թրթռան աղիք ցաւած սրտիս և քնարի,
Լոկ համբուրիկ մ՛ուզեցի քաղել այտէդ մեկ թարմ վարդ,
Ճառագայթ մը խնդրեցի աչերէդ երկնապուարթ,
Զըչացար դու, անգո՛ւթ, վարդ մը դժգոյն ճակտիս,
Եւ ճառագայթ մ՛այն անդունդին խոր սրտիս.
Ո՛չ, ես չ՛եմ կրնար ապրիլ կուրկ գրկէդ,
Ծիծառնիկն ապրի դուրս բոյնէն գէթ.
Տրտմալար քնարս կարնեմ ջախջախ,
Գոցեմ սիրտըս սիրաբախ...
Մնայք բարով, կո՛յս և քնա՛ր,
Կոյսին տեղ լա՛ց, քա՛ր,
Ճակատս նըսեմ
Հանգչեցնեմ
Մաշող
Հող։

**Translation.**

*To the Virgin.*

O tell me how long, o virgin, will my soul be your beauty's slave?
And how long must quiver my lyre and my heartstrings-
Only a little kiss I wished, one new rose to steal at your cheek,
A ray I begged from your eyes supernally gay,
But you refused my wan brow a rose, merciless,
No beam to plumb my heart profound,
No—I cannot live deprived of your embrace
Though the swallow outside his nest abide.
My sad-stringed heart a savage blow I strike

(10) And my heart that beats for love I close.
Farewell, maiden, and harp,
In her place, crying, and stone,
My forehead, dark
I lay me down to rest
In the ruining
Ground.

**Commentary.**

The date of the poem was unknown to Tchéraz, who wrongly thought it to be one of the poet's first compositions, "qui l'a créée comme un jeu d'esprit" (p. 11), perhaps because of its curious triangular structure. But the poem is in fact late and complex and not at all a game.

From breadth of hope and bird on the wind the poem literally narrows to immobility and despair: it is the opposite of the Psalmist who, straitened, called upon the Lord and was answered with enlargement. The first lines bedazzle with rays (*jarrakayt'*); the eyes, homologous to Suns as always, are "heaven-alert" (*ergna-zvart'*), the vivid compound evoking the angels (*zvartunk'*) and supernal light (Arm. *luys*): one of the beloved hymns of the Orthodox and Armenian Churches is *Luys zvart'*.[23] With the refusal, the mood turns from heights of delight to descent. The beam will not illuminate the dark and abyssal waters; so we have come to the Lake of Tourian's heart (cf. "Little Lake," *Lejag,* No. 22) where in the deeps of a mere a phantasmagoric sacred text is and is not aflame, is and is not there. The poet speaks of the abyss (*antunt*) of his heart, and the poem takes the literal shape of a pit, words and images relating to light and animation giving way to terms of darkness and hardness, the deeper down one goes: *ut poesis pictura*! As an iconic composition, the poem takes its rightful place beside the ekphrastic poems of Klee and Rousseau and Blake's "My

[23]On the word and name and its associations, see J. R. Russell, tr., Derenik Demirjian, *The Book of Flowers*, Belmont, MA: Armenian Heritage Press, 2003, intro.

mother groand!" analyzed by Jakobson.[24] The invention of the figure poem, in which the "text has the outlines of an object central to the poem," is generally attributed to the Greek Simias of Rhodes, *ca.* 300 B.C.; and the best-known Classical exemplar of the form is Publilius Optatianus Porfirius, fl. *ca.* 4 A.D. The European Baroque poets used the form, but one finds it in earlier poetry also, notably the cruciform type (see Tourian's "The Child to the Cross" and discussion).[25]

The imagery of the lyre compounds the grim mood: instead of the strumming and quiver of hope, it sounds with a discordant stroke (*chakhchakh*) like the hard, death-dealing cut of a sword; and to that marked reduplicative he links in rhyming irony, in the next line, his heart's epithet *sira-pakh,* "love-throbbing." But *pakh-el* means also "to knock"; so he will shut his heart, like a door. The very physical shape of the poem enforces the sense of waning, of words fading into silence. The word *k'nar,* "lyre," for instance, a loan from Hebrew *kinnor,* can be monosyllabic, as here, though there is in speech always a half-shva between *k'* and *n;* but a poet may lengthen it if he wishes to the fully disyllabic *k'enar.* The lyre, defined by the living vibration of its strings, is petrified—it turns to *k'ar,* "stone"—and its sound shrinks through the slight but sensed loss of the half-syllable -en that distinguishes the two words from each other. The stone then itself petrifies, from the metaphor of the hardened heart, to the literal gravestone. ***Jarrakayt',*** "beam of light," contracts and solidifies into ***jagad,*** "brow," whose primary meaning in the Middle Iranian from which is a loan is the stony brow of a hill. For as the poem reaches its vanishing point, Tourian disappears down into the *mashogh hogh,* the soil that makes one worn out. The recurrent theme of leaving an earthly woman who rejects the poet's love and going to the embrace of another woman, Mother Earth, who, archetypally and mythologically, accepts everyone and always,

---

[24]See Roman Jakobson, "On the Verbal Art of William Blake and Other Poet-Painters," in his *Language and Literature,* ed. K. Pomorsky and S. Rudy, Cambridge, MA: Belknap Press of Harvard Univ. Press, 1987, pp. 479-503.

[25]See Gerald Janecek, *The Look of Russian Literature: Avant Garde Visual Experiments, 1900-1930,* Princeton, NJ: Princeton University Press, 1984, pp. 8-9, citing examples by Bryusov, Shershenevich, and others.

must reflect the poet's bitter awareness of imminent death.[26] The two *o*'s of the last words lend that phrase an incantatory force, and provide also an ironic and hollow echo of the exclamatory *O!* of the start of the poem. The use of the marked and evocative reduplicative, the semantic contrast of near-homonyms, and the description of emotion through imagined flights and descents, are all hallmarks of Tourian's craft.

[26]In my article "The word *Chragamah* and the Rites of the Armenian Goddess," *JSAS* 5, 1990-91 (*AIS*, pp. 429-444), I discussed the sexual aspects of a chthonic cult involving the notorious "extinguishing of the lamps." Roberto Calasso has perceived in the myths of Alcestis, and of Eurydice, both involving beloved women and the descent to the underworld, encodings of the epithets of the rulers of Hades. (See also J. R. Russell, "An Epic for the Borderlands: Zariadris of Sophene, Aslan the Rebel, Digenes Akrites, and the Mythologem of Alcestis in Armenia," UCLA Conference on Sophene and Kharberd, May 1998, published in R. Hovannisian, ed., *Armenian Tsopk/Kharpert*, UCLA Armenian History and Culture Series, Historic Armenian Cities and Provinces, 3, Costa Mesa, CA: Mazda, 2002, pp. 147-183; *AIS*, pp. 951-988). The epithet *mashogh* given to earth by Tourian may have ancient resonances beyond poetic sound, too. Arm. *mash-em* "I wear smth. out" may be derived from Old Iranian *marsh-*, as in the last of the four epithets of the pre-Islamic god of infinite time, Zurvan: *marsho-kara*, "maker of decay." In the other three, he makes men live, thrive, and get old. So this is his death-epithet. Though Zurvan was never of very great importance to Armenian Zoroastrians in the Parthian period, the heresiologist Eznik of Koghb, fifth century, devotes much of his discussion of Persian religion to a refutation of beliefs concerning Zurvan, which were apparently of great importance at least to the Sasanian priesthood.

**16. "A Glance"** (*Nayvadzk' me*), 1871 (Sevak pp. 42-43)

**Text.**

ՆԱՅՈՒԱԾՔ ՄԸ

Ամրան տապէն ևս խոնջած՝
Թաւուտքի մը բիւր բիւր կայծ
Տերևներուն շուքն ինկած՝
Ո՛րչափ սիրեմ շունչն հովտաց՝
    Մեղմիկ
    Հողմիկ։

Արշալոյսին կանխուկեկ՝
Ո՛րչափ սիրեմ՝ ոտքըս մերկ
Կոխելով մարգ ծաղկաներկ՝
Լըւացուելու գտնել մէկ
    Հստակ
    Վըտակ։

Երբ միայնակ ես գամ ման,
Ո՛րչափ սիրեմ կրակներս այն
Ներշնչելու սէրս անձայն՝
Հոտոտելու կոյսի նման՝
    Քաղցրիկ
    Ծաղիկ։

Երբ հովանի աստղապարդ
Ըլլայ երկնից գմբեթարդ,
Որչափ սիրեմ ի սաղարթս
Երբ կը հիւսէ երգ ի վարդ
    Թրթռակ
    Սոխակ։

Բայց ասոնք չ'եմ փոխեր բնաւ
Մէկ նայուածքին հետ անբաւ՝

Թէ յուղարկէ ինձ հեշտեաւ
Իր աչերէն վառ ու սեաւ՝
Լուսիկ
Կուսիկ։

**Translation.**

*A Glance*

From summer's heat exhausted,
Midst the myriad glints in the glade
Of the leaves' shade fallen,
How I love the valley breathing its
Soft
Breeze.

Early, at the first dawn arriving,
How I love barefoot
To tread the flowering meadow
And find and bathe in a
Clear
Stream.

When alone I wander
How I love those fires
Of my silent love to inspire
Like a maiden scenting a
Sweet
Flower.

When star-adorned is the shelter
Of Heaven's dome
How I love when in the leafy green
To the rose his song he weaves, the
Lilting
Nightingale.

But ever all of them I'd trade
If a lone and endless glance
She might lightly convey my way
Out of those eyes dark and burning,
Luminous
Maid.

**Commentary.**

The poem begins with the pattern of shade from summer heat; the second stanza alters shade to cool water and heat to dawn. The third stanza might be expected to continue the conceit, but the poet instead takes the breeze of the first stanza and the flower of the second and has them fan the fires of his passion– which is a fragrance. Instead of taking shelter from the summer sun, he stokes the sun of love within him; and in the following stanza he invokes the ancient Near Eastern poetic symbol of beloved and lover, the rose and nightingale. In New Persian these form a rhyming figure, *gol o bolbol*, but Tourian prefers to use the Middle Iranian loans longer fixed in Armenian, *vard* "rose" (of which *gol* is in fact a later form) and *soxak* "nightingale," literally "speaker" (pron. in W. Arm. *vart, sokhag*). The final stanza seems to negate it all: for one glance from his beloved, Tourian would give up the whole universe he has evoked. But that glance is at once as infinite (*anpav*) and as dark (*syav*, "black") as the night sky and as burning bright (*varr*) as the midsummer noonday. Armenian also accepts the homology of (red) sun and (radiate) rose, playing further on *varr* and *vard*. The poet deflects these weighty correspondences from his image by stressing the lightness of the glance, which is given *heshdyav*, lightly– the word has also the underlying sense of sensuality and voluptuousness.

The words chosen to rhyme create startling patterns of contrast and association that intensify the imaginal world Tourian evokes. In the first stanza, the *gaydz*, "spark," should fly upward, as sparks do, but it rhymes with *ingadz*, "fallen"; and to the latter is added the Clas. Arm. gen. pl. *hovdats'*, "of valleys" to make the sense of falling large– the sparks of sunlight fallen between the leafy cover are not just under one tree, but all through many valleys. This anticipates and mirrors the image a few stanzas later of the dome—the valley-in-reverse, as it were—of heaven with its spangled stars at night (*kmpet'art, dzagh-gazart*). This curious inversion, deeply imbedded in the poem's imagistic structure, is a distant echo of the ancient Indo-Iranian idea that the night sky is a kind of inverted double of the earth.

In the second stanza there is a complex triad of alliteration m/n-r-g/k (final g in spoken Arm. is, unless stressed, often devoiced and thus similar to unaspirated k) that serves also to bind a contrastive rhyming pair: the poet walks with ***merg*** "naked" feet through a meadow, ***mark***, that is *dzaghga**nerg*** "painted with flowers." The result of this pattern is a kind of Edenic impression of the oneness of runner, meadow, and flowers, with the distinction between bareness and covering (as by painting something over) obliterated. The beloved is a little virgin, also—little, through the diminutive ending *-ig*: the alternation of this ending as *-ig* or *-ag* pervades the final adjective-noun pair of each stanza, like a refrain.

The final stanza has a contrastive rhyme, *heshdyav* "lightly" and *syav* "black." Black is, well, not light. It's dark, and it's also heavy. (There is implicit darkness and heaviness in the verb Tourian chose, ***h**ughargel*, "send," for the way the virgin conveys her glance, since this particular form of the verb is used of funeral processions.) *Heshdyav* is Classical Armenian, accepted and fixed as a rather formal adverb in Modern Arm.; but *syav*, a loan from Middle Iranian (in Persian it has become *siyah*) is wholly Classical. Since Tourian uses the new form, *sev*, very often elsewhere, of course, *syav* here is used either for rhyming purposes, or as a lingering Classicism without particular import, or as a marked term meant to make a different impression than the more common *sev*. Tourian loved Movses Khorenats'i's citations of the epic of Artaxias (Artashes) I, including the famous line *Hecaw ari ark'ayn Artašēs i seawn gełec'ik*, "Brave Ardashes rode (*hedzav*) a beautiful black (*syav*) [steed]" (Movses Khorenats'i, II.50). The word "black" alone is understood in Clas. Arm. to stand for a black horse, much as in English one can still speak in horsey company of "a grey," meaning a white horse. Note that Khorenats'i gives us our *-av* rhyme, too. So his usage removes from blackness its heaviness and endows the word with animation and vitality; and the passage continues to describe Ardashes lassoing Sat'enik, the princess of the Alans, whom he abducts and makes his queen. In Persian poetry, where the *kereshmeh*, "glance," is a perennial theme, the beloved's bangs or eyebrows can be lassos and polo-sticks; so perhaps there is an implication in this poem, too, of the captivating power of the glance that has a deep foregrounding in Tourian's reading of old Armenian epic tales of love.

**17. “Whispers”** (*Hdzdzyunk’*), 1871 (Sevak pp. 44-45)

**Text.**

ՀԾԾԻՒՆՔ

Երբոր վարդի փունջք հայեցի՝
Ծըլան տժգոյն ճակտիդ վերև,
Խոնարհեցիր աչերդ արև,
Քեզ այն օրէն ես սիրեցի։

Թերթեր հուզող սիւքի մը պէս՝
Թըռար սրտիս ծալքերն թոթուել,
Քընարի մը կըրակէ թել՝
Քեզ ձըգեցիր դու աչերէս։

Արդ կը փախչիս ինձմէ սիւքի
Պէս, շուքըդ տաս լոկ քընարիս,
Գիսաստղի պէս հեռուն կ’նայիս՝
Հովին տըւած մազերդ ոսկի։

Երբ աստղալոյց գիշեր է զով,
Շրջագայիս Պաղլար–Պաշի,
Գիտե՞ս թէ սիրտս ո·րչափ մաշի՝
Շրջազգեստիդ լոկ շրշիւնով։

Գայ սիւքն ապատ քեզ այցելու,
Նային քեզի աստղերն ազատ,
Ըստուերին մէջ մինակ ու պատ՝
Ես կը դողամ քեզ մօտելու։

Ո·հ, թող երթա·յ սիւքն իր ծաղկըց,
Նայի·ն աստեղք թող յ’Օվկեան,
Եւ թող մէկ մ’ե·ս ալ թալկանա·մ
Քու նայուածքիդ մէջ կրակուրոց։

Մահիկն երբոր շառագունած՝
Իջնէ լեռնէն ի հորիզոն,
Ալ կ՛անհետիս, չ՛ես շրջիր հոն՝
Կապին, հովին, աստղին դիմաց։

Գերեզմաննոցին ցուրտ ծառեր
Կը փըսփըսան մեռելոց հետ,
Շրջապգեստիդ շրշիւնին գէթ
Ինձ արձագանք մահահրաւէր։

Նըւապած են լոյս ու ժըխոր,
Դադրած շրշիւնք կանանց՝ անմռունչ
Արդ կը թաղուին համբոյր, մրմունջ՝
Աստեղապարդ անդունդին խոր։

Շրջապգեստիդ խշրտուքն յար
Կը փըսփըսայ դեռ ականջիս,
Հեծկլտալով իջնէ հոգիս
Արտօսրալից անդունդ մ՛ի վար…։

**Translation.**

*Whispers*

When I looked at the cluster of roses
That blossomed at your pallid brow
You lowered your eyes—the Sun—
And on that day I fell in love.

Like the petal-stirring breeze
You flew, and my heart trembled, stirred
As you strummed a fiery string of the lyre
Drawn from my inmost parts.

Now from me like a zephyr you flee,
Casting your shadow over my lyre alone,

Like a comet you glance, far,
Tossing your golden tresses in the wind.

When the star-enkindling night is cool
You stroll through Baghlar-Bashi.
Do you know how my heart expires
At the whisper of your skirts?

Your visitor, the breeze, comes freely,
Freely upon you the stars may gaze,
But separate and alone, in shadow,
I tremble with fear to approach.

O let the breeze attend to its flowers
And the stars at their Ocean stare!
And let me too, blasted, wither
In the blazing fire of your gaze.

When the reddened crescent moon
Goes down to the horizon from the hill,
You do not walk there—you disappear as well
Against the gaslights, the wind, the stars.

The graveyard's frigid trees
Have their whispers with the dead:
The rustling of your dress
Seem to echo death's summons to me.

The light and noise swoon,
Women's whispers cease-
Soundless, complaint and kiss are buried
In the star-adorned abyssal deep.

Forever the rustle of your skirts
Will whisper in my ear,
And in sobs my soul descends

(40) Down, tear-choked, to the deep.

**Commentary.**

A girl abandons her dying lover as easily as a passing breeze, for the embrace of all living nature: all that is left to him is the rustle of her dress mingled with the sound of the wind, and his own descent to the grave.

The poem exists in two manuscript copies; in the second, the first two stanzas are not recorded. The poem was published in *Meghu* ("The Bee"), 27 May 1871, no. 37—during Tourian's lifetime—and is in nearly all the editions of his works. There are insignificant corruptions and typographical errors in some of the latter, to which Yeghishe Tourian drew the attention of the writer and critic Arshag Chobanian, in a letter of 30 August 1891. The word *herrun*, "the distance" was, evidently for metrical reasons, replaced by *pats'* "open" in the 1872 edition, in the eleventh line, *Gisastghi bes herrun g'nayis*. The famous Soviet Armenian linguist and lexicographer Hrachya Acharian, a pupil of Antoine Meillet, suggested in an essay printed in 1947 that the meter and *herrun* be kept by reading *g'nayis* "you look" as two syllables (instead of prounouncing it as in conversation, *ge nayis*, with a shva after the *g*). Instead of the *kerezmannots'*, "cemetery," of line 29, the same editors printed *Shirmats'* [Clas. Arm. gen. pl. of *shirim*, "grave"] *michi tsurd tsurd dzarrer*, "the cold, cold trees amidst the graves," which Acharian rightly dismissed as well. Tchéraz translated the poem ("Murmures," pp. 62-64).

The opposition of harsh and gentle sounds pervades the poem, introducing other oppositions. Over and over the rustle of the girl's skirts (***shr****chazkesdi* ***shr****shyun*) merges with the trees whispering, for which Armenian has a like onomatopoeic word, *p'esp'esan*. The *shrshyun* of women is ***an****-mrrunch'*—sound**less**, without a murmur of protest—and this word serves to provide the foreground for a signature word denoting the expression of Tourian's own emotions of love, of pain, of protest against his fate, his loneliness: *mrmunch*, "complaint, murmur" (the title of No. 25, that work of Promethean rebellion). This protest is a negated and stilled sound, though, sharing the soft, reduplicative shape of the girl's whisper. It is buried, as is the lovers' kiss (*hampuyr,* the Parthian loan whose literal meaning is: sharing smell/perception). But the string of Tourian's lyre is ripped from his own guts; and his soul will be wracked with sobs (the rough, hacking word *hedzgldal,* line 39, an ironic reprise of the softer *hdzdzyunk'* of the title, perhaps).

The poem has two depths, two gardens. The girl's deep abyss (*khor antunt,* line 36) is the starry vault of heaven, a place of silence and peace; Tourian's abyss (*andund,* line 40) is the unquiet grave, echoing with sobs (it is *ardosralits',* "full of tears"; a variant has *ardasvalits',* a compound meaning the same thing but constructed with the plural, *artasuk',* "tears"). The Ocean of line 22, to which the stars are asked to turn their gaze, seems to stand between the two, mirroring literally the first and anticipating the dark downward horror of the second. As a corollary to all this astral and cosmic imagery, Tourian makes his beloved's eyes Suns, an intricate if common conceit of ancient Armenian and world poetry– and one that is seen frequently in his own verses. Her glance is the reduplicative-sounding *gragurots',* "fiery," from *grag* (line 24); but it has the overtones of the genuinely reduplicative Armenian word *geragur,* "food": she consumes him; and he, the consumed and the consumptive, will hear the rustle of her skirts for the last time, in line 32, as an echo (*artsagank'*) that is *mahahraver,* a summons to death. The construction of this line is in itself interesting, as it is paralleled and anticipated by the corresponding rhyme of line 30 in the quatrain, *Ge p'esp'esan merrelots' hed,* "They whisper with the dead." The three quiet syllables of Arm. "they whisper," two shvas and an a, turn into the stridor of the three long a's of Arm. "they echo"; and the equally gentle "with the dead," with its e's, o's, and open e ending (*merrelots' hed*), foreshadows the long blast of death's summons (*mahahraver*), with its overtones of Arm. *ah* "terror" and *arhavir-k'* "horror," and the cachinnating *ah-ah* of demonic laughter as the poet's soul plunges.

**18. "Small Dedications"** (*Tsonigk'*), 1871 (Sevak p. 46)

**Text.**

ՁՕՆԻԿՔ

Մինակ էր·
Վարդ մ'ըկգօն
Մատուցի
Նէրա ձօն։

Շիկնեցաւ
Նէ կըւարթ՝
Կ'ընդունէր
Երբ իմ վարդ։

Նէրա քով
Վարդն ո·րչափ
Էր անշուք՝
Գունաթափ

Նոյնպէս ձօնս
Համբոյրին
Զ'որ տուաւ՝
Չ'էր բնաւ գին։

**Translation.**

*Small Dedications*

She was alone.
A rose meek
I offered
A gift to her.

She reddened
When gaily
She accepted
My rose.

Beside her
How the rose
Lost its shadow
And its color fled.

So my gift
To the kiss
Which she gave:
It was past price.

**Commentary.**

The poem is written in terse lines of three syllables, and, like "The Child to the Cross," seems as simple as a nursery rhyme at first glance. Alice Stone Blackwell offers a pretty eight-line paraphrase of it in *Armenian Poems* (Boston, 1917, p. 33: "Little Gifts"). The beginning, "She was alone," introduces a state of lack—but it is the lover, not the beloved, who should feel this, so it sets one off balance at once. Then he gives her a rose, meekly (*vart m'zkon*). But the adverb, which should refer to the verb *maduts'i*, "I offered" in line 3, is attached to the indef. art. *me* modifying *vart*, "rose"; and *zkon* is more usually an adjective meaning "prudent, wise"; so the effect seems to be to endow the rose, which is the poet's sacrificial offering (*tson*: the verb *maduts'anel* is redolent of the Divine Liturgy and fixes the offering as more than a mere gift), with a sentient presence. Something *live* is being offered up—and maybe more than one thing, since the title of the poem is in the (Clas. Arm.) plural, another oddity masked by the precious diminutive -*ig*. (As for *tson*, Clas. Arm. *jawn*, it may be the native Arm. reflex of the same Avestan root *zav*- used in the terminology of Zoroastrian oblations.)

In the discussion in the Introduction of Tourian's poetics we considered the rich symbolism of the color red, and the importance to the poet of fragrance, Arm. *puyr*; and some of what was proposed may be repeated here. A rose by any other name may mean more than in English—at least the English of today. "Lo, how a rose is ever blooming, that from such tender root hath sprung," sang mediaeval Britons on Christmas. In Armenia, too, Christ is the rose. The word is of Middle Iranian origin, meaning originally simply a growing flower (Pth. *vard*, Mid. Pers. *gol*, possibly also the Arab. and Heb. loan *vered*): the name Vardan is an act. part., MIr. *vardān*, "blossoming, growing"; and St. Vardan, a *nakharar*-dynast of the noble Mamikonean house, the Armenian commander in chief who fell at the battle of Avarayr in 451 as a warrior martyr for the Christian faith, is celebrated in hymns as having shed his fiery (*vaṙ*) red (rosy) blood as martyr, armed (*vaṙ-eal*) as a soldier against death. One recalls that Tourian dedicated a poem to *Garmir* "Red" Vartan! The rose is a symbol homologous to the fiery red Sun, and Christ is the Sun of righteousness (*aregakn ardarut'ean*) that dawned on Armenia. The rose is also full of fertility, life, and joy: the Armenian summer festival of *Vardavaṙ*, "the bringing of roses" (cf. Gk. *Anthesterion*, Lat. *Rosalia*: in the Church it has become the Feast of the Transfiguration), may have old Indo-European roots, and came to be most closely related to the Iranian Ābrīzegān holiday, when revellers splash each other with water.[27] The concept of human beings as rational or prudent flowers endowed full of hot, life-giving, liquid blood, who lovingly allow themselves to be offered in sacrifice, is fully within the compass of Armenian religious imagination and traditional imagery.

The rose's scent is perhaps its most important sensual and emotional aspect: what other gift does one immediately make a show of smelling? The sense of smell is a primal component of sexual attraction, and of awareness generally. In Indo-Iranian, smell and awareness are linked by the same term: the base that produces Indic *Buddha*, "the aware, awakened One," is *baodha-*, "scent" in Avestan, with the Arm.

---

[27]On Vardan's place in Armenian tradition, see J. R. Russell, "The Credal Poem *Hawatov Xostovanim* ('I Confess in Faith') of St. Nerses the Graceful," in T. van Lint et al., eds., *Proceedings* of the Groningen conference "Redefining East Christian Identity," Apr. 1999, Peeters (forthcoming), and *AIS*, pp. 999-1032.

loan-word *boyr* "fragrance."[28] The fragrance of the rose of our poem will have registered in the Armenian reader's mind as *boyr*, W. Arm. *puyr*; so the kiss of line 14 will have a resumptive emphasis, since it is called in Arm. *ham-puyr*, to the modern Arm. ear implying a sharing of fragrance, though its original sense might have been a sharing of the life-force of consciousness in breath.[29]

In the second stanza of the poem, the beloved moves from loneliness into gaiety; in the third, the rose has lost its shadow (*shuk'*> *an-shuk'*), by which is meant presence, stature, personality, even life-force.[30] And its very color is poured away (*kuna-t'ap'*). Arm. *kuyn* (Clas.

---

[28] Parthian *bōdhistān*, "place of fragrance," i.e., garden, gives Arm. *burastan*; in Persian, a parallel form *bōyistān* becomes the famous *Bostān* (and from "rose," *Golestān* also), of Sa'dī. Students of Muslim mysticism note that the Persian poet Farīd al-Dīn *'Attār* was a *perfume maker*: William S. Burroughs *smelled* the mystical state at a point in the musical rite in Jajouka, Morocco (he explored the idea in his last, great trilogy, *Cities of the Red Night*). Of course stench has the same affect and spiritual content as fragrance. Middle Iranian renders "frightful" in the name of the archdemon Angra Mainyu as "stinking" (*gannāg*), and another Iranian language spoken in proximity to Armenian, Ossetic, replaces the common negating prefix *duš-* (Gk. *dys-*, Lat. *dis-*) with *fid-*, literally "rotten, stinky" (Old Ir. *duš-farnah-* "of bad glory" > Arm. l-w *t'šuaṙ*, "wretched, unlucky," but Oss. *fid-farn* "idem"). If enlightenment has a sweet scent, then ignorance and hatred create their own foul smell: medieval Christians believed they could detect a *foetor judaicus*, a "Jewish stench"—not realizing, one supposes, that it was their own unwashed bodies and souls that offended their nostrils.

[29] A kiss could involve smelling the nice perfume on each other's cheeks, but I think the word originally describes exchange of air through the mouth. Herodotus informs us that Persians of equal rank greeted each other with a kiss on the mouth (the king had an incense burner in front of him to guard his nostrils against lesser mortals; priests cover their mouths with a cloth [Arm. l-w *p'andam*] so as not to defile the holy Fire, and Achaemenian underlings covered their mouths with one hand before their lords, a practice still attested for Armenia in scenes on Cross-stones—see the commentary to No. 19 here). Did the girl kiss Tourian on the mouth, though? I think not: such behavior in polite Constantinopolitan Armenian society would have been unthinkable.

[30] It is possibly a calque upon a Persian usage, cf. the polite greeting *Sāh-e šomā kam našavad!* "May thy shadow [i.e., stature] never grow less."

*goyn*, from Old Iranian **gauna-*, "kind, color") has the primary meaning of color, but it has the overtone of force, too (the suffix *-kuyn* forms the superlative adj.)[31] The adjectives together assist one's perception of the rose as a being, with a face that can blush or blanch—which is what a lover's face does, so the imagery subtly emphasizes also the idea of sacrifice in the rose that is slain in place of the lover. (And this subtle manipulation is still within the frame of tradition, for Christ the rose is the world's ransom.)

When the beloved returns a kiss, Tourian apprises it above the sacrifice he made: so the kiss is not just a sharing, but an augmentation of the life and scent of the lover's gift. The kiss marks another, obvious transition: from the loneliness of the first line to communion. Roberto Calasso, citing the Sufi esotericist René Guénon, observes that sacrifice "reflects (and thus inverts) the *solve et coagula* ["separate and reunite"] of origins: what was divided in creation is now united again" (*The Ruin of Kasch*, Cambridge, MA: Harvard University Press, 1994, p. 151). This reapplication of the old alchemical motto is realized here in its primal way: the reunion of male and female. And the sacrificial cycle, by expense of energy, yields augmentation. But it's also just a girl, a boy with a rose, and a kiss.

---

[31]Prof. Bert Vaux, Univ. of Wisconsin at Milwaukee, has compared this semantic development to the well-known term "gunation," i.e., strengthening of forms, in Indic grammatology.

**19. "The Child to The Cross"** (*Manugn arr Khach'* ), 1871 (Sevak p. 47)

**Text.**

ՄԱՆՈՒԿՆ ԱՌ ԽԱՉ

Ով խաչափայտ
Դու քառաթև,
Որոյ ճակատ
Սիրոյ արև՝
Գամուած Յիսուս
Փըչեց խոնարհ
Հոգի և լոյս
Սէր ընդ աշխարհ,
Ընդունէ ւ'իմ հոգիս հեզիկ փառաճաճանչ
Թևերուդ տակ և սորուեցուր ինծի հաւատ,
Սէր, յոյս, որով միշտ բաբախէ իմ փափուկ լանջ,
Եւ փարատէ լուսովդ խաւար սրտէս վըհատ.
Սորուիմ աղօթք
Բառնալ քեզի,
Երբ խութից ոտք
Իմ հանդիպի
Սև Սատանին,
Որ ճգնի միշտ
Դիւթել կ'հոգին
Ի մութ, ի վիշտ։

**Translation.**

*The Child to the Cross*

O Tree of the Cross
Thou four-armed
Whose brow
Is love's Sun,
Jesus nailed

Breathed, humble
Soul and light,
Love towards the world,
Receive also my little meek soul, radiating glory
Beneath your arms, and teach me faith,
Love, hope, with which my tender breast may throb,
And dispel by your light the dark from my despairing heart.
May I learn prayer
To ascend to Thee
When the tripping foot
Makes me stumble
Of black Satan
Who strives ever eagerly
To bewitch the soul
To darkness and grief.

**Commentary.**

This is Tourian's chief poem with a clearly specified typographical shape corresponding to its theme—cruciform—together with his vanishing, triangular verse (No. 15), which is about disappearing, rather like the Abracadabra triangles of antiquity intended to make demons vanish; and a poem with the possible shape of a tombstone (No. 32).[32] Tchéraz comments in the note to his translation (pp. 39-40), which is in prose and does not reproduce the shape itself, "Le texte de la poésie suivante forme une croix. C'est le dernier jeu d'esprit du poète." Ekserjian writes that the poem was written deliberately for children; and Chobanian, in an article of 1893, dismisses it: տղայական խաղ մըն է, պէտք էր իր տաղերէն դուրս ձգել, կամ գոնէ հատորին ետևը, ծանօթագրութեանց մէջ դնել իբր հետաքրքրութիւն "it is a childish game that should have been excluded from the [collected] poems or at least relegated to the back of the volume and situated in the

[32]This chapter began as a lecture at a symposium at St. Petersburg State University in July 2001 to commemorate the anniversary of the conversion of the Armenians to Christianity; and a preliminary version was published as an article, "Bedros Tourian's Cruciform Poem and its Antecedents," in the *Journal of Armenian Studies* 6.2, pp. 27-45 (*AIS*, pp. 1101-1120).

footnotes as a curiosity" (Sevak, I, p. 250). But, as will be seen presently, the poem is a work of subtle artistic complexity with ancient and noble Armenian antecedents one might hesitate to dismiss as puerile.

To write a text in a shape corresponding to a theme is an old and widespread idea: anciently, there was an Orphic book called *Sphaira*; and Lobeck opined it was a *technopaegium*, written, that is, in spherical shape.[33] Amongst the modernists, Guillaume Apollinaire is famous for such inventions; and in American poetry we have the mantric entertainment "Bomb" of the Beat poet Gregory Corso, printed by City Lights at San Francisco as a broadsheet, the text in the shape of a mushroom cloud.[34] As noted, Tourian wrote poems in the shape of a tombstone and a triangle pointing down; the third document translated in the final chapter of this book suggests he could manipulate the shape of a text for purposes of playful mischief as well (pp. 336-37).

The Holy Cross is the pre-eminent Christian Sign, with or without Corpus symbolic of the World made flesh; and Armenian reverence for the Cross is so extreme—stone *khach'k'ars*, Cross-stones, receive blood offerings still—as to have been seen by some other East Christians as idolatrous. The symbolism of the cruciform and the corresponding quaternity is everywhere complex, and in Armenian exegesis still more so.[35] And as the Word was made flesh, the Cross was

---

[33]See M.L. West, *The Orphic Poems*, Oxford: The Clarendon Press, 1983, p. 33 and n. 99.

[34]It is reproduced in its original broadsheet form between pp. 32-33 of Corso's collection, *The Happy Birthday of Death*, New York: New Directions, 1960.

[35]On the Cross in Armenia see J. R. Russell, "The Four Elements and the Cross in Armenian Spirituality, with an Excursus on the Descent in Merkavah Mysticism," *Jewish Studies Quarterly*, Tübingen, Vol. 4.4, 1997, pp. 357-79 (*AIS*, pp. 851-874); where is translated and discussed the 65th meditation of the *Book of Lamentation* of St. Grigor Narekats'i, where the four arms of the Cross represent the four warring elements brought to harmony. J. R. Russell, "Raiders of the Holy Cross: The Ballad of the *Karos Khach'* and the Nexus between Ecclesiastical Literature and Folk Tradition in Mediaeval Armenia," in J.J.S. Weitenberg, ed., *New Approaches to Medieval Armenian Language and Literature, Dutch Studies in Armenian Language and Literature* 3, Amsterdam: Rodopi, 1995, pp. 79-93 (*AIS*, pp. 661-676), compares a folk ballad, attested in numerous and old variants, about a Cross two shepherds make, which im-

made word: there is a twelfth-century Byzantine lectionary on whose every page the text is Cross-shaped.[36] Or, we find an English Cross of walrus tusk densely worked with images and Biblical texts in positions corresponding to the symbolism of Christ's right and left, and of the above and below—a book in morse ivory.[37] The right hand is powerful;

---

mediately displays magical powers that help Armenians but destroy infidel Kurds who try to steal the object, to historical accounts of the same relic. There are numerous stone crosses and reliquaries with such traditions attaching to them in Armenia. They are listed in cruciform texts formed by the interlacing of successive lines with the narrative of the sacrifice of Isaac (which is believed to prefigure the Crucifixion) in talismanic scrolls (*hmayil*)(see J.R. Russell, "The Armenian Shrines of the Black Youth [*T'ukh Manuk*]," Le Muséon 111.3-4, 1998, pp. 319-43, esp. p. 329 and pl. 3, repr. in *AIS*). For a list of such Crosses, see also Abp. Norayr Bogharian (Covakan), *Haykakan xač'er*, Jerusalem: St. James' Press, 1991: on p. 49 is mentioned a Cross called *sk'anč'elagorc*, "miracle-working," and also *paterazmi*, "of war," from the Van area. The latter epithet corresponds to that of the miraculous *patrazin* or *paterazmin* Cross that alights on the fighting arm of the heroes of the Armenian Epic of Sasun, which in the oral narrative is probably a Christianized form of the supernatural *bāzūband* "arm-band" of the hero Rostam the Saka, in the Iranian epic cycle.

[36]New York, Morgan Library Cod. M 692: see Jeffrey C. Anderson, *The New York Cruciform Lectionary*, University Park, PA: Pennsylvania State University Press, 1992.

[37]See Elizabeth C. Parker and Charles T. Little, *The Cloisters Cross: its art and meaning*, New York: Metropolitan Museum of Art & Harry Abrams, 1994. The cross belongs to the Romanesque period. It shows the Ascension, appropriately, at the top, Easter on Christ's right (the right hand being powerful to work good, as is the Resurrection), and Good Friday at His left (sinister—His death). Adam and Eve cling to the base of the shaft, which is wrought in the shape of a palm—the Tree of Life. On the back of the object are the four Evangelists at the ends of the four arms, and Prophets from the Hebrew Bible, with Jonah at the bottom—for as he was in the belly of the great fish, so Christ descended at His death for three days into the inferno: the bottom of the Cross reaches Hell. Other texts and images liken the brazen serpent of Moses on a staff to the Crucifixion. Pilate and Caiaphas dispute over the *titulus*, which declares the Crucified one to be king of the Confessors (not the Jews); parallel Latin verses along the shaft compare Ham's mockery of Noah's nakedness to the Jews' laughing at Christ crucified. Genius, Pushkin wrote, is incompatible with evil. But this relic, like much else in Christian art, proves him wrong. The beauty of the cross becomes pernicious when one re-

the left, unlucky. The top is heaven; the bottom, Satan's realm.[38] There are many Armenian inscribed crosses and religious objects with cruci-

---

alizes it was made to illustrate derisive sermons, as an incitement to the anti-Semitic hatred that befouls English and European history. Except for the infernal symbolism of the base of the Cross, and of course that of the right hand, it is far from the innocence of Tourian's poem. My friend Prof. Marcus Moseley, a specialist in Hebrew and Yiddish literature, informs me that the great Jewish poet Uri Zvi Grinberg wrote in 1922 a cruciform poem in Yiddish, "*Uri Zvi forn Tselem*" ("Uri Zvi before the Cross"). Marc Chagall's painting of 1939 of the Crucifixion, now in the Art Institute of Chicago, portrays the dying Christ with a *tallith*—a Jewish prayer-shawl—as a loincloth. To His left is a burning synagogue; to His right, a village destroyed by a pogrom. Soldiers of the warring sides of the Russian Civil War march towards each other, banners flying. All around and above Jews flee and cry, their possessions fallen to the ground and ruined.

[38]The power of the right hand of Christ in Armenian folk belief is illustrated in a spell: *Ays girs gaylkap: Surb xač῾n ew xač῾ap῾aytn, K῾ristos bann ew knunk῾n, Yisusi yayrn kapeac῾ zəgayln i lerin aǰbt῾ov ew aǰčgət῾ov ew Mariamay k῾ałc῾r kat῾ov, kanač ew karmir narōtov. G heł asay ew G hangoyc῾ aray, cai̇̄ayis Astucoy ōgnakan ełic῾i ew pahapan* (text in A. A. Ōdabašyan, "*Xosk῾i hmayut῾yunn u cesn Axt῾ark῾um,*" *Lraber hasarakakan gitut῾yunneri*, Erevan, 2000.1 (601), p 49): "This is a wolf-binding writing: Holy Cross and Cross-tree, Christ the Logos and the seals, Jesus bound the wolf in a cave in the mountain with His right thumb and right little finger and with Mary's sweet milk, with green and red encircling fillet. Say 3 times and make 3 knots. Let it be a help and protection to this servant of God." Mountain caves are the dwellings in Armenian belief of the titans called *k῾aǰk῾*, and the apocalyptic figure Little Mher, covered in hair like Wild Man or werewolf, cast out by his father's ghost as Cain, is imprisoned in a cave on the rock of Van. Armenian tradition holds the Prophet Mohammed to have been a raving madman confined in a rock cave in Persia—like the tyrant Zahhak (Azhdahak) in Mount Damavand. So the spell partakes of local legendry. As for the power of Mary's milk, one might again note the power in Armenian epic and local Yazidi religion of the *kat῾nałbiwr*, the Milky Spring (see J. R. Russell, *An Armenian Epic: The Heroes of Kasht*, Ann Arbor, MI: Caravan Books, 2000, pp. 43-48). In the work by Aram Łanalanyan, *Haykakan zardarvest*, Erevan, 1957, fig. 468 is a line drawing of an Armenian medieval manuscript painting: at the center is a square altar with the Cross on its face. But the altar is a kind of magic spring, too, for four rivers flow from its base, two on each side. These must be the four rivers that rise from Eden in Genesis, for below is a tree with birds labelled *Ašxarhs ē*, "It is this world." Above the Cross and to either side are fabulous fruit trees—three in all—where birds in roundels nest: Paradise.

form inscriptions;[39] and the front cover of Armenian children's school copy-books often has a picture of the Cross with the prayer *Ōgnea inj Surb Xačʿ* "Help me, Holy Cross" or the like.

The most important cruciform text in Armenian, though, seems to have been virtually encoded by St. Grigor Narekats'i into the preface to his *Book of Lamentation,* a cycle of 95 mystical meditations or prayers—it is the most important religious work composed in Armenian.[40] The cruciform text was first studied by Avetik Bahat'rian, an

---

[39]A gilded silver cross from Tiflis, A.D. 1673, for instance, bears this inscription:

ԲԱՐԵԽ<br>ՕՍԷ<br>ՍԲ<br>ՆՇԱ<br>ՆՍ<br>ՄԷՆԷՆԴԽԱԹՈՒՆԻՆՀՈԳՈՅՆԱՌՆ<br>ԽՃՅՈՎԱՆԻՍԻՆՈՐԴՈՅՆՇԱՀԻՆԻՆ<br>ԻԴՈՒ<br>ՌՆՆ<br>ՍԲՅ<br>ՈՀԱ<br>ՆՆԻ<br>ՍԻՆ<br>ԹՎԻՆ<br>ՌՃԻԲ

"This Holy Sign is the intercessor for the Lady Mēnēnd's soul and that of her husband Yovanēs son of Šahin, at the gate [i.e., church] of St. John, in the [Arm.] year 1122."

A cope (*šurǰaṙ*) of A.D. 1601, provenance unknown, bears this cruciform inscription:

ՅՇՏԿԷ<br>ՍԲ ԵԿՂՑՍ<br>ՍԲ ՍԲ ՍԲ ՏՐ ՍԲ ՍԲ ՏՐ<br>ԶԱՒՐ ՈՒԹՑ ԶԱՒՐ ՈՒԹՑ<br>ՏՐ ԱԾ<br>ՅՍ ՔՍ<br>ԹՎ<br>ՌԾ

"This is a memorial/ of this holy church. / Holy holy holy Lord holy holy Lord/ Of hosts of hosts / Lord God / Jesus Christ / Date / [Arm.] 1050." (Evgine Mušełyan, *Hatkanšakan cʿucʿak tʿangaranayin žołovacuneri, prak 1: Hayeren arjanagrutʿyamb aṙarkaner*, Erevan: HSSṘ GA hrat. (Arm. Acad. Sci.), 1964, pp. 67, 88-9.) In the first example, the names of the owners are on the crossbar, perhaps to be sheltered by Christ's hand; one might imagine the outstretched wings of the angels as they sing the Trisagion on the arms of the second.

[40]See J. R. Russell, introduction to Grigor Narekats'i, *The Book of Lamentations (Matean oghbergut'ean),* Classical Armenian Text Reprint Series, Delmar, NY:

obscure schoolteacher from the Eastern Armenian province of Karabagh (Arts'akh): little is known of him, though he assisted the great linguist Hrachya Acharian to write his description of the local Armenian dialect.

Bahat'rian wrote a book, "The Art of Poetic Metrics among the Ancient Armenians" (*Hin Hayocʿ Tałačʿapʿakan Aruestə*). The manuscript was lost when bandits robbed the Tsar's Post at Aghstafa; a second copy was marooned at Constantinople in the hands of an envious and spiteful editor; and only after Bahat'rian rewrote the book a third time did it see its way safely to publication—at Shushi, 1891. But it seems to have languished in obscurity until the Soviet Armenian literary scholar Edward Jrbashyan discovered a copy in the library of the poet Yeghishe Ch'arents'.[41] It was reprinted by Erevan University in 1984, with a photographic reproduction and printed transcription of the following comments (in my translation, with emphases Ch'arents' own) scrawled by Ch'arents' in his copy in 1937 (the year the poet was arrested and murdered by the Armenian Communist regime): "This is a marvellous and ingenious book to have been written in the '90's by some unknown Shushi schoolmaster's hand ... *All* the problems connected to our ancient and modern metrical art are touched upon, and in part, by *ingenious* intuition, are resolved here—*problems* that thereafter were not only not posed and raised in our theoretical literature, but, till this day, were not even *understood*. This book is truly a remarkable *mine* discovered by an author *possessing an ingenious instinct*, who, sadly, indicates, points out solely by instinct the *existence of the mine*, sometimes even touching the mine's undisturbed *veins*—and how much *general culture* and *striving* is necessary, so that our literary scholarship, proceeding in

---

Caravan Books, 1981, and, most recently, "Armenian Spirituality: Liturgical Mysticism and Chapter 33 of the Book of Lamentation of St. Grigor Narekac'i," *REArm* 26 (1996-1997), pp. 427-439, with refs. (*AIS*, pp. 771-784)

[41]The book is No. 1067 (1193) on p. 36 of the typewritten handlist of Ch'arents' books (*Spisok knig lichnoi biblioteki Egishe Charentsa*, Dom-Muzei Egishe Charentsa, Erevan, n.d.), which my student Susan Barba was able to copy in Erevan, in the section *Haykakan grk'er*. The poet's well-thumbed copy of the Narek (I saw the book myself) is No. 1245 (1450) in the list.

the steps of these Bahat'rians, may open, *may be impregnated* with, and may *make use of* the wondrous features of our ancient metrics. II. In its essence, our modern literature (from Abovian[42] till today) has only *two original,* both *unique,* relatively *ingenious* figures, or names. They are *Gevorg Akhverdian*[43] and *Avetik' Bahat'rian*—the author of this same, *forgotten* book. Third. [*sic!*] It is M. Abeghyan,[44] but he is already learned in a European sense (of course very valuable), is *only a scholar,* and,

[42]Khach'atur Abovian, a native of K'anak'er near Erevan, wrote the first novel in modern spoken Armenian, *Verk' Hayastani* ("The Wounds of Armenia") about the war of 1828 in which Russia wrested control of the Khanate of Erevan from the Persians. Rule by a Christian power was hailed by Armenians as liberation, even though Nicholas I and his successors introduced repressive measures of Russification. Abovian studied at Dorpat University (now Tartu, Estonia) and accompanied Parrot on the ascent of Ararat, a mountain the Armenian Church regarded as sacrosanct. Abovian's secularist disregard of such superstitions made him many enemies in the establishment, and he disappeared under mysterious circumstances in the revolutionary year of 1848. Ch'arents' in his last published book, *Girk' chanaparhi* ("The Book of the Journey"), writes about Abovian in the poem *Depi lyarn Masis* ("To Mount Ararat").

[43]The author of the first printed collection and study, in 1852, of the songs of the mid-late-eighteenth cent. Armenian *ashugh* ("bard, minstrel") Sayat' Nova of Tiflis. Ch'arents' cycle *Tagharan* ("Canticles"), 1920, was inspired by Sayat' Nova in particular.

[44]Prof. Manuk Abeghyan of Erevan University wrote the essential *History of Ancient Armenian Literature,* in Russian and Armenian editions, and numerous other studies, including the invaluable *Armenian Folk Belief,* in both German and Armenian editions. These are works of great insight as well as encyclopedic scholarship, and I think Ch'arents' somewhat disparaging attitude is colored by an understandable ideological animus. The poet was already an outcast. By contrast, Abeghian accommodated himself to the Soviet regime readily, acceding to the reform of Armenian orthography, even though, as Acharian argued, the simplified spelling made Armenia's ancient literature less accessible—it was a break with the nation's own culture. Acharian for his courage was arrested and tortured; Abeghian in the 1930's enjoyed the perks of a Stalinist toady. (Maybe such amorality ran in the family: his brother Artashes Abeghyan, a professor at Munich, wrote a book late in the same decade entitled *Armeniertum-Ariertum,* attempting to prove to Hitler that the Armenians belonged to the "Aryan race.")

compared to the abovementioned, is merely a diligent toiler, ploughing with all love and stubborn determination the field of the literature of our fathers with the *spade of European Science,* accomplishing extremely useful work. But the above men are *native geniuses* in the arena of their labor, geniuses who more *grasp* and *discover* than accomplish assiduous, quotidian *scholarly* work. However, precisely in this they are ingenious, and, like every genius, are *unrepeatable...*"

By the 1930's Ch'arents', an Old Bolshevik deeply disillusioned with the puritanical tyranny of the Soviet state, had turned to the prayers of Narekats'i and to inner, mystical experience;[45] so a particular insight of Bahat'rian's evidently impressed him keenly. It was this: the teacher from Shushi saw that if you separate out the poetic lines Narekats'i's prayers can be broken into, according to their meter, and then stack them, you get shapes—the text itself becomes the description of the picture silhouetted on the page. The best example is the preface. Bahat'rian unfortunately reversed the order of the lines to produce what he thought was the real picture, but if we keep their actual order, with which he begins his analysis (p. 110, fig. 1), details of a word picture do emerge. Narekats'i arranged his text in an iconic pattern, so that as they were pronounced a word-picture of Christ's crucified body and the symbolism of the Cross would gradually unfold together.

---

[45]On these matters, see J. R. Russell, "The Armenian Counterculture That Never Was: Reflections on Eghishe Ch'arents'," *Journal of the Society for Armenian Studies* 9 (1996, 1997 [1999]), pp. 17-35, and "Ch'arents' the Prophet," *JSAS* 11 (2000), pp. 11-38 (*AIS*, pp. 737-756; 1073-1100).

Դրութիւնք յոգնաթախանձ
Բանից օգտակարաց
Ապաշաւանաց
Խրատուց անձին
Ստգտանաց
Զըղջականաց
Կանոնաց
Կենաց
Կամաւորութեամբ յանձնառութեանց
Աներևութից յայտնութեանց
Մեղանաց խոստովանութեանց
Ցուցմունք գաղտնեաց
Տարածմունք ծածկելոց
Սպեղանիք վօրաւորք Վիրաց անբժշկականաց
Դեղք ապդողականք ցաւոց անտեսականաց
Հնարաւորութիւնք բազմամասնեայ երկանց վտանգից
Ի դիմաց կարեաց
Ամենից բնութեանց
Առիթք արտասուաց
Պատճառք աղօթից
Ի խնդրոյ
Հայցմանց
Հարց
Միանձանց
Եւ բազմաց
Անապատականաց
Ասացեալ
Մատեան
Ողբերգութեան
Գրիգորի
Նարեկայ վանից
Վանականի։

**Translation:**

Theses of many supplicating
**Words** of use
In repentance
of **Counsels** for the soul,
Accusations
for regret
Canons
of **Life**
**Willing** undertakings
of invisible things, revelations
of sins, confessions,
Displays of secrets
Diffusions of things hidden,
**Cures** potent of **wounds** incurable,
Medicines capable of pains invisible,
Contrivances for conglomerate labors of danger
For the needs
of all **natures**,
Occasions of tears,
Causes of prayers,
At the request
and summons
of Fathers,
**Hermits**,
and many
Anchorites
recited:
Book
of Lamentation
of **Gregory**,
of Narek Monastery
a Monk.

If we travel down the text of St. Gregory's preface of theses, the Armenian equivalent of Greek *logos*, *ban(ic')*, is at the top, in the place of

Heaven: the incorporeal Word becoming flesh. On Cross-stones (*khach'k'ars*), as in other Christian art elsewhere, the position of the top of the Cross is the Heavens is stressed: the Sun, often shown atop its totemic eagle, is near the top of the Cross to Christ's right; the Moon, to His left with a bull. This portrayal of the two luminaries was an ancient convention of Christian art. It was gradually abandoned in Western painting, but some Renaissance painters returned to it. The symbolism is accepted to be that of multiple dualities—the Church *vs.* the Synagogue is one; the Old and New Testaments, another. Armenian art has always kept the sun and moon in scenes of the Crucifixion. In the specifically Zoroastrian environment of ancient Armenia, the waxing and waning of the Moon had been attributed to the emptying onto the earth of the life-giving semen of the Uniquely-Created bull slain by Ahreman, which is stored in the moon— the same symbolism of the bull's semen is differently treated by the Mithraists, a sect whose beginnings were in the Armenian area,[46] in the tauroctony, their principal cult scene.

The more corporeal *counsels* are beneath; and where the Lord's head is, we find *Life* and *will.* At His right hand are the potent *cures* and capable *medicines* of which that hand is capable (an inscription near it on some *khach'k'ar*s praise it as the hand that was stretched out to create the world, and on one Cross-stone He extends it down, off the Cross, for one of the worshipful family of donors to kiss it— others stand in prayer, and one kneels praying at the base, touching His feet); while in the middle of the line, the word *wounds* occupies the iconic place where the spear pierced His side (that spear-point, Arm. *gełard,* is one of the treasures of the Armenian Church). *Natures* may be at His loins. Crouching at the foot of the Cross in prayer are the hierarchical ranks of the clergy, with the humble author Gregory properly at the very base, waiting like Adam to be carried up from the death of sinfulness and the hell of himself to salvation and union with the God he loves. (On some Cross-stones, neither this world nor Hell is below the

---

[46]See J. R. Russell, "On the Armeno-Iranian Roots of Mithraism," in J.R. Hinnells, ed., *Studies in Mithraism*, Rome: Bretschneider, 1994, pp. 183-193 (*AIS*, pp. 553-564).

Cross, but a portrayal of the next life that pre-Christian noblemen hoped for: literally, the happy hunting grounds, where a splendid nobleman on horseback, restored to youth, spears a wild beast. On another, damaged *khach'k'ar* abandoned to the elements in the garden of the Van Museum, the nobleman sits his horse: servants on foot, their hands to their mouths in the ancient gesture of deference known from the court scenes of ancient Iranian rock reliefs, face him.)[47]

The iconic structure of Tourian's poem can now be deciphered with ease. The invocation in the first two lines alerts the reader to the shape of the poem (the Cross) and its multiple, coincident symbolic natures: it is a tree (*khach'**ap'ayd***), that is, the world tree with its head in Heaven and its roots reaching down to harrowed Hell. Its four-*armed* (*k'ara**t'ev***) shape calls attention to the width of the Cross (where the poem itself will widen), and its human aspect— for trees have branches, but only people have arms. Love is human, too, so love (*ser*) is stressed in line 8 just as the poem widens into its arms— and arms are mentioned exactly in the cross-bar lines, in line 10. Arms are used for a loving embrace, and they are also spread wide in the *orans* posture of prayer still common amongst East Christians. (Using a word

---

[47]On archaic elements on Armenian funerary monuments, see J. R. Russell, "The Scepter of Tiridates," *Le Muséon* 114.1-2, 2001, pp. 187-215 (*AIS*, pp. 1135-1164). In the spring of 1994 I visited the village of Narek (still called Narik by its Kurdish inhabitants, who remember also the Armenian shrines of the neighborhood, and their location, by their old names; the Turkish government, as part of its policy of obliterating the history of the nation it tried to exterminate, has renamed the village Yemishlik) and found a *khach'k'ar* on which the arms of the Cross were of equal length—perhaps of the tenth century or thereabouts, when Narekats'i lived. The stone bore incised prayers of later times and diverse hands. Armen Aroyan photographed the stone: when I returned to Narek in June 1997 with him and Abp. Mesrop Ashjian, the villagers told us that as soon as the authorities had got wind of our find, they sent men who smashed the priceless monument to bits. Nothing remained. Another Cross, that held by the angels between Christ and King Gagik on reliefs of the tenth-century church of the Holy Cross on Aght'amar island, in lake Van just opposite Narek, had been smashed to bits with a hammer (the pieces were lying below) between 1994, when it had been whole, and 1997. It is difficult to decide which is more criminal: the state vandalism itself, or the acceptance by the international community of the unrepentant Turkish regime.

borrowed from Middle Iranian meaning forearm in Armenian usage, Narekats'i describes the posture in the beginning chapter of his Book, *bazkatarac* "arms stretched out (wide)," perhaps a calque upon Zarathushtra's *ustanazasta, "idem"* towards the [canonical] beginning of his hymns, the *Gathas*.)

But Arm. *t'ev* means "wing," too—Narekats'i used a marvellously evocative compound of his own coining, *t'ewatrohat'ew*, "wing-beat-wing" to evoke angelic flight. (In early Armenian iconography the Cross often surmounts two outspread wings—in Sasanian art, such wings support and frame a sacred symbol. In later centuries, the wings in Armenia become acanthus leaves, arabesques, even waves.) The idea of flight appears in line 14, where the child begs through prayer to ascend to Christ. The word used is the infinitive *parrnal*, a term marked by dense and strong symbolism in Armenian folk belief: for from the aorist stem of the verb, Clas. Arm. *barj-*, is Arm. *ham-partsum*, "the Ascension," on whose eve Heaven opens and kisses the earth, a holiday when girls play the *vijagakhagh*, "game of lots," prophesying love in poetic quatrains. The imagery of Ascension encompasses Christ's harrowing of Hell below and His triumphant, glorious flight upwards through the parted clouds to Heaven: the scene is an important one in the program of Armenian Gospel manuscript illumination.[48] In Tourian's poem, the word *t'ev* anticipates the upward, winged flight of the soul of the praying boy standing below the "wings" of the poem.[49]

In the top part of the poem, still (line 3), is the word *jagad*— in Armenian, it means both the brow of the head, and the summit of a mountain, evoking height. And it is, properly, in Heaven with the Sun (*arev*, line 4), with the world (*ashkharh*) below in line 8. Between Heaven and the world is the act of Creation: instead of the Logos mov-

[48]See J. R. Russell, "The Song of Christ's Ascension (*tał hambarjman*) of St. Gregory of Narek," *St. Nersess Theological Review* 2.2 (1997), pp. 113-130, with refs.

[49]Sevak correctly prints բառնալ though, deplorably, even editions after his use the *lectio facilior* դառնալ , *darnal* "turn," which would give the whole the sense of repentance rather than ascension and deprive the poem of much of its intricate symbolism.

ing from the unseen to incarnation, Tourian inscribes in line 6 the *action* of the Word: *p'ech'ets'*, "blew, breathed"—the spirit of God wafting over the waters in Genesis, and the word of God commanding the universe into being; Armenians call the Bible itself *Asdvadzashunch'*, lit. "God's breath." With these multiple evocations of Heaven, divinity, and creation, the poem moves, broadens, to its Cross-arms. We have already noted the iconic mention of arms in line 10; and in lines 11 and 12, Christ's left side is visible in the verbal icon formed by the words *lanch*, "side, breast" and *srdes* "heart" (abl. sg. with 1st pers. sg. poss. pr.). The bottom side of the cross-bar, line 12, looks downward, to the darkness of Hell and the sorrow of mortal man (line 20: *i mut', i vishd*), and anticipates these with the word *khavar*, "darkness": *mut'*, at the base of the Cross and the end of the poem, is a completed, tenebrous state; but *khavar*, a loan from Iranian, while it can mean simply darkness, has also the nuance of a transitory state, as would be appropriate to the point of change of perspective from the light above to the dark below in the poem, meaning dusk, the setting of the sun.

The lower part of the poem and of the shaft of the Cross is marked by a foot (*vodk'*, line 15) where Christ's would be— part of the way down. But it is Satan's, which is unexpected; and the dramatic reversal of customary imagery is still more marked by the application of the verb *chkni*, "strives," to the prince of darkness, for the word refers usually to the vigilant (*čgnawor*) ascetic. Here, Satan (who is *sev*, black, line 17: this marks the transition of color from brightness to gloom, from illumination to darkness[50]) waits with monastic perseverance to trip up the unwary soul, then to charm and entice it (*tyut'el*, line 19) to perdition. The Clas. Arm. *diwtʿ* is a sorcerer, but the term also has the overtone of an Erlkönig-like seduction. The speaker, who is an innocent child (*manug*, in the title), presumably does not yet know the

---

[50]As in other cultures, Satan is in Armenian popular iconography a completely black man: see J. R. Russell, "Truth Is What the Eye Can See: Armenian Manuscripts and Armenian Spirituality," in T. F. Mathews and R. S. Wieck, eds., *Treasures in Heaven: Armenian Art, Religion, and Society*, New York: Pierpont Morgan Library, 1998, pp. 147-162 (*AIS*, pp. 909-924), where are illustrated talismanic scrolls showing devils and the child-stealing witch Lilith (Arm. *al* or *t'ebgha*) as pitch-black.

erotic sense of the word, but poet and reader do; so the multiple meanings that pervade the poem, linking it to tradition and bestowing upon it the might, accumulated over two millennia, of the central symbolism of the Christian faith, become here, in the base lines a lewd, corrupted *double entendre*, in which recognition is perverted, subtly but shockingly when realized, to a leer.

But this descent to darkness, to a cynical appraisal (and bitter protest) of the bare truth of death, is very typical of Tourian's endings generally. If we regard the shape of the poem as an image of the process of human life, then the first eight lines, of four syllables each, might represent earliest childhood, birth out of non-being; the arms of the Cross, then— four lines of twelve syllables each (a trinity of the syllabic count of the first!) are the expansion of the fullness of life. The final lines contract again—same number and syllabic count—to death. Twenty lines in all: and Tourian, in his twentieth year, knew death was upon him. After such knowledge, forgiveness is still possible, since the poem is a prayer addressed in faith to a loving God whose warm, human body glimmers through the lines, its resurrection and ascension the mystery greater than that of the worshipper's own imminent oblivion.[51]

The Cross is not only a mighty protector against evil. And contemplation of the Cross is meant not only to strengthen faith in a loving God in times of one's own agony or doubt. Is that heart still human that is so petrified as not to be broken by pity and love for the lonely, derided man dying in horror and shame in a gruesome place, and Heaven silent? From St. Ephrem the Syrian to Anania Narekats'i in Armenia, East Christian spiritual teachers have counselled shedding of tears as a means to open and cleanse the heart, to enable prayer and

---

[51]Leo Steinberg's studies of the sexuality of Christ are relevant here. Christian doctrine about the body is ambiguous: sometimes it is rejected as a tomb of the soul; sometimes it is the soul's temple (see Anthony Synott, *The Body Social: Symbolism, Self, and Society*, London: Routledge, 1993). But the figure on the Cross in art is more often sorrowful and piteous in His loveliness than tortured and frightful. Contemplating the God who took on human flesh and died for our sake, perhaps Bedros sometimes felt—despite the protest of "Murmurs"—that he was neither alone nor unloved.

repentance. Tourian was not the only Armenian poet to wrestle with the mystery of the Cross. Yeghia Demirjibashian, his fellow-Constantinopolitan and contemporary, to whom the poet Daniel Varuzhan was to dedicate a poem named after Tourian's own "Murmurs," wrote these astonishing lines:

ԽՈՑՈՏ ՀՐԵՇՏԱԿՆ
(Հարսն Աստուծոյ)

Վսեմագոյն ճիչն հուր հասաւ երբ յերկին՝
"Աստուած, Աստուած իմ, է՞ր, ընդէ՞ր վիս թողեր"
Եւ— խորհուրդ մեծ— թողուց ըվՏէրն անտարբեր,
Միակ քերոբն՝ որ ստեղծուած էր հուր կին՝

Մութին մէջ գաղտ սահեցաւ սև լեռն իջաւ
Սև պսակին, կիսեց փուշերն իր ճակտին,
Սև գամերուն գլխով փորեց իր մարմին,
Եւ Յիսուսին փարած՝ լացաւ ու լացաւ...

Երբ իրենց աչքը կոր ցայգն լուսոց փոխ կու տան,
Հրեշտակք բացին, կարմանալով կարմացան.
Ո՞վ այդ խոցոտ սերոբն հրաշիւք[52] հրաշագեղ...

Աստուածորդին ահա յերկինս համբարձաւ.
Որպէս խաչին վրայ՝ գթոյ քեռն փարեցաւ...
Խոցոտ հրեշտակն՝ հարսն Աստուծոյ էր անեղ...

*The Wounded Angel*
*(God's bride)*

When His mighty cry reached Heaven:
"God, my God, why? Why have you forsaken me?"

---

[52]The text has հրաշիւնք which is a misprint of հրաշունք and should in any case be հրաշիւք. I have restored the Classical Armenian orthography of the original throughout.

And, great mystery, He forsook our Lord indifferently,
One sole cherub, a woman fashioned of fire,

Glided in secret through the dark, to the black mountain came,
To the black crown, and shared the thorns upon His brow,
Pressed into her flesh by their head the black nails,
Clung to Jesus, and broke in sobs.

When their eyes that ring the luminaries' changes by night
The angels opened, they stood mightily amazed:
Who was that wounded seraph so wondrous fair?

Now the Son of God into Heaven ascends—
As on the Cross, now too the sister of mercy in His embrace,
The wounded angel, bride of God uncreate.[53]

It was being forgotten that Tourian feared even more than physical extinction. But with this subtle masterpiece he might proudly declare *Exegi monumentum!*—in every way, for the Cross for Armenians is of course and finally, the pre-eminent *maharjan,* the monument erected to immortalize the memory of the dead.

Finally one notes that Tourian's iconic and devotional poem connects him, not only to his Armenian predecessors, but to the tradi-

---

[53]Ełia Temirčipašyan (Demirjibashian), *Erker*, Erevan: Sovetakan groł, 1986, p. 80: "*Xocʿot hreštakn.*" In the final stanza is the word *hambarjaw* (pron. *hampartsav*), "he ascended," which affords a clue as to the train of thought that might have led Demirjibashian to this startling Passion upon Christ. Armenians believe that on the feast of Ascension (*Hambarjum*) Heaven and earth kiss. Heaven opens the night before, and young girls make rhymed prophecies about love and marriage. So Jesus goes up on Ascension with a bride. And her descent to Him would have been suggested, in part, by Christ's descent and harrowing of Hell. None of this robs the poem of its emotional originality and strength. The Seraphim and Cherubim are fiery; but one is reminded here also of the fiery female being Al who was created, according to Armenian myth, as Adam's first wife. The myth is a fusion of the story of Lilith and the Iranian and local belief in the demoness *āl*, who causes puerperal fever, with an imagined theology of pure love.

tions of Christian devotional and mystical poetry generally. A good example in support of this is cited by my friend Dr. Rodger Friedman, a scholar of the Renaissance and specialist in old and rare books. It is a poem of Herrick's that is rarely anthologized, so I cite it here, with grateful acknowledgement of my learned friend's help.

This crosstree here
Doth Jesus bear
Who sweet'ned first,
The death accurs'd.
Here all things ready are, make haste, make haste away;
For long this work will be, and very short this day.
Why then, go on to act: here's wonders to be done
Before the last least sand of Thy ninth hour be run;
Or ere dark clouds do dull or dead the mid-day's sun.
Act when thou wilt,
Blood will be spilt;
Pure balm, that shall
Bring health to all.
Why then, begin
To pour first in
Some drops of wine,
Instead of brine,
To search the wound
So long unsound;
And, when that's done,
Let oil next run
To cure the sore
Sin made before.
And O! dear Christ,
E'en as Thou di'st,
Look down, and see
Us weep for Thee.
And tho', love knows,
Thy dreadful woes
We cannot ease,

Yet do Thou please,
Who mercy art,
T' accept each heart
That gladly would
Help if it could.
Meanwhile let me
Beneath this tree
This honour have,
To make my grave.

**20. "Loving"** (*Sirel*), 1871 (Sevak pp. 48-49)

**Text.**

ՍԻՐԵԼ

Բոյլ մը նայուածք, փունջ մը ժըպիտ,
Քուրայ մը խօսք դիւթեց իմ սիրտ։

Ես ուզեցի լուռ մենանալ,
Սիրել փըթիթք, խորշեր թաւուտ,
Սիրել կայծերն երկնի կապուտ,
Առտըուան շաղն, իրիկուան բալ,
Ճակատագրիս սև գիծ կարդալ,
Խոկալ, սուզիլ, ըզմայլիլ սուտ։

Ո·հ, խուրձ մը վարս, եդեմ մը շունչ,
Շրջազգեստ մը շրշեց իմ շուրջ։

Ես ուզեցի լոկ ու մինակ
Սրտակցիլ ջինջ վըտակին հետ·
Յիշատակի չ'ունի նա հետ,
Սի·րտ մ'որուն մինչ սուզիմ յատակ,
Գտնեմ պիս հոն դժգոյն, հստակ,
Գաղտնի·ք մ'ունի— այն՝ անթիւ վէտ։

Եթեր մը տրոփ սրտի լսեցի,
Հծծեց.— կ'ուզե՞ս սիրտ, ե·կ ինծի։

Ես ուզեցի սիրել զեփիւռ,
Որ երկնքէն թռչի բեկբեկ,
Նա չը սիրեր խոցել երբէ·ք,
Հոգի· մ'որուն գաղտնիքն է բոյր,
Գիտէ շոյել երազներ բիւր,
Երկնի բոյրն յ'ուշ կ'ածէ առ հէք։

Ո·հ, փունջ մը բոց փըսփըսաց ինձ,
—Կ՛ուզե՞ս պաշտել հոգի մ՛անբիծ։

Ես ուզեցի քընարով մի
Լոկ սիրել հոս, հոս դալկահար,
Պաշտել, գրկել միայն քընար,
Սիրող էակ ճանչել կ՛անի,
Ըստ իմ քըմաց լարել աղի,
Եւ սրտակցիլ սիրողաբար։

Նէ մօտեցաւ յուշիկ, ըսաւ,
—Քնարդ է ցուրտ սիրտ և սէրըդ ցաւ։

Թօթուեց թևերն հոգիս մոլար,
Ճանչեց ըզնէ գեղ ու կըրակ,
Սիրտն անապակ՝ ինչպէս վըտակ,
Անմե·ղ՝ ինչպէս սիւք դալկահար,
Հաւատարի·մ՝ ինչպէս քընար,
Հրաժեշտ տըւաւ կեանքի մենակ։

Բոյլ մը նայուածք, փունջ մը ժըպիտ,
Քուրայ մը խօսք դիւթեց իմ սիրտ։

**Translation.**

*Loving*

A cluster of glances, a garland of smiles,
A crucible of words entranced my heart.

I wished to isolate myself, in silence
To love blossoms and thickets hid,
To love lightnings in the azure sky,
Dew in the morning, mist at dusk,
To read the black lines of my fortune,

Ponder, plummet, be entranced by its lie.[54]

Oh, tresses enwrapping, an Eden of breath,
Sound of their garment about me sweet.

I wished sole and lonely
With the limpid rill to share my heart,
That has no trace of recollection,
When to its heart's floor I dive
And find myself pallid, lucid there.
Whose secret is its numberless waves.

I heard a heart's ether of heartbeats
That sighed "If you want a heart, come to me!"

I wanted to love the zephyr alone
That flies from heaven and breaks apart:
It would never want to wound,
It is a spirit whose mystery is fragrance,
Knowing but to caress a myriad of dreams,
Reminding the downcast of the delicate scent of the sky.

Oh, a garland of flame whispered to me
"Do you want to worship an unblemished soul?"

---

[54]Tchéraz emends *sut*, "lie, lying," to *zut*, "pure," yielding "lire la ligne noire de ma destinée, et ne faire que méditer, m'absorber, m'extasier," which is pleasanter than the dark and ambiguous meaning established by Sevak, who has clearly chosen the *lectio difficilior*. Blackwell, "To Love," p. 19, has for the line "And dwell in meditation deep / And visionary joy." But what joy might the poet derive from scanning "my destiny's dark page"? It seems rather that Tourian is informed by fate of the coming betrayal and regards his present ecstasy as false. One might recall the lines of Sylvia Plath's "The Couriers": "A ring of gold with the sun in it? / Lies. Lies and a grief... / A disturbance in mirrors, / The sea shattering its grey one— / Love, love, my season." The typical harbingers of love are freighted with illusion; the real thing, love, is tremendous, strong, with a truth incapable of reflection, immediate, and therefore mirror-shattering.

I wanted with my harp, pale
But to love, here, here to worship,
To embrace but my harp
And see in it a loving thing
And to my taste tune its strings
And lovingly share with it my heart.

Softly she came close and said
"A cold heart is your harp and your love is pain!"

My soul in frenzy beat its wings,
Recognizing her as beauty, as a flame,
Her heart as undefiled as that stream
And sinless as the strengthless breeze,
Faithful as my harp.
And to life's loneliness it bade farewell.

A cluster of glances, a garland of smiles,
A crucible of words entranced my heart.

**Commentary.**

The poem should be read together with its despairing twin *Trzhum* "Betrayal" (No. 21), the mirror in which all the bright metaphors blacken and turn to poison. There are intimations that love will turn out badly: line 8, *khogal, suzil, ezmaylil sud,* "ponder, plummet, be amazed at its lie," produces a shock by introducing the syllable *su-* in *suzil* "dive, be engulfed, etc.," which is colored by the preceding *khogal,* "meditate, contemplate" to produce the sense of mystic profundity; the -*z*- stretches, encoded, into the equally dreamy *ezmaylil,* but the resumption of *su-* comes as the sharp monosyllable *sud,* "lie." (As noted, Minas Tchéraz emended *sud* to *zud* "pure.") What is the fortune (*jagadakir,* lit. "that which is written on the forehead") that belies his joys? His imminent death, or his beloved's impending rejection of him? Her words in line 34, *K'nart e ts'urd sird yev seret ts'av,* "Your lyre is a cold heart and your love, pain," would suggest the latter; and the repeated

***talg**ahar*, "wan," suggests the former—that the weakened Tourian is not long for this world. (But the epithet could equally be a pose of romantic languor: the Eastern Armenian poet Ch'arents' was to resume it with his famous, early songs to a *tkhra-**daluk*** տխրադալուկ "sad and wan" girl.)

Still, the reverie and anticipation of love creates typically Tourianic, sensuous rushes: lines 9-10, for instance, *Oh! khurts me vars, yetem me shunch', / Shrchazkest me shrshets' im shurch*, the bunched (*khurts*) tresses (*vars*) of the beloved become light as breath (***shunch'***). But the "encircling garment" linked alliteratively (***shrch**azkest*) and typologically (it rustles, ***shrsh**ets'*: the edition in the periodical *Meghu*, "The Bee," has the weaker *shrchets'*, "surrounded") to the hair that cascades over the boy in the girl's embrace is an Eden (*Yetem*). What encircles him is the garden of innocence; so his new garment is that of Adam's primordial purity with Eve (and in Armenian, as one will recall from previous discussion of this sound pattern so characteristic of Tourian, the Bible is called *Astvadza**shunch'***, "Breath of God"). In Eden, according to a tradition popular among Armenians, the first pair wore garments of light (Hebrew *or*); after the expulsion, they found it necessary to clothe themselves in garments of skins (Hebrew *'or*, with a glottal stop).

The heart of his beloved is a sea to whose floor he would dive (line 15, *suzim hadag*: in a strophe of the medieval Armenian poet Hovhannes T'lkurants'i, the beloved is an *anyatak* "bottomless" sea in which, paradoxically, the lover finds *gharar*, haven and anchor, by *ghargh*, drowning),[55] but it is a world, too, with a sky— an ether of pounding heartbeats, the expectant lover's agitation become an inward thunder. And her voice is a hissing, alliterative chorus of sparks (in p and ts/s) of fire: ***p'**unch me **pots'** **p'**esp'esats'* in*ts*, "a garland of fire whispered to me." He bids farewell to loneliness, but the paradise of union, like the self-extinction of the mystic in ecstasy, consumes him.

---

[55]See J. R. Russell, *Yovhannēs T'lkuranc'i and the Mediaeval Armenian Lyric Tradition*, University of Pennsylvania Armenian Texts and Studies 7, Atlanta, GA: Scholars Press, 1987, pp. 80-81.

**21. "Betrayal"** (*Trzhel*), 1871 (Sevak, pp. 50-51)

**Text.**

ԴՐԺԵԼ

Փունջ մը կնճիռ, բոյլ մը կայծակ,
Դըժոխք մ'անէծք խոցեց հոգեակս։

Ես ուզեցի պաշտել ըզնէ,
Սիրել ժպիտքն՝ փըթ·իթք անհուն,
Սիրել աստղերն սև աչերուն
Եւ այն խոկումն, որ մըթագնէ
Պայծառ ճակատը՝ այն ամպն է
Որ կ'ըշպարէ դէմքը լուսնոյն։

Գիշեր մը սուգ, անդունդ մ' հառաչ՝
Ցուցեց ներա հոգին ու լանջ։

Ես ուզեցի միշտ քովն ըլլալ,
Մըտիկ ընել թնդիւն սրտին,
Շնչել, խըմել ներա հոգին,
Եւ շօշափել լոկ ձիւնափայլ
Ծոծորակին վըրայ ծալ ծալ
Թափող վարսից ալեակք ծըփին։

Օվկեան մը տրտունջ լսեցի,
«Զ'իս կը նեղե·ս—» հծծեց ինծի։

Ես ուզեցի քընար մ'ըլլալ
Ներա ձեռքին տակ հնացող,
Ներա հոգւոյն խորն հիացող
Թեթև պատկեր մ'ըլլալ շարժեալ,
Մոռնալ զիս, լոկ ըզնէ· խոկալ,
Կ'վառէ երազ մ'որուն մէկ շող։

Ամպրոպ մը սաստ ցնցեց հոգիս,
Գոչեց— «սիրել չ'ես կրնար վ'իս»։

Ի վո·ւր սիրտըս մըխաց առջին՝
Խնկարկելու սիրտն անապատխ
Յուցի իրեն ճակատս գունատ,
Կուրծըս գոգած, մարն իմ աչքին,
Ի վո·ւր շուրթերս դողդոջեցին,
Ջ'ինքը սիրելս հծծեցին յայտ։

Նէ հեռացաւ ինձմէ, ըսաւ,
«—Բա·ւ սիրեցի քեզ, մնաս բարեա·ւ»։

Որոտացին խոկմանցս ամպեր,
Կայծակնահար ըրին հոգիս,
Մոխիր դարձան երազներս յ'իս,
Ճակատագիրս խնծղաց ի վեր,
Խորշ մը կար որ վ'իս չը ծաղրեր,
Այն լուռ փո·սն էր գերեզմանիս...։

Փունջ մը կնճիռ, բոյլ մը կայծակ,
Դժոխք մ'անէծք խոցեց հոգեակս...։

**Translation.**

*Betrayal*

A garland of frowns, a cluster of lightning
And a hell of curses pierced my little soul.

I wished to worship her,
To love her smiles, that are an endless blossom,
To love her dark eyes' stars
And that meditation that overshadows
Her shining brow—the cloud
That rouges the moon of her face.

A night of lamentation, an abyss of sighs
Agitated her soul, shook her sides.

I wished ever to be by her side,
To listen to the pounding of her heart,
To breathe in, drink her soul,
And but to touch the snowy gleam
Of tresses tumbling, waves
Cresting on her nape.

I heard an ocean of complaint.
"You hurt me," she murmured.

I wished to be a harp
Exhaling sighs beneath her hand,
To be a vignette moving
And charmed within the depths of her soul,
To forget myself, of only her to think—
One ray of which ignites a dream.

A thunder of rebuke shook my soul:
She cried, "You cannot love me!"

In vain before her my heart dissolved in smoke—
The heart on the desert its incense to spend!—
I displayed my brow to her, its color drained,
The blear upon my eye, my hollowed breast.
In vain did my lips quiver
And whisper their love to her cheek.

She abandoned me, and said
"I have loved you enough. Good bye."

The clouds of my thoughts roared thunder
And their lightning bolts stabbed my soul.

The dreams within me turned to ashes,
My fortune laughed down from above.
All that did not mock me was a hole-
It was the mute shaft of my grave.

A garland of frowns, a cluster of lightning
And a hell of curses pierced my little soul...

**Commentary.**

The title of the poem is literally the infinitive form of the verb, forming a darkly rhyming mirror with the title (and wording, and content) of the poem preceding it, *Sirel*, lit., "to love." The word *trzhel* has the emotional shock in Armenian of treason, of basest mendacity. In Avestan, the *Druj*, "Lie," is the personified cardinal characteristic of the archdemon Ahriman, the essence of his deleterious activity (Pahlavi *petyāragī*, from which is also the Arm. loan *p'at'erak*). Darius the Great in his victory inscription of 518 B.C. at Behistun, where the name "Armenian" is also first attested in history, explains the cause of the rebellions he has suppressed in the various satrapies of Iran simply by declaring "the Lie (Old Pers. *drauga-*) had become great in those countries." The word would have been borrowed into the vocabulary of Zoroastrianism in Armenia from Parthian, as **droyž*, with a secondary formation *druž* attested by the reduction in vowel alternation of -u- to zero. The Middle Iranian pres. act. part. *družān* appears as Arm. *družan*; there is a *pluralis tantum*, *držank'*; and the word is found in Arm. compounds with the Zoroastrian verb denoting evil speech (from the so-called "daevic" vocabulary), *daw-*: *dawadržoł*, "babbling untruth," i.e., fomenting deceit. The word also frequents the company of another marked loan from Iranian, *neng* "deception": the compound *sełananeng*, "luring into a trap at a banquet," which survives down to the tenth century in the writings of St. Gregory of Narek, echoing an epic scene of the second century B.C. preserved in the *History* of Movses Khorenats'i[56] conjures up in one word the political and social

[56]On this epic legend and its transmission and survival in a Northwest Caucasian version of the Ossetic *Nart* epic, see J. R. Russell, "Argawan: The Indo-

life of the Artaxiads. The word in Armenian that Tourian uses carries with it, thus, some of the force of its origins in the ancient cosmic dualism of Iran: it is not just not love, but love's opposite, the violent negation of love.

In English we may use different partitive terms: a pod of seals, a pride of lions, rather more preciously an exaltation of larks, and so on. The term denotes an aggregate of a particular kind of thing. In "Loving" the poet bathes our imagination in inventions of these: a garland of smiles and a cluster of glances, a crucible of words (like an alchemist's, producing precious gold), an Eden of breaths, an ether of heartbeats. In "Betrayal" Tourian phantasizes a grammar of the inferno: all the partitives are monstrous. A garland of frowns has the hideous undercurrent of waves frozen into wrinkles of hardened flesh that we see elsewhere. The effect of the line "a night of mourning or lamentation (*suk*) and an abyss (*antunt*) of sighs" is to evoke both sleepless agitation and the darkness of the pit—a dark premonition, for the hole in the black earth will turn out to be the sole thing that does not mock the poet at the end.

Tourian in "Loving" uses a string of alliteration in describing the beautiful long hair of his beloved. Here, too, the lines I have rendered as "And but to touch the snowy gleam / Of tresses tumbling, waves / Cresting on her nape" read *Yev shoshap'el log tsyunap'ayl / Dzodzoragin vera dzal dzal / T'ap'ogh varsits' alyagk' dzep'in*. The *sh-* of *shoshap'el*, "touch," introduces the sequence by reminding the reader of the sounds of *shunch'*, *shrchazgest*, and *shrshel* in the passage on her hair in "Loving." The unvoiced affricate *ts-* of *tsyunap'ayl*, "snow-shining," both links the adjective to *varsits'* "of tresses" (Clas. Arm. gen. pl.), which it modifies, and subtly anticipates the string of four voiced affricates, *dz-*, of the next line, and the final ***dzep'in*** closing the stanza. The phonetic gorgeousness of these lines is enough; but if you are willing to accept that the uninterrupted poetic literature of an ancient language can bear, even subconsciously, the patterns and thematic implications of its historical strata, then we can go somewhat further. Greg-

European Memory of the Caucasus," forthcoming in the *Journal of Armenian Studies*, 8.2, Belmont, MA.

ory of Narek, as was observed in the commentary to No. 11, used a similar alliterative pattern of the sound *dz-* (or *ts-*, in Classical Arm.) in his Ode to the Nativity to describe the eyes of Mary two eyes (*dzov*) laughing (*dzidzagh*) and dilating (*dzaval*) in the dawn, like shining stars (*p'aylagatsev*, փայլակաձև:we see Tourian uses a compound with *p'ayl* and the same *ts-*, ձիւնափայլ); and Grigoris of Aght'amar borrowed several of these images consciously to describe a seraph with beautiful tresses (*vars*, the same word Tourian uses, which he also marks with a Clas. Arm. declension instead of Modern *-eru*). Seraph and Mary. And the epithet *spitakap'ayl*, "shining white," was used of a god by the pre-Christian Armenians. Tourian's lines can thus achieve a multiple effect of divinity, purity, sensuality, and abundance. Though he never mentions the sea, unlike Narekats'i, the tresses become waves lapping at the shore—the solid turned to transparent liquid, the light-reflecting snow (*tsyunap'ayl*) preserving its luminescence as it becomes sea-waves crashing, full of life, on a sandy beach in love's summer. So he constructs the picture, and the very next line sweeps one, horrifyingly, from this joyful sea to the black oceanic abyss: *Ovgyan me drdunch*, "An ocean of murmur." And we have returned to the partitive grammar of hell.

**22. "The Lake"** (*Lejag*), 1871 (Sevak, pp. 52-54)

**Text.**

ԼՃԱԿ

Ինչո՞ւ ապշած ես, լըճա·կ,
Ու չ՚են խայտար քու ալեակք,
Միթէ հայլւոյդ մէջ անձկաւ
Գեղուհի՞ մը նայեցաւ։

Եւ կամ միթէ կըկմայլի՞ն
Ալեակքդ երկնի կապոյտին,
Եւ այն ամպոց լուսափթիթ,
Որք նըմանին փրփուրքիդ։

Մելամաղձոտ լըճա·կդ իմ,
Քեզ հետ ըլլա·նք մըտերիմ,
Սիրեմ քեզի պէս ես ալ
Գրաւուիլ, լըռել ու խոկալ։

Որքան ունիս դու ալի՝
Ճակատս այնքան խոկ ունի,
Որքան ունիս դու փրփուր՝
Սիրտս այնքան խոց ունի բիւր։

Այլ եթէ գոգդ ալ թափին
Բոյլքն աստեղաց երկնքին,
Նըմանիլ չ·ես կրնար դուն
Հոգւոյս՝ որ է բոց անհո·ւն։

Հոդ աստղերը չ՚են մեռնիր,
Ծաղիկներն հոդ չ՚են թոռմիր,
Ամպերը չ՚են թըջեր հոդ,
Երբ խաղաղ էք դու և օդ։

Լըճա·կ, դու ես թագուհիս,
Զի թ՚հովէ մ՚ալ խորշոմիս,
Դարձեալ խորքիդ մէջ խըռով
Զ՚իս կը պահես դողդղալով։

Շատերը կ՚իս մերժեցին,
«Քնար մ՚ունի սոսկ– ըսին.
Մին՝ «դողդոջ է, գոյն չ՚ունի–
Միւսն ալ ըսաւ– կը մեռնի·»։

Ոչ ոք ըսաւ– «հէ·ք տղայ,
Արդեօք ինչո՞ւ կը մըխայ,
Թերևս ըլլայ գեղանի,
Թէ որ սիրեմ, չը մեռնի»։

Ոչ ոք ըսաւ– «սա տըղին
Պատռե·նք սիրտը տըրտմագին,
Նայինք ինչե·ր դրուած կան...»
—Հոն հրդեհ կայ, ո·չ մատեան։

Հոն կայ մոխի·ր... յիշատա·կ...
Ալեակքդ յուպի·ն թող, լըճա·կ,
Զի քու խորքիդ մէջ անձկաւ
Յուսահատ մը նայեցաւ...։

**Translation.**

*The Lake*

Why are they, my little lake, amazed,
And your little waves leap not:
Perhaps in your mirror, impassioned
A beauty gazed.

Or could they be enraptured,
Little waves by heaven's blue,

By those clouds that in light bloom,
That are like your foam?

Melancholy little lake of mine,
Let us be close to one another;
May I love, like you
To be captivated, silent, and contemplative.

For every wave you have
My brow bears a furrow of thought;
As much as you have foam
My heart has myriad wounds.

But if into your bosom plummet
The multitudes of heaven's stars,
You still cannot compare
To my soul, an infinite fire.

There the stars do not die;
The flowers there wilt not.
The clouds there drench[57] not with rain
When you and the air are still.

Little lake, you are my queen,
For if you ripple in the wind,
Again in your depth, disturbed
You hold me as I tremble.

Many have rejected me:
"A lyre is all he has," they said.
One: "He shakes, he has no color."
Another said: "He's dying."

---

[57]Minas Tchéraz in his translation ("Petit Lac"), p. 69, suggests that *t'rcher*, "wet," should have read *t'rrch'ir*, "flies": "les nuages ne s'envolent pas." Sevak correctly does not make this emendation.

No one said "Poor boy,
Why does he burn?
If there were some lovely girl
And she but love him, he might not die."

No one said "Let's rip apart
This boy's sad heart
And see the writing it contains."
A blaze is there, no text.

Ash is there, and memory:
Bestir your waves, my lake–
For in your depth in agony
One bereft of hope stared.

**Commentary.**

The poem was translated into English by Blackwell as "Little Lake" (*Armenian Poems*, pp. 13-15), and reprinted in Zabelle C. Boyajian, *Armenian Legends and Poems*, pp. 18-19. Tchéraz translates it as "Petit Lac" (pp. 69-71), with the appreciative comment, "C'est probablement la meilleure des poésies du jeune écrivain." It is often asserted that Lamartine's "Le Lac" inspired Tourian's verses— Etmekjian compares the two poems, but goes on to emphasize, quite rightly, how different they are in all essential points.[58]

Lines 29-32 apparently have their source in a painful experience of Tourian's recalled by Azniv Hrach'ya, in the article "From my recollections," *Anahit*, April-May 1909, no. 1-2, p. 20, repr. in *Documents*, no. 46, pp. 86-87:

"... The first audition of the summer season was to take place at Scutari, in the same theater as before, the Aziziye. It was scheduled for 3 o'clock (that is, nine by European reckoning). But by 2:30 the whole

[58]James Etmekjian, *The French Influence on the Western Armenian Renaissance, 1843-1915*, New York: Twayne, pp. 206-207.

group had already assembled... To the left near the wings were seated some men; women, to the right— that is, the Karakash sisters and Theresa Chuhajian. The street door was ten feet away from them. I was sitting another ten feet away from the girls, on the side opposite the door. At that moment a youth entered: tall, with a long neck. He had a long nose. He was pale. He was dressed in very worn, ash-gray clothes, and carried a notebook under his arm. When he appeared, the actresses began to laugh, saying, 'Hey, Theresa, your boy's here!' [*K'a! T'ereza, k'ugint yeghav*] But Theresa replied, 'He's so pale I have no use for him— he's going to die soon.' [*Aynk'an kunad e, vor indzi bedk' ch'e, shudov ge merrni.*] I heard her words but didn't think the youth had heard them as well. That boy dressed in rags with one foot in the grave was Tourian, the poet we all loved. The notebook under his arm was the play *The Theater*, which he intended to read to Vartovian and was included in the repertoire. It was only when I read his poems, after his death, that I realized he had overheard Theresa Chuhajian's words, since he wrote, 'Many have rejected me...'"

In the first stanza is a recollection of Narcissus, who gazed upon his own beauty in the water's mirror and was unable to stir. Here the lake is a mirror because the waves cannot rise for amazement. But the lovely girl's emotions are unclear: *antsgav*, an adverb formed from the old instrumental singular of *antsug*, "narrow" could mean straitened in grief or impassioned (cf. the verse of the popular Armenian national song "Hayastan": *Yev antsgayryats' i k'ez husam, huys im miayn, Hayastan* "And burning with longing I hope in you, my hope alone, Armenia!"). "In my straits I called upon the Lord; the Lord answered me with enlargement," the Psalmist sang. A Persian sad for love is still *del tang*, "heart-narrowed." Is she impassioned, or grief-stricken? And if the first four lines have the lake itself acting, as Narcissus' never did, in the second stanza it is the lake itself that also does the looking, gazing up in rapture at heaven, which is like its blue water in color, and at the clouds, which are like its foam. And up to this point the images are gay: it does not matter that the waves leap *not*— the point is that the poet introduces the *thought* of leaping, and the movement is irresistibly upwards, towards a sky that seems itself growing. For the clouds are *lusa-**p't'it'**, blossoming* with light like flowers— and this short explosion of consonants for spring, all outward aspirations of breath and one front vowel, is a word Tourian especially loves.

But the third stanza resumes the theme of the lake's stillness, and introduces the person of the poet. With him, the color turns dark: Arm. *melamaghtsod*, "melancholy," contains the same Greek base as the English loan, save that the Western Armenian speaker, who also uses the Greek loan *melan* for "ink" (it is *t'anak'* in Eastern), will feel the coloration of blackness in the word more strongly than the English reader, for whom the word melancholy will conjure up not so much the color black, perhaps, as the dejected mood of Dürer's engraving. The poet asks for intimacy with the lake, and qualifies its outer stillness as a mental habit— brooding thought, care's burden (Arm. *khog-al*)— like his own. The wave (*ali*: he uses also the diminutive *alyag*; and see the discussion of *an-ali*, "waveless" in "Murmurs") is now the *khog*, "thought" of Tourian's brow. We do not think of a furrowed brow as liquid, rippling, moving: it is solid. So the waves are now still, not because they have not risen and the waters are calm and mirror-like, but because they are hard furrows, liquid no longer. The foam changes, horribly, as well: now it is likened, not to the clouds of spring up above, with their effervescent inner luminescence, but to the poet's heart— something dark and below and inside— with its wounds. With the change of color from sky-blue to depth-black and the spatial reorientation of the poem downwards, the lake-foam darkens in symbolism, to become the foaming blood of pain. The Armenian word for a wound is ***khots'***. Tourian links the image phonetically to another in the lines that follow: if the stars should fall (and once more he presses upon one the feeling of a movement *down*), they still would not rival the infinite fire, ***pots'***, of his soul. This fire should remind one of hell— it burns, rather than enlightens, and it is enclosed: it releases no light.

The poet then slips into a strange inner world where stars don't die, flowers don't wither, and clouds don't release moisture, when his lake is at peace (*khaghagh*). It is a desolate peace, a deathly landscape: the blossoms resemble the asphodels beyond Hades. And who has seen a star die? We see them move— above, they are made to drop— but this locomotion seems the only point at which they join our mortal career. They do not die, when they are not moving— their movements have been pitched to the sympathy of our own earthly career, so when still, they are already dead. It is an arid landscape, too: spring clouds bring showers. These do not. T. S. Eliot's clouds bringing rain, and the Himalayan thunder, relieve in the leap of an instant the desiccated despair and weariness of the last desert of the Waste Land.[59] The clouds in Tourian's inner inferno hang, leaden, spent, without the light energy to gush forth.

In the seventh stanza, Tourian closes the first part of the poem with a decisive rejection and reversal of the opening lines. There, a beautiful girl had gazed at the lake's placid ***surface*** in lovely surroundings. Now, it is the lake that holds (2 pers. sg., *bahes*) the poet atremble in its turbulent ***depths*** (Arm. *khork'*). And the poet has no beloved—Narcissus cannot be anyone's lover in any case: the lake, instead, is his queen. And as a monarch, she has power. If she is a lover as well, then her love and power must combine in the only way possible: for him to drown in her depths. Uniting with the beloved is, for Tourian, dying: we see this in "With Her" (*Nera Hed*) and other poems. With this shock, Tourian turns, abruptly, to the outer world.

"Many have rejected me": the next four lines have a long and bitter echo in the protest of the great Armenian poet of the twentieth century. In 1920, Ch'arents' wrote the fifteenth poem of his *Tagharan* ("Canticle").[60] In its use of heartless, public reported direct speech over inner anguish and protest, it is evidently inspired in part by this well-known poem by Tourian, and it contains the same word for despair (*husahat*)— though the setting is a festive gathering at Tiflis, not a pond near Constantinople.

When I came into this old world with my song, my *saz* and *kemancha*,[61]

---

[59]There is an excellent discussion of Eliot's use of this sudden rainstorm by Colin Wilson, *Poetry and Mysticism*, San Francisco: City Lights, 1970, p. 49. His insights, I think, anticipate those of Robert Bly's *Leaping Poems*.

[60]Text in Ełišē Č'arenc', *Erkeri žołovacu*, I, Erevan: Arm. Acad. Sci., 1962, pp. 240-241.

[61]The *saz* and *kemancha* are Iranian stringed instruments played by Anatolian and Caucasian minstrels (*ashugh*): Charents' *Canticle* is a tribute in imitation

"What will this hopeless fool do in the world?" they said.

But when at the parties of the crowd[62] I sang my sweet songs,
"Your words are sweet as summer's fruits,"[63] they said.

But at the heartless celebrations of the mob I remained alone and sad.
I wanted to leave, to go away. "He's proud, and he's wicked," they said.

In my heart's anguish and despair[64] I drank a glass of vodka.[65]

---

of the eighteenth-century Armenian bard of Tiflis, Sayat'-Nova, about whom Prof. Charles Dowsett of Oxford spoke his own *obiter dicta* in an erudite monograph, the only study of the poet in English.

[62]Ch'arents' uses the loan-words *khalkh* (<Arab. *khalq*, "people," lit. "creation") and *kef*—a word for partying, enjoying a sense of well-being—a score of Middle Eastern associations of moderate to boisterous pleasure. Such a party might also be called *mejlis* or *mehfil*. Men ate and drank, smoked tobacco with opium or hashish in water-pipes (on the practice in seventeenth-century Armenian life, see my article "The Demon Weed," forthcoming in the *Journal of Armenian Studies*, Belmont, MA), and enjoyed music and poetry. One writes this in the frigid, barren darkness of a Friday night in Cambridge, winter, middle age—here one might as well endeavor to evoke the customs of the men on the Moon. But then, Ch'arents' fared no better, in a warm and cultured clime where *kef* existed.

[63]A poetically less powerful, but more patriotic—and therefore, most popular—poem of the *Tagharan* is the one that begins *Yes im anush Hayastani arevaham barn em sirum*, "I love my sweet Armenia's fruit with the taste of the Sun." The Persian loan *bar* means "fruit"; native Arm. *barr*, with trilled *r*, "word." The latter *lectio facilior* inevitably appears on the bas-reliefs, plaques, and samplers emblazoned with the poem that the *khalkh* likes. In this line, though, fruit is fruit and word is word—but they are alike, in the public's appraisal of Ch'arents'.

[64]Ch'arents' uses the same word for a man in despair, *husahat*, that Tourian will in the last, ringing, anguished line of "The Lake."

[65]Arm. *oghi* could be the anisette called arak, too. But the cycle belongs to the poet's Moscow period, and is therefore most likely vodka.

"Ch'arents' is a raving drunkard, a tipsy fool," they said.

And in the midst of winter's blasts I was left, barefoot and bare:
"Outside it's cold, it's winter, but it's summer in your soul," they said.

I said: "You are men, after all— can you not see my wasted body?"
The soul of Ch'arents' in his songs is unbowed and defiant," they said.

They laughed and cackled only, that I remained naked so.
"The wonder of the ages is for your lofty songs," they said.

With the introduction of other voices, the deepening reverie of the poem, which, as we have seen, reaches a kind of conclusion in the seventh stanza, is interrupted. Again, Tourian employs a negative strategy: No one said, no one said—but we hear directly what they might have said, and in the context of the poem's sound-world, that is as good as the intrusion of loud and unfamiliar voices. At first, it is very clearly a chorus of three harsh, insensitive voices from the same crowd that Ch'arents' was later to imagine mocking him, each one with a rejection direr than the last: He's a useless poet! He's pale! He's dying! That is, his profession is useless, his body is useless, and his very life is useless: these three successive rejections (Arm. *merzhets'in*) seem grimly to parody the threefold recitation of abjuration (*hrazharumn*) of Satan in thought, word, and deed at the opening of the Armenian prayer-book: Հրաժարիմք ի սատանայէ՝ և յամենայն խաբէութենէ նորա, ի պատրանաց նորա, ի խորհրդոց նորա, ի գնացից նորա, ի չար կամաց նորա, ի չար հրեշտակաց նորա, ի չար պաշտօնէից նորա, ի չար կամարարաց նորա, և յամենայն չար զօրութենէ նորա՝ հրաժարելով հրաժարիմք։ "We abjure Satan, and all his deceit, his impostures, his designs, his ways, his evil will, his evil angels, his evil servants, his evil minions, and all his evil host—we abjure them utterly."[66] The next voices in the chorus are more intimate, and return to the image of a dark inner fire that Tourian has already introduced. The first wonders why the poet wastes away, or burns in

[66]*Žamagirkʿ Hayastaneaycʿ Surb Ekełecʿwoy*, Jerusalem: St. James', 1955, p. 5.

passion (*ge mekha*: the verb comes from *mukh*, "smoke," and is one he likes). He might become beautiful (*keghani*) if I loved him (*sirem*, 1st pers. subj. act.): here the device of direct speech is disorienting and strange, since till now only the poet has used the first person; it renders invisible the speaker, presumably a lovely girl like the *keghuhi* of line 4. Tourian himself becomes the lovely one through the similarity of *keghuhi-keghani*—as though he were gazing up at the girl through the mirror of the lake-water, out of its depths.

Those impossible depths out of which the poet is seen, that phantasmagorically still wave, the blood-foam, the blackness that has more true sight than light, are the truth. What first seemed the reality, is its shadow. The surface and the light are a mirror, not the thing in itself. Such disorienting uses of imagery to compel a reader to discover an imaginal reality behind what had previously seemed to him to be the real world of the senses are as old as Plato's metaphor of the cave in the *Republic*. The play of reality and reflection, of surface and interior, returns and reverses in ways that somewhat foreshadow Vladimir Nabokov's slain waxwing's ghost in *Pale Fire*.[67]

The fifth outer speaker recommends (or, does not recommend) tearing open the boy's heart to read what is written within. By this point, the reported speech is either wounded exaggeration—completely stilted and mannered, for who says such things?—or else a carefully-prepared phantasmagoria, outer voices bearing inner thoughts. (Imagine passers-by commenting on what you are saying silently to yourself in your head—or, more formally, a Greek chorus informing the audience of your thoughts.) I opt for fantasy over bad verse: the opening three voices seem both wholly real, and yet also a kind of liturgical text, a threefold condemnation sending the poet away and down to death. The next voice reverses poet, mirror, speaker; and this one, the fifth, makes the poet the depth to be plumbed. We have

---

[67]Brian Boyd in his monograph, *Nabokov's Pale Fire: The Magic of Artistic Discovery*, Princeton, NJ: Princeton Univ. Press, 1999, a work of magical insight and delight worthy of the masterpiece it investigates, demonstrates how key terms and reversals lead the reader to explore mysteries of vision and reflection that lead into depths of perception beyond apparent reality—something art can do and most other kinds of human endeavor cannot.

seen the waves turn to furrows; the depth itself is now his smoking heart with its dark fire. And—in agreement with the book-like implication of the initial voices—it should have writing. But when they (don't) cleave it open, almost as though it were the Red Sea parting, the waters to either side of the fleeing Israelites made into solid walls—but this is a malign miracle now, the solidity sinister rather than reassuring—there is a conflagration (*hrteh*), not a book. Tourian does not use the usual Armenian word for book, *kirk'* (and in his Lament for his friend Vartan Loutfian, No. 36, *madyan* and depth are there in lines close to these) but a strongly-marked term, Western Arm. *madyan*. Classical Armenian *matean* derives from Middle Iranian *mādag-dān*, Phl. *mād-ayān*, literally "container of a mother-text." Thus, Erevan's Armenian manuscripts—primary sources *par excellence*, as opposed to mere printed books, kept in a ***gr**adaran*, the usual "library"—live in the temple-like repository of the ***Maten**adaran*. The *locus classicus* in Armenian literature for the imaginative evocation of a tortured heart, of fires that illuminate not, is the *Matean ołbergut'ean* of St. Gregory of Narek, the *Book of Lamentation*. A conflagration, not a book—but *what* a book! One is forced simply by the juxtaposition of terms to imagine one with letters of fire, like Moses' tablets.

The final stanza enforces the image of such an extraordinary text, engraved with the burning script of an inner truth: the fire reduces the pages to ash (*mokhir*), but memory (*hishadag*) is also there, as though the book were read and consumed, paradoxically displaying its text by its very burning. (Remember Dante's souls made into animal-trees: they speak by having their branches torn, and the words emerge with the dripping blood.) Here the book is read by being destroyed—in "With Her," Tourian declares that to speak means to perish! The Armenian word for memory evokes that feature particular to manuscripts, the colophon (Arm. *yišatakaran*)—the Arm. word for which means "memory-container." There may even be an echo of the Book of Books in this not-book-but-fire, when one recalls that God inscribed the tablets with letters of fire, and that an early Greek appellation of the Gospel, "Memorial," may be found in Arm. if one explains *aweta-ran*< MIr.**ayād-dān* "a collection of memorial(s)," as Prof. C. de Lamberterie has argued. It is seen in other poems that Tourian, whose farewell to youth was not adulthood, but extinction, was obsessed with the fear of oblivion. So it is particularly suitable that his heart be a great text with its colophon—but one that is burning. And all this is happening in a lake.

Now the poem reaches its end, in a coda to the seventh stanza. Were a beauty (*keghuhi*) to look (*nayets'av*) in passion (*antsgav*) upon Tourian, he might revive. No, one in despair looked in anguish (*antsgav*)—a youth who never experienced requited love, whose utter passivity contorts the very syntax of that expressed hope. And he looked, not into the mirror, but past it into the depths—of the lake, of the heart. His sorrow from within, not the wind outside, drives the wave, makes it boil with the froth of blood and passion, and, possessed by his love, the lake, he drowns.[68]

[68]Though I do not think Tourian was consciously affected in the construction of this poem by Armenian epic and myth, the subconscious effect might have been there. Both the magic sword of the heroes of Sasun, the *T'ur ketsaki*, "Lightning Saber" and the mighty sword Havhaluni of St. Tiridates IV the Great, the king who was baptized by St. Gregory the Illuminator, were thrown into lakes, which then boiled—in both cases, the incident closes a narrative. Storms on lake Van were caused—so the local Armenians long believed—not by wind, but by the thrashing about of a *vishap*-dragon in the depths as the hero-divinity Vahagn extracted it, to burn it in the fire of the Sun. The lake is Tourian's queen: the heroes of Sasun are fathered by a rock in lake Van from whose milky fluid princess Tsovinar, whose name means something like Lady of the Lake, drinks. In Arthurian epic, which may contain remote echoes of Alan and Armenian epic lore, it is the hand of the Lady of the Lake that catches the sword Excalibur as it is thrown into the waves. Perhaps Tourian, drowning, finally finds and loves his *keghuhi*, who is death. (See J. R. Russell, "The Scepter of Tiridates," *Le Muséon* 114.1-2, 2001, pp. 187-215, *AIS*, pp. 1135-1163.)

**23. "The Turkish Woman"** (*T'rk'uhin*), 1871 (Sevak pp. 55-56); and **"The Armenian Woman"** (*Hayuhin*), undated (Sevak, pp. 92-93)

**Text.**

**ԹՐՔՈՒՀԻՆ**

Երեկոյ է. բոցավառ է հորիզոն.
Կառք մը կ'անցնի դագաղի պէս համրընթաց,
Գեղուհի մը ընկողմանած տրոփէ հոն,
Վերջալոյսի աղջի՞կ մ'է սա, ո·վ Աստուած։
Եթէ նայի·,
Կ'ըսես, հի·մա կը մարի։

Մեղրամոմէ անդրիանդի մ'է հանգոյն,
Ի·նչ դալկահար... կարծես հաջաղը վառէ
Պատան մ'է նուրբ ներա վարդիցը դժգոյն.
Աստուած ըվնէ կոյգ մ'աչերովն կը վառէ.
Եթէ ժպտի·,
Կ'ըսես— ո·հ, հի·մա կ'անցնի։

Նայիլ կ'ուզէ, բայց ա·ւելի կ'նըուաղի,
Սիրտը խունկի պէս կը մըխա· սիրավառ,
Նէ շողերու, բոյրերու է թագուհի,
Խոնջ թիթեռնիկ մ'որ կը խնդրէ ծաղկէ թառ.
Եթէ շարժի·,
Կ'ըսես— հի·մա կը թռչի։

Լանջն է յուզեալ օվկեանի մը նըման.
Կ'ուզէ սիրել... համբոյրի մ'հետ նըուաղիլ,
Մաշիլ, խամրիլ, խոնջած ընկնիլ գերեզման,
Քամել սիրոյ կրակէ բաժկին հուսկ կաթիլ.
Եթէ շիկնի·,
Կ'ըսես— հի·մա կը բռնկի։

Սրտի մեղո·ւ, ինչպէս կոչեց Լամարթին,

Որուն ծըծած ծաղիկը՝ սիրտ, մեղրն է սէր,
Ես կոչեմ վնէ կո·յս, որուն սիրտն է երկին
Անհուն սիրոյ, որ հորիզոն չ’ունի դեռ․
Եթէ խօսի·,
Կ’ըսես— հի·մա կը հատնի։

Նէ կը վառի, մի·շտ կը վառի, չը հատնիր
Տընանկ կընոջ տաճարն վառած ճրագին պէս,
Աստղերու նման գիշեր սիրէ՝ փողփողի·լ․
Կրակ մ’է փրթած կողէն սիրոյ բոցագէս…
Թէ իսկ մեռնի·,
Կ’ըսես— հի·մա կը ծընի։

**Translation.**

*The Turkish Woman*

It is evening— the horizon is ablaze—
A carriage passes, mute as a coffin it goes,
A beauty reclines within, her heart pounds,
O God, is she a girl of the dusk?
If she looks
You would say—Now she will flicker out.

She is like a beeswax bust,
So pallid... you would think her veil a fiery
Shroud upon her fragile, faded roses.
God kindles her eyes twain:
If she smiles
You would say—Oh, now she will pass away.

She wants to gaze, but her languor is too great,
Like incense her heart burns, with love aflame:
She is queen of scents, of rays,
Spent butterfly that seeks a flower as her nest:
If she moves,

You would say—now she will take wing.

Her bosom, like an Ocean vexed
Wants to love... with a kiss to faint,
Wear out, perish, exhausted drop into the grave,
Out of love's fire chalice to squeeze but a drop:
If a blush flush her cheek
You would say—now she will burst into flame.

Bee of the heart, as Lamartine called her—
The heart is the flower she sips, and its honey is love—
Virgin I call her, whose heart is an infinite
Heaven of love, whose horizon is seen no more:
If she speaks
You would say—now she wastes away.

She burns, burns eternally, never consumed—
Like the lamp in the Temple the poor woman kindled—
Like the stars that the night loves, that they glitter,
She is fire snapped from the rib of love, fiery-tressed,
Which if it dies
You would say—will now come to life.

**Commentary.**

Sevak notes (pp. 257-259) that in the 1893 edition the title was replaced by asterisks, since a Christian was not allowed to sing the praises of a Muslim woman in the Ottoman Empire. Other editions mechanically maintained the convention; and in 1940 the title "The Beauty" (*Keghuhi*) was used. The poem, which is a variant of "The Armenian Woman" (*Hayuhin*), was, according to Mak'sud Mihrdatyants', inspired by an incident: "I'll tell you a little story. There was a specialist in Turkish here who was dismissed and is now in Adapazar. One day he related to somebody—who told it, in turn, to me—that he, Tourian, and another boy—classmates, I think, went to Camlica and sat down under a tree. Shortly thereafter a palace carriage bearing a very beautiful Turkish lady came and passed right in front of them. The

Turkish woman, who was reclining in the carriage, tossed her veil to one side and fanned her face with a delicate fan. At the same moment Tourian, ravished by her beauty, pulled pencil and paper out of his pocket and produced, in instantaneous inspiration, the poem which we know by the title *T'rk'uhi*" (letter to Arshag Chobanian written at Armash monastery, Sunday, 8/20 November 1892, repr. in *Documents*, no. 39, pp. 73-74).

The poem is about an impossible love—it reminded Susan Barba of Baudelaire's "A une passante," which imagines a love that even in the pluperfect had not had the chance of beginning. She also noted the dictum of Walter Benjamin that beauty exists in its passing; and this idea she traces in part to the somewhat solipsistic Paterian notion—radical for its time—that the individual perceives art in an inner mental solitude after which he may perhaps radiate the strength of the experience in the heightened language of aesthetic writing.

Look, smile, move, blush, speak: the poem anticipates a meeting, builds towards it, dies. The images of death pervade the poem: the carriage is like a coffin, the woman's veil is like a shroud, her cheeks are like dead flowers, and she would fall into a grave. This preoccupation with death reflects Tourian's own state, of course, his sense of his own impending death and the wilting and decay of his own youthful beauty: in "The Lake" he speaks of his cloven heart as both a conflagration and a sacred text (*madyan*), and here the Turkish woman is likened to a lamp burning eternally in the Temple—the same mixture of the fiery and the hieratic. The burning, inner heart with sacred script is his.

The poem begins in the garish red light of dusk and ends with the lovely woman burning like the stars now aglow in the night sky: the movement of love from evening's anticipation, across speech, and into a fulfillment somehow linked to death, in a transfigured night, is the same here as in Tourian's "With Her" (*Nera Hed*). In "With Her," the poet describes himself exchanging kisses with a girl, who takes him in her arms. That poem culminates in nuptials at which Nature officiates, crowning the couple with stars: here, ecclesiastical images of virgin, chalice, incense, heaven, and Temple lamp, and the oblique reference to Adam's rib, taken together suggest the ritual of a wedding as well. The caresses and nuptials of "With Her" are pure imagination, and this fleeting vision of the Turkish lady passing swiftly by, one would think at first, might as well have been fantasy. But the fleeting glimpse engendered the poem.

With respect to this idea of a brief vision that the poet's passion and art transform into an encounter, into love and permanent beauty, I would like to speak for a while a of familiar poet of the Christian East. His parents were married at Constantinople in the spring of 1849, just before Bedros Tourian was born. Their son was thirteen years Tourian's junior, and was born and raised mainly in another great cosmopolitan city of the Hellenic Mediterranean, Alexandria, though he spent three years in the early 1880's in the Ottoman capital. He wrote one wry poem about Tigranocerta[69]—otherwise, his contacts with Armenians seem to have been only of the everyday sort. But, as we have seen, his deep sorrows, and his elegant transformation of the Greek poetic language from stilted *katharevousa* to flowing *demotike*, parallels Tourian's contribution to Armenian. In 1921, then, this greatest poet of Greece since Classical times, Constantine Cavafy, wrote:[70]

THEIR BEGINNING

The fulfillment of their illicit pleasure
Was over. From the bed they arose:
And they quickly dress without talking.
They leave separately, secretly from the house, and as

---

[69]For an English translation (the first and only one so far, it appears) and study of Cavafy's "Tigranocerta," see J. R. Russell, "The Lost Epic of Tigran: A Reconstruction Based upon the Fragments," in Richard Hovannisian, ed., *Proceedings* of the UCLA Symposium on Amida-Tigranakert (in publication; *AIS*, pp. 1031-1050).

[70]Translation mine, from the Greek text in G. P. Savvides, ed., K. P. Kabaphes, *Poiemata*, II, Athens: Ikaros, 1963, p. 22. The title is the same as the final three words, and I have tried to preserve this aspect of ring composition, a feature important in Cavafy's work. The best English translation of the poet remains Rae Dalven, *The Complete Poems of Cavafy*, New York: Harcourt, Brace, & World, 1963, p. 109.

They walk, somehow uneasy down the street it seems
They suspect something on them gives away
What kind of bed they fell into a little while ago.

Except how the artist's life has gained.
Tomorrow, the day after tomorrow, or years hence will be written
The powerful lines of poetry for which here was their beginning.

"In the beginning was the Word" (*En arkhe en ho Logos*) proclaims the Gospel according to John; and the title of Cavafy's poem, *He arkhe ton*, borrows some of that cosmogonic power, which it at first appears to contradict or lose, only to affirm it later in an unexpected way. One starts by thinking "*their* beginning" must be that of the two lovers, the start of an affair. But it is not—their love is immediately revealed as a brief, almost anonymous sexual encounter. Cavafy was homosexual, hence the adjective *eknome*, "illicit, outside the law," and in his era such love was a crime that had to be kept secret; and most encounters were furtive and short. But the poet's memory will preserve and transform the fleeting instant as beauty, and that beauty will be captured in "powerful lines" (*stikhoi dynatoi*). So the poetic *logos* is what beginnings matter for, after all: the *tekhnites*, the poet, is the demiurge. There is a hint of poignancy and defiance in Cavafy's claim, too, for he was well into middle age by the time he wrote the poem, his body no longer capable of attracting beauty—except, perhaps, for money—and he emphasizes the remoteness of the days of his carnal loves with the words *avrio, methavrio,* **e meta khronia**... "tomorrow, the day after tomorrow, **or after years**..." It must now be years. And we hear nothing of the boy whose body the poet quickly, fearfully, long ago caressed— it is as though it were not there, were only barely seen—the poet's own intense emotion of recollection is the sole reality to attest to what gratified desire might once have been. In "Half an Hour" (*Mise ora*),[71]

[71]Edmund Keeley and George Savidis, ed. and tr., C. P. Cavafy, *Passions and Ancient Days*, New York: The Dial Press, 1971, Greek text p. 48; English, p. 49. My translation is slightly more literal than theirs: they have "We who serve Art," which defines a relationship between craftsman and craft that the Greek expresses only with a genitive.

Cavafy writes: "I neither attained you, nor will I attain you / Ever, I suppose. A few words, a coming close / Like in the bar yesterday, / And nothing else. / It hurts, I admit. But we of Art / Sometimes with an intensity of mind, and certainly only / For a brief hour, create pleasure / Which seems, a phantasm, nearly solid." Here *emeis tes Tekhnes,* we of art, that is, the *tekhniteis,* create (*demiourgoumen*) matter (*hylike*).

In "Thus" (*Etsi,* tr. by Keeley and Savidis as "The Photograph"),[72] the poet looks at a pornographic picture he has secretly purchased and wonders what a vulgar life the boy must lead, what a cheap soul he must have. But twice he praises his dream-like face, and concludes the body was made for Hellenic love, and, the last line proclaims, "Thus for me you remain and my poetry pronounces you" (*Etsi gia mena meneis kai se leg' he poiesis mou*). The demotic "Thus" of the line, bearing the weight of the title-word of the poem, marks the point at which the poet makes his declaration. This declaration should be a logical conclusion of the foregoing, since "thus" introduces it, but in a way it is a departure. Cavafy was too much a Hellenist to be persuaded that the figure in the picture represented the love of Socrates or Alexander. It is his art that must uplift and transform it: belonging to *tekhne,* he is the demiurge whose *poiesis* speaks (*legei*: cf. Logos!) another reality into being. This poet deepens the past from which Cavafy's memory will construct an imperishable monument. In some poems it is only the bygone years of his youth he searches; but here, to invest the degraded picture with the dignity, no, the glory he wants, he must soar millennia back, into the pre-Christian heritage of the Hellenes, for whom homosexuality was not only licit, but the norm, the love of noble souls. Cavafy is the master of such time travel. Perhaps such tours de force of recovery of lost time are the special province of the homosexual writer, who has not the renewing present and serial immortality of a family, of new youth spawned—for vitality he must resurrect a boy frozen in the past.

The fleeting glimpse of beauty, impossible love, and, in the case of the Alexandrian poet, memory in old age, are the sorrow of loneliness and loss. This suffering, this mockery of our state, is what the real

---

[72]*Passions and Ancient Days,* pp. 36-37.

Demiurge has called into being by His Logos, and our decaying bodies are the *Hyle*—the material primordial stuff—molded by His *Tekhne*. Is it any wonder that the Gnostics declared the God of Creation a sadist and the author of all evil? So the poet rebels, storming Heaven and robbing God of His attributes. Now his is creative power, and word, and art, and matter to shape, in the only realm in which man has power: his mind and its language. The result, *poiesis*, literally "making," is an immortal voice creating an unchanging beauty. Constantine Cavafy—an old man nodding off in a bar in the port city of Egypt, ignored by the young things. Greek Alexandria—a dream of the past to be swept away by Arab nationalism, not long after Tourian's cosmopolitan Constantinople was to end. But Cavafy's Alexandria is better and more real in his poems than the city that stands; and without his living verse Greece would be less than alive—with it, her wounds are healed and past losses are restored. Antioch, Alexandria, and Byzantium become Greek again, the Sirens' song is heard, and the sun caresses the lovely archaic limbs cleansed of shame.

Now Bedros, at a lake at dusk, sees a woman, forbidden to him by time—by the swiftness of her passage—by the walls of her coffin-like closed carriage, by her veil and Muslim faith, and by the propriety of the day. But there is more to the distance between idea and reality, conception and creation, potency and existence, than these shadows. Cavafy at twenty, and for years after, tried the sensual loves he would later recollect (though not, I think, in tranquillity) and refashion. Bedros at twenty had never loved and never would: he saw a certain, soon grave before him, and in his pure and mourning solitude invented in these words that enable me to hear him now, a nuptial rite of love and resurrection like that of "With Her" in which the stars themselves and nature play. The loneliness of impending death, rather than the pariah-hood of homosexuality, fuelled his burning sorrow. But the cosmic reach of his imagery, which Cavafy—maturer, less lyrical—does not permit himself to employ, has something of Whitman, of the "Song of Myself" in it, an edge of extravagance in rebellion expressed in the scale of the poem's landscape.

*Fire*, snapped from the *rib* of love, which is snuffed out and seems as though it will ignite: Eve came from Adam's rib; but his first wife had been Lilith, who became a demon. In Armenian myth, Lilith is named Al, as we have seen, the crimson she-devil (or cherub!). She was a creature of *fire*: since Adam was of flesh, they could not mate. God saw Adam's frustration and made Eve from his rib.[73] The jealous, abandoned Al has hated womankind ever since, bringing red fever to mothers abed with child. Tourian has taken Eve's creation and Al's nature and fused them into a woman, but one of fire: to embrace her is to be consumed. But that death, if love be a part of it, is resurrection.

"The Turkish Woman" continues the theme of a fleeting encounter that Tourian had treated several years earlier in another, undated poem, "The Armenian Woman" (*Hayuhin*), Sevak, pp. 92-93:

ՀԱՅՈՒՀԻՆ

Աշնան մէջ էր, երեկոյ մը
Վերադարձիս յԻւսկիւտար,
օդը պարզ էր, հողմը՝ մեղմիկ,
Ծովուն ջուրերն ալ՝ հանդարտիկ։

Շոգենաւին սարաւանդը
Նըստած անկիւն մ'առանձնակի՝
Ուշադրութեամբ ես նոյն օրուան
Լըրագիրները կարդայի։

Մէկ մ'ալ յանկարծ սանդուխէն
Վեր ելնելու ոտնաձայն մը
Շըփոթեց զիս և աչերս
Դարձուցի դէպ յայն կողմը։

Հայուհի մ'էր վեր ելնողն,
Բարձրահասակ և գեղադէմ,
Անցաւ մօտէս նէ սիգաճեմ,

[73]See Manuk Abełyan, "Armenian Folk Religion," in *Erker*, VII, Erevan: Arm. Acad. Sci., 1975, p. 95; and J. R. Russell, *Zoroastrianism in Armenia*, Harvard Iranian Series 5, Cambridge, MA, 1987, ch. 14, with refs.

Նստաւ անկիւն մ'ինձ դէմ առ դէմ։

Ո՜հ, կարծես թէ նէ երկնային
Զրուարթուն մ'էր վար իջած՝
Լոյս սփռելու, սէր բուրելու,
Խռովելու սրտերն այրած։

Այլ չըգիտեմ թէ ինչո՞ւ
Կրկին աչերըս յառած՝
Իմ թերթիկիս վըրայ միշտ՝
Սիրտս էր ամբողջ խըռոված։

Մինչև մէկ մ'ալ նաւաստին
Խռպոտ ձայնով մը գալով մօտ,
Ըսաւ, «Հասանք յՒւսկիւտար,
Ալ ի՞նչ նստեր ես դու հոտ»։

Վեր վերցուցի աչերըս,
Ոչ ոք տեսի մէջ նաւին.
Մինակ էինք երկուքնիս,
Մէկ մ'ես, մէկ մ'ալ... նաւաստին։

*The Armenian Woman*

It was in autumn, one evening
When I was returning to Scutari:
The weather was clear; the breeze, gentle;
And the waters of the sea were calm.

On the foredeck of the ferry
Seated in a corner, alone,
Attentively I was reading
The newspapers of the day.

Then suddenly the sound of the step
Of one ascending on the stair
Disturbed me and I turned

My eyes that way.

An Armenian woman was the one coming up,
Tall of stature and lovely of face.
She passed by me with haughty gait
And sat in my corner, face to face.

Oh, you would have thought her a heavenly
Angel come down
To spread light, perfume the air with love,
Bewilder burning hearts.

I still do not know why
I again fixed my eyes
On my paper for the rest of the time:
My heart was so confused.

Till then the sailor
Coming by with harsh voice
Said "We've reached Scutari.
Why are you still sitting there?"

I raised my eyes.
There was no one on the ferry.
We two were all alone:
I the one, and the other... the sailor.

Sevak notes (pp. 286-287) that Kevork Pambukjian, the secretary of the archive of the Armenian Patriarchate of Constantinople, placed at his disposal Fr. Hmayag Ekserjian's article "Bedros Tourian's manuscript," published in the 1930s in *Aztarar* and preserved in the archive of T'oros Azadian. Ekserjian received the MS. of *Hayuhin* from Dikran Atamian in 1893 and was able to publish it only at the last minute in a few copies of his biography of the poet. Atamian gave the MS. to Yeghishe Tourian, as it seems, for Hagop Oshagan mentions the MS. found its way to Jerusalem, where he saw it, with *Sirets'i k'ez*—both in unrevised drafts (*Hamapatker arewmtahay grakanutʿean,* vol. 2, Jerusalem, 1953, p. 383n.). Chobanian considered the poem "an utter triviality" (*gadarelabes ch'nch'in pan*). Dikran Arp'iarian, writing in *Masis* no. 3966, 1892, p. 178, describes the circumstances of the poem's composition, worth quoting even though he was probably guided by the content of the text more than by an explanatory narrative of Tourian's:[74] "He wrote this poem on the steamship while travelling from one shore to the other and seated opposite a beautiful woman whose appearance exerted upon him a magnetic attraction. The timid youth ... wanted to speak with her through the tendrils of his heart; so he extracted pen and paper from his pocket and began to compose a poem ... but before he could finish the verse, the ship reached the dock; and while he still sought rhymes, his head hunched over, the lovely stranger had already vanished into the multitude of the ugly and disembarked." One recalls the on-the-spot *T'rk'uhin.*

As to the title of the poem, Eduard Kolanjian asserted in the journal *Luys* (Constantinople, 1908, no. 18, p. 605 n.) that it is not Tourian's own and the woman wasn't Armenian, either! Chobanian in his biography, p. 25, mentions that Tourian "in the springtime of his life" wrote a poem to a Turkish woman quite unlike the one that bears the title *T'rk'uhin*; and he cites one stanza, which is the fifth of *Hayuhin.* The former poem could be printed in 1893 only with a title consisting of three asterisks, since many Turks would then have regarded a love poem dedicated by a Christian to a Muslim as an offense. It is possible Tourian himself changed titles around; but the nationality of the beautiful stranger seems to have become part of her mystery.

What seemed banal and trivial to Chobanian may strike the contemporary reader, better attuned to the innovations in poetry since the nineteenth century, as refreshingly taut and crisply realistic. The poet has employed the vernacular tongue to evoke a vernacular experience

---

[74]Շոգենաւին մէջ, ափ յափոյ գրած է այս ոտանաւորը, անծանօթ գեղուհւոյ մը հանդէպ, որուն տեսքը մագնիսացուցած էր պինքը։ Երկչոտ երիտասարդն...կ'ուզէ սրտին թելերովը խօսիլ անոր հետ, թուղթ ու գրիչ կը հանէ գրպանէն և կ'սկսի քերթել։ ...դեռ ոտանաւորը չ'աւարդած, շոգենաւը նաւամատոյց հասած էր, ու մինչ ինք՝ գլխահակ վերջին յանգերը կը փնտռէր, անծանօթ գեղուհին՝ տգեղներու բազմութեան մէջ աներևոյթ եղած ու դուրս ելած էր արդէն։

readily recognizable to anyone who has spent his adolescence in a great city: being flustered at the apparition of a beautiful stranger on a ferry or bus or subway train whom one is unlikely to see again.

The English cannot reproduce the ironic ending: Tourian expected (and makes us expect) to see the Armenian woman—*hayuhin*—but she has vanished: instead there is the rhyming *navastin*, "sailor."[75] The poem requires little comment, save that in Armenian it is as casually conversational and urban as in English, and thus quite different from the heightened, densely lyrical style of most of his other work. From the standpoint of modernist poetry it holds up very well, though at the time it was written it would probably have been regarded as untried and choppy. Though it may foreshadow "The Turkish Woman" in very general terms, it is clearly a completely different sort of poem altogether—and maybe a better one.

---

[75]To a modern reader this scene will appear overtly suggestive, recalling perhaps Paul Cadmus' cheery painting of 1934 "The Fleet's In!" where sailors and male and female New Yorkers prepare to enjoy a polymorphous encounter in Riverside Park. On the painting and its reception, see David Leddick, *Intimate Companions: A Triography of George Platt Lynes, Paul Cadmus, Lincoln Kirstein, and Their Circle*, New York: St. Martin's Press, pp. 47-49; and especially the detailed study by Richard Meyer, *Outlaw Representation: Censorship and Homosexuality in Twentieth-Century American Art*, New York: Oxford University Press, 2002, pp. 37-59. Sailors and sex of all kinds always go together; so the replacement of *hayuhi* by the rhyming *navasti* seems more than ironic—unless Tourian was entirely naïve.

**24. "With Her"** (*Nera hed*), 1871 (Sevak, pp. 57-59)

**Text.**

ՆԵՐԱ ՀԵՏ

Համբոյր մ'առի ներանէ,
Համբո·յր մ'անհուն գորովի,
Երբ կարմիր շողք մարէին
Հորիզոնին վերևի։

Ձեռքըս տարաւ կուրծին՝ հոն
Սիրոյ երկին մ'որոտար.
Թոշնեցայ գիրկն ես իբրև
Համբոյր մ'անհուն, դալկահար։

Նէ պ'իս իր քով նըստեցուց
Գորգի վըրայ դալարեայ.
Հուսկ ճաճանչ մը կ'պլպլար
Ներա դիմացը վըրայ։

Թոթովեցի... դողացի...
Առի համբոյր անհամար.
«Խօսի·նք» ըսաւ— ո·հ, խօսի·լ,
Հատնիլ է լոկ ինձ համար։

Աչերու բոցն երբ մարի,
Դադրի տըրոփն երբ սրտին,
Լոկ այն ատեն հարկ է որ
Անպօր շուրթեր խօսին։

Հուր հորիզոնն մարեցաւ,
Երկինքն աստղեր փթթեցան,
Համբոյր մ'առի դարձեալ ես
Ց'անուն աստեղց ցիրեցան։

Նէ թողուց որ վարսքն ապատ
Սիւքը դէպ յ'իս բերելով
Միշտ հովահրէ բըըընկած
Ճակատըս պով բոյրերով։

Ո·հ, այն ժամը ոսկեզօծ
Անշուշտ սահած, թըռած է
Ճակատագրին անողորմ
Սև ձեռքերէն երկաթէ։

Մեր համբոյրներն պահեցին
Տերևները խարշափմամբ,
Եւ շողերու տըւին շուք
Աստղերն երկնից այն անամպ։

Ձեռք վերցուցինք աստղերուն,
Սէր ուխտեցինք իրարու,
Դողդըղացին աստղերն ալ
Մեր երդումէն ահարկու։

Լըսեց երկինք մեր ջերմ ուխտ,
Աստղեր սրսկեց ի գորով,
Բնութիւնն եղաւ պըսակիչ,
Մեզ պըսակեց աստղերով...։

**Translation.**

*With Her*

I took a kiss from her,
A kiss of endless tenderness
When the red rays were dying
On the horizon high.

She guided my hand to her bosom:
Love's heaven thundered there.
In her embrace I wilted

As a kiss, endless, wan.

She made me sit beside her
On the carpet of green:
A last sunflare blazed
Upon her face.

I stammered ... I shook ...
Innumerable kisses I took:
She said, "Let us speak." Oh, to speak
Means only to expire for me.

When the fire of the eyes is extinguished,
When the heart will cease to beat
Only then is it required
That the strengthless lips should speak.

The horizon of fire was extinguished,
The heavens blossomed with stars,
I took a kiss once more
In the name of the wide-scattered stars.

She let her tresses free:
The breeze bearing them to me
Ever fan my burning
Brow with cool perfumes.

Oh, that gold-leafed hour
Has slid away for certain, flown
From ruthless fortune's
Hands, iron, black.

The leaves by their sussurus
Our kisses kept,
And as the splendor to their rays
That unbeclouded sky's stars gave.

We raised up our hands towards the stars,
We swore to each other our love,
And the stars, too, were atremble
At our tremendous vow.

Heaven heard our promise fervent
And showered stars in mercy down.
Nature it was who married us;
The stars, our nuptial crown.

**Commentary.**

The poem was first printed as "A Night" (*Kisher me*) in the Constantinople paper *Yep'rad* ("Euphrates") on 11 Dec. 1871. The only significant variant reading is in line 10, where instead of a carpet of green the lovers are seated *pazmots'i vra togharyats'*, on a wobbly couch—or, if the setting is outdoors, a rickety bench perhaps. In the heroic Arsacid era this article of furniture was the seat for the *bazm*, or royal feast; but by the nineteenth century all it evokes is a tawdry seduction on the sofa. Fortunately, this reading was rejected in future editions and the lovers are situated on the grass.

It begins at dusk: the verb *marel*, of which Tourian is fond, is repeated to signify the dying of the day and of the light of the eyes. The sunset is a vivid, even lurid, red; and the girl's face is lit up by a final blaze—the poet employs the word *jajanch'*, "sunburst," the term used for the round, rayed reliquary of precious metal kept on the altars of Armenian churches. This ostensorium might ostensibly signify the climax of their kissing, and in the next line the girl, who is very much the active one of the pair, invites the poet to go a step further—to talk. But talk, he protests, would kill him. Only after death should one speak. And Tourian seems to be delicate and passive as a girl: death is his powerful, mastering lover.

1. The Sahilbent, the first steam ferryboat of the Shirket-i Hayriye's Bosphorus line, which was launched in 1851, the year of Tourian's birth (from Zeynep Celik, *The Remaking of Istanbul: Portrait of an Ottoman City in the Nineteenth Century*, Berkeley and Los Angeles: University of California Press, 1986, p. 85, pl. 52).

Tourian's poem "The Armenian Woman" and his prose-poem commemorating the 1863 Constitution were both inspired by ferry-crossings.

2. A view of Scutari (Üsküdar) (from Edmondo de Amicis, *Constantinople*, Paris, 1883, p. 381). The shore of the Bosphorus is clearly visible in the engraving: Tourian used to look out over the water to Constantinople.

3. The Karaca Ahmet cemetery in Scutari (from Edmondo de Amicis, *Constantinople*, Paris, 1883, p. 385). The towering cypresses of his home are a central image in Tourian's lyrics.

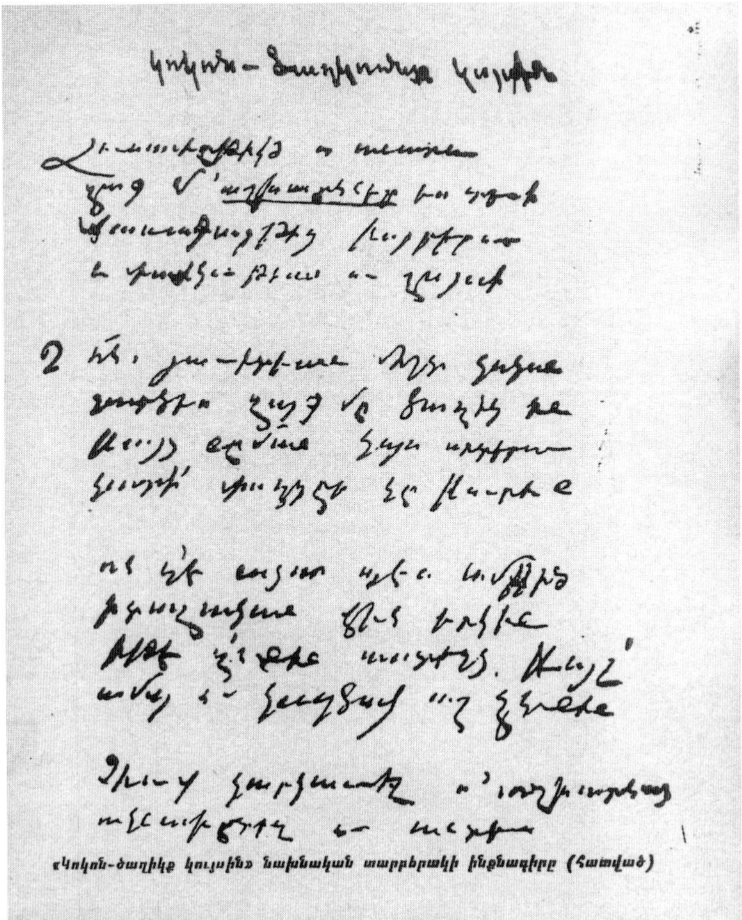


4. Tourian's draft of the poem "The Rosebud: Flowers of the Maiden."

Ἀπόδειξις πληρωμῆς ταξειδίου διὰ μίαν ὥραν ἁμάξης μὲ δύο ἵππους
3/4
Μεδζιδιὲ

Reçu pour une heure de Voiture a deux chevaux
3/4
Medjidiè

No. de la Voiture

Numéro
235 173

Date
4 OCT.

5. Metropolitan ephemera of Tourian's era: a one-hour parking receipt for a two-horse carriage, Constantinople, 4 October 1876.

The text is in, clockwise from top left, Greek, French, Armeno-Turkish, and Ottoman Turkish. The languages used reflect the cosmopolitan character of the city.

Courtesy of Mr. Mihran Adman, Long Island, New York.

6. Clockwise from left, the wonder-working image of the Ch´arkhap´an Surp Astvadzadzin ("Evil-Defeating Holy Theotokos"), Balat; a ten-para voucher of Tourian's parish church, Surp Garabed (St. John the Forerunner), Scutari; and a view of the altar of the church.

Courtesy of Mr. Berj Fenerci, Montréal, Canada.

7. There are no known photographs of Bedros Tourian, nor any picture of the poet made during his lifetime. These two pictures, from boyhood and early manhood, of Tourian's cousin Ghevont (1879-1933)—who was ordained an Archbishop and was murdered in New York City by members of the Dashnaktsut'iun—may afford some idea of how Bedros might have looked.

8. A horse-drawn araba, "carriage," with veiled Turkish ladies inside: perhaps the kind that inspired Tourian's poem "The Turkish Woman" (from Albert Smith, *A Month at Constantinople*, London, 1851, p. 75).

ԹՐՔՈՒՀԻՆ

ԻՄ ՄԱՀԸ

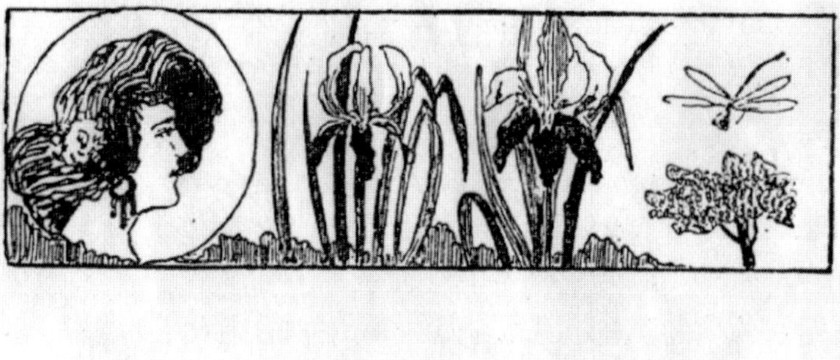

ՀԾԾԻՒՆՔ

9.-11. Illustrations from the Constantinople 1922 edition of Tourian's poems for (top to bottom) "The Turkish Woman,""My Death," and "Whispers."

THE WEDDING

12. Zabelle Boyajian's illumination (in her anthology *Armenian Legends and Poems*, London and New York, 1916) of the scene of the marriage of King Artaxias and Princess Sat′enik, from the History of the Armenians of Movses Khorenats′i with the fragmentary epic verses in Classical Armenian, Տեղ ոսկի տեղայր ի փեսայութեանն Արտաշիսի՝ տեղայր մարգարիտ ի հարսնութեան Սաթինկան։ "Rain of gold poured down when Artashes was groom; pearls rained when Sat′enik was bride." Tourian loved the epic and its imagery and employed them in his lyrics.

13. Albrecht Dürer's engraving Melencolia, I. The Romantics, especially Gérard de Nerval, were inspired by Dürer and by other artistic renderings of saturnine mood. They adopted the ancient, tragic image of the artist as a melancholic brooding beneath the rays of a black sun. Tourian, the Armenian Romantic, seems to have read Nerval, for he appropriates the latter image in a letter.

Պ. Դուրյանի տաղերի Ա տետրի շապիկի վերջին էջը՝
հեղինակի ձևավորմամբ

14. A sketch by Tourian in his first manuscript Notebook of cover art for a collection of his poems: on his deathbed, he implored his friends to publish the volume. On the left is a seraph, whose head is perhaps a self-portrait of the poet, with a lyre surmounted by two Crosses. On the right is a volume with the inscription Պ. Դուրեան, ՏԱՂՔ "B. Tourian, POEMS."

**25. "Murmurs"** (*Drdunchk'*), 1871 (Sevak, pp. 60-62)

**Text.**

ՏՐՏՈՒՆՋՔ

Է՜հ, մնաք բարով, Աստուած և արև,
Որ կը պըլպըլաք իմ հոգւոյս վերև…։
Աստղ մ'ալ ես կ'երթամ յաւելու երկնից,
Աստղերն ի՞նչ են որ, եթէ ո՜չ անբիծ
Եւ թշուառ հոգւոց անէծք ողբագին,
Որք թըռին այրել ճակատն երկնքին.
Այլ այն Աստուծոյն՝ շանթերո՜ւ արմատ՝
Յաւելուն պէնքերն ու կարդերն հըրատ…։
Այլ, ո՜հ, ի՞նչ կ'ըսեմ… շանթահարէ զ'իս,
Աստուա՜ծ, խոկն հըսկայ փշրէ հիւլէիս,
Որ ժպըրհի ձգտիլ, սուզիլ խորն երկնի,
Ելնել աստղերու սանդուղքն անալի…։
Ողջո՜յն քեզ, Աստուած դողդոջ էակին,
Շողին, փըթիթին, ալւոյն ու վանկին,
Դու որ ճակտիս վարդն և բոցն աչերուս
Խըլեցիր թրթռումս շրթանց, թռիչն հոգւոյս,
Ամպ տըւիր աչացս, հեք տվւիր սրտիս,
Ըսին մահուան դուռն ինձ պիտի ժպտիս,
Անշուշտ ինձ կեանք մը կազմած ես ետքի,
Կեանք մ'անհուն շողի, բոյրի, աղօթքի,
Իսկ թէ կորնչի պիտի իմ հուսկ շունչ
Հոս մառախուղի մէջ համր անշըշունջ,
Այժմէն թո՜ղ որ շանթ մ'ըլլամ դալկահար,
Պլլըւիմ անուանդ մռնչեմ անդադար,
Թող անէծք մ'ըլլամ քու կողըդ խըրիմ,
Թող յորջորջեմ քեզ «Աստուած ոխերիմ»։

Ո՜հ, կը դողդոջեմ, դժգոյն եմ, դժգո՜յն,
Փըրփըրի ներսըս դըժոխքի մ'հանգոյն…։
Հառաչ մ'եմ հեծող նոճերու մէջ սև,

Թափելու մօտ չոր աշնան մէկ տերև…։
Ո՛հ, կայծ տըւէ՛ք ինձ, կայծ տըւէ՛ք, ապրի՛մ.
Ի՞նչ, երապէ վերջ գրկել ցուրտ շիրի՛մ…
Այս ճակատագիրն ի՛նչ սև է, Աստուած,
Արդեօք դամբանի մրուրո՞վ է գծուած…։
Ո՛հ, տըւէ՛ք հոգւոյս կրակի մի կաթիլ,
Սիրել կ՛ուզեմ դէռ ւ՛ապրիլ ու ապրիլ.
Երկնքի աստղե՛ր, հոգւոյս մէջ ընկէ՛ք,
Կայծ տըւէ՛ք, կեա՛նք՝ ձեր սիրահարին հէք։
Գարունն ո՛չ մէկ վարդ ճակտիս դալկահար՝
Ո՛չ երկնի շողերն ժըպիտ մ՛ինձ չ՛են տար։
Գիշերն միշտ դագաղս, աստղերը՝ ջահեր,
Լուսինն յար կու լայ, խուզարկէ վըհեր։
Կ՛ըլլան մարդիկ, որ լացող մը չ՛ունին,
Անոր համար Նա դըրաւ այդ լուսին.
Եւ մահամերձն ալ կ՛ուզէ երկու բան,
Նախ՝ կեա՛նքը, վերջը՝ լացող մ՛իր վըրան։
Ի զո՛ւր գըրեցին աստղերն ինծի "սէ՛ր"։
Եւ ի զո՛ւր ուսուց բուլբուլն ինձ "սիրել"։
Ի զո՛ւր սիւքեր "սէ՛ր" ինձ ներշնչեցին,
Եւ զիս նորատի ցուցուց ջինջ ալին,
Ի զո՛ւր թաւուտքներ լըռեցին իմ շուրջ,
Գաղտնապահ տերևք չ՛առին երբէ՛ք շունչ,
Որ չը խըռովին երազքըս վըսեմ,
Թոյլ տըւին որ միշտ ըզնէ երազեմ,
Եւ ի զո՛ւր ծաղկունք, փըթիթնե՛ր գարնան,
Միշտ խնկարկեցին խոկմանցըս խորան…
Ո՛հ, նոքա ամենքը զ՛իս ծաղրեր են…
Աստուծոյ ծաղրն է Աշխարհ ալ արդէն…։

**Translation.**

*Murmurs.*[76]

Farewell, then, God and sun
Who coruscate above my soul.
I go, too, to add to the heavens a star—
What else are the stars but unblemished
And ill-fated souls' plaintive curses
That wing to burn on heaven's brow?
But for that God, root of lightnings,
They multiply weapons and martial trim ...
But what am I saying? Strike me down with your bolt,
God, shatter my clay's titan ponderings
Who impiously strive to plunge to the depths of the sky,
To ascend the heaven's unwavering stair.
Hail to Thee, God of the quivering being
Of the beam and tendril, wave and syllable,
You, rose of my brow and fire of mine eyes
Who extracted the flutter from my lips, took flight from my soul,
And set upon my eyes a cloud, gave my heart sighs:
They said, you will smile on me at death's door,
And surely you have shaped a life for me beyond,
A boundless life of rays and fragrances and prayer.
But if my last breath is lost
Here in the mute whisperless murk,
Then henceforth let me be a pallid lightning bolt
Writhing round your name and roaring without cease,
Piercing your side may I be a curse,
Let me proclaim you a "jealous God."

---

[76]I had chosen this English equivalent with some trepidation about its accuracy; Tchéraz preferred French "Murmures" for Arm. *Hdzdzyunk'*, No. 17; he entitles this poem "Plaintes." Susan Barba notes that the sound of English "Murmurs" also better captures the mood conveyed by the sound of the Armenian title.

O, I shake, discolored, pale!
My insides foam like very hell ...
Among the black, moaning cypresses I am a wail,
A dry leaf in autumn about to fall ...
O give me a spark, a spark! that I may live.
What? After dreaming to embrace the frigid grave?
How black is this destiny, O God—
Can it be it was traced by the tomb's filmy dregs?
O give a drop of fire to my soul!
I want to love still, to live on and on.
Stars of heaven, fall into my soul!
Life, lend an ember to your unlucky lover.
The spring spares no rose for my yellowing brow;
The rays of heaven smile not on me.
Night is ever my casket; the stars are torches
And the moon cries continually, scouring the abyss.
There are men who have none to lament them:
For them He established that moon,
For one close to death wants two things:
Life, first, then someone to lament him at the end.
The stars inscribed "love" for me in vain!
In vain did the nightingale teach me to "love."
In vain did the breezes breath "love" into me,
The clear wave a stripling display me.
In vain hushed the woods roundabout me,
The secret-sharing leaves not daring to breathe
Lest they disturb my high dream,
And let me dream her endlessly.
And in vain did the flowers new sprouted in spring
Cense my meditations' altar,
Oh, they all of them mocked me—
*God's mocking laugh is the World itself then.*

**Commentary.**

Above the first edition of the poem appeared the editor's note in parentheses, *Merts i mah krvadz*, "Written near death" (these words are not in Tourian's own manuscript). Several words in the text have been the subject of argument for over a century. Commenting on the word God in line 1, the critic Hagop Oshagan wrote in his *Chrestomathy of Armenian Literature,* Jerusalem, 1942, pp. 179-80,[77] "This word in this line is a bit strange. It is likely that the poem was written at night and begins with the starry sky seen from the window, so that half the word *Asdvadz,* God—*asd-* forms the body of the letters of the word *asdgh,* star. To the stars, as to the sun, the farewell is understandable (the whole poem is a feverish, living body's plaint to fire and the sun). Maybe the poet was thinking of stars but wrote God instead, which was just as powerful a reality dominating his thought at that moment. Such a state happens of writing just the opposite of what one intended when one's mind is afflicted by great panic. If we are to be forgiven for reading this line as 'Well, good bye, stars and sun,' the illogic is cleared up, since the main word of the next line, *blblal,* is explanatory of the light of stars (it is a verb of which Tourian is fond). If we keep in mind the addition of another star in the line after that, the supposition above appears more than probable. This way the contradiction is resolved that one encounters in saying farewell to God. A man does not say goodbye to somebody towards whom he's headed. Of course this explanation still does not allow us boldly to correct the poet's words." Janashian commented that Oshagan might have seen certain editions, where *asdgh* does appear in place of *Asdvadz.* The poet Vagharshak Norents' agreed that the emendation was both logical and inadmissible— later on he decided the emendation was altogether superfluous. Sevak asserts that no actual collection of Tourian's works has such an emendation, but Diaspora schoolbooks could have introduced it. V. Partizuni, writing in the Erevan literary weekly *Grakan T'ert'* on 5 March 1966, suggests a plural, *Asdgher,* could have been misread as *Astvadz*—but this is beyond the bounds of possibility, and Arshag Chobanian, who addressed the question of misreading from the manuscript, does not suggest this one at all.

---

[77]Cited by Sevak, with the other Armenian critical notices here, pp. 262-266. The translations are mine.

In my view, Oshagan's quibble about the word God is regrettable in its quiddity—what is worse, it seems that the critic, who is rightly venerated as one of the very greatest scholars of modern Armenian literature, if also as one of the most vituperative and eccentric, has somehow missed much of the message of the poem. Tourian addresses God throughout his verses. At first, he is frightened of his own bitter impiety, and asks Him to strike him. This Romantic pose owes something, perhaps, to the popular Lamartine, in whose ode to Byron one finds the declaration, "J'ai blasphémé ce Dieu, ne pouvant le connaître,/ Et ma voix, se brisant contre ce ciel d'airain..." ("I've blasphemed against this God, unable to comprehend Him,/ And my voice, breaking against this brass heaven [cannot stop destiny].") Then he muses on the trite bromides his religious countrymen (who remind one of Job's friends) have fed him about the afterlife, and, right in the upper middle right of the poem—where Christ's heart, iconically, would be (cf. my discussion of Tourian's cruciform "The Child to the Cross")—is the shocking, horrible twenty-fifth line, *T'ogh anedzk' m'ellam k'u goghk'et kherim*, "Let me be a curse piercing your side." Tourian becomes the *keghart*—the lance of Longinus stabbing the crucified Christ to death, in an utter reversal of Armenian Christian faith, for which that lance is a precious reliquary kept in the treasury of the Mother Cathedral of the nation, in the holy city of Echmiadzin. And it is right after this that Tourian turns from God almost altogether, addressing the created world in the second stanza, with the italicized summation that it is but an expression of the Divine sneer. When Tourian addresses God in line one, then, it would be intolerably pedestrian to regard his farewell as literal (*"Ts'desut'yun!" "Noren hramets'ek'!"*—"Au revoir" "Do come again," door slams, sound of car keys, God the father turns back from the entry hall towards the kitchen, where the Virgin Mary is washing up). It is a farewell to the idea of a loving God, a declaration that God is not good and is not worthy of worship;[78] and

[78]When I was a student at Oxford in 1975, I heard Professor Robert C. Zaehner of All Souls, a chain-smoking, gravelly-voiced, sarcastic scholar of Indian and Iranian religions (who looked as though he were in the last stages of physical decrepitude: he died—in the Cornmarket, it was said—a few weeks later) introduce a saccharine disquisition on Sufism by Professor Annemarie Schimmel—who after a quite successful early career as a graduate

it is a prelude to the rejection, in the second stanza, of earthly love, too, as all in vain.

---

student in Oriental studies in Nazi Germany had become the doyenne of things esoterically Islamic at Harvard. (Her enthused writings, brimming with *'eshq*, passionate love of God and sundry, say very little about Hitler as a part of Reality, nor do her published effusions about Turkey mention the fate of the Armenians there—in which the Kaiser had a hand. But if one wants to build a career around the idea of God as love, it is perhaps as well to gloss over inconvenient tragedies close to home.) Schimmel's lecture was delivered with hands clasped, eyes closed, and face turned heavenward, with all citations from the poets *verbatim*. It was quite a performance! Zaehner did not allow questions at the end of Schimmel's lecture, though, averring that mysticism brought out "the lunatic fringe." A fellow student told me of Zaehner's famous tutorial—generally limited, it was said, to comely young males—nothing terribly unusual in academia—on God. The system was that you wrote an essay every week on a different idea about Divinity. At the end of term, said the student, Zaehner would deliver a summation with his own Idea: "But I, my dear, I think God is a thug." His book, *The Savage God*, with its chapter "God: Mad or Bad?" presents a learned and entertaining review of the matter. Only man is vile, concluded the poet in a survey of the world; but then Nature, too, is red in tooth and claw. And that is just the world we can see. There are demons, and hell, too. After the Armenian and Jewish holocausts, with all the other sorts of suffering of sentient beings thrown in for good measure, one can hold, stubbornly, to the Old Time Religion (Zaehner's essay "Why not Islam?" is good on the most recent of these monotheisms, which answers imponderables with the dictum *bi-la kayf*, literally "With no 'How'")—*Credo quia absurdum!*—or choose atheism (from Raffi's petulant novels hectoring the Armenians to give up the Church and stop turning their cheeks, to Shahan Shahnur and others, this has been an honorable alternative in Armenian letters). Or one might consider the Older Time Religion of cosmic dualism, when the prophet of Armenia was Zradasht—Zarathushtra—and the Creator God Aramazd—Ahura Mazda—was thought to be entirely *good*, but not entirely *powerful* (Daniel Varuzhan and the young Ch'arents' liked Vahagn and the other pleasant divinities of the old pantheon). Theodicy is a knotty problem. Tourian comes closest to Zaehner's view in "Murmurs," but there is something of the love of Christ, too, in "The Child to the Cross." And—forget the prudence of Pascal's wager, which still reduces faith to a kind of *sauve qui peut*—I must agree only with F. M. Dostoyevsky, and out of sheer love cleave to the broken, derided man on the Cross who died for me—even if He was wrong. Even if He never rose from the dead. Even if the Father who forsook him never existed and does not exist.

I think support for the reading of the poem as an accusation against God is to be found also in Tourian's letter of 5 July 1871, written at Scutari, to his friend B. D. Atamian, on the death of their friend Vartan Lutfian (1851-1871).[79] (See also poem No. 36 here, which is a lament at Lutfian's grave.) The letter restates the relevant themes and wording of "Murmurs" quite unambiguously, and in the last line Tourian mentions the "conflagration, not a book" of his famous Lake reverie, as well; so I translate it here in full:

"Mourner!

Do not bury that boundless groan: let the heart's storm erupt... You had reminded me to scatter a bouquet of flowers on the ground heaped above his grave. I shed a hell of curses over God's name—haven't I done better [thereby]? Flowers fade, but my curse pierced God's side![80]

Ah, he loves—we loved—him. I am the lamp burning in his memory, I am the ocean of his grief, I am the chasm of his mourning, I am his tomb... No, I shall not scatter flowers over his sepulchre: the flower is cold and without feeling, but the tear pressed from my soul is hot. That will I shed, will I shed by the handful... The eyes in grieving are oceans of tears, those same that in pleasure are stars.

They piled cold earth over him, but we will embrace and keep, keep warm, keep always his memory in our moans...

You curse the world, my friend, but it is already accursed. The world must be either a sigh of the boredom of God (from the time when He dwelt in Chaos) or a tasteless joke of Hell ... Whatever the case, it is enough that it is a gateway into sorrow.

You inquire after my state. I'm sufficiently improved: I was in a bad way during the days I wrote this letter, and it greatly pained me to have agitated you. For the time being Dr. Kyatibian is still looking after

[79]Sevak, letter 5, pp. 164-165. See also Tourian's eulogy for Vartan Lutfian, and another letter to Atamian about him, in Part V of this book.

[80]On the lance, see discussion above. One is reminded of Rimbaud's uncannily similar curse, that Christ's wounds burst and bleed.

me. Ah, let me shock [*tghrtem*] God with a groan from the soul ... I've lapsed into the infinite, so I must be silent ...

Repose your hope in friendship—you say you impel me to greater grief, but where are my friends? ... Why are you so far away? ...

We should meet, lips to lips [*bedk' e vor shurt'n arr shurt'n desnvink'*] ... then you will see I am a conflagration [*hrteh*] ... Ah! I have so many things to say...

Au revoir,

B. Tourian."

Much ink has been spilt also in arguments about line 12, *Elnel asdgheru santughk'n anali* (Sevak corrects the last word to *ahali* "frightful"). Modern Armenian uses most often for the singular of "wave" the *plurale tantum, alik'*, with *-ner* added to form a plural; but Tourian uses *ali* as a singular, with Classical gen. pl. *alyats'* elsewhere. So *an-ali* means "without a wave" (as P. Ekserjian explained, *p'okhanag eselu arrants' alyats', vor alik' ch'uni*, "instead of saying without waves, or not having waves"). Janashian says *anali* is "a word with the meaning not susceptible of ascent, which Tourian created" (*Turyane horinvadz parr men e anelaneli imasdov*). Sevak, though he prints *ahali* in his edition, restates in the notes his support of *anali* from his *Grakan T'ert'* article of 1962, which is translated on pp. 329-335 from the reprint in his *Collected Works*. V. T'erzibashyan (*Petros Duryan*, Erevan, 1959, p. 162 n.) considers *anali* "one of those incomprehensible words of Tourian's that remains obscure till now" and adds, "it is a result of the erroneous reading of the manuscript: apparently the letter *h* was confused with *n*, since the two of them can in handwriting easily be mistaken for each other. So one must not read *anali*, which is a meaningless epithet, but *ahali*." I looked to Alice Stone Blackwell's lovely, and, on the whole, faithful translation, entitled "Complaints" (pp. 35-37, with the note "This poem and the next were written on successive days, a short time before Tourian's death"), but was disappointed to find she simply avoided the problem: "Thoughts of an atom in thy universe / Whose spirit dares defy its mortal bars, / And seeks to dive into the depths of heaven, / And climb the **endless** [emphasis mine—JRR] stairway of the stars." Zabelle C. Boyajian, (*Armenian Legends and Poems*, 1916, New York: Armenian General Benevolent Union reprint, 1958, pp. 82-83, "Complaints") has even less: "And e'en to climb to the stars has striven!"

The stairway to heaven is Jacob's ladder, which, tradition has it, stood on the *locus classicus* in every sense, Jerusalem. This vivid Biblical image became very important to the mystical systems of the three Abrahamic religions. The Jewish greater treatise on the heavenly mansions, *Hekhalot Rabbati*, a mystical work, describes a truly pious man as one "who has a ladder in his house" (ch. 15). There are seven such halls or mansions through which one passes before arriving at the divine throne, and the sixth has the appearance of a multitude of **waves**. The mystical traveller must be aware that the effect is produced by the radiance of the marble walls, and not cry "Water, water!" lest the angels deem him ignorant and unworthy to proceed.[81]

By the early Christian period or even before, the ladder had become a metaphor of mystical ascent; and later on it was to symbolize the acquisition of higher stages of knowledge, and even the soul itself. The angels ascending and descending were taken to represent different methods in philosophy. The Hebrew for "ladder" is *sullam*: Ethiopic translates it as *ma'ṭ reg*; and the latter word is borrowed by Arabic as *mi'rāj* : this word, which becomes English "mirage," means "ladder" but is used specifically to refer to the ascent of the Prophet Mohammed to Heaven following his ride on the magic steed Burāq from Mecca to "the further mosque" (*al-masjid al-aqṣā*, a place not specified in the *Qur'an*: the Muslims, with no little contempt for the Byzantines, who had left the place a waste, chose later as the site of al-Aqsa the Temple Mount in Jerusalem—where Jacob's Ladder had stood). In Islam, too, the word *mir'aj* came to be applied to mystical ascents generally,

---

[81]See Peter Schäfer, *Hekhalot-Studien*, Tübingen: Mohr, 1988, p. 245. So waves and ladder both find a place in one early schema of the ascent. Milton's *Paradise Lost* (3.499-522) envisions a ladder outside the wall of Heaven thus: "The stairs were such as whereon Jacob saw / Angels ascending and descending... / Each stair mysteriously was meant, nor stood / There alwayes, but drawn up to Heav'n sometimes / Viewless ..." The rungs here seem wavy, imbued with motion.

though there was a feeling that the Prophet's should be cherished as unique; so the Iranian Sufi Abu Yazid of Bistam was expelled from his home town for claiming to have had one.[82] On the eve of the revelation of Islam, St. John Climacus (whose book earned him his epithet, from Gk. *klimax*, "ladder") wrote at the monastery of St. Catherine on Mt. Sinai a manual for contemplatives consisting of thirty "steps" to spiritual perfection.[83] The ascent of souls up the ladder, with good angels helping the saved and devils tugging the condemned from its rungs, became a popular theme for illustration in manuscripts and on icons. There is an Armenian translation of the treatise of John, but it is relatively late, belonging to the Cilician period.

For Tourian in Constantinople, a city teeming with Greek Orthodox Christians, the image was as recognizable as the words "she's

---

[82]See A. Altmann, "The Ladder of Ascension," in *Studies in Mysticism and Religion presented to Gershom G. Scholem*, Jerusalem: Magnes Press, Hebrew University, 1967, pp. 1-32. The Hispano-Jewish mystical theologian Moshe ibn Ezra wrote a poem on illumination in faith, *Heqītsotī tənūmath ra'ayōnai*: "I wakened my thoughts from their sleep / That they force the passions of my baser soul, and my eyes, to slumber. / And I reviewed in my heart the cycles of time / That my ears hear future things. / Then knowledge recounts greatness to me, / Setting before me the miracles of God, my Rock, / And tells me profound mysteries / Till I think myself to live among the angels / And my intelligence have vision of the Almighty, / And I know God to be close to me, / Whose precious self is hidden treasure, / But in His works to my thought is revealed. / In my mortal flesh He has set light... / By that light I will search the chamber of wisdom / And ascend without a ladder to the garden of Eden (*bəlī sullām elē ginnath 'adēnai*)." Given Ibn Ezra's close acquaintance with Arabs, the final line seems to me to chide the Muslims, whose Prophet needed a ladder—Rabbinic and mystical Judaism enables the faithful to reach God mentally, without one.

[83] See Archimandrite Lazarus Moore, tr., St. John Climacus, *The Ladder of Divine Ascent*, London: Faber and Faber, 1959. The Persian mystic Farīd al-Dīn 'Aṭṭār, *Mantiq al-ṭayr* ("Conference of the Birds"), has precisely thirty birds, i.e., soul, set out on the quest to find the king of the birds, a magical creature called *Sīmorgh* who represents the Divine essence. The creature's name actually means "eagle"; but by popular etymology, Pers. *sī morγ*, "thirty birds" means the seekers themselves. The Kingdom of Heaven is within you. Nascent Muslim mystical practice and symbolism obvious drew from a rich Jewish, Christian, and Zoroastrian store—including the thirty rungs of Climacus.

climbing a stairway to heaven" (from the song by the rock band Led Zeppelin, "Stairway to Heaven") would be to any Englishman or American my age—but *anali,* which I render as "unwavering," makes the picture rich and strange. For what does he mean? That the ladder has no rungs; or the stairway, no steps—a chute or slide, a steep ramp that you can climb when gravity no longer holds you down? Or does he have the ripple and swell of a moving wave in mind (as elsewhere, including in this poem, when he mentions waves)? Surely he does not mean to say the stair is not an escalator (which did not yet exist, and anyway the stairs of one are unmoving in relation to one another), but then does he imagine a staircase on which the steps themselves move? Since there is no such stairway, except perhaps in the frustrating panic of a nightmare, then why negate the possibility to start with? Or is the image intended to be one of fixity, of a kind of existence where even waves are frozen—where water is solid? There is a precedent for the latter, again in Jewish mystical visions adopted by the Christians. R. Akiva and his companions traveled to heaven and saw water that is solid, like marble: St. Gregory of Narek elaborates this phantasmagoric image in a prayer whose repetition is meant to enable a celebrant of the Divine Liturgy physically to see light from Heaven descending.[84]

Tourian's murmurs of complaint echoed far beyond the grave. Three decades later, Daniel Varuzhan[85] wrote a poem with the same title, *Drdunchk'*. The complaint of his poem goes beyond Tourian's, though. He grieves for the fate of his nation, which has failed to heed his warnings and exhortations; and he appeals no longer to a Christian God, but to the abstract state of Nirvana.

---

[84]See J. R. Russell, "Armenian Spirituality: Liturgical Mysticism and Chapter 33 of the Book of Lamentation of St. Grigor Narekac'i," *REArm* 26 (1996-1997), pp. 427-439 (*AIS*, pp. 771-783).

[85]Taniel Krikori Chabukkarian, *nom de plume* Varuzhan, born at Brgnik', near Sebastia (Sivas), Western Armenia, 20 April 1884, arrested with 250 other Armenian artists, politicians, and intellectuals on the night of 24 April 1915 at Constantinople by the Ottoman Turkish Government and murdered in the Armenian Genocide on 26 August of the same year.

*Murmurs*

To Yeghia Demirjibashian.[86]

"My soul is sorrowful unto death."
—Jesus[87]

On this grievous evening, O Yeghia,
I come to pound upon the star-studded gates of your Nirvana.
You bore my sorrow; you can comprehend it,
My death-wishing gloom derided by men.
Only genius could give it a moment's relief.
And I have no wish—for an instant worthy of your love—
To enclose but the flicker of your immortality in my expired breast.
My life goes up the silent chimney; my death, to Nothingness as well.
When the Lord wished to share his heaven-rich treasure's store,
He gave the stars to talents; the Sun, to genius,
But I wished to tiara my vainglorious brow
With the shooting stars that sparkled for a second and then died,

---

[86]Yeghia Garabedi Demirjibashian, born 8 May 1851 at Constantinople—a contemporary of Tourian. He died there by suicide on 19 July 1908. See his essay on Bedros and Abp. Yeghishe Tourian, in the final chapter of this book. Demirjibashian was an educator, philosopher, and public servant, as well as a poet. He never actually went to India, but his poem "Nirvana" contains an epigraph attributed to the Buddha Sakyamuni: "My soul is entirely full of compassion for the sickness of the world," which Varuzhan seems to echo in his epigraph from the words of Christ. In "Nirvana," Demirjibashian leaves the shores of the Bosphorus on a spiritual quest that takes him through the Holy Land of Israel, on his way to Benares, skirting the Altai on the way. He beholds Siddhartha, "Maya, thy son of miraculous birth" (*Maya vortit hrashadzin*), and declares "from afar, Sakyamuni, you guide [the world] / to Nirvana from those bottomless deeps" (*i herusd, Sak'ia-Muni, tu vares / Nirvanayin ayn hanhadag i khorots'*), and prays "I desire this: the extinction of my ego" (*yes zayn ts'angam, zaneats'umn im yesin*) (see Yeghia Demirjibashian, *Erker*, Erevan: Sovetakan grogh, 1986, pp. 49-54). See pp. 177-78 above.

[87] Matthew 26.38. (Arm. Մատ. ԻԶ.38` Տրտում է ոգի իմ մինչև ի մահ։)

Died never to return, yet today I persist in believing
That of my slashed lyre-strings and marauder-picked remains
My Sorrow is left unconquered; and immortal, my Despair.

See! I come from the spring, from the roses' fatherland:
May once boisterously bloomed before my threshold.
At the lip of my white font my doves[88]
With red-passioned beaks in kisses entwined.
But unspeakable pain like a tombstone, black
Sealed my heart against the vernal sap
And of May's roses round my head there remained
A stabbing crown of thorns drawing blood from my brains.
You, O Indian, one day gripped by your genius' agony
In the lake of Moda[89] with fragrances brimming
Wished to vanish beneath the light-dripping pearls:
You never saw how all around the splendor
Of Nature laughed, the acacias on the shore
Snowing blossoms on the abysses over which they bent.
You did not hear the nightingale when she moistened her wing
And summoned you in passion from the enchantment of the deep
To the divine bacchanal beneath the Sun shooting darts of light.
You never pondered whether it's worth it to live at all,
To gaze at the stars, to meditate on God,
Whether it's worth it to give your heart to song and bequeath it then
To immortal ages—in a few simple chords strummed.
So, Yeghia, you can well understand
How awful it is to pass through life's springtime and go
With tears in your eyes alone,
Your coattails brushing the roses, touching your brow to the laurel
Only to carry away naught save the thievish nettles' stings.

---

[88]*Aghavniners esbidag avazanis yezerk'in*: This blends the images of the baptismal font (*awazan*), with its purity, and perhaps the white fountain, or Milky Fountain (*katʿnałbiwr*) of Armenian epic, where heroes came to drink to attain physical size and strength, and to bolster their reckless courage.

[89] Moda burnu is a locale in Constantinople.

Like you I sat on the bank of those lakes
Or sailed the pond of a perfumèd evening—
But, never drinking in the peace, I plumbed the deep
And begged my boat to be my coffin, to reach
The breast of the Unknown by a storm's savage breath.

Yet it was still worth living!.. and I assayed to love,
To cleave to another's breast to feel my heart's beating.
Did you, Yeghia, not do the same, when the Holy Woman came
to sit upon your Hindu mat (*p'ost*) and rest her head upon your knee,
And listen like an angel to your turbulent melodies?
And you, owl-eyed, perused the *Rig Veda*.
Surely you found her little head of greater grace
Than the lotus blooming at Maya's shining breast.
And when her waterfall of tresses spread
Upon your book, for certain they recalled to you
The deeply mystic susurrus of the forests in Hindustan.
But one day, too, She—tired of amazement
And of observing your mental flight into the infinite—was bored,
And failed to arrive to kiss the lofty forehead of the Sun.
Which soft turtle dove did rest the eagle's brood
Enfolded in her wings, bestowing living warmth,
Which woman's heart was able to give genius fortune?
Love and genius of the World twin shapers be,[90]
Tyrants are they, are at odds with the aim of felicity:
One, a storm of thoughts; the other, hearts' fire—
One creates stars; the other gives them flame,
Beneficent to the cosmos, yet rivals to each other,
With mutual blood the Great Ones they generate.
Oh, poet, how may I relate to you my love's tragic lay?

---

[90]*zuyk hastich'nern Ashkharhi*: *Astuac* (pron. *Asdvadz*), "God," is the one who—according to an Armenian folk etymology which may actually be right—*(h)asteacʿ* "created" and *hastateacʿ* "established" (<**hast-hasteacʿ*, a reduplicative form) the cosmos. By unsubtly encoding the Divine name into his line, Varuzhan sets his poetic Demiurge up in opposition to the Biblical God.

To remember it for me is to be new bloodied.
How to say that I once worshipped too a woman of magic beauty:
Above her tresses' flood with lyre of ten thousand strings
My fingers strummed love, streamed like molten wax of the honeybee.
A year's length submerged in her pupils' deeps
Drunken I spread wide my blood-bespattered wings
As wide as one may stretch them in infinity.
It was a whole year's labor in my cell
To tune my lyre's strings, head placed against my breast
My songs' great mysteries my heart's profundities to seek.
Then with her through the door ajar
A myriad of ages' springs smiled in,
Pungent roses of the past and sacred doves of ancient shrines[91]
Returning to my roof, in its sooty rafters
Diffusing the warm smells of their white nests.
The rustle of her dress already from the steps below
Made my blood bubble over, my heart race,
And for an instant I felt the approach of an angel[92]
To give tidings that I am earth's happiest being.
However, our passion promised immortality in vain:
From too much stroking the butterfly expired in my palm.
In vain at her bosom did I hide my battered head:
Within my breast I felt the halting of eternity.
In vain I betrayed to supple arms my pliant neck
And lost my head and worshipped her love's deceit.
Below the nectar-brimming cup I took from her round hand,
A viper crouching spitting death's poison through its fangs.
She betrayed, and covered her betrayal with a kiss;
That heart which I opened one day was locked by another key.
As she laid my head upon her knee she fixed her gaze

---

[91]*Isg serpeni dadragnern mehyannerun hinavurts'*: Arm. *mehean*, lit. "place of Mithra" is the word for a pre-Christian temple, and the allusion here is perhaps to the mixed sensuality and chastity of the customs surrounding Anatolian worship of Anahit-Aphrodite.

[92]*zevart'un*: the same word Tourian uses when he asks Love what she is.

Upon a stranger in her soul whom she did ponder.
And another day I—O moment grim as the agony of death—
Cried, fallen to her navel aglow—my doubt I cried.
I saw her belly leap with laughter, hidden and profane.
Upon my mouth the kiss she gave was another's kiss.
The heart pressed to my heart throbbed for another,
And, O horror! when she came surrendering to my arms,
I smelled on her body another bed's scent.
A clamor in my soul's waste sounded then—
And, Yeghia, its immortal echo is this poem.
The woman abandoned me forever, and her footfalls'
Derisive thud upon my grief receded from the lane.
In shock I flung myself from heart and cell.
April was bursting over my doorstep into flower:
Between cypresses, the broad cemetery road,
Perfumed by Mary's grass,[93] stretched out before my steps.
Then I heard a voice out of my life's ruin,
Saying, Go wander midst the mouldering bones—
What matters Spring, when your heart was not its swallow?
What matter roses, when they can but recall your wounds?
Go, surely you will find a hole ready dug,
And what woman would not hasten to pile the dirt upon you?
We live to die, but happy alone is he
Whom the fewest springtimes death hunts down.
Heeding that voice, I hastened towards the graves
But did not find an empty one in which to bury my weary head.
The martyrs had filled them all!
Maybe I was base, wanting but to live
For my own heart's sake, to fill it with joy
When it had already split open with the fire of my tears.
Perhaps fate for another had defined me
And my life's aim was for another's life.
And from my cross at the crucified Man I gazed

---

[93]Arm. *maremakhod* "Mary's grass" or *khngadzaghig* "frankincense flower," Tk. *Maryam otu*, Eng. Cat thyme.

As you, long suffering Seer, had done,
When like a sacrifice immured within the Mosque
You let flow from your lyre-striking fingers that caress the stars
Your heart's songs, nay, the seas of your heart
Towards your brothers consumed by fire in chains.
And so that you might bequeathe to future generations
A lyre atremble with grieving speech like the tremor of a storm,
You had anointed it long before with your genius' despair.
To the hopeless its sound is now a consoling sister.
Some find solace in it; others imitate—
But its sole power is to harmonize his song to your own:
He who feels his heart to be the axis of the universe,
Whose blood-drenched head touches Nirvana.
My need was devotion, and then I beheld
Beyond my own lacerations, deeper pains and wounds.
They were murdering the nation that with a hammer in its hand
Was shaping an age of marble upon these times of clay.
They my dejected heart steeled itself in lightnings
And my heart's desolation brimmed with storm.
My will, overcome by my pain, invigorated a pain-wracked other.
I sensed the nation that beat beneath my breast.
Oh! A God had come to dwell within my chaos then,
And into my deep furnace, which was barren of all egotistical loves,
He cast the immortal Idea, and in gold foaming forged—
And there was I, where men in soot-blackened hovels
Curse the morrow's light, which will flash freeze
In their famished, fainting, death-desiring eyes.
There was I, where workers' arms excavate the mine
To open the golden vein, and find in ill-omened accident
Their graves, having as shrouds the wanderer's
Ripped shirt, stained by streaming sweat.
I was there where the multitudinous stepchildren of fortune
Demanding the great and just right to life
Set fire to the palace towers in their rage.
Theirs was the mob's thundering charge through the streets;
And my words broke like a thunderbolt upon its brow.

It made them surge forward, hold back; consoled or cajoled,
And caused rays of flame to burst forth from the masses' womb.
Oh! Bold beating of the Ego in the hearts of millions!
Oh! My lightning-clutching hand that rained fire
Upon the uplifted heads of a mass of men spreading as a sea.[94]
O, my ascent, the regal seal[95] upon the nation's shoulder.
I rode the nation like an untamed stallion,
And with my eyes, founts of light, fixed upon the goal,
I dragged it, storm-driven, down from its thrones.
Now I lacerated its flaming flanks with my goads;
Now I anointed with my fingers its soft mane with cooling flow.
Straining beneath my whip, for three years it galloped
Out from beneath the ruins of tyrannical law.
For three years it wet its hooves in the blood of trampled skulls,
Feeling the hiss of boiling blood on its flanks.
But one day the horse bridled, questioning my quirt,
And just as it was about to neigh upon
Salvation's adamantine summit, it shied
And tossed me from its back, shattering my ribs on the rocks.
And now, Yeghia, at Nirvana's gate
It is the blood of my mounted flight that marks my brow.
The nation defined by freedom lost its discipline,
Tired of its striving, and preferred ignoble creeping,
And so that it might luxuriate in its servitude,
Donned the skin the serpent shed, and dwelt in the burrow of a mole.
Why wet my claws in bloodshed, it said:
Better to draw the carriage of my gluttonous masters—

---

[94]Arm. ծովածաւալ, *dzovadzaval*, lit. "sea-dilating," which, with the associated images of lightning and fire, recalls St. Gregory of Narek's hymn of the Nativity: *Ach'k'n dzov i dzov dzavalanayr harravodun, / yergu p'aylagatsev arekagan nman* "[Her] eyes, sea into sea, dilated in the dawn/ like two flashing-formed suns." The irony is palpable: the tenth-century poet imagined the proud Theotokos, not a Romantic firebrand inciting the urban proletariat to revolt.

[95]Arm. *varaz*, lit. "wild boar": the ancient Zoroastrian totemic animal of Verethraghna/Vahagn gives its name to the Arsacid royal seal it adorned.

A carriage piled not with marble pure, but with gilded dross—
Why sweat, it said, free beneath the sun?
My legs' shackles do not impede the cup
Of foaming wine I raise over my strumpet's curls now and then.
And, Yeghia, one day in godlike pride
I garlanded that cup with the nettles of my contempt.
My hand was not used to clasp the hand that, in weapons untrained
Bore willingly the rusty stamp of chains.
The mob's fury had been well; this celebration, base,
And after my lightning, my smile did not dawn upon its face.
And when they wove a laurel wreath to crown my glory,
I turned my stony back upon their flattery.
I went away, entered my hut, put out my final hope,
And, desiring death, O Indian, I summoned you.
Now against nature, devotion, and love
I have shut fast my gates, and sealed them with despair.
Ivy of sorrow has overgrown my windowpanes,
And the nightingale comes no more to its former nest to sing.
The moon beyond, before it gains my parapets, wanes;
And on my casements the breeze's sweet pinion breaks.
I, driven from my life, shed my tears in the dark:
Now I thirst for the earth, I long for oblivion.
And the air that moves my veins, and the light enamelled in my eyes
I curse! ... And now, mind crazed, I pound against
Nirvana's starry door, and gnaw its threshold.
O Adom,[96] must one still live, in indomitable despair,
The golden ground once firm beneath my feet now turned to dust?

---

[96] Adom Yarjanian, *nom de plume* Siamant'o, 1878-1915, Armenian poet. He is best known for his collections Դիւցազնօրէն (*Tyuts'aznoren,* "In the Heroic Mode"), Հայորդիներ (*Hayortiner,* "Sons of Armenia"), Հոգեվարքի և յոյսի ջահեր (*Hokevark'i yev huysi chaher,* "Torches of Death Throes and of Hope"), and Կարմիր լուրեր բարեկամէս (*Garmir lurer paregames,* "Blood-Red News from My Friend"). He praises the Armenians' ancient valor and exhorts his countrymen of the present day to emulate their ancestors; but the strongest poems evoke the horror of the massacres of Armenians by the Ottoman Turks.

Must I nourish this useless body, against
My heart's immortal suggestion, that heeds now only death?
O Seer, is there hidden joy,
Or can I gird myself in some unknown thought
And dress my wounds in the honey-steaming light of a new star?
Can my wounds heal? Can I be embalmed?
Declare to me! ... But, godlike, you are silent.
Your fingers dewed with light point only
To the holy sacrificial noose, which your death bequeathed my end.
I understand, that only intertwined with it
My heart becomes the sphinx; my grief, her secret:
And like the scattering smoke of a holocaust I attain,
Nirvana and Thee, eternal Peace ...

Tourian and Varuzhan, children of bourgeois Armenian Constantinople, moved from the conventional piety of their surroundings to a stance that is more Promethean than atheistic—and maybe too morbid for the primordial Prisoner of the Caucasus. Yeghishe Ch'arents' lived out the fantasy of revolution and nihilistic rejection of religious faith in his youth, only to turn to ancient springs of Armenian Christianity on the threshold of middle age, disillusioned by the Stalinist monster he and his contemporaries had helped to fashion. His murmur of complaint, with an irony Clio must have relished, is part of a prayer. Shortly before his arrest and murder, which he foresaw all too clearly, Ch'arents' wrote in 1937 a poem variously titled "Last Prayer," "My Prayer on the Mountain," and "Prayer on the Mountain of Torments," which includes these lines addressed to God:

Ո, վոչ դու չես լսել յերբեք տրտունջս իմ
Վոչ հոգնության, վոչ չար հերյուրանքի հանդեպ,
Թեկուզ իջել յեն ծանր, որհասական ամպեր
Իմ ուսերին խոնջած և անտերունչ շնչին...

"O, you have never heard my murmuring complaint
Gainst weariness, gainst wicked calumny,
Though heavy clouds of doom descended

Upon my tired shoulders as I panted, in despair ...

Cited by Anahit Č‘arenc‘, *Č‘arenc‘i jeṙagreri ašxarhum* ("In the World of the Manuscripts of Ch'arents'"), Erevan: Armenian Academy of Sciences, 1978, p. 127: I have restored the Soviet Armenian orthography of the 1930's that Ch'arents' actually employed. There is little doubt that the word *drdunch* in his poem echoes Tourian's protest.

**26. "Remorse"** (*Zghchum*), 1871 (Sevak p. 63)

**Text.**

ԶՂՋՈՒՄ

(Օր մը վերջը)

Երէկ երբ պաղ քրտանց մեջ
Սև մըրափ մը կ'առնէի,
Եւ թոշնած կոյգ մը վարդեր
Այտերուս վրայ կ'այրէին,
Անշուշտ ճակտիս վրայ մահու
Դալկութիւն մը կը պլպլար,
Եւ մահու թռիչ մ'ունէի,
Լըսեցի մօրս հեծեծում...
Բացի աչերըս խոնջած,
Մօրըս արտօսրը տեսի·...
Ո·հ, ճշմարիտ գոռվի
Մարգարիտներ սուտ ու կեղծ...։
Մայրըս անհո·ւն ցաւ մ'ունէր,
Այն սև ցաւը ե·ս էի...
Ա·հ, գըլուխըս փոթորկեց...
Այս սև հեղեղն դըւի դուրս...
Ո·հ, ներէ· ինձ, Աստուած իմ,
Մօրըս արտօսրը տեսի...!

**Translation.**

*Remorse*

(A Day Later)

Yesterday when in a cold sweat
I lapsed into a black slumber,
And the pair of wilted roses

Burned on my cheeks,
Of a certainty upon my brow death's
Pallor shone,
And towards death I flew,
I heard my mother's sobbing:
I opened my exhausted eyes
And beheld my mother's tears! ...
Oh, true tenderness'
False and lying pearls ...
My mother had an endless pain,
And that black pain was I!
Ah, my head in storm
This black torrent flooded forth ...
Oh, forgive me, my God:
I saw my mother crying.

**Commentary.**

The subtitle "A day later" indicates without a doubt that Tourian wrote the poem after "Murmurs." Sevak notes (p. 269) that Tourian wrote the poem without rhyme—Felekian, thinking such a poem impossible, revised it to rhyme. Ekserjian restored the text but retained some of the distorted forms. In a letter to Arshag Chobanian of 30 August 1891 (published in *Banber Erevani Hamalsarani* [Erevan University Herald] 1967.1, p. 168) Yeghishe Tourian ridicules Felekian's grotesqueries. Tchéraz in the preface to his translation, "Repentir (Un jour après)" (p. 75) comments simply of the poem, "Le poète, ame pieuse, se repent d'avoir, la veille, maudit la Providence, dans un crise de désespoir." This is trite and misses the point altogether.

The regret of the poet has more to do with having hurt his mother than with offending God. It would seem that Tourian's mother was distressed not only by her son's mortal illness, but also by the hideous despair out of which the protest of "Murmurs" emerged. The latter would have sounded not just bleak, but utterly blasphemous, of course, to a pious Armenian woman of the nineteenth century. Yet in this poem of the remorse of conscience—that agenbite of inwit, the image of tears as the lying, false pearls of true tenderness sounds exceedingly strange. Tchéraz, relying as it would seem on a bowdlerized version, is able to evade the issue entirely: "je vis les larmes de sa pitié; son baiser reposait sur mon visage comme un dernier souvenir sacrée." Blackwell ("Repentance," p. 38, has much the same thing.) Twice Tourian expresses horror at having seen his mother's tears (lines 10 and 18, identical in the Armenian); he begs God to forgive him, with the shame of a Ham who has uncovered the nakedness of a parent. How can the tears of a mother's grief over her son's suffering be fake pearls? Perhaps the falsehood inheres not so much in the tears themselves as in Tourian's vision of them, which is informed by his awareness of having provoked them, of having employed his art in self-pity to manipulate emotion and excite compassion. His description of his own cheeks—it is onto the cheek that tears fall—as twin wilted roses is self-conscious almost to the point of parody. So one may construct parallel and opposite themes: Tourian's raging poem, his pseudo-Endymiac nap, are the contemptible **outward** causes of his mother's **visible** tears, which bespeak his own false and deceitful machinations; the true source of her sorrow (marked as *sev*, "black") is **within** Tourian himself, and the true tears are his own **inner** flood (also marked as *sev*) of pure remorse.

**27. "I Worship Her"** (*Z'ne bashdem*), 1871 (Sevak pp. 64-65)

**Text.**

ԶʼՆԷ ՊԱՇՏԵՄ

Ճառագայթի ու վարդի
Փթթումներով վեհապանծ՝
Ես չը սիրեմ սա դէմքը
Սիրոյ ժպտով մը օծած։

Ես չը սիրեմ, երբ կոյսի մ'
Աչերը կ'իս բուրվառեն՝
Զերթ հուր ամպոց կոյգ մը հիւս
Հօնիցը տակ մեղմօրէն։

Գիսաստղի պէս հերարձակ՝
Ես կը սիրեմ սա վըճիտ
Կոյսն, որ դէմքէն կը փթթին
Լուսնի դալուկն ու ժըպիտ։

Ես չը սիրեմ՝ հանդիպիմ
Երբ կոյսի մը հեզանազ,
Որ եդեմ մը կը բուրէ,
Կ'վառէ երկինք մը երազ։

Ես հը սիրեմ սա կապոյտ
Զոյգ մ'երկիններն գինովցած,
Որ մէկուն մէջ պաշտի նա,
Եւ միւսին մէջ ալ Աստուած։

Ես չը սիրեմ սա օտար
Ժըպիտները յուսաշող,
Որք ծաղիկներ են սուտ սոսկ
Սրտի անդունդը ծածկող։

Ես կը սիրեմ իմ Պ...
Ինձ կը բաւէ իր սրտին
Մէկ ճառագայթը միայն,
Եւ մէկ վարդն իր ժըպիտին։

Թէև սև աչքն հեղեղեն
Անթիւ աստեղց միշտ բոյլեր՝
Իր սև հօնից շուքին տակ՝
Զ՛որս ութ օրն է Նա գըծեր։

Լուսինը ո՛չ ներա վարդն,
Եւ ոչ ալ վարդը ունի
Ճառագայթումը ներա,
Ճառագայթո՛ւմ սիրողի։

Ես կը դողդողամ իր վըրայ,
Նէ իմ վըրայ գորովի,
Իսկ թէ մոռնա՛յ զ՛իս օր մը...
Ա՛հ, այն օրը քա՛ր կտրի...։

**Translation.**

*I Worship Her*

In high flowering glory
Of sunflare and roses
I love not her visage
Gilded by love's smile.

I love not when
The maiden's eyes like twin
Clouds of fire consume me as incense
Softly 'neath her knitted brows.

Comet-like, tresses shaken free,
I love not this clear
Maiden on whose face flowers

The moon's smile, pale.

I love it not, to meet
A maiden of blushing grace
Exhaling an Eden of fragrance
And igniting a heaven of dreams.

I love not these sky blue
Twin heavens, drunken,
In one of which is worshipped She;
And in the other, also, God.

I love not these strange
Smiles agleam with hope
Which are but blossoms false
Concealing the heart's abyss below.

I love my B...
And but a single beam
Of her heart suffices for me;
Of her smile, one rose,

Though from her black eyes flood
Endless hordes of eternal stars
In her black brows' shade
That He traced on the eighth day.

No moon has that rose of hers,
Nor has the rose
Her radiance, that is
The radiance of the lover.

I tremble over her
And she is tender over me,
But if she forget, one day,
Me, then petrified that day be! ...

**Commentary.**

I agree with Tchéraz, p. 57, in translating *paštem* as Clas. 1st pers. pres. ind. act. rather than as Mod. Arm. subj.: such classicisms are too common in Tourian's usage to merit special discussion. This makes the entire poem rather declarative, however, depriving it of a gentler and more tentative, even elegiac quality that the subjunctive mood might have imparted. Tchéraz in the penultimate stanza corrects *vark'n* "life," from the 1872 edition–the word is solemn and is used often in the hagiographical sense—to *varsn,* "tresses," which is more sensuous and appropriately evocative of comets and the like, in view of the stanza just above. But Sevak rejects both of these for *vard,* "rose." With his emendation, Tchéraz achieves "La lune n'a pas sa chevelure, ni la rose son rayonnement, ce rayonnement d'amoureuse!" The metamorphosis of human *chevelure* into a solar *rayonnement*—that is then denied to the rose's ray-like red petals, for She is (nothing like?) the Sun!—is elegant and intricate. But the retention of the better reading *vard,* "rose," allows an almost syllogistic chain: Moon (A) does not have Rose (B); Rose (B) does not have Radiance (C); the Lover (D) has C and is superior thereby to A and B also. This is finer than Tchéraz's reading, because it saves from triviality the image of the Moon, whose special characteristic amongst the luminaries of heaven is that it reflects light, rather than radiating it. The act. pres. part. *sirogh,* lover (a word usually implying in Armenian, as in many other tongues, the boy rather than the *amoureuse* girl, *pace* the shade of Tchéraz!), is the source of the light that causes the Beloved to shine. And this explains the foregoing Shakespearean litany of I love nots, all of which preface an image that is in one way or another unsettlingly violent in its undertones: the girl's cosmic beauty is qualified as sunflare (stanza 1), fire cloud (2), comet-like (3), igniting (4); stanzas 5 and 6 speak of drunken dualism and the deception of the heart's abyss; and in 8 her blue eyes hollow to black infinities made outside Creation's sanctified week. There is something of the *femme fatale,* of Lilith and Astarte, in this object of Tourian's perilous idolatry. It is the poet's light that illuminates; that of the She-goddess, that consumes.

Who is the mysterious P (B)? On pp. 272-3, Sevak dismisses the name restored by several editors on shaky grounds as *Pistos,* and leaves the ellipsis of the gentleman lover, who never tells. Some sterile speculation: the ending *-istos* in Greek, a language known in some measure by every Constantinopolitan, is that of the adjectival superlative: cf. Arabic *akthar,* "most abundant," Turkified *via* Persian as *ekser* and present in the name of Tourian's friend and editor B. Ekserjian! But it was to H. Janfesjian that Tourian gave the poem; and in any case its object was surely a girl, perhaps one with the mostest. J. received, E. edited—and *tertium non datur*!

**28. "The Rosebud—Flowers of the Maiden"** (*Gogon—dzaghigk' guysin*), 1871 (Sevak pp. 66-67)

**Text.**

ԿՈԿՈՆ– ԾԱՂԻԿՔ ԿՈՅՍԻՆ

Լուսափըթիթ ւ՛անարև
Զոյգ մ՛աշխարհներ ես տեսի
Ճառագայթից, բոյրերու
Եւ փափկութեան ու լոյսի։

Ո·հ, չ՛է· նոցա պէս անբիծ
Իտալական վեհ երկին,
Եթէ չ՛ունին աստեղց բոյլ,
Ամպ ու կայծակ ալ չ՛ունին։

Ո·հ, յաւիտեան միշտ կոկոն
Կարծես ցոյգ մը ծաղիկ են,
Բայց նըման կոյս սրտերու՝
Կարի քաղցըր կը բուրեն։

Ձեռք կարկառել ս՛աշխարհաց
Ակնախըտիղ ու անտես՝
Յանդուգն ըլլալ է լոկ քան
Զ՛աշխարհակալն Արտաշէս։

Ի՞նչպէս արդեօք կերտեց Նա
Լուսագունդներս այս դողդոջ,
Նա աշխարհի քան ըպկերտ՝
Մտածեց ոգի տալ կընոջ։

Կը դողդողան իմ շուրթեր
Հըպիլ սիրոյ այդ խըռով
Կոկոն– ծաղկանց՝ խամրելու,
Արատելու երկիւղով։

Այլ որ շուրթերն յանդըգնի
Հըպել հրաշից այդ լուսէ,
Կ'երթնում յ'աշխարհն աստեղաց,
Թ·է նա դա·ր մը կը ծըծէ։

**Translation.**

*The Rosebud-Flowers of the Maiden*

Blossoming light yet sunless
Twin worlds beheld I
Of radiances, of fragrances
And of delicacy and luminescence.

O, not unblemished as they
Is the Italian noble sky;
And if they have not its myriad stars
Neither have they cloud and lightning.

O, ever and aye, the rosebud
A pair of flowers seems,
But like virgin hearts
Their fragrance is fiercely sweet.

To stretch out my hand to these worlds
Invisible yet tickling the eye
Means but to be bolder still
Than Artaxias cosmocrator.

How did He fashion then
These luminous, tremulous spheres?
Rather than to the world's frame
Thought He to grant to woman a soul.

My lips are atremble
Bestirred with that love to touch

The rosebud—and wither its flowers,
Sully them with fear.

But the lips that dare
To touch these miracles of light
To the world of the stars I swear
Will suck of them a hundred years!

**Commentary.**

The great linguist Hrach'ya Acharian thought the globes of light (*lusakuntner*) in the poem breasts.[97] In the final line, the victorious lover sucks them (*dzedzé*). But one can drink of a kiss, too; and it seems that by two rosebuds might also be implied the twin lips of the imagined girl. At first it would seem, since they sprout (*p'et'it'*) light, that the roses are eyes: it is an ancient Armenian and Indo-European poetic conceit to liken, sometimes in an intentional paradox, the two eyes to the single Sun of heaven; and the redness of roses is homologized to the Sun's red fire. In the hymn of the birth of Vahagn preserved by Movses Khorenats'i, the eyes of the god are "little Suns" (*aregakunk'*); and in the Melody of the Nativity of Narekats'i, cited above, the Virgin's eyes are *erku p'aylakadzev aregakan nman*—"like two fiery Suns."[98] An early Christian stele of the fourth or fifth century A.D. from Garnahovit, Armenia, depicts a woman rising out of a base of stylized acanthus leaves. She holds aloft a box or frame containing two rosettes—like Tourian's twin rosebuds! The relief has been interpreted as symbolizing the beginning of spring, but its meaning is unclear.[99] But I think the mention of stars in the open Italian sky could have been

---

[97]Cited by Sevak, I, p. 276.

[98]See J. R. Russell, "A Poem of Grigor Narekacʿi," *Revue des Études Arméniennes* 19, 1985, p. 438; and J. R. Russell, "Carmina Vahagni," *Acta Antiqua Academiae Scientiarum Hungaricae*, t. XXXII, fasc. 3-4, Budapest, 1989, pp. 317-330 (AIS, pp. 31-36; 357-370).

[99]See B. N. Aṙakʿelyan, ed., *Hayastani mijnadaryan kotʿołayin hušarjannerə* ("Memorial monuments of mediaeval Armenia"), Erevan: Arm. Acad. Sci., 1984, plate 9.

meant to introduce a simile to the pearly teeth in the mouth of the beloved—were she to part her lips and open it. The aroma of the flowers can also refer metaphorically to lips as petals, since the sweetness of the latter is a common conceit in mediaeval Armenian poetry.

But the two worlds of the fourth stanza are called *agnakhedigh u andes*, and the line is connected by rhyme to *Z'ashkharhagaln Ardashes*. A woman's breasts are both alluringly visible beneath her clothes yet modestly concealed: one touches their nakedness in sexual conquest. The Armenian king Artaxias I, in the second century B.C., subdued enemies to the east and west, and lassoed, captured, and married the princess of the Alans, Sat'enik. It is plain Tourian loved Movses Khorenats'i's narrative of these legendary events, with ample quotation from oral epic: the fourth line of No. 11, "I loved you" (*Sirets'i k'ez*), reads *Deghar markrid yev vosgi* (*tełar margrit ew oski*), which is a paraphrase of the citation of the Artaxiad oral epic by Movses: *Teł oski tełayr i pʿesayutʿeann Artašisi, tełayr margarit i harsnutʿean Satinkann*, "A shower of gold rained when Artashes was groom; pearls rained when Sat'enik was bride."[100] Khorenats'i explains that it was customary to shower newlyweds with coins at a wedding and to sprinkle pearls in the nuptial bed. There seems little doubt that such a custom existed. However, as was noted in the Commentary to No. 11, the verse echoes also a famous Greek myth that is relevant to the theme of abduction and sexual possession: Acrisius, king of Argos, was told that the son to be born to his daughter, Danae, was fated to kill him. To keep this from happening, he confined the girl in a tower. But Zeus, who desired her, transformed herself into a shower of gold in her chamber; and in time she bore Perseus. The Armenian bard either borrowed from a version of

---

[100]Movsēs Xorenacʿi, *Patmutʿiwn Hayocʿ* ("History of the Armenians"), Echmiadzin, 1913, repr. Delmar, NY: Caravan Books, 1981, ch. 50, p. 179, lines 10-11. Movsēs explains that the Roman consuls scattered gold coins at weddings, and queens scattered pearls in the bridal chamber: Prof. Thomson, in the notes to his translation, offers references which suggest sources for Movsēs' explanation (R. W. Thomson, tr., Moses Khorenatsʿi, *History of the Armenians*, Cambridge, MA: Harvard Univ. Press, 1978, p. 193, notes 8, 9). The verse is illustrated, in keeping with Xorenacʿi's explanation, by Zabelle C. Boyajian, in her *Armenian Legends and Poems*, London: J. M. Dent and Sons, Ltd., 1958, p. 48.

the Greek tale he had heard, or else employed an image drawn from native mythology, probably kin in its origin to the Greek.

**29. "Black! Black!"** (*Sev, sev!*), 1871 (Sevak, pp. 68-70)

**Text.**

**ՍԵ·Ի, ՍԵ·Ի**

Երբեմն հոգիս աստղի մը բոց
Եւ թիթեռնի մ'ունէր թևեր·
Վերջալոյսի նըման ամպոց
Երազներ հո·ւր ճակատս վառէր։

Արդ սառոյցներ դառն արտօսրի
Կը քարանան կուրծիս ներքև,
Եւ բարդք ամպոց սևաթորմի
Կ'ուզեն խեղդել սիրտս ու արև։

Հավիւ քանի մ'օրերն կեանքիս
Ոսկեզօծեց իմ բախտը վատ,
Որո·նք եղան լոկ օվասիս
Մեղմող կեանքիս դառն անապատ։

Մենանայի օրեր ցըվերջ
Երբեմն՝ հովտի ծաղկանց ւ'երկնի
Չինափըթիթ ամպերուն մէջ,
Կեանքի մըրուրն ես թափէի։

Ծըծէի սէ·ր, ծըծէի կեա·նք,
Մինչ վերջալոյսն կը հըրահրէր,
«Մնաս բարովի» սա կարմրորակ՝
Տըխուր կըրակ ւ'երկնի բոցեր։

Ունէի ես երբեմն առատ
Վարդեր, առատ աստղեր նոյնպէս,
Ճակատագիրս սև տեսաւ շա·տ,
Բրցուց, քաղեց վ'անոնք սրտէս։

Ունէի ես իմ սիրուհին,
Որոյ թէպէտ աչքն էին սև,
Սակայն սըգալ չը գիտէին...
Հրեշտակ մ'էր նէ, հրեշտակ անթև։

Սև երազ մը օր մը դողդոջ
Մըղեց վ'իս սև· փոսի մ'առջին,
Ուր քար կտրած՝ սիրտ ի դողդոջ՝
Դագաղի մ'աչքս յառած էին։

Աւա·ղ ներա վարդքն ու աստղերն
Լուռ պիտի տար կուլ այն սև փոս,
Ցուրտ համբոյր մը առի ճակտէն,
Ներա վերջին ձօնն էր ափսո·ս։

Եւ լըսեցի յայնժամ՝ թի թի
Սև սև հողեր կոշտ թնդեցին
Տըխուր քողքին վըրայ փայտի...
Դըժոխք մ'անէծք այն սև· օրին։

Այն ցուրտ հողերն յ'իմ դատարկ սիրտ
Լըցուցին, փոսն գոցելնուն հետ՝
Եւ այս աշխարհն ալ անժըպիտ
Գոցեցին իմ առջև յաւէ·տ...։

**Translation.**

*Black! Black!*

Once my soul possessed the fire of a star
And had a butterfly's wings:
Like clouds in crepuscular light
Glowed my brow, with dreams aflame.

Now, salt tears' mountains of ice
Petrify within my breast,

And black clouds in sullen mass
Would strangle my life's sun and my heart.

My evil fortune gilded
But few days of my life;
And they proved but an oasis
To palliate my life's bitter wastes.

I would retire till the end, passing
My days among the valley's blossoms
And heaven's clouds' snow flowers,
And pour out all my life's dregs.

I would suck at love, suck at life
Till the sunset blazed
Its incarnadine "Farewell!"
Of sad fire and heavenly flame.

Once I had abundant
Roses, and no fewer stars:
My fate beheld vast darkness
And tore and plucked them from my heart.

I had a beloved of mine own,
And though her eyes were black
They had not yet learnt to mourn...
An angel was she, an angel without wings.

One day a black dream, wavering,
Thrust me towards a dark pit looming,
Where I turned to stone, my heart pounding:
My eyes upon a sepulchre were fixed.

Alas! for her roses and stars
That the black pit was silently to swallow:
A cold kiss I took from her brow

That was her final gift of woe!

Then I heard spade on spade clang
Ringing rude on the soil, black, black!
Upon the grim wood coffin lid...
A hell of curses rain upon that black day!

The cold clods clogged my vacant heart
As they mounted up to fill the pit
And also sealed, unsmiling,
This world before me for eternity.

**Commentary.**

The poem is rich in alliterative effects that bridge its violent contrasts: the stars' *pots'* ("fire") and the red evening glow reflected by the clouds, *ambots'*, establish a strong initial O sound. In the middle stanzas the fire-theme is carried by the milder, open *herahr***er** ("flamed") and *pots'***er** (pl., "fires"). The final stanzas then take up the linking O sound in a chain of movements expressive of fear and trembling (*toghtoch, t'entoch*), to the pit (*p'os*) that causes them, and the cry of woe (*ap'sos*). And in the final lines, the poet expresses the sound of the gravediggers' shovels' ringing with the doubled monosyllables *t'i t'i* (lit., "shovel by shovel"), falling in the next line into the hollow mirroring, title words: *sev, sev*. And the clods falling in the grave whose horror sound and color thus repeat, echo a last time the signature O: *hogher goshd*.

The theme of a lost love is typically Romantic; but the insistent physical description is macabre enough to suggest shades of Ligeia–the possibility, that is, albeit unlikely, that Tourian had read Baudelaire's recently-published article introducing Poe to the European reader: even then, it was recognized as epochal.

**30. "To May"** (*Arr Mayis*), 1871 (Sevak p. 71)

**Text.**

**ԱՌ ՄԱՅԻՍ**

Ծաղիկներու մայրի·կ դու կոյս՝
Ո·վ իմ Մայի·ս ծաղկահանդերձ,
Սա երփներանգ ծաղկօքդ հանդերձ
Է՞ր չը բերիր Ծաղիկն հոգւոյս։

Ո·հ, միթէ կա՞յ այլ վըւարթուն
Մայիս հոգւոյ Ծաղիկներու․
—Նա փողփողէ վերև գլխու,—
Մի դալկահար Մայիս անհուն։

**Translation.**

*To May*

Thou, little virgin mother of the flowers,
O May of mine, attired in blooms,–
Why does she, with her blossoms multihued
Not bestow her Flower upon my soul?

Oh, could there be another gay
Soul's flowers' May?
—Above your head it is ablaze:
An endless, pallid May.

**Commentary.**

In line one Tourian addresses May as though in a prayer to the Blessed Virgin; and in line two, the poet intensifies the religious and prayerful mood by introducing a vivid—and, in context, aretalogical—epithet *dzaghgahanterts*, literally "flower-clothed": Genet's Notre Dame des Fleurs! The third line breaks the epithet down into the common and less striking phrase *dzaghgok' hanterts*, "with flowers," where the specific meaning of the second word, "clothing," is dulled to the plain postposition meaning "with." The breaking of the epithet accompanies the descent of the poet's mood, from the first two lines of glorification to his complaint that the Flower, that is, love, has not been given to him.

The second and final stanza of this brief verse contains a reversal and irony that are signatures of the poet: he looks up again from his dejection, but the springtime that exists for him, though it shines, belongs to a world beyond the grave, which, one must imagine as yawning below and not above; and, unlike the sky of Constantinople in springtime, this upside-down sky is death's—endless in time and pallid as a corpse. This May is consumptive, an angel of death.

**31. "The Violet"** (*Manishag*), 1871 (Sevak, pp. 72-73)

**Text.**

ՄԱՆԻՇԱԿ

Ո՜վ մանիշա՜կ, մանիշա՜կ,
Ինչո՞ւ այդպէս գլխիկոր
Նայիս հողին սըգաւոր...
Ո՜հ, ինչի՞ այդ նըշանակ։

Միթէ դու կո՞յս մը տեսար,
Որուն աչաց քով կապուտ՝
Ըկքեկ գըտար այնչափ մութ,
Որ կը սըգաս սևահար։

Եթէ դու ալ վարդին պէս
Ունենայիր դոյկն բոսոր,
Կը շիկնէիր, ինչպէս որ
Շիկնեցաւ այն վարդը վէս,

Երբ տեսաւ օր մը ներա
Վարդերն անբիծ այտերուն։
Շուշանին պէս դալկութիւն
Եթէ ըլլար քու վըրայ,

Դժգունէիր որպէս նա,
Ինչպէս որ օր մը շուշան
Դժգունեցաւ աննըշան՝
Տեսաւ ձեռներն երբ ներա։

Եւ դէռ ըսե՞մ... օր մ'երկին
Ամպոտնեցաւ... է՞ր արդեօք...
Երբոր կ'ընէր նէ աղօթք,
Վերն յառած աչքն ու հոգին։

**Translation.**

*The Violet*

O violet, violet,
Why thus with head inclined
Mournful at the ground you stare?
O what means the sign?

Perhaps you saw a maiden
In whose sky-blue eyes you found
Your own reflection, so dark
That, stricken by its black, you mourn.

If only like the rose
Abundant crimson you possessed:
Then you might blush, just
As the rose flushed haughty red

When one day it saw her
Roses, on her unblemished cheeks.
Were you a pallor
Upon them, like the lily,

Then you would lose your color
Like that lily one day, when
It paled imperceptibly
At the sight of her hands.

More dare I say? One day heaven
Was beclouded... was it that
When she prayed
Her eyes and soul upward strained?

**Commentary.**

The poem employs a web of nice chromatic conceits: the violet's bent head betokens shame; the rose's haughty red, a blush; the lily's pallor, color drained from an abashed face; and the clouds, God shielding His face at the sight of Her. The latter corresponds to Tourian's feeling, elsewhere variously expressed, that if female beauty did not exist, there would be nothing to inspire prayer. And the progress of violet to blue to black to crimson to rose-red to lily-white to the pale hue of the cloud provides a pictorial accompaniment to the poem's shifting movements and moods.

**32. "My Rest"** (*Im Hankiste*), 1871 (Sevak, p. 74)

**Text.**

ԻՄ ՀԱՆԳԻՍՏԸ

Եթէ մօտի հողակոյտիս,
Թուխ—մոխրագոյն ւ'աչեր ներա
Թէ ջուխտ մարգրիտ թափին իմ վրայ,
Չը ցաւագնիր ոսկերոտիս.
Ա·յս իմ հանգիստ,
Իմ լըռանիստ
Ա·յս օթևան
Խաղաղութեան։

**Translation.**

*My Rest*

If at my tumulus near,
Black-ashen, and her eyes
If those twin pearls upon me fall,[101]
Then my bones grieve not.
This is my rest,
This the silent seat
And inn
Of peace.

**Commentary.**

The poem has the brevity of an epitaph and possibly the shape of a gravestone (the wider top, for the inscription, and the lower tongue inserted into the soil): monument and memory are constant

[101]Tchéraz, p. 69, emends passive *t'ap'in*, "fall," to active *t'ap'en*, "shed": "si ses yeux gris foncé laissent tomber sur moi deux perles," making it tears from ashen eyes that fall, and not the gaze of two eyes that are themselves pearls upon an ashen tomb.

preoccupations of the poet, and "The Child to The Cross" also is laconic, and iconic in shape. Tourian manages to fuse and confuse the two colors modifying "tumulus" (*hoghaguyd,* lit. "earth-heap") with "eyes" through the line break and reduction of the conjunction *yev* "and" to a nearly imperceptible *v'*. The distance between the dead poet and the beloved, unnamed "she" (*ne*: he uses the gen. *nera*) closes: she does not gaze from a distance; her eyes instead seem to touch the mound and share its color. A beloved's eyes are often black (*sev* or *t'ukh,* the latter word being used in this poem), and the color can be an endearment: the Armenians have shrines to a *t'ukh manuk,* "black youth"; and Turks call a beloved boy *karaoghlan.*[102] Tourian places "black" closer in the text to the mound than the other color modifier, "ash-colored" (*mokhrakuyn*), which has greater funereal overtones and is less likely to be used as a color of the eye in poetry. The poem begins with the word *yet'e,* "if"; so the *t'e* of the third line is resumptive; but it has the added effect of separating the "eyes" (*ach'er*) of the preceding line from what these eyes grammatically *are*—"twin pearls" (*jukht markrid*). Rare black pearls, perhaps, that shine in the hypogean dark—and now comes a possible contrast, for the poet's skeleton (*vosgerodi*) will not be sad. Bones, of course, are white. A girl's grieving visit to Tourian's grave becomes an imagined, though impossible, union of opposites, through the manipulation of color, image, and word order.

The next four lines, even more laconic, seem the narrow part of the tombstone that is inserted into the ground, and the stanza seems to **be** the earth: a silent and restful place of peace. The rhyme scheme of the first stanza, ABBA, allows a middle swelling, and has the sounds *is,*

---

[102]The Black Youth seems to be a figure of Indo-European antiquity in Armenian mythology: see J. R. Russell, "The Armenian Shrines of the Black Youth (*t'ux manuk*)," *Le Muséon,* vol. 111, fasc. 3-4, 1998, pp. 319-343 (*AIS,* pp. 925-950). I have compared him to Balakrishna, the Dark Youth of the Indian pantheon, the cowherd and lover; and to an analogous Greek figure, the Black Hunter. One can now add to the schema of this Indo-European mythological type an attestation from the Iranian area as well: the Siyāh Gāleš, "Black Cowherd" spirit of the folk belief of the Taleshi-speakers of the SW Caspian littoral (see Viktoriya Arakelova, "Siyakh-Galesh—chyornyi pastyr' (Obrazy dukhov-pokrovitelei skota v verovaniyakh novoiranskikh narodov)," *Iran and the Caucasus* 1, 1997, pp. 121-123).

*a, a, is*: the scheme of the second is one of narrowing, A′A′B′B′—and I suggest primes rather than a new ordination of CCDD because the sounds *ist, ist, yan, yan* are the initial sound made heavier by consonant clusters—subtly enforcing the downward thrust into the heavy ground of the grave monument. The word I have chosen to translate as "inn," Arm. *ot'evan,* could mean an abode or dwelling, but its primary meaning is closer to that of a hotel. Calling the earth this reflects the Christian belief that the rest of the departed is not eternal—the graves will give up their occupants at the resurrection of the dead. This aspect of hope adds to the positive tone of peace and rest, though one is reminded again of Tourian's grief-stricken conviction that requited love will come to him only in death.

**33. "New Black Days"** (*Nor Sev Orer*), 1 October 1871 (Sevak pp. 75-77)

**Text.**

ՆՈՐ ՍԵՒ ՕՐԵՐ

Մինչ բռնութեան՝ ընկա·ն արեան դարերը,
Աշխարհ մը կայ արցո·ւնք թափող սարերը,
Արեամբ պղտո·ր դեռ գետերուն ափունքը,
Չը դադրեցաւ դեռ այս երկրին սև սուգը·
Աւերակոյտն այս ահարկու,
Աշխարհ մոխրոց ու նոճերու։

Հայ դիւցազանց, որ հոն ընկան ի վաղուց՝
Ոսկերոտիքն՝ արմատնե·րն այն վըրիժուց
Ա·հ, դեռ բողբոջ մը չ'արձըկած հո՞ղ դարձան...
Ուրեմն հիմա աղիք չ'ունի Հայաստան...
Ա·յ, դալկահար դու հայրենիք...
—Եւ դեռ Քրդի՞ն ալ խոնարհինք։

Մառախուղ են հագեր դաշտքն ու լերինքը,
Չը գեղգեղեր Հայ հովւուհւոյն սըրինգը,
Հայուն համար չը փալփըլիր աստղիկը,
Արցունքներով թոռմեր հոգւոյն ծաղիկը,
Դադրեր անմեղ խինդ, թինդ ու պար,
Շողայ ապա·տ Քրդին տապար։

Դողդոջ մտնէ առագաստը գիրգ հարսը,
Արտասուաթոր՝ դէմքին ծածկած հոյլ վարսը՝
Որ չ'ըլլայ թէ յանկարծ սիրոյ մրմունջը
Խափանէ վատ Քրդին տռփոտ մըռունչը·
Սէրը փեսին արեամբ կարմրի,
Հարսը Քրդին կ'երթայ գերի...։

Մի·շտ կը ցանէ Հայն, չը հնձեր... անօթի·...
Իր դալկահար դէմքէն երկու շիթ կաթի,

Արտօսր ու քիրտ միանգամայն... ո՛վ Աստուած.
Նա ճաշակէ տրտմած սրտով ցաւ ու հաց.
Այս տարաբախտ ազգն է Հա՛յը,
Մեր արի՛ւնը, մեր եղբա՛յրը։

Ա՛հ, ոտնակոխ Հայուն սիրտը և տաճար
Հրացանն յ՛ուս սա կոշտ Քրդին անդադար,
Եւ մեր չ՛եռա՞ր կարմիր մէկ ալին
Կամ մէկ փրփուրն հայրենեաց սուրբ երակին,
Որ սառոյցի վէրթ որդիներ՝
Մեր աղիքները չ՛ենք թօթուեր։

Ի՞նչ սիրտ է այս, որ հոս գամեր է Աստուած,
Մինչ չը սիրեր նա հայրենիքը ցաւած...
Չ՛ունի ներսը Հայն իր նախնեաց տրոփը,
Լըքե՛ր է կ՛ինք ճակատագրին Սերոբը.
Երես դարձուց Հայն սուսերէն,
«Սև» ժառանգեց լոկ պապերէն։

Սառէ աչեր, քարէ լեզու, ա՞յս մընաց
Բիւր փառքերէն մեր գոռ ու պերճ հայրենեաց,
Սևագլուխ խումբ մը ագռա՞ւ մընաց լոկ՝
Կամ խումբ մը կոյր խըլուրդ՝ ըստրո՞ւկ փառքի սոսկ.
Ա՛հ, այն արծիւ ժողովրդէն,
Որ հարուածուի արդ կոշտ Քրդէն։

Ի՛նչ, սև ձեռքեր հըպին վըճիտ ճակատին
Հայ կուսիկին նըուիրական լաչակի՛ն,
Դըժոխք մը տարփ թոշնեն վարդը կուսութեան,
Կարծես ծաղիկ մը կոխկոտեն— կ՛այս կըզգան,
Ինչպէս որ Հայ կը մորթեն,
Կարծես թէ հաւ մը մորթեն։

Է՛հ, մի՛ վախէք, ասեղ մ՛անգամ պէտք չ՛է մեզ,
Այլ հայրենի սոսկ ըզգացում մ՛աղեկէզ.
Ժանգոտ սուր մը, պատռած դրօշ մը թէ չ՛ունինք,
Կուրծերնուս տակ տըրոփող սի՞րտ մ՛ալ չ՛ունինք։

Օ·ն, ոտքերնիս վարնե·նք գետին,
Յայտնե·նք մեր ցաւը ահագին։

Մեր քերց վարդերն և արևներն մեր եղբարց՝
Մեր տաճարաց խաչերն՝ պատի·ւն հայրենեաց
Մենք պահանջենք, բարօրութի·ւն մեր ազգին.
Ջ՛ա·յս պահանջե·նք՝ կ՛ա·յս Սուլթանէն սրտագին,
Մեր պատիւն ու Քուրդը կ՛ուզե·նք,
Եւ կամ նորա պէնքին դէմ պէ·նք։

**Translation.**

*New Black Days*

As long as bloody centuries of tyranny have lain
Upon the land its mountains weep,
The rivers' shore with blood are dimmed,
The black mourning of the land does not subside.
This frightful mound of ruins,
Country of cypresses and ashes.

Armenian heroes fallen long ago—
From their bones does revenge take root,
Or have they turned to earth without a sprout?
So Armenia has no vitals now.
O, fatherland enfeebled thou—
Shall we submit to the Kurd now?

Hill and dale are clothed in gloom,
The Armenian shepherdess' flute will not sound.
For the Armenian no twinkle of the little star,
His soul's flower in tears rots.
The innocent laugh and antic hay stop:
Freely glints the Kurdish scythe.

In nuptial bed enfolded, trembles the bride

In tears dissolved, her face in abundant tresses hid
Lest suddenly love's murmur
The lewd Kurd's bestial bellow interrupt.
The bridegroom's love incarnadine;
A captive to the Kurd, his bride.

The Armenian sows ever, reaps never ... hungry!
From his wasted face two drops stream—
Sweat and tears together ... God!
He sups his weary heart's pain with his bread.
This Armenian is a star-crossed brood,
Our brother, our blood.

Ah, the Armenian's heart and temple underfoot
The rude Kurd, musket at his shoulder, ever tramples.
Does not a red wave mounting in us roar within,
Foam of our fatherland's holy vein—
Or are we sons of ice
That our innards do not shake?

What sort of heart has nailed God here
That loves not its fatherland in pain,
Whose ancestors' beat the Armenian has not within—
The Seraph of his fortune has abandoned him!
The Armenian has turned his face from the sword,
The "Black" of his forebears his only inheritance.

Eyes of ice and tongue of stone—is this what remains
Of our haughty, splendid fatherland's abundant fame?
A black-headed crows' flock alone remains,
Or a sightless crowd of moles fit for the glory of a slave,
From that eagle nation
That now the rude Kurd smites.

What? Shall black hands touch the clear brow
Of the Armenian maiden, her sacred veil,

A hell of lust blast the virgin rose,
As though the blossom were crushed: they feel
When they slaughter the Armenian
That they throttle a chicken.

Hey—we don't need a needle, don't be afraid,
Just patriotic sentiment that kindles our vitals.
We have neither rusted sword nor tattered banner,
But is there not even a heart that beats within our breasts?
Hey! Let's stamp our feet upon the ground,
Our frightful pain to sound.

Our sisters' roses, our brothers' suns,
The crosses of our temples, our fatherland's glory—
We demand our people's benefit.
From the Sultan, heartfelt we demand it:
We want our honor and the Kurd,
Or else against his guns—to arms!

**Commentary.**

This is one of several patriotic poems that issued from Tourian's impassioned pen. The expression "trampled underfoot" in it (*vodnagokh*) is to be found also in the first couplet of Michael Nalbandian's ode *Mer Hayrenik'* ("Our Fatherland"): *Mer hayrenik' t'shvarr anter / Mer t'shnamyats' votnakokh* "Our wretched headless fatherland / Trampled underfoot by our enemies." The poem celebrated the Italian uprising against Austria. Armenians subsequently modified it as a national(ist) anthem: when Soviet power dissolved and the second Armenian Republic was formed, the song became official, with the couplet cheerfully upgraded to *Mer hayrenik' azat ankakh / Vor aprel e dare dar* "Our fatherland, free and independent/ Which for ages has endured."

Full of romantic bombast about deflowered virgins, "New Black Days" (which seemed to two of one's students a good name for a rap group) leaves much to be desired as poetry. I fear that my translation reflects the tone of the original faithfully. But the poem reflects fairly also the naive view of Tourian's contemporaries that the Kurdish depredators of the Armenian homeland were somehow a force separate from the Ottoman Sultan, of whom they were of course the agents. The indifference the poet bewails, at least, was to be replaced soon by direct concern—and within a quarter century it was the relatively secure Armenian community of the capital who were to be the victims of government-sponsored pogroms. There is a nascent militancy in the final stanza of Tourian's poem. The "Black" inheritance he refers to is the reverend clergy; and the "crows" have to do with them and with the Armenian folk legend that Noah first released from the Ark a crow (*Noyi akrrave*), who, perfidiously, did not return. Tourian implies that the Christian doctrine of turning the other cheek has unmanned the Armenians, who have forgotten their ancient heroes' valorous repute. In this century, the poet Avetik' Isahakyan drew a similaly invidious comparison between the medieval historians, who, he claimed, were pessimistic monks, and the folk bards, who exhorted the people to a war of liberation in the spirit of David of Sasun.[103]

It may still come as a surprise to the present-day reader that the Kurds, not the Turks, are the enemies of Armenia here. The Kurds are speakers of a Western Iranian language: organized in *ashirets*—clan-based coalitions—to this day, they belong to diverse sects, some with only the most tenuous connection to Islam. Most Kurds, for most of their history, have been illiterate nomads. Armenian sources call the Kurdish language *mareren*, "Median," however, and Kurdish nationalist scholars trace their ancestry to the Medes of antiquity. By the Sasanian period, though, they were much as they are now: the *Gestes* of the dynasty insist that Ardeshir fled the Parthian Arsacid court and took refuge in the hilly wilderness, with *kurdigan shobanan*, "Kurdish shepherds." In the unsettled conditions of the tenth century, they migrated north from the Zagros mountains of Western Iran into Armenia, where they have lived ever since, sometimes in uneasy symbiosis, but just as often as predators of the indigenous Armenian population. During the genocidal campaigns of World War I, Turkey enlisted the

---

[103]See my article "Revelations of Darkness: Medieval Armenian Apocalyptic in the Epic of Sasun and the Visions of Yovhannes Kozern," *Journal of Armenian Studies* 6.1, 1998, pp. 3-15 (*AIS*, pp. 875-887).

Kurds to exterminate the Armenians, much as Nazi Germany later on was to employ Lithuanian and Ukrainian fascists, for example, against the Jews. After Mustafa Kemal ("Atatürk") consolidated power, he murdered his Kurdish confederates and set about creating a unitary state based upon the fiction that Turkey had no national minorities: the Kurds became "mountain Turks," forbidden to use their language or to celebrate their distinct culture. Some Kurds and Armenians have now become political allies, since Turkey is a common enemy,[104] though maps of "Kurdistan" include the Armenian capital, Erevan.

---

[104]In my book *An Armenian Epic: The Heroes of Kasht*, Ann Arbor, MI: Caravan, 2000, a study and translation of a folk epic transmitted by Karapet Sital, I have discussed the new Armeno-Kurdish amity, which was in the case of that text a reflection of Communist official policy.

**34. "My Pain"** (*Im ts'ave*), 1871 (Sevak pp. 78-79)

**Text.**

ԻՄ ՑԱՒԸ

Սուրբ տենչերով լոկ ծարաւած՝
Ցամաք գտնե·լ աղբերքն յամայր,
Ցամքի·լ ծաղիկ հասակի մէջ,
Ո·հ, չ’է այնչափ ցաւ ինձ համար։

Ջերմ համբոյրով մը դեռ չ’այրած
Սա ցուրտ ճակատըս դալկահար՝
Հանգչեցնե·լ հողէ բարձին,
Ո·հ, չ’է· այնչափ ցաւ ինձ համար։

Դեռ չը գրկած էակ— փունջ մը
Ժըպտէ, գեղէ, հուրէ շաղեալ՝
Գրկե·լ սա ցուրտ հողակոյտը,
Ո·հ, չ’է· այնչափ ցաւ ինձ համար։

Քաղցր երազով մ’յըղի մրափ մը
Չ’անդորրած գլուխս մրրկահար՝
Ննջե·լ հողէ վերմակի տակ,
Ո·հ, չ’է· այնչափ ցաւ ինձ համար։

Հագնիլ հիւղին մուր—անունը,
Ծըծե·լ նորա մըրուր— օդն յար,
Միշտ ցաւի·լը միանգամայն,
Ո·հ, չ’է· այնչափ ցաւ ինձ համար։

Հէգ մարդկութեան մէկ ոստը գօս՝
Հայրենիք մը ունիմ թըշուառ,
Չ’օգնած անոր՝ մեռնի·լ աննշան,
Ո·հ, ա·յս է սոսկ ցաւ ինձ համար։

**Translation.**

*My Pain*

Athirst alone with sacred striving
But to find once more the sources dry,
To dry indeed at the age when I should flower—
That is not for me so great a pain.

This cold, wan brow of mine
Still by warm kiss never burned
And laid to rest on a pillow of earth—
That is not for me so great a pain.

No creature yet within my arms—a garland
Of smiles and loveliness and of fire comprised,
And to clasp the cold tomb's clods instead—
That is not for me so great a pain.

My storm-wracked head unquieted
By sweet dream in sleep aborning,
To slumber beneath earth's blanket instead—
That is not for me so great a pain.

To put on the sooty garment of the tomb
And suck its dregs forever as air,
And at each breath to suffer ever,
That is not for me so great a pain.

A withered branch of humanity poor,
I have an ill-starred fatherland:
Without assisting it, to die unknown,
O, that alone for me is pain.

**Commentary.**

The theme and emotion of the poem are familiar: the dying boy complains about the joys he will not live to have–the patriotic ending may seem somewhat disconcerting, but one must recall that Tourian often combines private anguish with concern for his fellow Armenians. He was a nineteenth-century liberal, and an idealistic adolescent as well. The ideological dictum of the 1960's in America—The personal is political!– had as much to do with the canonization of epicene culture as with Herbert Marcuse's eroticized Marxism. Tourian's phantasmagoric partitives are here in the poem, too: garlands of smiles and fire that evoke the complex Armenian homology of Sun-Rose.

Paleness is so common a feature of Tourian's descriptions of himself and others, and of things in nature, also, that one may look forward into the future he paved for Armenian poems. So, line 6 of the Armenian text, *Sa ts'urd jagades talgahar,* "This cold, wan brow of mine," is noteworthy, because his favored word "wan" (Clas. and E. Arm. *daluk,* here with *-har,* "stricken") might have served to inspire the name the sixteen-year-old Yeghishe Ch'arents' gave to his first cycle of poems, *Erek' erg tkhradaluk aghjkan,* "Three songs to a sad, wan girl" (1913).[105] The precocious poet uses terms, and strikes numerous romantic notes and themes, that he would have encountered in Tourian's lines (though not exclusively there): estrangement, bitterness, and the waning and sickening of a love that ends in death. There are differences, of course: Tourian's *siècle* was long past its *fin,* so the influences of Symbolism are strong and one feels some Modernist chords as well. Knowing how the poetry of Ch'arents' changed, acquired its own, confident voice—of which only a little is heard yet, here—and moved to perfection, one cannot help but wonder how Tourian also might have changed, had he lived past his own adolescence.

*THREE SONGS TO A SAD, WAN GIRL*

To Astghik Ghondakhchian.

---

[105]I translate here the entire cycle, from the text published in Eghishe Ch'arents', *Erkeri zhoghovatsu,* vol. 1, Erevan: Arm. Acad. Sci., 1962, pp. 11-17.

Et c'était le dernier amour du soir antique... –Albert Samain

1. On the Road.

The carriage like a cradle rocking sped
Across the plain, on its muddy road.
It was damp with a cold, monotonous, soaking rain.
Gentle, dejected, the sick day died.

The carriage like a cradle rocking ran and ran,
The coachman singing some kind of song.
A consumptive woman beside me was coughing hard
As darkness embraced the west and the east.

It was damp with a cold, monotonous, soaking rain.
The crows crossed cawing.
The consumptive woman sobbed in grief.
The wind passed, singing someone's lament.

And the coachman, rocking, long
Sang the colorless song of his days.
We were going, I don't know where, without end.
We went. Speechless. Soundless. And unable to sleep...

2. On a Sleepless Night.

I cannot sleep...
Just now, when I want to sleep so much,
To remove everything, everything from my mind.
My unclosing glance wanders, silent,
And my uncertain mind strays through dark
Sad plains.

In the blackness' embrace my wavering
Lantern's light cries like the last gasps
Of a young girl dying...

One knocks at the door of the past
And I remember you.

Like the melody of a forgotten song
My soul trembles beneath the fingers of light
And one by one before me are arrayed
Scenes and faces immemorial
And lost.

There in the dark now appears
Your pale, sad, wan visage,
From the unknown mist of days arisen,
Pale visitor.

And I recall a rainy day,
An ancient evening:
The exhilarating rhythm of faraway songs,
A wedding feast in progress.
Beneath the drops from a rainy sky
I was standing...

Oh, to sleep, to get to sleep...
I'll close my eyes and shut them tight
And not think about anything at all.
"Weren't we together once?"
"O sing me a lullaby, softly, lullaby."
I want to sleep, but night is past...
"Was it a dream, delirium, or pain?"

Of course it was pain, pain!
You never, never smiled at me,
Your very smile seemed a pain
Upon my fragile spirit...
I called for you a long, long time
But you never came, never–
I wanted to stand obedient before you,

A captive without will,
And all my love brought you was boredom...

My soul was alien to you, like
A bouquet brought from strange meadows:
Roses of torment, blossoms of emotion,
Stars of dream, glimmerings of hope—
And red, red opium poppies of pain.
I offered my soul wreathed in these flowers to you as a gift
So that your virgin soul might grieve with me.
And I do not recall how one day—
Alien, incomprehensible—
I lost you on a new life's threshold...

No, you went away, I don't know where.
I went, too. Of course, there—where you lived so long—
There was no living there.
There was no seeing the lights in your house,
There was no seeing your broad street
That I have not forgotten till now...

Ah, let's leave it. What does it matter?
Nobody, after all, knows
Why life turned out like this:
Love was tears and blood for us.
Love for us bears the price of death,
But for a woman that is wine of exultation...

This sleepless, sleepless, silent night,
Ah, I don't want to recall yet again
The senseless, inconsolable past.
So why do you keep coming back,
Wanting late at night to bore
Your way through my weakened soul?

Is that why you came,

Deceitful spectre?
Would you excavate the wounds of my soul
When you spurned the treasures there?
Oh, repulsive woman,
You want a soul of vanity and blemish
To laugh at in your hearty malevolence,
To roar with all your soul in sheer delight...
Shall I tell you how suddenly
Every single thing for me was changed
And I lost the road of dream?

It was a dark night. It was raining.
Darkness had descended upon my shadowed soul.
Barrenness sobbed there
Where ancient dreams of no return had been.
And I went out. In the muddy street
I walked a long time.
I don't know where. For me there was
No road left any more...

I walked a long time.
And before me was—a long street.
Faraway indistinct yellow fires were burning.
And I went towards those fires,
Which brought ancient tidings to me...
Ancient tidings kept secretly in my soul—
So gingerly I crossed the threshold...

And... this I remember:
An old bed buried in the fog
And a naked body
And my pained, choked sobbing
And then I went out.
All I felt was how cold it was, the wind,
And how life was a joke for me, as well...

Everything sacred to me died.
Go away, my darling!
Let life storm over my head
And scatter ashes,
For no regret can now restore
My ancient dream...
Go away, my darling!
And for a moment let me get you out of my brain,
Since I want to fall asleep, to fall...

3. The Dead.

The evening was rainy and wet;
The streets, empty and silent.
And the wind swept past,
Swift and damp.

And the dark night was descending,
In the tenebrous distance appeared
The street lights, wavering,
Betrayed to shame and to lying.

And I walked with deaf tread,
Repeating your name to myself.
Somebody faraway burst out laughing
In the street's rain-washed dream.

And in my heart I blessed
Your dark, forgotten tomb.
Someone said I was lying, lying—
And faraway was heard another's helpless cry...

Charents spent several of his younger years in Moscow and returned there and to the northern capital, Leningrad, very often throughout his short life. He was as fluent in Russian as in Armenian; so it is very unlikely he did not read Bryusov's *Anthology*, in which there is an abridged translation of this poem of Tourian's (the first three stanzas, and the final, sixth one) by the famous Russian poet Konstantin Dmitrievich Bal'mont, on p. 441. In the Table of Contents, Bal'mont's translation is marked with an asterisk, as a reprint from an earlier publication. Of course Charents read *Im ts'ave* in Armenian anyway–Ch'arents' was editor-in-chief of the Transcaucasian State Publishing House till the mid-1930's, and there were three copies in his personal library of the Erevan edition of Duryan, P., *Tagher* (i.e., Bedros Tourian, "Poems"), 1932. Charents also possessed copies of books by both Bal'mont and Bryusov—but not, it would seem, the *Anthology* itself.[106] Bal'mont is so important a poet that his faithful but free version merits our attention.

МОЯ СКОРБЬ

Я не о том скорблю что в жажде сновидений,
Источник дум святых иссякшим я нашел,
Что прежде времени мой нерасцветший гений
Сломился и поблек под гнетом тяжких зол;

И не согрел никто горячим поцелуем
Ни бледных уст моих, ни бледного чела;
И, счастья не познав, любовью не волнуем,
Смотри- уж предо мной зияет смерти мгла...

Ни не о том скорблю, что нежное созданье,
Букет из красоты, улыбки и огня,-
Не усладит мое последнее страданье,
Лучом своей любви не озарит меня...

Я не о том скорблю...Нет, родине несчастной-
Все помыслы мои ... О ней моя печаль!

---

[106]Nos. 1072-1074 /1198-1200/ on p. 36 of the typewritten handlist of the *Spisok knig lichnoi biblioteki Egishe Charentsa* ("List of books of the personal library of Yeghishe Charents"), Dom-muzei Egishe Charentsa ("House-museum of Yeghishe Charents"), Erevan.

Не в силах ей помочь, томясь тоской напрасной,
Безвестно умереть,- о, как мне жаль, как жаль!

Translation:

MY SORROW

I do not grieve because in thirst of dream-visions
I found the spring of holy thoughts had run dry
Or because before my time my unblossomed genius
Broke and faded under heavy evils' oppression;

And no one warmed with a hot kiss
My pale lips or pale brow;
And, having known no happiness, by love, unstirred,
See: the murk of death already before me looms...

And I do not grieve that a gentle creation,
A bouquet of beauty, a smile, and fire,
Will not sweeten my final suffering,
With the beam of her love will shine no light on me ...

I do not grieve for that ... No, for my unfortunate motherland
Are all my thoughts ... My sorrow is for her!
Unable to help her, languishing in vain longing,
To die unknown—O that, that is my regret!

**35. "Memorial Gift to B.H. Janfesjian"** (*Nver hishadagi arr B.H. Janfesjian*), 6 October 1871 (Sevak pp. 80-82)

**Text.**

ՆՈՒԷՐ ՅԻՇԱՏԱԿԻ ԱՌ Պ.Հ. ՃԱՆՖԵՍՃԵԱՆ

ՅՈ·ԻՇՔ

Սա խաղաղ Մայր- Օվկեանին,
Ուր փողփողեն աւապք ոսկի՝
Մեր երապոց վառարանին՝
Թ'եպրէն՝ վարդից մէջ աճիւնի
Երբ արևը շողշողէ,
Դու իմ սէրը միշտ յիշէ՝։

Թաւուտքէ մը կանաչ ու մորչ,
Որոց շուքը սիրէինք միշտ
Նստիլ, խօսիլ շրթամբք դողդոջ,
Ծըծել անյագ իրարու սիրտ,
Երբ տերև մը խարշափէ,
Դու իմ մրմունջքը յիշէ՝։

Առաւօտներն գարնանային,
Ո·հ, հորիկոնն ալ վարդավառ՝
Յ'այց ելնելուդ ծաղկած մարգին,
Ուր կը գտնես մորչ չոր մացառ՝
Երբ թռչնիկ մը ճըռւողէ,
Դու իմ իղձերը յիշէ՝։

Պաղլար-պաշի ելած ատեն՝
Եւ կամ սա·րը Չամլըճային՝
Սիրո·ւն վայրեր ուր միշտ արդէն
Ճեմել հոգիք մեր սիրէին՝
Երբոր պեփիւռ մը փըչէ,
Դու իմ հոգին միշտ յիշէ՝։

Եւ առօրեայ աշխատանքէ
Վաստակաբեկ վերադարձիդ՝
Եւ կամ սիրոյ արշաւանքէ
Դարձած ատեն տըրոփ ի սիրտ՝
Երբ հորիզոնն հրդեհէ,
Դու իմ կրակները յիշէ՛։

Ամրան գիշեր մ՚երբոր գտնես
Աստղերն առատ գլխուդ վըրայ՝
Եւ լուսինը լապտեր ընես
Դողդոջ քայլից դէպ ի Մոտա,
Երբ շրջազգեստ մը շրշէ,
Իմ մաշած սիրտը յիշէ՛։

Տրտում նստած դու պատուհան՝
Յառած երկնից այն սևերես՝
Սև մըտածմանց լոկ վառարան
Տժգոյն ճակատդ և աչերդ վէս՝
Տըխուր կոչնակ մ՚երբ հնչէ,
Մըտերմիդ մա·հը յիշէ՛։

**Translation.**

*Memorial Offering to B. H. Janfesjian*

REMEMBER!

When upon this peaceful Mother, Ocean,
Whose golden sands are aglitter,
Hearth of our dreams,
Or upon the roses that blossom in my ashes by the shore
The sun shines down,
Thou! my love ever remember!

When in the verdant woodland green
In whose shadows we always loved

To sit and speak with trembling lips,
Imbibing insatiably each other's hearts,
A leaf is stirring,
My murmurings, then, remember!

When on springtime mornings,
O! the horizon itself is festive rosy flame
And to tarry in the flowering meadow you go out
And there find a dry bush green
Where the little bird is trilling,
My longings then remember!

When you go to Baghlar-bashi
Or to the hill at Camlica—
Lovely places where ever
Our souls delighted to ramble still,
And the soft breeze blows:
My soul, then, remember!

And when from daily work,
Broken by your labor, you're returning,
Or when from amorous conquest,
Heart still pounding, you come home
And the horizon is a conflagration,
My fires, then, remember!

When on a summer night you discover
The stars in abundance overhead
And make the moon your lantern
On your hesitant way to the Moda
And a woman's dress rustling you hear,
My worn out heart, then, remember!

When seated by the window, sad,
You fix your haughty eyes, pale brow
'Gainst dark-faced heaven, the focus

(40) Of black musings only,
And the grim bell is tolling,
Your bosom friend's death remember!

**Commentary.**

The poem refers to the death of Vartan Lutfian, 1851-1871, a poet, playwright, translator, and student of the imperial medical academy at Constantinople: he was a dear friend of Tourian's. The Lament for him (No. 36) pursues at least one powerful image adumbrated in this poem. Hovhannes Janfesjian, a relative and close friend of Tourian's, to whom this poem is addressed, was a member of the Armenian Philanthropic Society for the Indigent (*Aghk'adasirats'*) of the district of Yeni Mahalle, Scutari. He later became a successful businessman, and died in the 1920s. Several places are mentioned in the poem: *Moda burnu* was the seaside promenade and main street of Scutari; *Camlica* is the highest point in Scutari, a place where Tourian used to sit with friends and watch the colors of the city below change towards evening; *Baghlar-bashi*, a favorite haunt of Tourian's, was a park in the same town: Tourian is buried in the cemetery of Baghlar-bashi. Ekserjian changed *khaghagh* "peaceful" in line 1 to *gabuyd* "blue," even though Tourian had corrected the latter to the former in his drafts.

I have translated the subtitle *Hushk'* "Memories," following the syntactical intent suggested by the exclamation point, as though it were an imperative verb, cf. *hishe!* "remember!" within the poem. One is reminded by the repetition of the injunction, of the famous ghazal of Hafez whose lines are still for the Persian reader the archtypal cry of longing for the fellowship of the past: *Rūz-e vaṣl-e dūstdārān yād bād, yād bād ān rūzgār yād bād ... rāz-e Hāfez baʿd az īn nāgofte mānad, Ey darīγā! rāzdārān yād bād* "May the day of association with friends be remembered! / Be remembered! That time be remembered! ... After this, let the secret of Hafez remain unsaid, / Cry woe! may the keepers of the secret be remembered!"[107] Hafez is the survivor, and his memory proceeds from the broad circle of friends to the mystery (*raz*) of the depths

[107]For a translation, see H. Wilberforce Clarke, *The Divan-i-Hafiz*, repr. Bethesda, MD: Iranbooks/Ibex Publishers, 1998, p. 454.

of his heart—for those who knew its interior, its mystery (they are called *razdaran,* lit. "mystery-keepers"), are themselves now gone.[108] Tourian's poem moves similarly from a wide vision to a grief-laden, constricted one of the interior of the heart: its images proceed from the vast, romantic, and nearly abstract to the narrowly specific and quotidian, in two halves whose various oppositions impress upon the reader the change. The first three stanzas evoke the ocean, then the forest, then a vernal meadow—all in the daylight. The final four name Baghlar-bashi and Camlica, then one's trip home from work or from a date, then departure for a prowl along Moda Avenue, and, at last, a session of sad silent thought at home by one's window—and the setting deepens from day to dusk to dark night.

One may compare two descriptions of the sky in these contrasting large sections of the poem: in line 14, the horizon is *vartavarr;* in 29, it is a *hrteh,* "conflagration." The first word by folk etymology can seem to mean "rose-and-burning" (with the verb *varrel*);[109] and, as discussed previously, it is the name of an ancient Armenian spring festival—the same Zoroastrian celebration that is called in Persian *Abrizegan,* "Water-sprinkling"—which became associated in the Christian calendar with Pentecost. On Vartavar, Armenians energetically drench each other with buckets of water; so Tourian's word has a festive connotation and brings together the diverse associations of dawn—rosy color, the burning fire of the sun, and the cool dampness

---

108Persian *raz,* "secret, mystery," appears as a loan in Arm. *eraz,* "dream," that is, a vision whose hidden mystery is to be unlocked; and from the loan of *raza* into Aramaic from Old Persian we even have a Kabbalistic *angelus interprans* for the purpose, Raziel. See J. R. Russell, "The Dream Vision of Anania Shirakats'i," *REArm* 21, 1988-1989, pp. 159-170; and "'Sleep' and 'Dreaming' in Armenian," in J. Greppin, ed., *Proceedings of the Fourth International Conference on Armenian Linguistics,* Delmar, NY: Caravan, 1992, pp. 147-169 (*AIS,* pp. 293-304, 477-499).

109The actual etymology is "bringing roses": the ending *-varr* has nothing to do with burning here, but comes from Iranian *-barana-,* "carrying, bringing," cf. Arm. *burvarr* "thurible" and Sogdian *vodhvarn "idem,"* both from **baodhabarana*—"incense-holder": see J. R. Russell, "The Etymology of Armenian *vardavarr,*" *AArmL* 13, 1992, pp. 63-69 (*AIS,* pp. 469-475).

of dew (cf. the manipulation of *vart* "rose," *shogh* "sunbeam," and *shagh* "dew" in poem No. 11, *Sirets'i k'ez* "I loved you"). So here Tourian has added a misty veil of fine water—dew and spray—to the sensual collocations of redness and fragrance and passion central to his imagistic palette. The verb *hrtehe* from *hrteh* in line 29 describes a flaming dusk, not dawn—the dying, not the nascent, day. And it has none of Vartavar's joyful overtones—the conflagration is fire as consuming destroyer only. And when the speaker then summons his surviving friend to recall the fires (*gragner*) of his heart, one must recall Tourian's startling description in *Lejag* ("The Lake") of his heart's depth, identified with the dark waters of the still mere, as ***hrteh*** *voch' madyan* "a **conflagration**, no book." All the contrasts of the earlier image of Vartavar are here, forming an exact and subtle parallel structure: rose-fire-water—but all have a negative marker. This symmetry can be discerned in other sense impressions: at the end of the third stanza, that is, the end of the first, positively marked, half of the poem, a bird trills; but at the end of the seventh, the second, dark half, a funeral bell tolls. The first is light and swift; the second, heavy and slow: the poem moves from widening expanse, light, and youthful swiftness to constriction, slowness, and dark—the road all follow down into death.

Line 10: ***Dzdzel*** *anhak iraru sird*, "(We loved) insatiably to suck/imbibe each other's heart(s)." Tourian develops this image in the Lament for Vartan Lutfian, no. 36, in the stanza constaining line 27 and following: *Sev* ***dzdzeink'****: suk anhadnum!* "We sucked/imbibed black: mourning inexhaustible." Arm. *dzdzel*, "suck," has the overtone, as everywhere, of a child at the breast; and as will be seen in the Lament, Tourian takes the contrasting images of blackness and milk and introduces the image of *sev gat'*, black milk, in line 30—anticipating the remarkable *Todesfuge* of Paul Celan.

**36. "At the Grave of the Most Beloved Vartan Loutfian"** (*I gerezmann amenasirelvo Vartan Lut'fyani*), 1871 (Sevak pp. 83-85)

**Text.**

**Ի գերեզմանն ամենասիրելւոյ Վարդան Լութֆեանի։**

ՀԵԾԵԾՄՈ՛ՒՆՔ

Ո՛հ, երկնքի ժապաւէններ՝
Ճառագայթնե՛ր՝ միացուցած
Էին սրտերը մեր միմեանց՝
Մեր սրտերը սիրանուէր։

Նոքա միմեանցս համար քանի՞
Էին անհո՛ւն բա՛ց մատեաններ,
Հոն ամեն բառ խորք մը ունէր
Իր ներքևը սիրոյ, ցաւի։

Ո՛հ, կը յիշե՞ս, Ճամլըճայի
Սարը նստած լո՛ւռ մըխայինք,
Ուր շուք տային մեկի նոճիք՝
Սև հովանոցք վշտահարի։

Ըսթամպոլի կապոյտ գօտւոյն՝
Վոսփորի ծուփը դիտէինք,
Ուսկիք և մերթ կ'անամպ երկինք–
Ո՛, ախորժնե՛ր լուռ մեր հոգւոյն։

Այն հիւսկէնները երկնքին՝
Այն ամպերը ձիւնաթորմի՝
Մինչ երեկոյ, ո՛հ, մի առ մի
Մեր նայուածքը գըրաւէին։

Չ'էինք խօսեր, խօսքն մեր հոգւոց
Անհունութիւնը կը պղծէր,

Մենք վերթ երկու տժգոյն բոցեր
Իրարու մէջ կ'այրէինք սոսկ։

Մեր հոգիքը նոճիներու
Թուխ թիթեռներ էին տրտում,
Սև· ծըծէինք՝ սո·ւգ անհատնում,
Նայէինք միշտ երկրէս հեռու։

Անյուսութի·ւն, գերեզմանի
Այդ սև կաթը շատ ըմպեցինք,
Քեզ յափրեցուց այդ ըմպելիք,
Եղար երկնից տժգոյն որդի։

Քու դալուկըդ՝ պիս ցաւցուց շա·տ,
Եւ նայուածքըդ վերջին նըուաղ՝
Զ'որ ուղղեցիր ինծի, աւա·ղ,
Բևեռացուց յ'իս յիշատակդ։

Երջանի՞կ ես հոդ թէ թշուառ,
Զուարթնոյ թևով լուր մ'ինձ ղրկէ,
Ա·հ, այս աշխարհը միշտ տաղտուկ է...
Ցաւերու մեծ մայր մ'է աշխարհ։

Ո·հ, եթէ հոդ ծառի մը շուք
Կայ և նորա քով մեկ վըտակ,
Եթէ կայ հոդ սէ·ր անապակ,
Կան ապատ օդ, ապատութիւնք։

Ո·հ, կը թօթուեմ ես այս աղտոտ
Ձորձն հոգւոյս՝ կեանքս՝ մինչ իսկ այսօր,
Հող կը հագնիմ, հո·ղ սըգաւոր...
-Ա·հ, ուպածներս, Վա·րդան, կա՞ն հոդ...։

**Translation.**

*At the Grave of the Most Beloved Vartan Loutfian*

LAMENTS!

O streaming rays of heaven
That joined our hearts
To one another,
Our hearts dedicated to love!

How much they were for one another
Boundless, open books
Where every word had a nether
Depth of love and pain.

O do you recall how we sat
Silently, smouldering, on the hill
Of Camlica, the cypresses
Affording us their black and grieving shade?

We looked upon the undulating blue
Of Stamboul's girdle, Bosphorus,
From there, too, the cloudless sky:
To our silent souls, what delight!

Those filaments of sky,
Those snowbound cumuli,
O till dusk, one by one
They captivated our gaze.

We did not speak: our souls' talk
Would have defiled the infinite—
Like two discolored flames
Within each other we burned, instead.

Our souls were the cypresses'
Black butterflies grieving,
We sucked the black of inexhaustible mourning,
From this earth ever gazing far away.

Despair! That black milk
Of the grave we drank deep:
That drink sated you entirely
And you became heaven's sallow child.

Your paleness often grieved me
And your final, expiring glance
Upon me, Alas! was your memory's nail
Driven into my side.

Are you happy there or sad?
Send me tidings on an angel's wing.
Ah! This world is ever weary...
This world is a mother of great pain.

O, if the shade of a tree there
May be found, and a rill besides,
If imperishable love is there,
If there are freedoms there, free airs...

O, I toss in the filthy raiment
Of my soul, my whole life until today:
I clothe myself in earth, the mourning soil ...
Ah, Vartan, are the things we longed for there? ...

**Commentary.**

The poem exists in one of Tourian's notebooks, where, however, the page with the last six lines is missing. In a letter of 14 October 1871 to Dikran Atamian (d. 1908; the letter is translated in my notes to No. 25, "Murmurs," p. 228), the poet writes that he is sending him the poem; so it is likely he had finished it sometime earlier in the same month. The lament has been published in most of the Armenian editions of Tourian's works. Tchéraz (pp. 51-53) translates it, with this note: "V. Loutfian, un des amis intimes du poète, est mort, comme lui, de phtisie et à l'àge de 20 ans." The two youths were close indeed: in the first lines of the poem, Tourian declares that *yergnk'i zhabavenner*, "ribbons of heaven" united the friends' two hearts, which were "devoted to love" (*siranver*): the image is a potent one, reminding a reader versed in the culture in which Tourian was raised of the *narod*, the ribbon-like band tied round the heads of bride and groom at the wedding ceremony of the Armenian Church. The hearts of Bedros and Vartan were devoted as much to each other as to any ethereally glimpsed ideal of the Goethesque *Ewige Weibliche*.

Tourian regarded his bosom friend's early death as a foretaste of his own, which was indeed not far off; so it is reasonable that some of the images of their time spent together should resonate also with impressions of Tourian's solitary musings in "The Lake": ashes, the heart a book (in both poems, the strongly-marked term *madyan* is used—a word evoking the Bible and the Lamentations of Narekats'i—rather than the common *kirk'*) with depths. Blackwell provides an accurate and pretty, but not altogether literal, translation (pp. 30-31). Tourian deleted these two draft stanzas from the poem:

Նոճիներու սև շուքը ինկած,
Բաւ տքնեցանք ու հեծեցինք.
Եւ մեր ողբոց բաւ արձագանք
Տըւին Մասեաց հսկայ լերինք։

Նոճիներու սև շուքն ինկած
Ոսկրներով՝ մոխրով ծանօթ
Յիշատակն էին սևցած քարեր...

"The cypresses' black shade fallen
Upon us, full vigil we kept, grieving;
And the titan mountains of Ararat
Gave multitudinous echo to our lamentations.

"The cypresses' black shade fallen
On the memorial stones, blackened, old,
That knows ashes, bones ..."

The lines are variants, as Sevak astutely observes (I, p. 281), of lines 9-12 of the poem *Hdzdzyunk'*, with its evocation of the poet's beloved Camlica—the perch from which he used to gaze at the Bosphorus and Constantinople—and its cypresses. In his final draft, Tourian removed the heavy gravestones of the second of the omitted draft stanzas, whose presence would have been an irrelevant intrusion—*de trop du mort*—upon the hilly, wooded setting of the two youths gazing in dreamy Romantic rapture at the Bosphorus below. As for the titan mountains, *Azat* and *P'ok'r* Masis (Classical *Masik'*, genetive plural *Maseats'*, as here) are Greater and Little Ararat; but Tourian has the Classical Armenian nominative plural *lerink'*, "mountains" that points directly to the phrase *i lerins Araratay* "in the mountains of Ararat [scil., Urartu]" of the story of Noah in *Genesis*—all of them, where the Ark rested. Tourian presumably concluded that this image, too, would not work. Why, indeed, should the quiet musings of a private colloquy on the gentle hill of Camlica, over the soft evening and twinkling lights of the great sea-girt city suddenly assume patriotically stentorian volume, carry an Ark, and echo across the Anatolian land mass?

Lines 25-28: ... *nojineru / t'ukh t'it'errner ein drdum, / Sev dzedzeink': suk anhadnum...* Tourian employs a complex strategy of alliteration to underscore the image selected for the final version of the poem: the crack of the three aspirated t's of the first two words of line 26 fades at the end of the line into two soft echoes, the d's of *drdum*, "sad"; while the u of the latter word echoes and thereby stresses the u of the first word of the line, *t'ukh*. The latter word is a synonym of *sev*, "black," evidently chosen both because it merges in alliteration with *t'it'err*, "butterfly" and because it introduces but does not upstage the entrance of the other word for black, upon which a larger image will be constructed. The following line—the third of the stanza—begins, indeed, with *sev*, as the object of *dzedzeink'*, "we sucked," which makes one think of a child suckling at his mother's breast (this use of *dzdzel* is adumbrated in the preceding poem, in which Vartan's soul admonishes his surviving friend to remember him everywhere they spent time together). This anticipates the image to come in the following stanza, but in apposition to the object, *sev*, is not milk here but "unbroken mourning," *suk anhadnum*, whose two stressed u's recall the pattern of u's enclosing the previous line. The double consonants of *dzdzel*, "suck," recall the double of *t'it'err* in the preceding line; and it is perhaps noteworthy that the strong sound *dz*, Clas. Arm. *ts*, comes indeed in the third line after the basic imagery of the stanza has been established. In the oldest known Armenian verse, the Song of the Birth of Vahagn preserved by Movses Khorenats'i, the phrase *tsovn tsirani*, "wine-dark sea" (Western Armenian *dzovn dzirani*) comes in the third line to complete and complicate the pattern of the first two. The Song is octosyllabic, as is Tourian's poem (he ensures that an eighth syllable will be read, indeed, by inserting a written *shva* between the first two letters of *dzdzeink'*—the *sugh vang* of Arm. prosody).[110]

The black butterflies chosen for the final draft of the poem, then, provide an image at once deeply symbolic and startlingly contradictory: butterflies are light, and their color is generally imagined to be correspondingly bright. They are delicate summer creatures, not harbingers of death. Even when the moth is imagined in Persian poetry as a lovesick soul consumed by its longing, it is the candle flame that extinguishes its life: light still dominates the pair of lovers, the *parvane o sham'*. And the image is anciently evocative of the immortal soul, too: for the brilliant butterfly, bursting forth from the caterpillar's cocoon-tomb, the prison-house of the chrysalis, is the emblem of enfranchised Psyche, the soul born into the afterlife.[111] Tourian's butterflies are thus

---

[110]On the poetics of the Song of Vahagn generally, see this writer's, "Carmina Vahagni" (*Acta Antiqua* 32.3-4, Budapest, 1989, pp. 317-330), and note the discussion of *yergin-dzov* in the section on Tourian's poetics, in the Introduction to this book; on the complexity of the *ts*- and other patterns, see my "Sound as Symbol: The Case in Pagan and Christian Armenian Poetics" (*Le Muséon* 109.1-2, 1996, pp. 113-126) (*AIS*, pp. 357-370; 713-726).

[111]The image is central to Vladimir Nabokov's short story, "Christmas" (*Rozhdestvenskii rasskaz*, 1928, tr. in *The Stories of Vladimir Nabokov*, New York: Knopf, 1995, pp. 131-136): Sleptsov (the name contains Rus. *slepoi*, "blind man") goes in winter to the family estate, where everything of the last summer reminds him of his young son, a butterfly collector, who has just died. The man lights the stove in his son's room and the heat quickens the gestation of a beautiful moth from a cocoon the boy had placed in a box. Nabokov believed strongly in subtle and elegantly artistic intimations of the afterlife, Rus. *potustoronnost'* (lit. "on-the-other-sidedness"), to which the hero is blind.

arrestingly vivid as images, phantasmagoric and sinister, and chromatically resonant with the scene: the lengthening of tenebrous shadows, the somber masses of cypresses—themselves an emblem of beauty in the Orient as well as a favorite fixture of romantic landscapes of death.[112] The cypresses are marked as *sev*, "black," in line 12. The trees' dark spires, like cathedrals of beauty and mortality fused, soar heavenwards, and midst their dark spires wheel the black-winged butterflies of the soul.[113] One is reminded of Sylvia Plath's lines, nearly a century later: "This is the light of the mind, cold and planetary. / The trees of the mind are black... / The grasses unload their griefs on my feet..."[114] All set the scene for Tourian's most astonishingly vivid image, a great contradiction possible only in poetry: black milk.

Lines 29-30: ... *kerezmani/ Ayt sev gat'e shad embets'ink'*: for "black milk," Blackwell has "dark-hued milk" (and not of the tomb, but of hopelessness, though the latter word is in the vocative in the text); Tchéraz translates, precisely, "ce lait noir du tombeau." Ekserjian, with surprising insensitivity to poetic invention, comments, "In one verse, through a typographical error, *arbets'uyts'* ["caused to drink, made intoxicated"] and *sev gat'* ["black milk"] should be regarded as incongruous (*anhamatsayn*). But when we observe that Tourian had written *hap'rets'uyts'* ["satiated"], we will then say that Tourian had not made a mistake" (Sevak, I, p. 281). I cannot see what difference it would have made, though it is gratifying that the editor settled on the *lectio diffi-*

---

[112]Arnold Böcklin's painting *Toteninsel*, 1880, for instance, shows Charon rowing a standing, white-shrouded figure into the cypress-shaded lagoon of a semi-circular isle of pale sepulchres (illus. in *La revue du Musée d'Orsay* 48.14, Paris, Automne 2001, p. 56, fig. 6, with discussion on p. 65 ff.).

[113]Tourian's extreme sensitivity to color is what one should expect in a poet; yet still his strong evocation of blackness here reminds one of *chyornyi barkhat*, "black velvet," the insistent and concrete symbol of death in Osip Mandelstam's *V Peterburge my soidyomsya snova*, "In Petersburg we shall come together again": in the Russian poet's work the source seems to have been the black velvet hangings around the catafalque of an official at the Italian Embassy on the Moika, which Mandelstam saw as a child.

[114]See Frieda Hughes, ed., Sylvia Plath, *Ariel: The Restored Edition*, New York: Harper Collins, 2004, p. xii.

*cilior*. Milk has two primary associations: whiteness[115] and motherhood. The soil of Mother Earth, where the grave is dug, is black; so may her milk be. Yet the image of *sev gat'* is still startling, arresting. Modern European readers know it, not from Tourian's work, but from a poem by Paul Celan. Could he have got it from Tourian? Though there was a very large and thriving Armenian community in Romania, it is most unlikely—one may say, impossible—that the German-speaking Jewish poet Paul Celan (born Antschel), who grew up in Czernowitz, Bukovina (postwar Chernovtsy, Ukraine) ever read or even heard of Bedros Tourian. For it seems relations between Jews and Armenians in the poisonous atmosphere of fascist Romania were generally cool.[116]

---

[115]This is so intuitive that two examples chosen at random will suffice to make the point. G.M.A. Grube, in the Introduction to his translation of the *Poetics* of Aristotle, uses "white milk" as the example of an unnecessary epithet permissible in poetry but best avoided in prose (G.M.A. Grube, *Aristotle on Poetry and Style*, Indianapolis: Bobbs-Merrill, 1979, p. xi). Since the Islamic Revolution, the inspired observations of the Founding Ayatollah, many of them so commonplace as to seem tautological, have adorned the blank walls of Persian buildings. One satiric wag's subversive contribution, *Mast sefid ast—Imam Khomeini* ("Yoghurt Is White.—Imam Khomeini"), was, so Tehran urban folklore has it, not erased for some time, since it was feared the dictum might be genuine.

[116]The Romanian Jewish writer Mihail Sebastian in his diaries of the 1930s and early '40s mentions a number of Armenian acquaintances in Bucharest: like the famous scholar of religions Mircea Eliade and other Romanian intellectuals, who ostracized the shocked and despairing Sebastian from their company, they tended in varying degrees to be pro-Fascist and anti-Semitic. Catholicos Vazgen II, who guided the Holy See of Echmiadzin through the postwar years in the Armenian SSR, grew to maturity in Fascist and Nazi Romania without, to my knowledge, making any protest as the country's Jewish community was slaughtered with an enthusiasm that took some fastidious Germans aback. A Romanian-Armenian woman, a classmate and friend of mine at Columbia University and a great lover of Arab culture (her family moved to Alexandria when Romania became Communist), spoke once without noticeable irony of her family's friendship during the Occupation with a German officer, "a very idealistic Nazi" as she put it. This characterization rather disturbed one, though a postcard she wrote from Alexandria one summer during my infatuation with Lawrence Durrell's *Alexandria Quartet* remains an unforgettable and delectable memory of youth. The pleasure

Yet Tourian has anticipated the most extraordinary image of the most powerful strophe of Celan's most famous poem. Celan's family were murdered in the Nazi Holocaust; and at the end of World War II he wrote *Todesfuge*, "Death Fugue," a poem about the Nazi death camps that has been called "the *Guernica* of postwar European literature." The poem begins with the line in which is embedded its most powerful and best-known metaphor, one surreal and contrary to fact, a metaphor which is, in John Felstiner's characterization, "extreme, bittersweet, nullifying the nourishment vital to humankind": *Schwarzes Milch der Frühe wir trinken sie abends*, "Black milk of dawn we drink it at dusk." Though the image *Schwarzes Milch* had been used in a book published in 1939 by Rose Ausländer, a Jewish poet of Czernowitz whom Celan knew, it is not known whether he found it there, or somewhere else, or came up with it independently.[117] Celan's poem continues: *wir trinken sie mittags und morgens wir trinken sie nachts / wir trinken und trinken / wir schaufeln ein Grab in den Lüften da liegt man nicht eng* "We drink it at noon and in the morning we drink it at night / We

---

outweighed the disquiet, but both have remained. These examples illustrate the deep chasm that divided Romanian Jews and Armenians before the Second World War: it is all the more unlikely that the young Celan would have had Armenian friends to recommend Tourian (presumably in Tchéraz's 1913 French translation) to him. The situation in Romania will have been typical of Armeno-Jewish relations generally in Eastern Europe outside the USSR. One recalls that the Yiddish code word for Armenians is a kind of Cockney-slanging term, Hebrew *timkhe*, the second half of the Biblical injunction *yemakh timkhe* "may he be utterly blotted out" against the murderous tribe of the Amalekites. It has been suggested that Yiddish *timkhe* comes from Georgian *somekhi*, "Armenian," or is based on a local tradition of descent from Amalek amongst the Armenians of Amasia in Pontus. But when one reads such compositions as the Armeno-Turkish novel "The Jewish Wife," with its visceral anti-Semitic hatred, or considers the fomenting by local Christians of the Damascus blood-libel riots against the Jews in the 1840s, it is plain that Yiddish *timkhe* simply expresses contempt for an ethnic rival in the Ottoman world.

[117]See the chapter "A Fugue after Auschwitz (1944-45)," pp. 22-41, in John Felstiner, *Paul Celan: Poet, Survivor, Jew*, New Haven: Yale University Press, 1995; for the text and translation of *Todesfuge*, see Felstiner's *Selected Poems and Prose of Paul Celan*, New York: Norton, 2001, pp. 30-33.

drink and drink / We dig a grave in the air one does not lie cramped there." We drink and drink—the same image of grotesque satiety or even sardonic intoxication of Tourian's verb *hap'rets'nel*; and the grave (German *Grab*, Arm. *kerezman*) is there, too. Later in the poem, Celan contrasts the golden hair of Margarete, the girl evocative of Goethe's *Faust* and all that is Germanic, with the ashen hair of Shulamith, the beloved of the *Song of Songs* and the personification of Jewish and Biblical beauty. But the tresses of the maiden of Jerusalem are gray with humbling age, burnt by the crematoria; while the camp commandant, animated by satanic energy, plays with serpents and writes letters home to Germany, to the heart of darkness, to the still-youthful Margarete.

In Felstiner's translation of Celan's poem, words and phrases easily understandable to speakers of English appear in the original German (*dein goldenes Haar*—"your golden hair," etc.) and multiply towards the end: the German language partakes in the thickening evil of the demonic fugue. Celan, writing within German, could deploy such possibilities of what must have become for him to some extent a tainted language, only through his images themselves. Many Armenians of the Ottoman period before the Genocide—probably more than is generally supposed—spoke Turkish as their native or principal language, even as most Jews of Europe spoke Yiddish (Judeo-German), and German, too, before the Holocaust.[118] The idiomatic Armenian of

---

[118]For example, my first teacher of Armenian, Mrs. Maritza Tsaggos, née Boyajian, was the daughter of Armenian Turcophone parents from Kayseri (ancient Caesarea-Mazaca of Cappadocia). In the Dutch television documentary of 1997, "The Wall of Silence," the brother of Vahakn Dadrian, the well-known historian of the Armenian Genocide, explains that their family, which was very prominent in Ottoman Armenian society, spoke only Turkish at home in Corum, and began to speak Armenian only after moving to Constantinople. Cilicia in particular had a large Turcophone population and Armeno-Turkish press; but in general the prevalence of Armenian amongst Ottoman Armenians in Western Anatolia before the Genocide is probably exaggerated in hindsight. Rather, the pre-eminence of Armeno-Turkish should be compared to that of Judaeo-German amongst the Jews of Europe before the Holocaust. *Mutatis mutandis*, the renascence of Hebrew, promoted with urgency by Zionism, and the restoration to exclusive use of Armenian (and cleansed of loans from the languages of Muslims, at that) reflects the salutary

Istanbul in which Tourian forged his poetic medium was very strongly informed by Turkish word formation, syntax, and lexical loans. It is an ironic accident that Celan writes in a language that must, after the very events to which it refers, seem at best a sardonic medium for Jewish literature; so has Turkish become for Armenians writing after 1915. The German painter Anselm Kiefer has based a series of remarkable paintings on Celan's poem and on the Kabbalah; but no Turkish artist has yet emerged to encounter creatively the unexpiated horror and guilt of the Genocide. The writer Arp'iar Arp'iarian, born in Constantinople the same year as Tourian, lived to 1907—far enough for a long retrospective of the Armenian literature of the nineteenth century; and he asks, in a poignant paragraph, *Inch' bidi ellar? Kaghdnik'e kerezman darav.* "What would he have become? He bore the secret to his grave."[119] Both men, had they lived to 1915, would have been murdered with Varouzhan and Siamanto, or, had they survived, would have found themselves in a city become alien and overshadowed by unimaginable mass murder. *Sev gat', schwartzes Milch ...*

Since the poem bears the title of a lament (*hedzedzmunk'*), one seeks a possible inspiration for the imagery in the Book (*madyan!*) of Lamentation (*voghp-ergut'yan*) of St. Gregory of Narek. There is no exact precursor there to Tourian's remarkable vision of black milk, though milk is contrasted in the *Matean* with ashes, and with blood; and in one passage even a Black Sun rises:

Այս մայր հոգևոր երկնաւոր լուսաւոր, քան թէ երկրաւոր շնչաւոր մարմնաւոր, պիս գգուեաց որդի· կաթն ստեանց սորա՝ արիւնն Քրիստոսի։
(Բան ՀԵ.ժդ, էջ՝ 240)

---

intention to dissociate oneself from a linguistic and cultural context compromised by murder.

[119]See Arp'iar Arp'iarean, *Patmut'iwn ŽT: daru T'urk'ioy Hayoc' grakanut'ean* ("History of the Literature of the Armenians of Turkey of the XIX Century"), Hamazgayin series 1, Cairo: Yusaber, 1943/1944, p. 61.

This mother, spiritual, heavenly, and luminous rather than earthly, breathing, and corporeal, nurtured me as her child: the milk of her breasts is Christ's blood.[120]
(Ch. 75.14, p. 240)[121]

Իսկ ես զերախտիսն Աստուծոյ լքի զայսքանեաց բարեաց արարողի, և չարին զկնի միտեցայ՝ հայել ընդ նմին յատակս դժոխոց… կաթնս հոսեալ ի կոյտս մոխրոց, այրս մահու ի յարեաց գնդից։
(Բան Կէ·բ, էջ՝ 171)

But I abandoned the gifts of God, Maker of all these many good things, and followed my inclination to the Evil one to contemplate with him the nethermost floor of hell... pouring my milk out onto heaps of ash, I the man of death, expelled from the hosts of the noble-and-manly.[122]

---

[120]The mother of the passage is the Church, but Christ is the giver of milk. Christ nourishes us with His blood; and when He was stabbed with the lance, blood and water flowed from His side. Early Christian literature has occasional references to the milk of the male God's breasts: see, e.g., the strange, gender-mixing nineteenth poem of the so-called *Odes of Solomon* in Syriac: *kāsā də-halvā etqarav lī... wa-hū d-ethəlev abā* "A cup of milk was given to me ... and he who was milked was the Father" (see J. H. Charlesworth, ed. and tr., *The Odes of Solomon*, Oxford: Clarendon Press, 1973, p. 81).

[121]Page numbers refer to the edition used for the 1975 Erevan *Concordance* to the Narek: Grigor Narekats'i, *Matean Oghbergut'ean (Book of Lamentations)*, Buenos Aires, 1948, facsimile repr. with an Intro. by J. R. Russell, Delmar, NY: Caravan, 1981.

[122]The usage, with *ayr* "man" played against the gen. pl. of itself and another word, *areac'*, is strikingly archaic, typical of deep structures in the *Narek*: Arm. *i yareac' gndic'* referred of old to the cohort (*gund*) of the *Arik'*, i.e., the armies of the *Aryas*—the noble ones, as the ancient Iranians called themselves. Middle Iranian *Eran ud Aneran*, Iran and the rest of the World, as it were, is Arm. *Arik' ew Anarik'*; but *ari* is also an adj. formation upon *ayr*, "man." And in Iran, just as in India down to the Buddhist scriptures, *arya-* has the sense of moral nobility as well as martial valor. In the narrative of the conversion of the Armenians of Agathangelos, king Tiridates invokes *ari Aramazd*, "the noble/manly Ahura Mazda." In a recent Erevan publication in which this writer is generously praised as an Iranocentrist, Mr. Armen Petrosyan proposes, for no particular reason, and with no evidence, to see the names *Ara* (the Beautiful) and *Aram* (probably the Urartean king, thought by Movses Khorenats'i to

(Ch. 67.2, p. 171)

Ըմպանակք երկու յերկոսին ձեռին, մինն արեամբ և միւսն կաթամբխ երկու բուրանոցք կայծակնաւորք, մինն խնկով և միւսն ճենճերիւ… արեգակունք երկու ի յերկուց ծայրից, մինն խաւարի և միւսն կիզման։ (Բան Լ.բ, էջ՝ 73-74)

Two chalices he holds in his hands twain: one full of blood; the other, with milk. Two thuribles there are, flashing lightning: one with incense; the other, with acrid smoke ... two suns rise from opposite horizons: one of darkness; the other, of burning.
(Ch. 30.2, pp. 73-74)

Narekats'i's phantasmagoria exceeds the visions, in places, of modernists and surrealists; but the sun of darkness, the black sun, is a very ancient image the Romantics adopted. Tourian would have encountered it in the Armenian passage above and, most likely, in the famous poem of Gérard de Nerval, "El Desdichado." In a letter of 10 December 1871 to his friend B. A. Lusinian the poet, very close to death, speaks of "the Joining of the Sarcophagus Bird and the Sun of Night": the letter is translated in full, with discussion, in the final section of this book.

---

have been Armenian) somehow encoded into the Zoroastrian divine name and epithet—to make it more Armenian and less Persian, presumably (with the result that St. Gregory the Illuminator is persecuted more by an Armenian than by a Mazdean, *pace* a millennium of hymnology on the Parthian lineage of the king). One thinks Petrosyan, a popular autodidact, wastes such light impressionism on scholarship: philology, including poetry, is, to pursue the *ayr/arya* word, *er maydani*, men's serious business. Still, as Jake Barnes tells Lady Brett in *The Sun Also Rises*, "Isn't it pretty to think so."

**37. "My Death"** (*Im mahe*), 1871 (Sevak, pp. 86-87)

**Text.**

ԻՄ ՄԱՀԸ

Եթէ դժգոյն մահու հրեշտակ
Անհուն ժպտով մ'իջնէ իմ դէմ...
Շոգիանան ցավքս ու հոգիս,
Գիտցէ·ք որ դէռ կենդանի եմ։

Եթէ սընարըս՝ իմ տիպար
Մոմ մը վըտիտ ու մահադէմ,
Ո·հ, նըշուլէ ցուրտ ճառագայթ,
Գիտցէ·ք որ դէռ կենդանի եմ։

Եթէ ճակտովս արտօսրապօծ
Զ'իս պատանի մէջ ցուրտ կերթ վէմ
Փաթթեն, դընեն սև դագաղը,
Գիտցէ·ք որ դէռ կենդանի եմ։

Եթէ հընչէ տըխուր կոչնակ՝
Թրթռուն ծիծաղն մահու դժխեմ,
Դագաղս առնէ իր համըր քայլ,
Գիտցէ·ք որ դէռ կենդանի եմ։

Եթե մարդիկն այն մահերգակ
Որք սև ունին ու խոժոռ դէմ՝
Համասըփռեն խունկ ու աղօթք,
Գիտցէ·ք որ դէռ կենդանի եմ։

Եթ' յարդարեն իմ հողակոյտ,
Եւ հեծեծմամբ ու սըգալէն
Իմ սիրելիքը բաժնըուին,
Գիտցէ·ք որ մի·շտ կենդանի եմ։

Իսկ աննըշան եթէ մընայ
Երկրի մեկ խորշն հողակոյտն իմ,
Եւ յիշատակս ալ թառամի,
Ա·հ, այնատեն ես կը մեռնի·մ…։

**Translation.**

*My Death*

If the angel of the discolored hour
Descends before me with deep smile,
My pains and soul evaporate—
Know that I am still alive.

If on my pillow my face
Waxen, wasted, stamped with death
Is struck by the flash of an icy ray—
Know that I am still alive.

If with my brow tear-plated
They wrap me in a stone-cold shroud
And place me in the black coffin—
Know that I am still alive.

If the sad rattle sounds,
Ill-favored death's rising cackle
As my casket takes its muted steps—
Know that I am still alive.

If those men who sing the dirge
Who have faces black and grim
Scatter prayer and incense wide—
Know that I am still alive.

If they tamp my earthen mound
And with sobs and lamentation
My loved ones part—

Know that I am forever alive.

But if without a sign remain
The corner of earth that is my grave,
And if the memory of me decay—
Then, then I die!

**Commentary.**

"Death be not proud." "Do not go gentle into that good night." Much human lyric is Promethean protest against death—and most poets did not have to compress all they had to say into a twentieth and final year. But Tourian, dying of consumption, was facing death constantly. His images, which would be unremarkable in modernist poems of two or three generations later, here have the original force of vision and nightmare.

With the end the distinctions of space and time flee; so the hour has a foul color (*tzhkuyn*)—as though time were a thing one could see. Death does not descend as restful, dark sleep, or even black oblivion, but as a cold ray (*ts'urd jarrakayt'*). Given the standard portrayal of inspiration as a man struck by an illuminating beam of light, Tourian's cold ray seems to bring with it dread awakening and terrible realization. Then comes the first image with any hint of warmth, of bright golden yellow light: that of the dead poet's forehead, glistening with the tears shed by his loved ones with their parting kisses: it is "tear-plated" *ardosra-zodz*, a striking compound immediately evoking the more common *vosge-zodz*, "gold-plated." And there is an uneasy ambiguity to this qualification of tears, too. For intrinsically they are springing, welling, trickling, falling drops, always seen and felt in movement, the human heart's dew, emotion's rain. But gold plate (or any plate) for all its shine is a static thing that fixes, even freezes a picture in an illuminated manuscript. There is light in the image, but though it is warm, it is immobile.

And there follows swiftly another contradictory, arresting vision that fuses the above concepts of cold and immobility together: the material of a shroud must be supple, winding; but Tourian's shroud is cold (as the ray of death was), and cold as what? As bare mountain rock (*ts'urd zert' vem*)! Nothing is harder, more unmoved and unyielding. This phantasmagoric image has justice, though; for the corpse and shroud in earth will be forever motionless. One is reminded of the stone folds of the garments of the lord and his lady on the relief of the Arundel tomb in Philip Larkin's poem: "They had not thought to lie so long." The images encountered so far have religious overtones: God is praised by the Psalmist as "my Rock, in Whom there is no unrighteousness." Armenia was baptized by St. Gregory, called the Illuminator (*Lusavorich'*); and rays of divine inspiration are a commonplace in the depiction of Evangelists and native saints (Mesrop Mashtots', Gregory of Narek, etc.). And Tourian continues with explicit references to the trappings of religion, for the clergy mediate our death.

The priests of the Armenian Church and their ritual objects seem more agents and instruments of death in the poem than providers of sanctified rest. Not only their robes and pointed hoods, but their faces, too, are black. The Armenian wooden clapper that was used before bells becomes a death rattle. Everything in the poem, in fact, brings death, and the poet's defiant refrain is a kind of challenge to fight. This invites one to consider more closely the angel in the first line (who is the part of the same company as the priests, after all). The Armenians regard Gabriel as the *krogh* (Clas. *grol*), the "writer" who notes men's deeds and brings the divine decree of death to them. (More rarely, Armenians call the angel of death Azrayel, from the usage of surrounding Muslims.) On talismanic scrolls (Arm. *hmayil*), Gabriel is often portrayed as a winged warrior, scroll and sword in hand, his eyes rolling horribly, standing on a corpse and holding the freshly extracted soul—a tiny, swaddled baby very like a white-shrouded corpse in miniature.

A popular Armenian ballad relates that one Prince Aslan (the name is Turkish and means "Lion") feasted and made merry and knew nothing of death. One day he sent a servant out for provisions. On his way, the servant came upon the funeral of a pauper and gave the money he had to the mourners. Because of this he returned late: his lord was angry, and, having found out the reason for the delay, challenged Gabriel, the angel of death, to fight him. Aslan actually won, so God Himself intervened and defeated him. The prince, knowing now that he must die, asked his parents and other relatives to accept death in his place, but they would not. Only his wife agreed to sacrifice herself for him; and God rewarded her devotion with double the three score and ten years of man's life span for them both. The story illustrates the very life cycle and psychological maturation of a human being. A person may think himself immortal—or simply not think of death at all. Some struggle mightily against the cold beam of illumination, refusing to grow up, fighting the inevitable, and fleeing to those who had seemed in the past a bulwark of strength, only to realize that they are not only also mortal, but maybe even a little selfish. So a man shakes childhood off him, and discovers that he must sustain himself in his life through the relationship of love and commitment he himself has made. This summation makes Prometheus a man in arrested adolescence, but then, many epic heroes are just that: the Now of man's maturity always must be the time after the end of a heroic age.

The oldest literary elaboration of this mythological type in the Near Eastern area is the Greek tragedy of Alcestis. The eastern Anatolian folk hero of Byzantine and later times, Digenes Akrites, dies in some versions of his epic after such a contest with the angel of death. But it is not Gabriel: the job has gone to the old pagan ferryman of the Styx, Charon. Denizens of the opium dens (Greco-Turkish *tekedes*) of Constantinople at the turn of the twentieth century, and certainly in Tourian's day as well, offered Charon, as lord of Hades, three grains of hashish with an invocation.[123] The last of the heroes of the Armenian

---

[123]They said, *Ya sou Khare, na kharis to mavro sou skotadi,* "Greetings, Charon, may you enjoy your black shade." I learnt of these songs and the culture behind them from the Iranist Prof. Martin Schwartz of the University of California, Berkeley: his annotated compact disk recording *Greek-Oriental Rebetica, Songs and Dances in the Asia Minor Style, The Golden Years: 1911-1937,* Folklyric CD 7005, Arhoolie, 1991, is the authoritative work—and a source for some of the sound of Tourian's city. In the invocation, note the pun: Charon and charity! One can observe such courteous verbal magic meant to disarm and appease the dangerous, in the name *euxeinos* "hospitable" that the Greeks professed, a bit disingenuously perhaps, to hear in the Old Persian designation *akhshaina* "dark" of the definitely inhospitable Black Sea that washes Hellenic Asia Minor's northern shores.

epic of Sasun, too, P'ok'r Mher ("Little Mithra"), naively fights the angel of death and loses when God steps in.[124]

When all the rest leave, or forget, who is Tourian's Alcestis?[125] In the final stanza, he expresses the fear that his grave will be *an-neshan*, "without a sign, unmarked." The Cross is the *surp Nshan*, "Holy Sign," but he would have doubted that the crow-like clergy would omit to erect a Christian tombstone,[126] that the memory of him will "wilt"

---

[124]For a study of the mythologem of Alcestis and its development in Armenian epic literature and balladry, with texts, see J. R. Russell, "An Epic for the Borderlands: Zariadris of Sophene, Aslan the Rebel, Digenes Akrites, and the Mythologem of Alcestis in Armenia," in R. Hovannisian, ed., *Armenian Tsopk/Kharpert*, UCLA Armenian History and Culture Series, Historic Armenian Cities and Provinces, 3, Costa Mesa, CA: Mazda Publishers, 2002, pp. 147-183. The Armenian ballad is illustrated in a remarkable and rarely-reproduced fresco by the painter E. T'adeosian, published in *Anahit: revue arménienne trimestrielle*, Paris, 6.1-2, N.S.,1935, p. 21. Regrettably it did not appear in the Hovannisian vol., but is included with the reprint of the article in *AIS*, pp. 951-988.

[125]In the view of Tcheraz, p. 61, the French translation of Tourian's poem is meant itself "répandre sa réputation parmis les peuples civilisés!"

[126]In the event, a monument was erected at his grave near the wall of Baghlarbashi cemetery with a poem by the poet's brother Mihran Tourian in Classical Armenian:

ՔԵՐԹՈՂ
Աստ հանգչի մարմին Պետրոսի Դուրեան,
Որ քըսանամեայ էջ ի գերեզման,
Երկաթագործի սա ծընաւ որդի,
Բանաստեղծ թըռեաւ ի կենաց աստի,
Ի տարաժամու յունվար քըսանի
Հազար ութ հարիւր եօթասներկի,
Արեւըն իւր էր դէռ առաւօտին,
Օրհասին սեաւ ամպք ըզնա ծածկեցին.
Մահ նորա բնաւից իւրոց սիրելեաց
Սուգ անմխիթար և կսկիծ էած.
Վըշտըմբեր կենաց իւրոց սոսկ վըկայ
Կըճեայ մահարձանս աւասիկ աստ կայ։

"POET. / Here rests the body of Bedros Tourian, / Who at age twenty descended to the tomb: / He was born an ironworker's son, / And as a poet from this life he flew. / Untimely on January 20th / 1872. / His light stood yet at its morn, / When black clouds of doom hid it away. / His death for all who loved him / Brought inconsolable mourning and grief. / Sole witness to the sorrowful life he bore, / This monument of death of marble here stands."

(*t'arami*). This verb is used of roses, of course—the rose given by the poet to a girl fades in the poem "Small Dedications" (*Tsonigk'*), and brightens the bloom on her cheek. Tourian's sign is the seal set upon the arm and heart of the beloved in the *Song of Songs*: (only) love is as strong as death. Death's hour takes the color of life, warmth, youth away from him; but if it does not fade in memory of him, then the cold dominion is overcome, and death itself must die. For years after Tourian's death, Armenian boys and girls came to the grave leaving poems and offerings; the grave is visited still—like another at Pére Lachaise.

---

Many pilgrims left messages in pencil and ink upon it for decades after. Arshag Chobanian's estimation that it is a rather flat poem seems just. In 1898, Mihran—by then Yeghishe—had the final stanza of this poem, "My Death" (*Isg anneshan yet'e mena...*) engraved on the west face of the stone. In recent years, it was reported to Sharurian, the Turkish municipal authorities destroyed the monument to widen a road (A. S. Šaruryan, ed., Aršak Č'opanyan, *Petros Duryani kyank'n u gorcə*, repr. Erevan: Mitk', 1967, p. 84 and n. 77, 78). This report is contradicted by others who tell me they have seen the monument: it was moved, undamaged, to the center of the cemetery and Armen Aroyan photographed it in June 2005.

**38. "What Are They Saying?"** (*Inch' g'esen?*), 1871 (Sevak p. 88)

**Text.**

**Ի·ՆՉ Կ'ԸՍԵՆ**

Ինծի կ'ըսեն– ինչո՞ւ լուռ ես–
Ո·հ, միթէ բառ կամ խօսք ունի՞
Արշալոյսը, որ կը բոընկի,
Զի անհուն է այն ալ ինձ պէս։

Ինծի կ'ըսեն– միշտ տխուր ես–
Ի՞նչպէս չըլլամ, մէկիկ մէկիկ
Թօթափեցան գլխուս աստղիք…
Արշալոյս մը չ'անցաւ սըրտէս։

Ինծի կ'ըսեն– կրակոտ չ'ես,
Լըճակի մը պէս ես մեռած,
Դալկահա·ր դէմքդ ու հայեցուած։–
Ո·հ, յատակն են իմ փրփուրներս։

Ես ինձ կ'ըսեմ– ժամդ է հասեր,
Քու երկրորդ սև մօրդ գընա գոգ,
Գերեզմա·ն, հո·ն գտնես դու գոգ
Վարդեր, թրթռում, թռիչ ու աստղեր…։

**Translation.**

*What are they saying?*

They say to me, Why are you silent?
Oh! does the dawn speak
When it bursts into flame?
For it is infinite, like me.

They say to me, You are always sad.

One by one, the stars upon my brow
Are brushed away: how could I be otherwise,
My heart's dawn not yet past.

They say to me, You lack fire:
Like a mere, you're dead,
And your visage and mien are wan.
Oh! my agitations are deep below.

I say to myself: The hour has come–
Go to the bosom of your other mother, dark,
The tomb: you'll find embraces there,
Roses, shivers, soaring, stars.

**Commentary.**

The text of Sevak has Arm. *inch'* ("what") in the title with an exclamation point ( · ) rather than a question mark ( ՞ ), however I find that my translation of the title as a question agrees with Tcheraz, p. 68, "Que dit-on?" As in other poems of Tourian's, there is a complex and transition of imagery between heaven and earth, sky and water, which doubles backward in ironic repetition and echo: the first stanza introduces the movement of the dawn in color, as it bursts into flame (*prrengi*); in the second, dawn is situated in time, as it extinguishes the stars and one is told it has not yet blossomed into day. The third stanza resumes the fire-imagery of the first stanza but in reverse, with a negation: Why is the poet not *gragod*, "fiery"? The negation continues with a image reversing and contradicting the sky-vision of the preceding lines. The poet is not the star-spangled sky consumed by the fire of dawn bursting, but a still, dank tarn. The word used is a key, though: *lejag*, "little lake," the title of Tourian's famous poem (No. 22). As though this hint were insufficient, Tourian points us to the image of the lake-bottom (*hadag*), where his agitations are: the word he uses for these is *p'rp'urners*, literally, "my foamings." This word refers to the froth on waves, and as such can only mean the surface of water, its top, not its bottom. But poetry can do what nature cannot. The depth is the height, the truth of Tourian's emotional reality; and one recalls then the astonishing declaration in *Lejag*, where the poet's heart—the bottom of his dark lake, as it were—is torn open to reveal, not a book (*madyan*), but a conflagration (*hrteh*). So this impossible foam is also a roiling book of fire.

When a poet declares you will not find a book, and uses, besides, not the common word for a book, *girk'*, literally a group of writings, that one's eye might slip past, but precisely the marked Classical Armenian word *matean*, literally, matrix, the mother of all books!—it is a *book* you must think of: cf. the psychological experiment which begins with the request that the subject not think about white bears. Poets write books: if Tourian's heart is inwardly aflame, then it is an unconsumed, burning book that provides the fuel, a book whose every letter is metaphysical fire. In the present poem, the *leitmotif* is not the printed aspect of the poet's craft, but its aural one: saying. They say ... they say ... and ask why he is silent. But his very poem is an act of saying; the saying, the cleaving of the heart, the plunge to the ground of truth, from the unfinished conflagration of early dawn to the esoteric tossing of watery flames in darkness in the inner book, the mystic *volumen* no less phantasmagorically divine than Ezekiel's. And, like a Prophet, he is not heard. So in speaking his poem out loud (the word *asats'ogh*, pres. act. part. from *asel*, W. Arm. *esel*, "sayer," is the term for the man who chants the Armenian oral epic of the wild men of Sasun), he simultaneously deploys the conceit, in the final stanza, of addressing himself.

The dying boy whose terrible cries about his coming death have brought his mother to tears—the sight of it torments him anew—takes the final plunge: dawn sky, tarn, *earthen lake* (with the old English meaning of a pit in the ground). In that anti-sky he will discover all that one would least think to be there: the fire-sun hue of the opening rose, the shudders of orgasm in an erotic embrace never achieved within life, enfranchised flight, and stars. Again, stars: these were blotted out earlier, in dawn's greater light, so their reappearance is not merely the signifier of the new dark of black Mother Earth, but a reversal in time, the sky spinning backwards from the dawn, retreating from the diurnal moment when, before he may even behold that dawn fade to the light of common day, Tourian will expire. But his winged soul, like Nabokov's waxwing slain, will live on, fly on, in the inverted—the reflected—otherworld.

**39. "A."** 1871 (Sevak pp. 89-91)

**Text.**

Ա.

Երեկոյեան բալն կը սողար բարդիլ խաւ,
Աստեղազարդ անդունդն հիւսիլ լուռ ու սեաւ,
Տըխո՛ւր ըստուեր, կոր կը ձըգէր իր ետև
Լուսափըթիթ օրն սիրայնոց կարճատև։
Կը նըշմարուէր հազիւ երկնի կապուտակ
Գմբեթին խոր փայփլող ւ'այլոյն ջինջ ալիք։
Մառը մտնող արփւոյն մարէր հուսկ շառայլ
Սառնամանուտ սարերու վրայ քայլ առ քայլ,
Ինչպէս հիւծեալ կոյսի մ'ակնարկ առ դամբան,
Ուր պարէն ցուրտ ծիծաղք սիրոյ դառնութեան,
Ինչպէս և իմ դիւթեալ ակնարկս առ արօտ,
Զոր մըթագնեց մառախուղ մի նախանձոտ,
Ի'այլ չը կրցի ընդնշմարել էակն ան,
Զոր գգուէին ճաճանչ, վեփիւռ իրիկուան.
Հողմածածան իր շրջազգեստն ու հոպոպք
Դեղձան վարսից գիրգ ուլան շուրջ ոսկի ծոպք,
Կարծես ծաղիկ մ'էր երազի հիասքանչ,
Կը կոխկըռտէր այն ծաղկալից մարգաց լանջ.
Թողէ՛ք կոխել պի կը փթըթէ աւելի.
Երբոր հովիկն իր այտէն գոյն գեղանի
Եւ իր ամբիծ լանջէն առած քիչ մը հոտ՝
Տանի սփռէ անապատներն աւազոտ,
Ի'ահա փթթին խաղիկներ բիւր առաւել.
Անոր համար ի՞նչ է ծաղիկ փթթեցնել,
Մինչդեռ սիրոյ կէս դիակներ կը յառնեն՝
Երբ սև աչքէն սըլաք մ'ուղղէ բոցեղէն։

Լուսինն արդէն կը գողազգէր՝ պըճնէր վինք
Նուրբ ամպիկով, ուսկից ուսան թրքուհիք
Ծածկել իրենց դէմքն հաջաղով նրբաթել,

Անոր նըման տժգոյն ըլլալ և դիւթել։
Լուսի՛ն, գըտիր լոյս ցօղելու ցածուն հիւղ,
Ուր գէթ ցամքած է կանթեղին առկայծ իւղ.
Մի՛, մի՛ սորուիր գաղջ արևէն ձըմեռուան
Մոռնալ հիւղն, ուր ամայի է վառարանն,
Եւ լոկ սրտերն հոն կը մըխան յուսահա՛տ...
Ծագէ հիւղն այն՝ բանաստեղծն ուր աղքատ
Ինք լոյս, կըրակ ոչ մէկն ունի գըրելու.
Սարն իր աստեղց թո՛ղ դըղեակն ալ ջահերու,
Գընա՛ ցօղել լոյս տընակին այն ցածուկ,
Ուր մայր մը գիրկն առած կայտառ մի մանուկ՝
Ցոյց տալ կ՛ուզէ քեզ Աստուծոյ վերթ պատկեր,
Դու որ միայն սիրահարաց ես լապտեր։

Տերևներուն մէջէն արծաթ լի լուսինն
Կը դիտէի՝ ինչպէս որ դէմքն հարս կուսին՝
Երբ կը ծածկէ քողքն հիմենեան ոսկեթել,
Բայց սա վարդի փոխան գիտէ լոյս փթըթել։
Ալ աստղն աղոտ և կարծես թէ աւելի
Երկընքի լուրթ խորը սուզած կը փալփլի,
Եւ վերջալոյսն ալ կը մարի որ դեռ հոն՝
Հրդեհի նման բոցավառէր պհորիզոն։
Եւ դուք՝ կրա՛կք սիրոյ, մարիք շուտ և դուք,
Տևէք ինչպէս վերջալոյսն այս բոցաշուք...։
Արդեօք արևն այսօր ո՛րքան սիրաբոյր
Կուսից լոյս դէմքն այրեց, ուսկից մեղմ համբոյր
Քաղել դողաս, կը վախնաս թէ կը թօշնի
Իր այտերուն վառ վառ վարդեր գեղանի։
Թաւուտք այսօր շուքերնուն մէջ առանձին՝
Խորհրդաւոր ի՛նչ փըսփըսուք լըսեցին,
Ի՛նչ խոստումներ, ի՛նչ մըմունջներ սրտմաշուք,
Իսկ դո՞ւք, մացա՛ռք, հովանոցա՛կք, ա՛հ, իսկ դուք.՞.՞.՞։
Ո՛հ հովանի՛ք, թաւո՛ւտք, խորշե՛ր անմարդի՝
Ուր դայլայլիկ թռչնոյ, խորշիւն սաղարթի
Եւ երբ լըսուի շրջապգեստի մը շրշիւն
Չոր տերևոց վըրայ՝ սըփռէ կորս աշուն,
Երբ շուքին տակ կոյս մ՛առանձին ընէ ման,

Եւ տերևոց ետև դողամ անոնց նման,
Որ չըլլայ թէ դիպիմ աչքին բոցեղէն,
(Պէ՞տք է դողայ միթէ տերևն արևէն)
Երբ ծիծառնուկն ինձ հետ հեծէ աղեկէկ,
Ո·րչափ ատեմ քաղքին ժխորն, սիրեմ Ձեկ։

(Հիւեանս պատճառաւ ընդհատուած)

**Translation.**

*A.*

It crept and thickened, massed, the crepuscular mist,
Woven silent and dark upon the starry abyss—
Sad shade, that the lovers' short-lived
Day of light unfolding its petals cast in its wake.
Barely seen was heaven's vault's azure
Deep scintillating floor, wave-tossed, clear,
Reflecting the night's first-born star,
Which the Bosphorus' limpid swells swiftly clasped in their embrace.
The final gleaming of the sun sinking into misty darkness died
Step by step, upon the ice-bound mountain peaks
Like the glance of a maiden wasting away cast at her tomb
Where cold cackles of love's bitterness whirl in the dance,
Like my glance, too, bewitched, upon the meadow
That a jealous fog reduced to murk—
So I might no longer make out that being
Whom sun's corolla and evening's zephyr stroked.
Her skirt and ringlets aflutter in the wind,
Saffron ruffles round her soft neck, tresses gold,
Were like the flower of an astonished dream
As she trampled underfoot the bosom of the meadows dense with blossoms.
Let her tread, for she makes more bloom
When the little breeze stealing from that cheek its gorgeous hue
And from her innocent breast, slight fragrance,

Conveys and sprinkles it over sandy wastes:
Look! more than a myriad of flowers open.
And what is it to her to make the flowers grow
When corpses half-dead of love arise
As she shoots at them fiery darts from her black eyes?

The moon had already donned her mask, embellished
In that fine wisp of cloud from which Turkish women
Learnt to conceal their faces behind the gauzy veil
To appear pale-hued like her, to work enchantment.
Find, Moon, light with which to bedew the humble hovel
Where the oil of the lamp is flickering, almost dry.
Do not, do not learn from the pallid wintry sun
To forget the hut whose hearth is barren,
Where only hearts bereft of hope are smouldering ...
Dawn over that hut: there the penniless poet
Has no light, no fire by which to write.
Leave the mountain its stars; the palace, its torches—
Go and pour light down as dew upon that humble home
Where a mother cradles her brave child,
Wanting to show him to you as if an image of God,
To you, who lend your light as a lantern only to lovers.

The moon replete with silver from the leaves' midst
I spied like the visage of a virgin bride
When the gold-spun veil of Hymen hides her:
But this one knows how to make light, instead of roses, bloom.
The star is still pale, as though deeper
Sunken in the sea-green gulfs of heaven it glimmered,
And the last light of evening there waning
Enflames the horizon in conflagration.
And you, fires of love—you, too, swiftly die,
Lasting no longer than this flame-shadowed dusk ...
Could the sun today have burnt so
The love-scented shining faces of maidens
That you tremble to reap a tender kiss, fearing

That the burning beauteous roses will wilt upon her cheek?
Alone in the thickets' shade today:
They heard such mysteries of whisperings,
Such promises, such heart-rending murmurs of complaint—
And you, canebrakes, leafy shade, ah, and you?
O shady woods and untenanted lairs
Where but the warbling of birds is heard in the soughing of the green,
When the rustling of skirts is heard
Upon the dry leaves that autumn scatters,
And a maiden strolls alone in the shade,
And behind the leaves, like them I shake
Lest I meet her eyes' fiery gaze
(But must then the leaf at the sun's sight quake?)
When with me the swallow piteously cries,
I love you then, even as the city's tumult I despise.

(Interrupted by reason of my illness)

**Commentary.**

The manuscript of the poem, on a single sheet of paper, is kept at Jerusalem. Sevak has corrected various corrupt readings in printed editions, e.g.: line 2, *asteghazart* restored from *ayn lusazart* ("that light-adorned"); line 8, *chinch* restored from *khonch* ("tired"); line 9, *marre* instead of *mare* ("dusk"); line 29, *k'oghazger* from *k'ogharger* (meaning the same thing—veiling—but with "cast" instead of "clothe"); line 66 read *zor derevots' vera sep'rre merg ashun* ("which bare autumn scatters over the leaves"); etc. The word *asdgh*, "star," was changed to *luys*, "light," in some editions of the Ottoman period lest the former word be considered a subversive reference to Yildiz ("Star") Palace (Sevak, I, p. 285)—not entirely unreasonable, since a *teghyag*, fort or palace, is mentioned in line 40, in contrast to the dwelling of the poverty-stricken poet. In his translation, Tchéraz wrongly altered *partil* and *hyusil* in the first lines to infinitives of active verbs, in *-el*. This seems to have been Tourian's last poem. It was also to have been his longest. The text originally had no divisions; and the poet changed several words in the text: line 34, *maradz* ("extinguished") to *ts'amk'adz*; line 43, *anor* "to her" stricken after *ts'uyts' dal*; line 71, the Turco-Persian loan *belbuln*, "nightingale," replaced by Arm. *dzidzerrnugn* "little swallow"; etc.

The lines describing the poet's humble home and hard circumstances, which are contrasted to the life of palace-dwellers, echo No. 5, "Love one another"; and line 37 echoes a letter of 22 January 1871 Tourian wrote to Bp. Khoren Nar-Bey requesting aid: Կոյր մը չէ Ձեզ դիմողը որ աչերը բանաք, այլ մէկը որ ճակտին վրայ սև ամպ մ'ունի, հիւղի մը հառաչն է այն, հոն ուր վառարանն ամայի է և սիրտ կը մխայ, հոն ուր կեանքը կը լռէ և քնարը կը հեծկլտայ։ "It is no blind man who appeals to you that you open his eyes, but one who has a black cloud upon his brow. It is the groan of a hovel whose hearth is barren and a heart smoulders, where life is silent and the lyre is sobbing."[127] The other themes of the poem are familiar: the poet escapes from the bustle of the city to seek peace in the solitude of a wood and to commune with the mutually-reflecting depths of the Bosphorus and of heaven. But he trembles with the leaves and cries with the birds when he hears the rustle of the skirts of a girl walking: her luminous sight is both the life-giving sun of spring and the death-dealing heat of summer. The *danse macabre* of line 12 is redolent of Poe; whilst the paradisiacal dream-flower of line 19 faintly recalls Coleridge's musings.[128] Overall, the poem seems proto-Symbolist, though—perhaps a hint of how the poet's style might have changed, had he lived.

---

[127]Text of letter in Sevak, I, p. 160 (letter 3); Nar-Bey is the *nom de plume* of Khoren Kalfayan, 1831/2-1892, an Armenian educator, administrator, and cleric at Pera.

[128]Coleridge wondered what might happen, were a man to wake holding a flower that had been given to him in a dream of Paradise as proof he had been there: see J. R. Russell, "A Scholium on Coleridge and an Armenian Demon," *JSAS* 10 (1998, 1999 [2000]), p. 70 n. 26 (*AIS*, p. 996).

**[40] (Undated) 2. "Now soars the joyful day"** (*Aha srana orn yerchanig*) (Sevak pp. 94-95)

**Text.**

Ահա սրանայ օրն երջանիկ՝
Ի յիշատակ ոսկեղենիկ,
Յորում լըցան հէք հոգւոյս իղձք,
Ետուն տեղի սրտէս թախիծք,
Թարմացան հոյլ վարդք ոսկեփունջ
Կենացս պատեաց բուրում վիմ շուրջ,
Եւ կարէ ոչ սրտիկն իմ վառ՝
Գոլ գոհ, յագիլ լոկ ի կիթառ,
Զհոգիդ ըզսիրտ և ըզբարիս,
Դու որ յարտօսր զհիքօք փարիս,
Փրկչին մերոյ արձան տիպար՝
Փոյթ թշուառաց ի մըխիթար,
Դու որ սփռես զդամբանօք վարդ,
Տաս ցոյց զերկին յակնարկ զըւարթ,
Երգես սոխակ ի գիշերի,
Ո·հ, ի գեղգեղդ սոսկումն ցըրեմ
Գերեըզմանաց խօլ արհաւիրք,
Պարզես զբարեաց զյաւերժ երկինք։
Քև·, քև· շնչեմ ես յայս յաշխարհ,
Եւ քոյդ ի շունչ մըխիթարար
Սիրելեացս խոր փակեցան փոսք,
Աստեղք յերև գան լուսահոսք,
Յորչափ են թիւ՝ կեա·ց առ յապա
Աստեղաց վառ՝ ցորչափ նոքա,
Եւ ի յալիսըդ ձիւնափառ
Ըսփոփես զհէքս հոգեբարբառ,
Եւ ի դամբանս եկ առ ի գութ՝
Ըզփըրկութեան մնչել պաղօթ։

**Translation.**

Now soars the joyful day
Into gilded memory,
In which my poor soul's longings were fulfilled
And sorrows retreated from my heart.
The roses' throng freshened in gilded garlands
And compassed me roundabout with life's bouquet;
Yet my burning heart cannot
Be satisfied, satiated with the strains of a guitar.
You who cleave unto the wretched in a tear!
Image and semblance of our Savior,
Hasten your soul, your good, your heart
To the unfortunate for consolation.
You who scatter roses round the tombs,
Who shewest thy alert and joyous glance as the sky,
Who singest, nightingale, in the dead of night,
Oh! against your beauty I strew
The sense-bereft terror of the grave,
As heaven's eternal goodness thou openest wide.
Through thee, thee I breathe in this universe,
And by thy consoling breath
Were sealed the grave-pits of those I love.
The stars rise into view, streaming with light.
Live on, to the measure of their number—
As many as the burning stars—
And in thy breakers snowgloried, bright,
Thou consolest my lowly spirit's speech
And come then in pity to my grave
To murmur a prayer, my soul to save.

**Commentary.**

The poem is composed in fairly pure, pleasant Classical Armenian, and because of this Sevak has preserved in his edition the original, pre-Soviet orthography. It is not known whether the manuscript has been preserved; and Sevak cites (p. 289) the judgement of Arshag Chobanian, who disliked it and doubted its authenticity as well. He wrote: "Its Classical Armenian (*krapar*) is so rancid, so archaic, so overblown, clerical (*vartabedagan*) and arcane, that it could not be Tourian's. And even if it were his by some chance, still it should not be included in the works of the person who was the first to write verse in the pure vernacular (*ashkharhapar*)" (*Hayrenik*, 1892, no. 246). There is perhaps in this criticism something of an animus towards Classical Armenian and its connection with the obscurantist institutions of Armenian society—it is telling he singles out the clergy. In later years Chobanian modified this opinion, and considered the poem the maiden effort of a schoolboy. Neither Tchéraz nor Blackwell includes it in their translations. But it sounds themes and presents images to be refined in the vernacular poems. There is something of the spirit of "The Child to the Cross" (*Manugn arr Khach'*) in its prayerful descent from the sunlit spaces of the upper world to the confining, tenebrous grave. The evocation of stars and waves just at the latter point is a contrastive touch typical of Tourian's imagination; and the concatenation at the beginning of gorgeous gold and rose colors must remind one of Tourian's hymns to the dawn. The verb Tourian uses of the day of happiness that drove his sorrows away for a time, is *sranal*, which has the sense of soaring, but also of being sharp; and by the very second line of the poem it becomes plain that the day has sped away—it is already a memory.

Within the arcane convolutions of *krapar* rhetoric there is an intricate profundity of thought, too. Whom does the poet address with the familiar "thou"—a human maiden who is exalted the object of his love, or Nature, or God? Who is the fairest eidolon of our Savior? The nightingale (*sokhag*) addressed at the exact midpoint of the poem focusses this ambiguity: the bird introduces the impending dark, the appearance of the stars, all in contrast to the brilliance of the fleeting day. But at the same time the bird is, like the poet himself, a creature shaped solely to sing—Prof. Anahit Perikhanian has pointed out that Arm. *sokhag* must derive from a Parthian form meaning literally "the speaker," with the OIr. base *sah-*, "speak"—and, in human hearing, to express love and longing. The infinite stars of the night become the years of an otherworldly eternal life; and though the singer die, the song does not. It becomes a prayer to save his soul, which is itself linked to speech (*hoke-parparr*, line 26). And the breath (*shunch'*) of consolation of line 20, with obvious reference to a funeral, must be the readings of the Armenian Apostolic Church service from the *Asdvadzashunch'*, i.e., Holy Scripture, literally "the Breath of God." That breath, and the soul's speech, and the nightingale's song, display the unity in poetry of Divine language, personal creation, and nature's voice. This triune being, both source of inspiration and audience of the poet's lyric, the object of his love, becomes also the vehicle of his immortality in his poems. Awkwardly classicizing as the style and diction may seem, then, there is still in this poem an early statement of Tourian's *ars poetica*.

**[41] Fragments** (Sevak, p. 197.)

**Texts.**

1. ՊԻՏԻ ՄԵՌՆԻՄ ԵՍ

Ինչո՞ւ մռնչէք, նոճիք սևագէս,
        Պիտի մե·ռնիմ ես·
Սիրելիքս բոլոր խոյս տուին քովէս,
        Պիտի մե·ռնիմ ես·
Տխուր գերեզման, ո·րչափ ինձ մոտ ես,
        Պիտի մե·ռնիմ ես։

2.

Ես մեռնիմ նէ, մի· գար, մի· լար իմ տապան,
Հողը, լեռը, սարը, ձորը պիս կ’ողբան։

**Translation.**

1. *I will die*

Why do you moan, black-tressed cypresses?
        I will die!
All my loved ones have fled from my side:
        I will die!
Sad tomb, how close you are to me!
        I will die!

2.

If I die, don’t come, don’t cry over my coffin:
The earth, the mountain, hill and dale will sing my lamentation.

**Commentary.**

Sevak, p. 352, offers the following notes: in his booklet "We build our cemetery or tombs" (Constantinople, 1885), P. Ekserjian mentions that "amongst the unpublished works of B. Tourian of blessed memory there is a most affecting lyric entitled 'I will die.'" Arshag Chobanian published the text (1) that Sevak has published. The other verse (2) was printed first by Ekserjian, then by Chobanian. The former testifies (see the accounts of Tourian's last days and death in the third section of this book): "Hovhannes Janfesjian says that there was another song [besides (1)] that he [Tourian] had and had set to a sad melody: in 1871 he would sing it whenever he saw me or another friend." See p. 342, *infra*.

# Documents, Letters, and Critical Essays

The materials I have translated from Armenian in this chapter provide documentary testimony to the public and private life, death, and cultural inheritance of Bedros Tourian. They include theatrical announcements, reports, articles, and letters to the editors of Armenian and Armeno-Turkish newspapers, in Constantinople and abroad; letters from Tourian to friends and a potential benefactor; essays on Tourian by other Armenian poets, and verses dedicated to his memory; and a variety of reminiscences and speculations. Many are culled from the painstaking biography of the poet by Arshag Chobanian; and most selections come from A. S. Sharuryan's *Bedros Tourian in Documents and the Reminiscences of Contemporaries,* Erevan: Erevan University Press, 1982 (Ա. Ս. Շարուրյան, խմբ., Պետրոս Դուրյանը վավերագրերում և ժամանակակիցների հիշողություններում, Երևանի Համալսարանի Հրատարակչություն, 1982 թ.).

Tourian emerges from these documents as a youth much loved by a large circle of friends, with an enchanting singing voice, a talent for mischievous fun. We see him at the opera, at a cafeteria at dawn, at a coffee house whose owner cherished his company, proofreading his own eulogy from his sick bed, complaining bitterly about his sickness and impending death. His friends remember the haunting graveside songs he composed and sang, as if staring down into the pit at his own lifeless form; and these few lines add to the sum of his lyrics. Though his love life remains most obscure, the documents perhaps add to our knowledge of the life of his mind—he seems to have read Gérard de Nerval. The various documents are presented in more-or-less chronological order, except for Paruyr Sevak's essay. The explanatory material to each selection is introduced in parentheses; citations of Armenian are in square brackets within the text, as are my own comments or explanations. The latter are initialled [—JRR].

## 1. Paruyr Sevak, "The Herakles of Our Lyric Poetry."

(Sevak wrote this essay in 1962: it is reprinted as *Mer k'narergut'yan Vahagne,* in Paruyr Sevak, *Erkeri zhoghovatsu* ("Collected Works"), vol. 5, Erevan: Hayastan, 1974, pp. 156-163. Vahagn is a Middle Iranian form of the Avestan Verethraghna, lit. "he who smites opposition"—Bahram and Vahram are later forms of the same name. Vahagn is a Zoroastrian divinity of the pre-Christian Armenian pantheon who was equated, both anciently [as for example at Nimrud Dagh, where he is named Herakles-Artagnes in Greek inscriptions] and later, by the Classical Armenian historian Movses Khorenats'i, with the Greek Herakles. Statues of the latter were reconsecrated to him as well in Iranian and Armenian *bagins,* or temples containing sacred images. Vahagn is principally a martial champion against the forces of evil, and this function is exemplified by his slaying of dragons, Arm. *vishap.* These combats, evocative of his heroism and strength, are reflected in his cult epithet *vishapak'agh,* "reaper of dragons." On Vahagn, see J. R. Russell, *Zoroastrianism in Armenia,* Harvard Iranian Series 5, Cambridge, MA, 1987, ch. 6. Sevak uses the name to indicate the titanic power and vitality of Tourian's work and vision, the mythopoetic character of his life. Sevak seems to encode his own name into a description of Tourian's physical appearance: he identifies with his subject; and in retrospect, is to be identified with him—one recalls Sevak's early and untimely death in 1971, half a year short of the centenary of Tourian's own passing. Sevak's funeral, like Tourian's, became a spontaneous, gigantic outpouring of national mourning.)

There are poets who conjure the image of a whole world and are called great—indeed, they are. But they age fast, because the world itself, fortunately, changes into something new. And then there are poets who invent a new world: its substance is theirs, and they are its maker. This is how the good, purposeful spider spins her web, and the bee, without honor of an epithet, shapes his honeycomb. These poets are condemned after their death to misfortune: not only do they become obsolete, but gradually they are forgotten, since those whose task is memory are under no obligation to relive an unreal or alien world.

Then there are also those poets who neither depict a world nor create one. They open up *their* world—and these are not forgotten, since they do not grow old. And if they do, then they do so only the way morning also fades. They do not become obsolete, for life in its renewal renews them, too, just as morning ever dawns anew. Bedros Tourian: he neither depicted nor fashioned a world, but revealed his own, which was then called after him, and will bear his name yet. What was it? "A multitude of glances, a bouquet of smiles," "an ether of heartbeats," "an Eden of breath." Or, "a night's worth of mourning," "an abyss of sighs," "a hell of curses."

It is true that "a word defiles the infinitude of our souls," but the master of the world named after Tourian was not heavy of tongue, as Moses was, nor, like Aaron, a deft echoer of the commandments. For Tourian, "speaking means only to be drained." And in reality his life was nothing other than a wasting away through the expenditure of words and a speaking into exhaustion.

Therefore that world was a "crucible of speech," one that exerted an alchemical effect upon our hearts and became our own speech. Thereby that world was transformed into our own.

That world had a moon, one that in Tourian's times was fashioned of paper. Even the great Beshigtashlian did not have the strength to tear himself free of that paper moon. It was up to Tourian to arrive and yank the mask of "a delicate cloudlet" away from the moon. Many perform such a task with pleasure, but the cloudlets were also of paper. Tourian had to come along to deduce from that "delicate cloudlet" masking the moon how "Turkish women learnt / To hide their faces under finely-woven veils, / To be as pale as she, to cast their spells." From that day forth, the reign of the paper moon was over. In the same way, Tourian revived those bookish stars that twinkled also with a paper light. "We lifted our hands to the stars, / To each other, pledged our love, / And the stars trembled together / At the frightful vow we swore." It is not enough to say that the stars are alive here—here an additional life is bestowed upon them. And only here? So as not to be too far diverted, let us be satisfied for now with the recollection of one line: "To ascend the unwavering stair of the stars" [*Yelnel astgheru santughin anali*].

In the epoch of moons cut out of paper and of stars that cast a papery gleam, only sheer genius could employ such a turn of imaginative thought. "To ascend the unwavering [*an-ali*] stair of the stars:" *an-ali,* that is, without waves [*ali-k'*], that is, a stair without steps—is that "ether of heartbeats" by which Tourian anticipated those who were to come, by at least half a century. This is a line enraptured by future generations, and it is not at all strange that Tourian's contemporaries were incapable even of reception of his image, assuming the word *anali* to be a typographical error. And they even corrected that "misprint": so for many years *anali* became *ahali* ["full of fear"].

Till full half a century had passed, till the great Varuzhan arrived, who could write these lines? "By her breath she thought in sacrifice to slay me, / But Alas! she stirred myriad sparks of my love instead." And who was there to compare "these alien smiles agleam with hope" to the "fake flowers" that concealed "the lonely heart's abyss"?

Till half a century had passed, till Medzarents' and Teryan came, who could feel that in the embrace of his beloved "a light, a wind in my arms went out," or "a spirit passed across my heart and left its shadow there"? The reception of the living body as light or wind, the incarnation of an insubstantial spirit and the consequent perception of that spirit as casting a shadow—those are the palaces with northern and southern exposure that form the gateway into the Tourianic world.

So it is scarcely worth adding that the ruler of such a world could not have been content with the animation of the moon and stars. In the Tourianic world, and for the first time in our modern lyric poetry, lightning and tears, thicket and rill, "early morning mist" and "crepuscular fog," flower and soul, are animated—not to mention red rose and blue violet.

From his vantage point of about a century in the past, Tourian still turns to us with a question: "Were the rose of spring / Not the type / Of the virgin's cheek, / Who would render it esteem? // If ethereal blue were not the semblance / Of the virgin's eyes, / Who would favor heaven with a glance?" This is what he asks, and we, a hundred years on, have nothing to say in reply, since many of us still trade in paper roses, violets, deer, and so on.

In Tourian's world there is a "little lake"—and what a lake! If by some malign miracle all the lakes of the world were to be reduced to steam, one could restore them by means of the poem *Lejag* ("The Lake").

By his example he familiarized us with that melancholy mere, even as he taught us how to "be captivated, be silent, and meditate." We learnt, again, from him "to meditate, to be immersed, to be amazed at the lie." Again by his words he whispered to us "a bouquet of flame": "Do you wish to worship an unblemished soul?" We suffered alongside him the "disease of heaven," and together with him cried out, "Oh, give me a spark, a spark, that I may live!" Becoming with him "a pallid bolt of lightning," we prosecuted the dispute against a "jealous God" and thought for a despairing moment that "The world is God's derision, then."

He was not twenty when like a star he went "to augment the heavens." Others write imitative poems at his age, barely maintaining elementary rhyme and meter. At his age the best offer promise, not finished work. At his age they are beginning to recognize the world, but they do not have a world about which it might be said, "The stars there do not die; / Nor the flowers wilt, / Nor clouds fall as rain ..." A world he was able to define in its entirety, whose master he made himself: "There is a conflagration there, no tome!..."

The millennial history of world literature knows very few names that can be inscribed next to Tourian's, murmuring like him, "My beginning, woe to me, became my end!" Living for all of two decades and creating for all of one or two years (1869 and 1871), close to death throughout his conscious life, Tourian with his "bouquet of smiles" and his "bouquet of groans" became one of those happy ones through whom all mankind does not recall its youth, but relives it every time. Tourian's brief life was a ceaseless death. And in the world it has been the fortune of but a few to turn their death into immortality [cf. Yeghishe on Vardan—JRR]. Tourian is one of those very few.

In the ill-starred history of our people there have also been some strokes of good fortune. One of our national good fortunes is Tourian, our certificate of nobility in the world. His advent was a thing like a miracle, especially if we consider the state of our modern poetry beneath the Mekhit'arist pen and in the pages of *The Northern Lights*. [Sevak refers to the Armenian Catholic order's classicizing tendency and to the Russian-Armenian journal *Hyusisap'ayl*, to which the democratic revolutionary Michael Nalbandian was a major contributor. Tourian in an early poem laments Nalbandian's death in Tsarist exile.—JRR] The youth at death's door came and advanced our poetic thought by a century beyond his predecessors; and he left behind a standard that many of our poets—and not just the metric, rhyming ones—could not maintain even half a century later.

He came, in order to become the bridge tower from which, in a giant catenary descending to either shore, the *hayrens* and Varuzhan, Sayat'-Nova and Teryan were to be united. [The *hayren*, or "Armenian (song)," is a short love lyric of the late mediaeval period: the sixteenth-century *ashugh*, or folk bard, of Van, Nahapet K'uch'ak ("the Boy") is the master of the form. On Daniel Varuzhan, see the commentary on poem No. 25 in this volume. Sayat'-Nova, the last and greatest Armenian *ashugh*, died at the close of the eighteenth century. Vahan Teryan was a Russian-Armenian Symbolist poet of the early twentieth century. —JRR] He is the first great poet of our modern lyric tradition but will always stand alongside its latest exemplar, since he does not age, any more than smiles or sighs, laughter or crying do. Images, similes, epithets, metaphors—the froth of poetry—become obsolescent. But did not Tourian himself cry, "Oh, my foam is at the bottom!" That is why, being our first great, he'll always be with the last ...

In one of his letters Tourian exclaimed, "Can one sob aloud a Hosanna?" Truly it is an impossible thing. But genius begins just at the point where the supposedly possible ends. And Tourian, indeed, made the impossible possible. His lyric poetry, while being a sob, is at the same time a Hosanna, both mortal affliction and exaltation of life, a storm of grief and a surfeit of love. And Tourian himself knew, and he himself stressed this. "I am sad and gay, no, I am atremble and happy ..."

It is absurd, and, in general, inexcusable in poetry to epitomize; but despite this rule one of the masterpieces of Tourian's oeuvre and of the world's lyric poetry is "The Turkish Woman." And the poem is not just about a Turkish woman. If we substitute the usual pronoun for the Tourianic "she" [*Yet'e duryanakan "ne"-n p'okharinenk' sovorakan "na"-ov*: Armenian has no grammatical gender, so the third person singular pronoun is W. *an*, E. *na*; Tourian employs the artificial feminine *ne* "she" of the classical grammarians who attempted to explain in Armenian the analysis of Greek of Dionysius Thrax.—JRR] and change two or three words in all, the poem will become a splendid portrait of the author. It's Tourian himself, who "if he but looks, you'll say, Now he'll die out!... / If he smiles, you'll say, Now he'll fly!... / If he blushes, you'll say, Now he'll burst into flame!... / If he speaks, you'll say, Now he'll expire!" And all these ifs are accomplished in Tourian before our eyes, and all these metamorphoses take place in his lyrics.

He really "burns, he ever burns, he doesn't burn out / Like the lamp the destitute woman in the temple lit... / But if he dies, you'll say, Now he is born!" Yes, the lamp the poor woman lit in the temple burns and burns, and is not consumed. And that poverty-stricken woman could not have been Tourian's mother of blessed memory. That poor woman can be only Mother Armenia. Only the lamp she lights cannot burn out. Only she could give birth to such a son as Bedros Tourian.

Bedros Tourian!

A hundred and ten years have passed since his birth, but it is already unbelievable that he ever lived, much less was born. And if ever he was born, then he was born when "Heaven was in labor, earth was in labor, / In labor was the wine-dark sea, / The sea's labor seized the small red reed ..." [These are the first lines of the pre-Christian song of the birth of Vahagn/Heracles, with three more and various phrases cited below: see J. R. Russell, "Carmina Vahagni," repr. in *AIS*, pp. 357-370.—JRR] He didn't live long enough to grow a beard, and even if he was black-haired and black-eyed [*sevakn*: Sevak has encoded his own name here.—JRR], it's all the same: "He had hair of fire, / A beard of flame, / And his little eyes were suns." That is how we picture him, since he is the Herakles of our lyric poetry, the "blond youth" who spreads around him the smouldering smoke of the "reed stalk" that was his life, a life already unreal and mythological today; and the reed stalk's flame is his eternal presence, "a crucible of words" but also "a thunder of reproach." "A Thunder of reproach," so that we might achieve the merit to be termed his followers without setting fire to our lives in art in the "disease of heaven" and to leap up emerging "from the flame ..."

**2. A Night at the Opera, and Tripe Soup at Dawn.**

(Arshag Chobanian, cit. in *Documents*, no. 48, pp. 95-96. This class trip from Scutari to Pera seems to have been one of the high points of Tourian's brief, youthful life. The poem "The Armenian Woman" is about a ferry crossing, too; so the associations of the Bosphorus ferry were for Tourian all love and adventure—we have seen, in the introduction to this book, how the ferry served as a symbol of the progress of the Armenian people towards a freer, better life. If Tourian had met Edna St. Vincent Millay and read her "Recuerdo," they would have understood each other at once. She, too, was a Poet of the City: the city is New York; the ferry, the Staten Island line. "We were very tired, we were very merry— / We had gone back and forth all night on the ferry. / And the sky went wan, and the wind came cold, / And the sun rose dripping, a bucketful of gold.")

Serapion Tghlian invited Bedros' whole class to the performance of his play *Eleonora,* which was to take place at Pera. I don't know how his father's extreme severity softened sufficiently on this occasion for him to permit his son to spend a whole night in Pera. But there was the fact of an invitation from a teacher; and for many uneducated fathers the teacher possessed tremendous significance ... Serapion Tghlian, whose practical lesson in literary scholarship I heartily applaud, gave his pupils a box, into which they crammed like sardines, one on top of the other. At the end of the play Tourian and his comrades, their mouths agape in wonder at the finery of the theater-goers and the stage sets, left the theater with no idea of where to go. They hung around on the street, without much money in their pockets or any destination in mind. It happened to be winter, too, so even the most stout-hearted could not withstand the bitterly cold weather. The whole group went into a cheap café to while the night away over a twenty-*para* cup of coffee. Laughing and joking, with Tourian the master of the revels, they saw in the sunrise. At last! But now they were ravenously hungry, and the money left was barely enough for their ferry tickets. Heads drooping in the rainy gray dawn, they paced the sidewalks before the slumbering great houses. What was to be done?

Suddenly, one of them espied the newly-opened shop of an *ishkembeji* in the street of the Holy Trinity church. [Tk. *ishkembe chorbasi* is tripe soup, which people in Turkey still enjoy at daybreak after a night of drinking; the *ishkembeji* is a cook whose establishment specializes in the dish.—JRR] The people who plied that trade had the custom of serving up their juicy fare for free on the opening day of a shop. Without waiting for an elaborate invitation, they all piled into the restaurant with much laughter and clamor, in a frontal assault on the *ishkembejis,* and concluded their extraordinary night with a gluttonous repast.

### 3. Tourian's Amusements.

(Chobanian, repr. in *Documents,* no. 48, p. 99. A number of Tourian's poems have the graphic shape of their subject: from the testimony below it is apparent that he could employ physical manipulation of his texts to comic purposes as well.)

One of Bedros' mates, a medical student, was in love with a girl. In order to amuse his other friends, Bedros composed letters in French addressed to the girl by the young man, filling them with errors in spelling and grammar, and then read them out to the company ... Dikran Atamian has one letter of Tourian's, which when folded in half at the middle, yields a different meaning—a clowning, risible one.

Janfesjian remembers a satirical poem Tourian had written about the clergy of Scutari, which is, unfortunately, lost.

Tourian loved singing as much as, certainly more than, joking. He had a sparkling voice and sang Armenian, French, and Turkish songs pleasingly. He was one of the favorite singers in his school days, and many attest that he sang our melancholy hymns [*sharagannere*: the medieval spiritual songs of the Armenian Church—JRR] most sweetly ... He sang so well that a European lodger on the upper story of their house came downstairs, full of admiration, stood outside and listened, not daring to enter the room: the next day he asked that they allow him to come in and listen when Bedros sang.

**4. Tourian's Passions.**

(Chobanian, repr. in *Documents*, no. 48, pp. 101-102.)

The aspect of Tourian's life that has remained the most obscure is the history of his passions ... According to M. Boghigian, Tourian's loves were Platonic feelings, indefinite desires that emerged and perished in shadow without ever seeing the light of the sun. Janfesjian, who was a daily companion of the poet unto death, does not recall the name of a single girl to whom Tourian might have shown preference; he does not know of any being to whom the poet's love songs might have been dedicated. Dikran Atamian says the same thing.

But the story that is the most unusual, romantic, unverified, and unnatural, is the following, which Dr. Kosma, one of Tourian's friends, relates: When Tourian was at school he supposedly fell in love with the daughter of a family with whom they were acquainted. She was a student at the same school, fell in love with him, had assignations and exchanged letters with him. After their graduation, their love continued to burn in Tourian's heart and became so ardent that the poet dared to ask the girl's hand in marriage. Her parents rejected the proposal with contempt, on account of his poverty, and made it impossible for the two lovers to see each other thereafter. The girl fell ill of heartache. The doctor ordered that they allow Tourian to come and visit her a few times at least. But the girl, seeing Bedros was not to be her own, could not contain her grief and at last expired of her illness, the very same disease that Tourian was to come down with and suffer, six months after her death.

... There is no proof of the veracity of this most poetic tale. I regret that Dr. Kosma, who lives far from Constantinople, gave me no facts and clarifications despite several letters I sent to him requesting these. On the other hand, Tourian's closest friends, and Janfesjian in particular, reject outright the existence of such a romantic affair.

**5. A Theatrical Advertisement.**

(*Manzume-i Efkar*, no. 1152, 7 February 1870, repr. in *Documents*, no. 9, p. 14. The reckoning of time here is according to the old Ottoman Muslim system: the hours are counted from sunset. So in late winter, the hour of 2 1/2 would be about 8 P.M. I thank my friend and colleague Professor Wheeler Thackston of Harvard for this explanation. D. Chukhajian, the Armenian Verdi, wrote an opera based upon the account in the *Buzandaran* of P'awstos of the stormy passions and political intrigues of Arshak II, Arsacid king of Armenia in the mid-fourth century A.D. The opera exists in two versions: Chukhajian's original, tragic one, and a cleaned-up Stalinist version upholding Arshak as the contemporary embodiment of the *Führerprinzip*. The San Francisco Opera, despite protests from local patriots, staged the former version in September 2001.)

The Osmaniye Theater
at Gedik Pasha
1870 February 7, Saturday night at the hour of 2 1/2
Directed by H. Vartovian
An extraordinary and glorious production
A national event
The Fall of the Arsacid Dynasty

The play has interludes of song, in six acts and three scenes with a silent conclusion (*tableau vivant*)

Author: B. Tourian
Music: D. Chukhajian

**6. Missy Eugénie on Love and Verse.**

(Dikran Arp'iarian, *Arevelk'*, 18 July 1892, no. 2544, repr. in *Documents*, no. 37, p. 69.)

But the most arresting thing the lady has to offer us is the estimation and intimacy with Tourian that she enjoyed, which reveals the difference in morals and taste when one compares these to the habits of some contemporary poets. The new ones—the new of today, that is—experience a kind of pleasure, a savor, from reading the poems that describe those secret feelings, even when they are still fresh, to their intimates, in some group of youths enamoured of literature; in homes; on a steam ferry; in a restaurant; and even... on the street sometimes—wherever it might be possible to find heads nodding in agreement and an assemblage of lips murmuring *"Vivat!"* Tourian—who would be numbered amongst the ancients, were he alive today—to the contrary, comprehended the pleasure of poetry. For them, enjoyment consisted in concealment: he wanted to preserve the inner harmony that had arisen between the heart and the virginal poem. Poetry was his; he, poetry's. And if with trembling hand and pounding heart he dared on some occasion to offer his verses to some adored creature who had inspired him, that remained a secret he bore with him to the grave.

Missy Eugénie alone was an exception, sharing the knowledge of his excitations, of his hidden life. The twenty-year-old poet deferred humbly to that fifty-year-old woman, who, gripping a pen in her bony fingers, and shaking her head, would correct this or that line of a poem. Who knows what losses those delicate, quivering poems suffered from these excisions and improvements! But Tourian was always satisfied, since he held in esteem the lady to whom he consigned his writings. And later on the woman was not without pity: more approval than criticism passed her lips. She did not drive the poet to despair—she encouraged him. Along with a particular fondness for sermons, she loved and admired Tourian's writing. Sometimes her admiration led her to betray confidences: Tourian happened to meet at her house one day a radiant young lady, one of those noble beauties who leave a profound impression upon one at first sight. The youthful poet, who had already achieved a measure of renown, was greeted approvingly by the young lady, but the conversation that followed was hesitant, even timorous. While the girl did not feel her expectations had been deceived, Tourian still had not measured up to the magic of his name. A few weeks after this meeting, Missy Eugénie went to pay a call on the young lady and removed from her pocket a letter addressed to the girl, in which the poet's pen had attained its zenith. Tourian, who lay sick, had penned the epistle in bed, in order to express his admiration and likable impression of the girl in whose presence he had been tongue-tied. The publishers of Tourian's works will surely append a comely page to the volume they are compiling, if only they succeed in locating this letter, which I myself have sought in vain. Missy Eugénie, pocketing it again, took it away with her. And all this happened over twenty years ago ...

**7. Secret Love, and a Visit to the Doctor.**

(Dr. A. Finjanian, letter to Arshag Chobanian, Constantinople, 17 October 1891, repr. in *Documents*, no. 36, pp. 66-67.)

Since you are Bedros Tourian's biographer it would perhaps not be superfluous to inform you that Mr. Tourian loved a young lady by the name of S[at'enik?]—Sharuryan's suggestion. JRR], who has since married and passed away. He refers to her in many of his verses. His love was, however, poetical or intellectual; and the girl was entirely unaware, to the best of my knowledge, that she was loved by so great a poet.

Another point concerning his life that I recall is this: Bedros Tourian toward the end went to Pera, to the now-deceased Dr. Katibian, for care, paying a fee of one *mejidi* per visit. Once Mr. Tourian recommended I go to the same physician—I was then a student—so that Dr. Katibian might examine me more attentively. We went. After Katibian had examined his sick patient, I and the doctor remained alone together. I declared to the doctor, among other things, that my friend was a considerable poet with promise for a great future, but that at the moment he was a bit strapped for cash. The doctor, of blessed memory, smiled sadly at my mention of the word "future" and fell silent ... Thereafter I learnt from Mr. Tourian that Dr. Katibian from that day onward would never accept a fee from Bedros Tourian for a visit—a fact that brings as much honor to the departed doctor as to the lamented Tourian.

**8. Tourian's Last Year.**

(Arshag Chobanian, repr. in *Documents,* no. 48, pp. 102-106. The Armenian coffee house on Camlica is still there. The texts of the two poems or songs are given also at the end of the second chapter of this book.)

At the top of Camlica hill there was an old Armenian coffee-seller [Tk. *kahveci*], a dear little man, whom Tourian knew and loved. Every Sunday when he saw the poet coming he would run to spread the straw mat [*p'siat'*] out on the ground, brew coffee, and sit down next to him to listen—doubtless without understanding much—to Tourian's talk. And Tourian spoke very mellifluously and fluently, as his friends attest ... "There was no strain," Janfesjian says, "when he spoke. The words welled forth abundantly from him and flowed out of his mouth with the lightness and alacrity of the waters of a fountain, yet we felt that every word was draining his strength at the times he held forth so generously."

... In June 1871 he began to spit blood ... In the autumn of that year Avedis Koranian's mother once saw Tourian looking very sad and asked him, "What's the matter with you, Bedros?" Tourian laid his hand upon his breast and said, "There's a fire here, such a fire as cannot be extinguished; and it will not go out till it has consumed me." [Հոս կրակ մը կայ, անանկ կրակ մը, որ չմարիր և պիտի չմարի, մինչև որ զիս հատցնէ։]

His friends relate that he wrote songs of lament over himself, composed melodies for them, and would sing them to himself or his comrades. Here is one such melody which Janfesjian remembers:

"If I die, don't come and cry over my coffin:
Earth and mountain, hill and dale will lament me."
[Ես մեռնիմ նէ, մի՛ գար, մի՛ լար իմ տապան,
Հողը, լեռը, սարը, ձորը պիս կ'ողբան։]

And here is part of a song of the same kind, which I found in the possession of Mrs. Zabel Donelian (Sibil) [1863-1934, poet, writer, teacher—JRR] :

"My loved ones have all fled from me.
I will die!
Why, black-tressed cypresses, do you moan?
I will die!
Sad tomb, how close to me you are!
I will die!"

[Սիրելիքս բոլոր խոյս տուին քովէս,
Պիտի մեռնի՛մ ես.
Ինչո՞ւ մըռնչէք նոճիք սևագէս,
Պիտի մեռնի՛մ ես։
Տըխուր գերեզման, որչա՛փ ինձ մօտ ես,
Պիտի մեռնի՛մ ես։]

A month before his death he asked Boghos Telpian, who had come on a visit, to write his funeral oration. Telpian, horrified, refused. But Tourian insisted, nearly begging ... Tourian entreated him so insistently that Telpian composed the eulogy, which Tourian not only read through, but corrected.

During the final days Dikran Kalemjian [1844-1920, playwright—JRR], the prompter at the Armenian theater, called upon him a couple of times. And here is how, in telling of the impressions culled from his visits, he describes the house where Tourian lived and died: "When you went in the door there was an earthen-floored court; next to it, a ground-floor room. To the left—a stair of five steps. Above was a hall [*sufa*] and two rooms. Tourian lay in the room on the left. The hall looked out onto the Bosphorus, and it was there the poet worked when he was well, at a wooden table, looking out over the enchanting scene and writing. The bedroom, bare of all adornment and furnishing, had only a low couch on the floor, with the upholstery torn and the straw stuffing spilling out. Near the bed, standing in the corner, was a square table-stool [*at'orrag-seghan*] on which medicines, books, and papers were heaped in disarray. In place of a bookcase there was a little chest and a niche [*mihrab*] in the wall. The curtains were closed."

Kalemjian tried to comfort the patient during his visits, but Tourian was inconsolable. Because of his impending death he pondered all the more his sad life: he was departing from the world without having lived! His bitterness on account of this deprivation was so great that now he did not want to die. He cast his gaze over his entire existence and saw nothing there save the poverty that had curtailed his flights, the incomprehension of contemporaries who had failed to appreciate him at his true worth and the savagery of a few who had hurt him, the utter absence of a kiss from the beautiful girl he had worshipped, who might have given him his fair share of bliss—a life utterly empty and cold. And the poor deprived boy was to die with his eyes wide open, embittered against mankind, the world, even sometimes against God. "They did not recognize the honor due me," he often repeated to Kalemjian, "but they will seek me yet." [Յարգս չգիտցան, բայց պիտի փնտռեն զիս։] And like a refrain he always added, "Ah, at least publish my work, so that I'm not forgotten!" [Ա՜խ, գոնէ գրածներս տպեցէ՛ք, չմոռցուիմ։]

On the day before his death, he was visited again by Kalemjian. "Do you need anything?" he asked. "What could I need?" the sick man retorted with grim sarcasm. "All I've got is my bed. They'll bear me away with it." And, shaking his head, he repeated, "They'll seek me, they'll seek me yet!"

**9. Tourian's Eulogy for Vartan Lutfian.**

(21 May 1871, Scutari. Arshag Chobanian writes, "Tourian, who had decided to read a eulogy over the grave on the day of Lutfian's burial, entered a café that same day, asked for pen and paper, and wrote for a few minutes." Ekserjian says Tourian "did not have the courage at first to write and recite [a eulogy] but then gave in to the request of others, and wrote it out in pencil on the way, in great haste." After "sighs" (*harrach'ank*), Tourian had added, then crossed out, the words "and the prayer of the venerable clergy"—Lutfian had not received last rites. See Sevak, I, pp. 348-349. If that is the case, then Tourian's reference to the impatient gravediggers anticipated the scene at the cemetery but was not an actual reaction to it.)

Esteemed participants in this ceremony,

I pray you remain a bit longer: do not part yet from this lamentable casket, whose pale traveller has heard in calm the sighs of his friends. Listen, then, you, too, to the high echo of his life, which he imparted to a friend's sincere heart. Hear the weak voice of a bosom friend declaring his great memory, daring to let it resound through the tomb's frightful archway.

Vartan Lutfian, our wonderful friend, is dead. He died on the earth, more than the lifeless marble of the tombs beaded with perspiration, more than the flower which from year to year is reborn. He died and dried in his twentieth spring. But shall we now cry? We make a great error, which I will always repeat: instead of bewailing a man at his birth, we cry over a dying man, though it is into an abyss of grief he is born and he dies at the zenith of blessing.

Let us not say that the universe is the mockery of a God. [A reference to his own "Murmurs"? —JRR] Never! The cosmos is the mine of souls.

Vartan Lutfian was one of those who always detect the fragrance of heaven in their lives. He was one of those happy ones who breathe out a pure and brief life.

In this shaken multitude there are very few who know his heart and genius.

There is only one thing we have here to lament. Vartan was disposed to be a revolutionary of ideas; but when his hand lifted the luminous edifice, when that hand conveyed it to his fresh, ingenious brow, death bathed it in cold sweat. That is what is so painful.

But do you wish his soul to remain now undisturbed? He bequeathes to you his fire and memory. You, who are his friends, carry forward the work he began, if you love him.

Yet one aspect of this grief-stricken assembly amazes me. I notice in pain that the gravediggers, spade in hand, wait impatiently to fill up the black pit of our dear one. They think they are burying one of those men whose tomb is an abyss, who die with their memory. Tell them, you who know Vartan, tell them that this one is not one of those men. This one is a soldier of light and cannot be buried, no matter how much cold earth they pile upon his corpse. This one belongs to a nation of the nineteenth century and is one of the rays of light.

Can a ray of light be interred?

Especially, why this grave, when his friends' warm hearts are open to receive him hospitably?

Be shut, you black sarcophagus, / For Vartan belongs forever to us! [Գոցուէ·, դու սև գերեզման, Վարդան մե·րն է յաւիտեան։ *Kots've, tu sev kerezman, / Vartan mern e havidyan*]

B. Tourian

**10. Letter to Bishop Khoren Nar-Bey.**

(22 January 1871, Sevak, I, pp. 160-162. The letter was published in *Endanik'* ("Family"), 1 March 1884, no. 12, pp. 189-190, with this editorial note: "The following is from the unpublished works of the Armenian poet B. Tourian, who died young. It was sent to a revered priest in order to seek his patronage. We publish it in order to provide to ladies and girls enamoured of literature some taste of the style of the abovementioned poet." The original manuscript belongs to the Armenian Patriarchate of Jerusalem; and handwritten copies by M.

Mihrdatiants' and H. Janfesjian are also extant. Nar-Bey had read Tourian's poems addressed to the Little Father Khrimian and had promised him help in finding work and publishing his verses. Nar-Bey did not fulfill his promise, since the poems dealt with the subject of falling in love, and he did not want people to castigate him for assisting their publication. Nar-Bey wrote poems himself; and his translations of Lamartine into Armenian were published. He also penned patriotic feuilletons.)

Most Honored Lord,

Those shining emanations of genius and brotherly love, that splendid unity of the rays of the brow and of the heart, by which you soar aloft, encourage me to apply to your Holiness, to you, whose soul is so composed [*gazm*, other copies have *badrasd*, "ready," Sevak] as to be eager to give bread to the destitute and to offer a spark to the corpse. It is a thurible of God's temple, a lamp erected in the abysses.

Most honored lord, you have both Christ's radiance and the pinion of genius: this is no blind man approaching you, that you might open his eyes, but one upon whose brow a black cloud hangs. It is the groan of a hovel whose hearth is cold, though the heart smoulder; where life is still, and it is the lyre that sobs.

Often in the storm of genius, the planks of the decrepit hut shake, and when the storm is quiet, in the miserable dusk a dry leaf plummets from a tree outside. The boards are the cold spade tamping down the grave-mound of oblivion; and perhaps that leaf is the shadow of a star, fallen from a constellation.

How many talents, plummeting down to that threshold of chaos, have burnt out, expired—there are graves in the cemeteries of common folk that might have been volcanoes, yet their spark was entombed in the thick darkness of the heart without ever having been fanned to life ... Genius in the shaft of the grave is a skull that was unable in humanity's aether to become a comet.

I, too, have been trembling for some time upon that threshold, sparkling without attaining genius; and instead a roving, bloody eye observes warily the sparks from the massed cumulus of the revolutionary volcano of humanity, as a tiger eyes the blood pouring from the victim he has mauled. I desire from that volcano of revolution, from that forge of love, from that human dawn, from that Golgotha to strive towards the chaos, the barren root, the dim horizon of the last light setting on mankind—to my hovel.

But I have kept vigil with but a lamp of clay, contesting with the stars only with the sparks of my lone heart plunged in silence, and have felt the freezing of every drop of sweat upon my brow. Now I test my feet beyond that humble threshold, seeking first the assistance of your office of Love.

Your Holiness, aside from your granting me the honor of the noteworthy occasion of a sympathetic interview, I am animated by a joy that is like the gift of a tear [*arts'unk'*; some versions have *artsakank'*, "echo," Sevak] to a straitened heart. It is a promise whose sweet demand I have kept for the proper occasion: now that occasion presents itself to me.

Pardon, most honored lord, this volcanic heart that lingers by your sublime lyre and prepares to shed a droplet, a dewdrop, into your heart.

Most honored lord, I beg you accept this assurance of my previously mentioned, most profound, esteem.

B. Tourian

**11. Letter to B. D. Atamian.**

(6 July 1871, Sevak, I, pp. 165-167. The letter was published first in *Arevelk'* no. 1607, 1889; the unanswered letter seems to be one dated 5 February 1871.)

Friend, sharer of my heart,

It has been some time since I wrote to you a letter which has remained without reply. I was not pained by this; I understood you either had not the means of replying or else did not consider it important to do so. Though I might have written a second letter then, what was I to write? What can one write, when one's heart is empty? You might naturally infer from my writing now that my heart surely must be full...! Yes, it is replete with the tears of a grieving memory.

I slept almost peacefully, whilst on the black night of 21 May *he* [Tourian refers here to their classmate and friend Vartan Lutfian: see also the letter to Atamian on Lutfian in the commentary to poem no. 25, "Murmurs"—JRR] was bathed in sweat, when a soul was wailing, caught in between human hearts and the grave.

Now his bones have rotted, and the mound over his grave is flattened and indistinguishable ... I did not want to believe he was going to die, till the time when he sent me one of his last, expiring glances, and it fell between us before it reached me, and died ... till when his strangled voice died out in a sad "Farewell" ... Ah, there are memories that in their continuation perpetually retain the very same lightning bolts ... In the recesses of my heart I have been able to keep only one sturdy interstice for the recitation of his sad funeral oration.

As I said in another place, [in the letter of 5 February 1871: "Where does our fortune remain—the fortune that united us in childhood, that hearth of fellowship called school?" Sevak] in one of the hearths of humanity, in school, black fate brought our heads together and compressed them in an iron diadem [*bsag*: the image is of the diadem or *narot,* with which the heads of bride and groom are bound together in the wedding ceremony of the Armenian Apostolic Church.—JRR] kneaded into one our ideas, and made of our boyish talents a single pale bouquet composed of bolts of *lightning* [*talgahar shant'eru p'unch m'erav*: the phrase echoes multiple images in the later poems.—JRR]. And one of the coruscating flashes of that black fate is now entirely extinguished, appearing in the guise of a mournful dusk deep in the hearts of those he loved.

A sad confession!

I am Vartan's continuation.

Noble friend, in the winter I wrote to you that I was ill with a cold; now I tremble, blood is always coming out of my mouth, I'm wasting away, and on my brow life's ruddy smile is going pale. I dip my lyre ceaselessly, in an endless farewell to those who did not open up to me their inner depths but glowed only from without, and first of all to a woman! ... the mistress of my imagination ... to that multihued star of dream or flower like the corolla of the sun ... no, more, the queen of all radiance, of every scent ...

Ah, but one beam of her ignites a reverie, her single fragrance fills the tenebrous nave of the heart with the smoke of incense ... To die, fresh and dreaming! ... To die without a furrow traced [*kdzvelu*: another version has *tskelu*, "left," Sevak] upon a marble brow, without one's lips having burned with a kiss, without one's soul enflamed by a smile, to die!!! That is sad, still ...

. . .

I am very grieved—if only you could come here as before, but black fate has stretched out again towards us its sanguinary hand, disrupting everything. I don't know whether there is any plan ready for your coming back. It's some days since I saw your brother; and I've not asked him.

Ah, I'd like to see you. I'm the same as ever, except a little inclined towards the grave, my gaze fixed on that summit of my meditations. I hope to get a letter from you, or to see you here in a few days ...

Your friend,

B. Tourian.

**12. Letter to A. Lusinian.**

(13 August 1871, first printed in *Arevelk'* no. 1607, 1889, repr. Sevak, I, pp. 168-169. The "she" (gen. sg. *nera*) is Aghavni Vartanian, whom Tourian defended against criticism in the press. He refers here to a speech she delivered on 8 August at a gathering in Scutari.)

To the Hon[orable] A(rak'el) Ef[fendi] Lusinian.
Constantinople.

My brother,

Forgive me.

I wished in fact to praise Her fame, but I found my pen and feelings weak and numb before so noble a subject ... Ah, can one sob a Hosanna? These days my perpetual wound breathes beneath my breast, that black star of my firmament. Release your hold upon the collar of this "child of the cypresses," this "pianoforte owl" who is sometimes struck dumb before the sublime, whose heart is agitated [*g' aledzp'i*: literally, "crashes in waves," cf. the imagery of "The Lake," and note subsequent play upon images of solid and liquid.—JRR] in the abyss, whose lips are petrified, who ever gazes upon his wound, even as one enamoured of glory looks to his star ... Pardon this "wan intimate of yours..."

I am to blame ... but no! Approach my wound, my brother, this terrifying abyss ... however only the black brow of the cliff and star of heaven can look upon it.

I hope you will have forgiven me even before these lines reach you; and you will certainly have understood what I was unable to explain; for the arrow of a poet's meditations can penetrate the layers of the heart. There is much else I wished to write, but in that respect I am limitless, and besides, my brother delivered your letter to me only just now—but he, too, was constrained by circumstances to act as he did.

I await your letter.

Au revoir,

Your brother

B. Tourian.

**13. Letter to B. N. Janfesjian.**

(Scutari, 5 September 1871, published in *Arevelk'* no. 1607, 1889, and often reprinted; repr. in Sevak, I, pp. 169-171. The lines "You wish to bestir ..." were deleted and substituted with others by Eghishe Tourian in an 1893 edition.)

My intimate friend,

I sound now the note of the boundless Farewell. I wanted to see you—want, for me, means thirst. I directed my tottering steps towards your house, asked after you, and, even as I was asking, looked immediately at the place where your shoes should be. [In Armenia, Russia, Iran, and other civilized countries, one leaves one's street shoes at the door and puts on slippers.—JRR] Your mother—and the empty space—rendered me sad answer: He's not here. Spontaneously I echoed, My brother isn't here! ...

I know that the bitter symmetry of life did not grant that you see one time your brother, your wan and trembling guest. But what is one to say to the blackness of that fortune, that refused to reward my infirm steps and compelled me to turn my feeble tread correspondingly away, sad and pained? Whither? To seek a corner where my burning tears might be hidden from men's eyes.

My condition, my brother, is one of despair. But I am calm, and of course rather gloomy. Every human desire in my heart has wilted—desire, that is the gilt surface of this world. All my hopes have turned to ashes; I live almost like a machine. I've lost my intellectual fire, and my thoughts are brief and dark.

But do not be pained, my friend; be thus persuaded that your brother enters, instead of the grave, the ark of Noah, to be spared the world's deluge of blood ... No, this black thought never weighs as heavily upon my soul as a single tear does in my eyes.

Oh, how pleasing it is to sit beside [*arrent'eragts'elov*] you and to suck at a few hours of the last blaze of a wan sunset ... but I know that in this illness I am a little nauseating [*noghgali*] ... when somebody looks at me I see lines of commiseration form on his brow.

But you, friend, heart of my heart, I know you always love me, equally and unshakeably, in all my smiles, pains, health, and sickness, when pitying me you wish to be commingled within me [*nerk'ins g'uzes kharrnel*] ... You wish to bestir a soul burdened with a skeleton ...

to agitate an abyss of terrifying dreams that is my heart, where the silence of death reigns and only heaven's echoes are there to dissolve the stillness: sound your sweet speech there, too, my friend. For a grave, the soughing of a cypress is sufficient, and when we meet hereafter I will not speak much, but be content with mere looks.

Never think I am bereft of hope. Do not be at all frightened by a poet's death. I should have the right to feel pain only all were immortal, and I alone were mortal.

Be thus persuaded!

Till our sweet meeting,

B. Tourian.

**14. Letter to B. A. Lusinian, and an Image from Nerval.**

(Scutari, 10 December 1871. Ekserjian published the letter in two separate parts in 1892. The lines "To be young and sing; / To be old and pray" are from Lamartine. Lusinian studied at the Nubar Shahnazarian School; A. Vartanian—who is the "she" of the letter, also—at the Agapian Ladies' Academy founded by P'anosian, who criticized Tourian's writing. Tourian refers in the letter to several articles submitted for publication: see Sevak, I, pp. 345-348. The source of the "sun of night" is ancient alchemy: in European art it is exemplified by Albrecht Dürer's esoteric *Melencolia* [1514]. Dürer's shaggy, brooding hero of the mind and spirit is himself a precursor of the Romantic rebel. But the more contemporary Romantic *locus classicus* that is most likely to have inspired Tourian's reference to the image is a famous poem by Gérard de Nerval, who was born at Paris 22 May 1808 and took his life there on 25 February 1855—his suicide inspired Gustave Doré's "La rue de la Vieille Lanterne." Nerval visited Constantinople at the time of Tourian's birth. He translated Goethe's *Faust* into French from German: his focus on the dream, mysticism, and the nocturnal comes out of German Romanticism. His sonnet of 1853, "El Desdichado," whose Spanish title means "The Disinherited," was dedicated to the opera singer Jenny Colon, whom he loved and whose untimely death unmade him.

The speaker in Nerval's poem has lost the inheritance of love and life, yet he still lives; so he regards his bereavement from a vantage point of contradictory states and identities. He is a prince, but his domain is a relic of the past. His heavenly lyre is star-spangled; yet the night is that of the tomb, his true star having been snuffed out. The sun that rises there is black, the opposite of the luminary of day. Voices of demon and fairy clash—perhaps Yeghia Demirjibashian's imaginal picture of Tourian in the essay translated in this chapter, was also inspired by Nerval. Orpheus hangs between the sunlit earth and the paths of Hades—how strongly such a sonnet would have appealed to Tourian! Orphism, with its collocation of song-world-harmony, and its conviction that poetry is the voice of the universe, became popular in the late eighteenth century, entering the Romantic inheritance. The poem contains other arresting images that are echoed in the dying Tourian's letter: the night of the tomb—Virgil's own, on Mt. Posillipo, near Naples—crossing Acheron, the sighs of the saint. Tourian would have been alert, too, to Nerval's mention in line 9 of the Crusader king of Jerusalem, Guy de Lusignan, 1129-1194, with his Armenian connections. And Tourian speaks of melancholy.

Je suis le ténébreaux,—le veuf,—l'inconsolé,
Le Prince d'Aquitaine à la tour abolie:
Ma seule *étoile* est morte,—et mon luth constellé
Porte le *Soleil noir* de la *Mélancholie*.

Dans la nuit du tombeau, toi qui m'as consolé,
Rends-moi le Pausilipe et la mer d'Italie,
La *fleur* qui plaisait tant à mon coeur désolé,
Et la treille où le pampre à la rose s'allie.

Suis-je Amour ou Phébus? ... Lusignan ou Biron?
Mon front est rouge encor du baiser de la reine;
J'ai rêvé dans la grotte où nage la syrène ...

Et j'ai deux fois vainquer traversé l'Achéron:
Modulant tour à tour sur la lyre d'Orphée
Les soupirs de la sainte et les cries de la fée.

Tourian anticipated Modernism in various ways; and Nerval may thus mark a significant nexus with T. S. Eliot, 1888-1965, who cites the second line of the sonnet at the end of *The Waste Land*. Most recently, Lawrence Rainey, ed., T.S. Eliot, *The Annotated Waste Land with Eliot's Contemporary Prose*, New Haven: Yale University Press, 2005, pp. 123-124, provides the full text of the sonnet—with several misspellings of the French corrected here—but he fails to mention Dürer in his meager explanatory notes. No study of Tourian I have seen mentions Nerval.)

My brother,

Forgive my tardy reply. Though again my hands tremble over the pen, my heart fades out instead of feeling emotion, and instead of seeing I grieve; but I want to make the heroic effort of a doomed man and write two more lines.

My brother, the intent of your last letter was to comfort me; and you said, "Put out of your mind all this idea that you're sick, and you'll be entirely cured." Ah, my brother, there's a volcano erupting beneath my breast. The fires are scorching and roasting me. This fire is like one cast down from heaven: it doesn't go out and won't, till it's consumed everything.

Yes, I, too, believe now that I'm being *devoured*. I know I won't live much longer. Ah, my brother: here's a youth who's come into the world only to see and feel his own death and misery.

I don't know what to write. I feel a lot, but there's some difficulty writing. it's as though I were speaking from inside the tomb. I'm the ray of a setting sun. I am an extinction. I am a destruction. I know these lines are the last and will be the last, but how can I collect my scattered thoughts and speak? I'm not a poet, but I love poetry: I, who loved only songs in the world, desire that my last breath be a song as well.

They say that the swan at his last breath declaims its most harmonious cry [*ir en nertashnagavor jich'e*]. Let me pass out of this world like that swan, too.

Your missives of recent days have given me great consolation and pleasure. We'd barely managed a few gay strolls in the leafy shade, in the lovely, breezy fields and meadows of Scutari, and now I've fallen again, in hopelessness—doubtless not to rise again. But keep writing, my brother: your words are sponges that absorb my sorrows. Yes, I know you've never loved sadness. And often you hasten away from particular places in order not to see objects that give birth to or awaken the idea of sadness. But you love my sadness, since it is poetic. Ah, how sweet your words were: "I love to observe the pallor of melancholy on your brow more than a beauty's rosy cheeks or her forehead's shine." I have done my living in the world and like you I have loved only to be a *voice*. Like you, I loved to sing. He who has no song or knows not how to sing, has not that sweet capacity to touch the ideal of the beautiful and the lovely, of the harmony of sense.

Song is man's emblem; the most Primordial voice is song, and all nature is a song. Yes, my brother, you once said to me most specially, "Song is nothing but a harmonious bouquet of voices." Yes, I, too, say: "To be young and sing! / To become old and pray!" [*Yeridasart ellal yev yerkel, / Dzer linil yev aghot'el*]

This is life!

Ah, there is another, beautiful life: it is love. "To sing, pray, and love!" Ah, what a poetic life, what a perfect life! You sing, you love, and you pray! The greatest savor of souls in the world is to love. You know this in a more choice and lofty form than all men in the world: you love and are loved. You love beyond the grave. You are loved from the other side of eternity. My brother, how pleasant and desirable it would be for me to behold your love's appointed Occasion. If I am not to enjoy the boundless sweetness of it on earth, then I must have the dream and striving to whisper therein as the breath of a zephyr blowing from the Fatherland of the Stars and Angels—how hopelessly do I speak! Forgive me, brother, I shall confess all to you, albeit confusedly. Ah, I implore and beg providence, together with you, that life and death be commanded for a moment to lay down their arms that I may see, too, the Joining of the Sarcophagus Bird and the Sun of Night... [Տապանի թռչնիկին և գիշերուան Արևին Աջակցումը *Dabani T'rrch'nigin yev kishervan Arevin Achagts'ume*] What heart-lifting moments!... That joining is a meeting of lightning and flower. Sun and cosmos will behold a happy new nuptial pair. Happiness is the fortune decreed for you. Men will only admire as much as they envy you.

You are unblemished and pure. Whoever sees you as black and corrupt is black and corrupt himself. From you will emanate the first breath and daybreak of the future sodality of the Graduates of the Noubar and P'anosian schools. You must love P'anosian as much as Shahnazar. You said to me one day, though, that "P'anosian is on the one hand a foundation for me, a verity, he is also a great man of action." It does not matter that he had contempt for me, too. Nor does it matter that you yourself counselled me that if P'anosian is aroused to passion, whether it be the apple of his eye or God who comes before him, he'll either trample him underfoot and pass or tell him to step aside—that's normal for every man. One must forget *Discord* and the enmity between *Norayr* and *Armenag*, since on the far side of the grave, after all wrath everything is forgiveness. Let us pardon and be pardoned, Brother! These are the last murmurs of a man on his deathbed: I must say everything in sincerity, for I no longer rely upon, nor have regard for, the world or my own scruples.

My brother, now I am descending, or am close to the point of descending, to the black floor of that abyss they call the grave. What will they say of me beyond the grave? Surely: Here is an unfortunate youth who came into the world and felt only his own dying, and died [*ashkharh yegav yev miayn ir merrniln zkats' u merrav*].

I've written some tearful lines on a few scraps of paper. Surely my friends will honor them and they will see the light of the Sun. Did you speak to Zartarian about the publication of my latest work? My mind is distraught, my brother.

They are death's sacrificial altar. I step forward to be beheaded. I believe in God, I believe in the future life to come. Happy is he who believes! In the world only the faithless man is bereft of happiness, hopeless, and unfortunate. Perhaps friends and readers will find me mystical or allegorical [*misdikagan gam aylapanagan*] in my lines. I am already a metaphor, a thought. This is my being; that is my essence.

My brother, why do you not come? When I see my friends by my bedside, it is as though I saw angels of hope and life.

I know I will die in a short time: instead of tears over my casket, a few words; instead of sighs, two breaths of prayer for my soul; and instead of grief, two bouquets of flowers upon my grave. I will not be dead, then; I will remain ever verdant and alive [*yes al merradz ch'ellam bidi, mishd talar u gentani mnam bidi*]. I pray do not grieve at these doomed and despairing lines.

There is no more strength left in my fingers. It is as though I were all exhaustion. I grip your hand in tenderness and send Her this final greeting of respect: grow and flower!

Alas! Yes, my beginning was Alas! and my end was a cry of Woe!

Fortunate are you, fortunate you will be, and when I go to heaven before God and the angels I will plead for your happiness. Enjoy it! ... Farewell!

Your Brother,

B. Tourian.

**15. An Ominous Dream.**

(Yeghishe Tourian, "A dream (memory of childhood)," *Masis*, 20 January 1907, no. 9, p. 161, repr. in *Documents*, no. 44, p. 83.)

It was in November of that year
He lay sick in bed.
And I, a heedless boy
Who played with fire,
Not even suspecting
The impending sting of death,
Went to tell my dream to him.
He listened, meekly.

"Brother," said I, "last night
In our garden, on that plum tree
You know, I saw four fruits growing.
But they weren't plums,
Red and plump, or green,
But elongated like pears—
Or that's how it seemed—
With these crystalline stems,
Silvery, and they gleamed.
One of them suddenly, all by itself,
Broke off the branch, and fell."
My fevered Beteg [a diminutive of Bedros—JRR], sad and sweet,
Interpreted my ominous dream:
"The four fruits are my brothers four,
And the one that fell into the ground was me."

**16. The Death of the Poet.**

(Letter of Mak'sud Mihrdatiants' to Arshag Chobanian with Yeghishe Tourian's responses to Chobanian's queries, repr. in *Documents*, no. 33, pp. 61-63.)

As was customary, the members of the household gathered on Thursday evening, too, in the sick man's room. His little brothers were next to the bed, drawing minarets on paper and exchanging childish talk, saying, "What is the mollah saying?" Tourian heard this question, and in his fevered imagination he began to preach about God: "That is God, who in his superhuman power ..." and similar things. But Fr. Yeghishe (who was then a little boy named Mihran) doesn't recall them.

Everybody went to bed. At midnight he called father to turn him over from one side to the other. Father did this and he relaxed. "Let the *hajji* come upstairs," he said. The hajji was his elder brother, who had gone with father to Jerusalem that year and had just returned. [Armenians use the Arabic term for the pilgrimage to Mecca, *hajj*, for a trip to the holy city of Jerusalem; and one who has been there is called either *hajji* or *mahtesi,* the latter from Arabic *muqaddasi,* one who has been to the holy—*muqaddas*—city.—JRR] His maternal aunt, when she overheard this, understood that the sick man's condition was serious: in order not to overexcite the hajji's heart, she herself hastened to the patient's bedside. Tourian, thinking his aunt the hajji, gripped her hand and directed his words to her, starting this way: "You have gone to Jerusalem; I am going to the heavenly Jerusalem. You have seen the places where the Savior walked; I shall see Him." That kind of thing. The family were already wide awake and were gathering in the room. "Call Janfesjian!" he ordered them. His two younger brothers lit a lantern and went off to Janfesjian's house, which was a fair distance away: they roused him from sleep and brought him. Of course this took over an hour. During that time he was unable to be present to hear Tourian's talk. When Janfesjian arrived and sat down, Tourian began to speak: "There's no more Bedros," he said, "this will be your Bedros," pointing at Janfesjian. After that he gave several orders: he desired that his works be published, and requested that his burial rites be performed with dignity—you already know this. "Look after Mihran well!" he said. His maternal uncle arrived during the final moments. When he stepped through the doorway, Bedros made an effort to recognize him but did not speak. He went over and sat down on the bed. He [Tourian] blinked his eyes again, stared, recognized him him this time and smiled in sign of recognition. "Won't you speak?" asked his uncle. "Bedros, can't you speak?" asked his mother, who was sitting by the bed. "Your uncle's come." "I have no more time left" [*Al zhamanag ch'unim*] he replied—and those were his last words. His head fell back onto the pillow and his eyes closed. But what is remarkable is that after his eyes had shut, he brought his right hand gently to his head thrice, doubtless at the cost of supreme effort, as a sign of farewell, and that was the end.

"*Allah*! A doctor!" shouted father. "Quiet, you, too," said his brother, and took him aside. During his illness he had apparently said farewell to everyone. Very often he had even let his gaze rest upon a corner of the ceiling, and, fixing it there, had recited "Farewells" [*Mnak' parov*] in the precise tone priests use in church for repetition of the "Lord have mercy" [*Der voghormya*]. Once during his illness he was changing his shirt and saw how loose it had got around the neck. Throwing it to one side he cried "Is this what was to become of me?" [*Yes aysbes bidi ellayi*] and burst into tears. That was the only time in the course of his sickness that he shed tears. During the last days he used to say, "Someone is coming, remember to him my greetings." Afterwards they thought this to mean Dikran Atamian, who had been away from Constantinople, and arrived only on the day of the funeral. Twenty or twenty-one days before his death he said, "I'll celebrate a fine New Year with you this year," meaning that it was to be his last. On the contrary, the disease worsened during the holiday, but Tourian, raising himself from bed on a cane, got up and came to the downstairs room, where he sat down in the corner (*bujakhe*).

Fr. Hovhannes, the pastor of Yeni Mahalle, who has by now passed away, said to Fr. Eghishe, "Your brother made a confession, the like of which I had never heard before." Little Father Khrimian was at a wedding banquet when he heard of Tourian's death: he flung down his fork. Afterwards, on another occasion when he was going to their house he said, "Many wrote about me when I was Patriarch, but there was nothing like what he wrote." He also asked why the poem "My Rest" had not been inscribed upon his tombstone; and thereupon, tossing his head back, he recited the poem by heart.

**17. A Report on Tourian's Funeral.**

(Letter to the Editor of *Manzume-i Efkar*, 24 January 1872 by the journalist Dikran Papazian, repr. in *Documents*, no. 17, pp. 22-23. Other articles on Tourian's funeral stress forcefully, in flowery language, how the obsequies honored the literary genius of a boy from an indigent family, rather than wealth or nobility. Vahram Torkomian, 1858-1942, who was to become a physician and literary scholar in later life, was able as a small boy to squeeze through the crowd into the room where Tourian's body lay, as the funeral procession was about to begin. He remembered [*Documents*, p. 89] that Tourian's father was crying, and the latter's brother was consoling him in Turkish: *Ah, gözümin huri kardashim, aghla, ne kadar aghlarsan, az dir: amma bir defa soka'a bak—ölen Sultan Mahmud ola idi, böyle insan denizi yapilmaz idi,* "O brother, light of my eyes, cry! However much you cry, it's still too little! But just look for a moment at the street—if the dead man were Sultan Mahmud, such a sea of people still would not have gathered." It was plain to the family, the press, and the public that this was an extraordinary moment in the history of the Armenians and their literature.)

To the Editor:

Yesterday was a day of mourning and sorrow for all of us Armenians. The sad ceremony following the death of the young poet Bedros Tourian, who by his talent of genius had claimed the highest rank in the field of literature, was enacted at Scutari.

It was eight when the body of the deceased was taken directly from his home to the Church of the Holy Forerunner [*Surp Garabed*], where Bishop Hovhannes Setian pronounced a short eulogy.

Two bands provided accompaniment to the chanting of the choir boys. The first was hired in honor of the young poet by the Society of Lovers of Reading [*Ent'erts'asirats' engerut'iun*]; Mr. Vartovian had brought the other. A group of young people draped the coffin with a black veil.

We deem it proper here to make mention of Mr. Avedis Koranian, who devoted much effort and labor to the arrangement of the event. A crowd of about 3000 people accompanied the procession. This was a fitting honor to a great talent.

Finally the deceased was conveyed to the cemetery, where Fr. Khoren Pehlivanian delivered a written oration, after which the young Messrs. Lusinian, Telpian, and Melikian pronounced affecting eulogies, one by one, and with that the proceedings were concluded.

The untimely loss of the brilliant writer B. Tourian in the twentieth year of his age is truly a bitter blow to all Armenian hearts, especially for those people who have seen and read his theatrical compositions and beautiful verses.

It is our desire that the Society of Lovers of Reading of Scutari, which wishes to immortalize the name of this young man, will hasten to bring into print all of his works, which can indeed add notable luster to Armenian literature. We hope to see these intentions take shape in reality, for the immortal poet of genius, B. Tourian.

**18. A Poem by a Friend.**

(Boghos Telpian, d. 1881, was Bedros' classmate; he later became a teacher. The poem was printed in *Yep'rad* ["Euphrates"] no. 53 on 12 February 1872, shortly after Tourian's death; it is repr. in *Documents*, no. 22, pp. 32-33. The "comet of Transfiguration," *kisastghig Vartavarr*, combines the images of the brightness of Tourian's life's star, the tragic suddenness of its brilliant passage, the Romantic tresses of the poet, and the joyful Armenian holiday of early summer, on which roving bands of young men drench passersby with water. Vartavar, meaning "the bringing of roses," is popular understood as "burning roses": the fusion of water and fragrant, rosy fire is apposite to Tourian's own usages.)

On the Death of Tourian.

The dark clouds of a grim dawn, alas, have descended on Byzantium;
A storm wind's blast out of the gloom envelops Armenia ...
Ah, death's merciless talons have their revenge at last.
The star is dimmed, bright star, the Armenian's love's nightingale
And myrtle, and green branch and comet of Transfiguration.
Silent is the eloquent speaker; silent to the world, the Armenian's sad brother.
To death, the weakened and the hopeless;
To death, the sick man in the stony mountains.
Dying is for the old—
Why has the green tree died?
Just a month ago, when I said, "Let's talk," he said, "I am to die, speak death."
He imposed a debt: "When I die, recite a speech above my grave," he said.
"When you come next year to Baghlar-bashi, shed tears over my black earth," he said.

Woe, silent youth! Am I to be the one who sings your soul's songs? My speech is stricken mute, too.
Inseparable were your lyre, your love, your sorrow;
Immortality is to be your station, now.
Alas, advance! Only woe and yet more woe
Is the speech, the eulogies pronounced above your tomb ...

Your grieving friend,

B. Telepian [*sic*].

**19. A Eulogy for Tourian.**

(From an article by Dikran P'ap'azian entitled "Bedros Tourian" published in Masis no. 1197, 3 February 1872, excerpted in S.A. Shtikyan, *Hay nor grakanut'yan zhamanakagrut'yun, 1865-1875* ["Chronology of Modern Armenian Literature, 1865-1875"], Erevan: Arm. Acad. Sci., 1991, p. 359.)

If there is any immortal thing in this world, it is genius. That vivid talent which sketched its birth pangs on a scrap of paper and departed, immortalized his own name forever. History, that sublime teacher of future centuries, knows to memorialize a destitute man of literature rather than an ignorant rich man glutted with gold and possessions. The writer's life and glory begin on the other side of the grave. Yes, the life and glory of our dear friend, B. Tourian, have begun on the other side of the grave. Even though B. Tourian, our noble friend, left us in early youth and went away, he still left with us such unforgettable memorials—even a man who lived many centuries could not leave so many. And these are a myriad [*khel*] of choice literary works fit to contest against the revolution of time better than gigantic monuments, and to immortalize their author's name.

**20. Bowdler's Touch.**

(Arp'iar Arp'iarian, 1851-1908, a writer and public figure, employed the *nom de plume* Hraztan—i.e. northwestern Iranian Hrazdan, from Avestan Frazdanu, the name of the sacred river where the Prophet Zarathushtra converted King Vishtaspa to his visionary new religion. The name was given by Armenian Zoroastrians in ancient times to the river that runs through Erevan. This protest, published in *Hayrenik'* no. 45, 28 September 1891, Constantinople, is repr. in *Documents,* no. 30, pp. 41-42. Simon Felegian [var. Felek'ian], 1835-1904, was a teacher, editor, and poet. As to Bowdler, he was of course the editor who gave Victorian Britain a "family" Shakespeare. Felegian had criticized Tourian's poems when Bedros was his pupil at school; after the poet's death, he still could not leave them alone.)

Everyday Life.
Moral Advice.
By Hraztan.

One of our Armenologues, Mr. Simon Felegian, told a friend of mine the following the other day: "When they were about to print Tourian's poems," said he, "they brought them to me to look them over. Sir, I saw a lot of things to be changed there. There were immoral lines. I took it all, shaped it, fixed it, polished it, and made of it a proper thing that gives it a clean face and renders honor both to the departed and to literature."

... Is there really anything for me to add to this tale? Those who wish to do violence to writers in the name of 'morality' should always remember that it was in the name of morality that Tourian was corrected by Felegian, that is to say, was desecrated.

**21. The Two Tourians.**

(From an essay, "Bishop Yeghishe Tourian," by the poet Yeghia Demirjibashian, published in *Arevelk',* Constantinople, 25 November 1898, repr. in *Artsag echer, namagner, k'ert'vadzner* ["Prose pages, letters, poems"], Paris, 1955, pp. 229-234; and *Erker* {"Works"], Erevan: Sovetakan Grogh, 1986, pp. 368-373. Daniel Varuzhan dedicated to

Demirjibashian a long poem bearing the title *Drdunch'k'*, from Tourian: it is translated in its entirety in the commentary to No. 25. After a hiatus of some two decades after the poet's death, a lively interest in Tourian's work revived. Arshag Chobanian made far-flung inquiries in his research for a biographical study; and his correspondence with the poet's surviving younger brother was particularly extensive. Mihran Tourian had received the name Yeghishe at ordination.)

He is entirely black without; equally white within. The stereotype of a cleric? His calling to the priesthood is as powerful as his short-lived, immortal brother Bedros Tourian's was to poetry. An ill fortune? Bedros Tourian used to wander around the cemetery of Scutari [Baghlar-Bashi—JRR] throughout his brief life, and it was as if by accident that he went home in the evening, instead of entering a tomb. Yeghishe Tourian's fate was nearly the same: he spent the years of the springtime of his life within the walls of a seminary or monastery; and it is as if by some mistake that he sometimes descends to this world, instead of departing for the next. But how many men living at the very bosom of the world, at the heart of its bustle, do you know who render greater service to it than the ever-grieving, newly-ordained Bishop Yeghishe Tourian?

Both are dedicated to the book, to writing, which engenders the thought of mankind. Both glorify the written word—a glory less transitory than all other glories are. What wet nurse sang their lullaby? They themselves were both singer and midwife to the youth of the Armenian people. Thoughts beget the true; souls, the beautiful—through the lyrics of Bedros and the lectures of Yeghishe. Bedros' pupils were the birds, released by the great lyric poet to carry harmony into open windows, to diffuse it beyond the poet's nest. Fr. Yeghishe's pupils were doctors of theology, impatient to leave behind their seminary classrooms and to spread the truth of the Logos outside the monastery, in the world, to the meek and the poor in spirit in the world.

In his wonderful book *Creation,* Edgar Quinet [1803-1875, French historian and romantic nationalist whose repeated denunciations of the influence in society of the Roman Catholic church led ultimately to his dismissal from his teaching post—JRR] writes that birds listen timorously to the sound of the lyre and correct and augment accordingly all that is deficient in their own music. Now, could all the birds of the shores of the Bosphorus find a master of the lyre greater than Bedros Tourian? During the poet's lifetime, and especially after his death, their sensitive hearts fluttered to the cadences of his lyre and developed their own melodic power. Bedros Tourian's poetry possessed the ardor of groans and the struggling languor of consumption that passes from smoke as it is dispersed into a fire gathering strength. He was a white swan, arrow-stricken, whose every wing-beat with its arching spray of blood behaloed in red his gentle head, its gaze strained heavenward; and with his burning cries he plowed a furrow through the air and men's hearts. When for a time the exhausted poet's head would hang in peace, a black cloud or fillet of white, a vulture or dove, a demon or angel—sweet reveries or ominous dreams vexed by fever—would descend, surround, press against him like an iron band or caress his face with downy feathers, his precious tears yet uncreated, or else already melted away ...

Could Bedros Tourian, who in a few verses visibly sensed his own greatness, could even he have foreseen that one day Bedros and Yeghishe Tourian were to be summoned together in the same greatness and glory? ...

**22. Homage from the Future: A poem by Misak' Medzarents'.**

(This poem was first printed in *Masis*, no. 6, 2 April 1905, p. 94, and signed with the poet's *nom de plume* Shavasp Dziadzan. Misak Medzarents', whose native surname was Medzadourian, was born in Jan. 1886 in the village of Benkean near Akn, Western Armenia. After study in the local school and at Sepastia/Sivas, he attended Anatolia College at Marsovan/Merzifun, moving thence to Constantinople in 1902 to be with his father and to attend the *Getronagan* ("Central") School. Ill health forced him to abandon his studies in 1905, however; and he died of tuberculosis on 4 July 1908. He published his first poem in 1903; his first collection, *Dziadzan* ("Rainbow"), appeared in 1907. *Nor tagher* ("New Lyrics") came out only a few months later:

Medzarents' knew his death was imminent and wished to secure his literary legacy. The obvious parallels between his brief life and Tourian's add poignancy to the poem he dedicated to his predecessor. On Medzarents', see, in English, James Etmekjian, ed., *An Anthology of Western Armenian Literature,* Delmar, NY: Caravan Books, 1980, pp. 198-202; and Kevork B. Bardakjian, *A Reference Guide to Modern Armenian Literature,* 1500-1920, Detroit: Wayne State Univ. Press, 2000, pp. 156-157 and 417-419, who lists numerous translations (but only one short selection in English, by H. Kelikian in *Ararat,* Autumn 1961) and critical studies. A. S. Sharuryan edited the complete, critical edition of his works (*Erkeri liakatar zhoghovatsu*), Erevan, 1981. If Tourian epitomizes in Western Armenian poetry the tendencies of the Romantic age; it is Medzarents' whose work exemplifies the influence of French Symbolism in Armenian literary Constantinople. Prof. Bardakjian has noted, in comparing Tourian to Medzarents', that while both experimented with the language, creating new compounds and endowing old words with new nuances, the latter was not overcome at the prospect of death by black depression, responding to life instead with "elevated and deeply moving insouciance" and an "unalloyed, boundless altruism.")

*BEDROS TOURIAN*

From the silent marble sepulchre's depths
Unblinking, the eyes of genius gaze
With the heavenly luminous spirits' life,
Apart at last, too, from all tumult vain.

He is dead, no more to chant impassioned loves;
Still minds forever will be entranced
By his ringing lyre, and his songs will enthrall
Us forever in ancient reverence.

Impassioned he died; he lives on, remembered,
Vivid as the trees by his tomb

That rise fresh and green.

Amazements follow in his train...
And memories of him, forever inspiring
And forever right, shall forever remain!

8 July 1903

Միսաք Մեծարենց

ՊԵՏՐՈՍ ԴՈՒՐԵԱՆ

Լուռ, մարմարակերտ դամբանին խորէն,
Հանճարի աչքերն անքոյթ կը նային,
Լոյս ոգիներու կեանքովն երկնային,
Ա·լ մեկուսացած ունայն ժըխորէն։

Մեռա·ւ, խանդավա– սէրերն երգելէն՝
Ու պիտի յաւէտ միտքերն հըմային
Իր թունդ քընարէն, ու երգերն ալ հին
Պաշտումով ըպմեպ միշտ պիտի գերեն։

Ցոյպով մեռա·ւ ան, յուշքով՝ կ'ապրի դեռ,
Ծառերուն նըման՝ որ թարմ ու դալար,
Իր գերեպմանին կ'ելլեն քովն ի վեր։

Հիացքներ կ'երթան իրեն ետևէն...
Եւ իր յուշքերն ալ, յաւէտ անմոլար
Ու միշտ ոգևոր՝ դեռ պիտի տևե·ն։

8 յուլիսի, 1903 թ.

# Index